GERMANY'S SECOND REICH

Recent studies of Imperial Germany emphasize the empire's modern and reformist qualities, but the question remains: To what extent could democracy have flourished in Germany's stony soil? In *Germany's Second Reich*, James Retallack continues his career-long inquiry into the era of Bismarck and Kaiser Wilhelm II with a wide-ranging reassessment of the period and its connections with past traditions and future possibilities.

In this volume, Retallack reveals the complex and contradictory nature of the Second Reich, presenting Imperial Germany as it was seen by outsiders and insiders, and as it has been seen by historians, political scientists, and sociologists ever since.

(German and European Studies)

JAMES RETALLACK is a professor of History and German Studies at the University of Toronto. In 2015 he was awarded Research Fellowships from the Killam Trust and the John S. Guggenheim Memorial Foundation. His most recent book for the University of Toronto Press was *The German Right, 1860–1920*.

GERMAN AND EUROPEAN STUDIES

General Editor: Rebecca Wittmann

Germany's Second Reich

Portraits and Pathways

JAMES RETALLACK

UNIVERSITY OF TORONTO PRESS
Toronto Buffalo London

© University of Toronto Press 2015
Toronto Buffalo London
www.utppublishing.com
Printed in the U.S.A.

ISBN 978-1-4426-5057-2 (cloth)
ISBN 978-1-4426-2852-6 (paper)

Printed on acid-free, 100% post-consumer recycled paper with vegetable-based inks.

German and European Studies

Publication cataloguing information is available from Library and Archives Canada.

Cover illustrations: (front) "Durchs dunkelste Deutschland – Crimmitschau," by Thomas Theodor Heine, *Simplicissimus* 8, no. 43 (19 January 1904), 337. © Estate of Thomas Theodor Heine/SODRAC (2015). The caption in *Simplicissimus* was "We need more policemen on top. The wretches haven't been pressed soft yet." (*"Es müssen noch mehr Schutzleute herauf. Die Luder sind noch nicht weich gedrückt."*) Crimmitschau was the centre of Saxony's textile industry. From 22 August 1903 to 18 January 1904 it was the site of one of Imperial Germany's longest and most bitter strikes. Industrial employers from all parts of Germany, working with state authorities, eventually forced the striking workers to break off their action. The strikers included a large number of female textile workers. The term *"Luder"* has multiple connotations, some of them gendered; but they all convey Heine's sympathy for the broken strikers.

(back) This busy painting shows shopping centres and other buildings erected during the "founding era" of the early 1870s, together with bustling trams and pedestrians, all of which provide a shimmering, nervous impression of everyday life in a modern city. But we also catch glimpses of throne, altar, and state. On the left is the Hotel "Imperial" at König-Johann-Str. Nr. 12. Policemen mingle with well-dressed burghers. In the background two shadowy towers loom: the pinnacle of the Baroque *Frauenkirche* and, to its right, the squat turret atop the new police headquarters, which was erected at Schießgasse Nr. 8 between 1895 and 1900. *Pirnaischer Platz. Vor 1914*, by Ernst Richard Dietze. Städtische Galerie Dresden – Kunstsammlung, Museen der Stadt Dresden, Photograph: Franz Zadnicek.

University of Toronto Press acknowledges the financial assistance to its publishing program of the Canada Council for the Arts and the Ontario Arts Council, an agency of the Government of Ontario.

 Canada Council Conseil des Arts
for the Arts du Canada

University of Toronto Press acknowledges the financial support of the Government of Canada through the Canada Book Fund for its publishing activities.

This book is dedicated, with love, to

Stuart Adler Graham Retallack
and
Hanna Elizabeth Graham Retallack

Contents

List of Maps and Figures   ix

Preface: The Kaleidoscope of German History   xi

Pan

1 Forging an Empire: Economy, Society, Culture, and Politics, 1866–1890   3
2 British Views of Germany, 1815–1914   44
3 Digital History Anthologies on the Web   86

Focus

4 King Johann of Saxony and the German Civil War of 1866   107
5 Julian Hawthorne's *Saxon Studies*   138
6 Bismarck and Engels: *The Role of Force in History*   186
7 Heydebrand and Westarp: Leaving Behind the Second Reich   202

Twist

8 Get Out the Vote! Electioneering without Democracy   237
9 The Authoritarian State and the Political Mass Market   258
10 Society and Democracy in Germany: Why Dahrendorf Still Matters   280
11 Democracy in Disappearing Ink: Suffrage Robbery as *Coup d'État*   293

Acknowledgments 325

Index 333

Maps and Figures

Maps

1 The German Empire, 1871–1918 xvi
 © James Retallack/German Historical Institute, Washington, DC. Cartography by Mapping Solutions, Alaska

 Readers may also wish to consult maps in the *German History in Documents and Images* project, available online on the website of the German Historical Institute, Washington, DC. These include:

2 Central Europe (1815–1866)
 http://germanhistorydocs.ghi-dc.org/map.cfm?map_id=373

3 Creation of the German Empire (1866–1871)
 http://germanhistorydocs.ghi-dc.org/map.cfm?map_id=374

4 Germany and Europe in the First World War (1914–1918)
 http://germanhistorydocs.ghi-dc.org/map.cfm?map_id=2177

Figures

1.1 Krupp's Steelworks in Essen, 1890   9
1.2 Wedding Photograph   13
1.3 Gottlieb Daimler's First Automobile, 1886   31
2.1 "Prize Question," *Simplicissimus*, 1911   59
2.2 "Diplomatic Training," *Simplicissimus*, 1903   67

3.1 Belching Smokestacks, 1876   99
3.2 Nazi Rally, 1935   100
4.1 Prussian Troops March into Dresden, June 1866   113
4.2 Sewing the New Germany Together, September 1866   119
4.3 King Johann Returns from Exile, October 1866   126
5.1 A Poor Family of Day Labourers   143
5.2 Washerwomen in Dresden   160
6.1 Bismarck and Dresden Burghers   191
6.2 "Our State Ministry in Uniform (with one exception)," *Lustige Blätter*, 1889   194
7.1 Ernst von Heydebrand und der Lasa   204
7.2 Count Kuno von Westarp   205
8.1 "The Only Jew-Free Hotel in Frankfurt"   248
8.2 "A Philistine Voter," *Gartenlaube*, 1881   251
9.1 Crown Prince Friedrich Wilhelm of Prussia   263
9.2 Tavern Scene   268
10.1 "Progress in the Education System," *Simplicissimus*, 1911   285
10.2 "Voting-Magic, East of the Elbe," *Ulk*, 1913   287
11.1 "A German Socialist Propounding His Bloodthirsty Ideas"   297
11.2 Paul Mehnert, Jr   301

Preface
The Kaleidoscope of German History

This book is about how Germans saw themselves, how others saw them, and how each side understood the changes wrought by the arrival of modern times between 1866 and 1918. Those changes are surveyed in chapter 1, which also introduces the themes that run throughout this volume. Interpretive couplets provide another means to explore the range of German reactions to change, including joy in stability or reform, conflicts between authority and "subversion," protests against inequality and injustice, celebrations of what it meant to be German, and uncertainties about how Germany's past and present might determine its future. As such this book is quite different from an earlier collection of essays I published with the University of Toronto Press in 2006. I hope the present work will be seen as more speculative, at times more playful, than the last one.

The changes and the range of responses I consider in these chapters did not begin or end in the age of Bismarck and Kaiser Wilhelm II. Recent scholarship makes clear that German history from 1500 onward, including the period of the Holy Roman Empire, was free from none of those joys, conflicts, protests, celebrations, and uncertainties. Historians are exploring their relevance during Hitler's "Third Reich" more intensively than for any other period. That trend will not change anytime soon. Nevertheless, it is to embed these portraits of Germany in the longer path of German history – and to rethink real or alleged discontinuities – that I have chosen a title that alludes implicitly to Germany's first and third "empires." I cannot think of a single subject considered in these pages that does not also resonate in the periods before 1866 and after 1918.

This book examines attitudes and outlooks in a second way. In the Foreword to *The Essays of E.B. White* (1977) we read that the essayist can choose to be "any sort of person – philosopher, scold, jester, raconteur, confidant, pundit, devil's advocate, enthusiast." (Of these I prefer the last two.) No one wants to read a wilfully arbitrary selection of writings, especially if they upbraid other scholars or recount familiar truths. For that reason I have chosen the subtitle "portraits and pathways" to signal that this book differs from my other writing, some of which has been published, or soon will be, in edited volumes and monographs devoted to subjects treated here tangentially or not at all.

Certain portraits in this book might better be called miniatures – those of Otto von Bismarck and Friedrich Engels, for instance, in chapter 6. Others are broader than their subjects, at first glance, seem to warrant: the study of Julian Hawthorne and his 1876 rant against everything German in chapter 5 fits this category; so does the megalomania of Kaiser Wilhelm II, considered in chapter 11. I have also included portraits of "another country" that appear to gaze on Germany from afar through a telescope but, paradoxically, turn out to be panoramas. These include British views across the North Sea, as in chapter 2, and digital histories, discussed in chapter 3. Other portraits focus on important turning points. Thus chapter 4 is devoted to Johann, King of Saxony; but the "uncrowned king of Saxony," Dr Paul Mehnert, Jr, makes an appearance in more than one chapter. Both had their own little crises to solve, as did Saxony's King Albert, as we see in chapter 11. By and large they succeeded in taming their circumscribed worlds of endeavour. By contrast, the "uncrowned king of Prussia," Ernst von Heydebrand und der Lasa, could accomplish no such conjuring trick, as we discover in chapter 7.

Pathways are conceived temporally and territorially. In the latter sense they appear as borders, boundaries, transit zones, routes of exchange, voyages of discovery, lines in the sand. Temporally, pathways lead into and out of Germany's Second Reich. But in both senses they help guide the reader of this book from its beginning to its end. Section One tackles the problem of deciding how we want to sketch the outlines of a big picture. Chapter 1 provides an overview of the period between 1866 and 1890, emphasizing the materiality of everyday life in the new nation-state. At the same time it plants signposts pointing toward detours where Germans celebrated or despaired about their nation's future. In later sections those detours will twist and turn. But before that happens, chapter 2 takes readers in straight lines back and forth across the North Sea. Readers hop around the world and across decades in chapter 3.

Section Two of this book asks that we focus on narrower paths: bridges and intersections, for example. We consider one monarch's reluctant entry into the North German Confederation in chapter 4; one author's acceptance that he was a second-rate hack in chapter 5; one account of Bismarck's rape of German liberty in chapter 6; and one small part of the great divide that separated the Second Reich from the Weimar Republic in chapter 7. In the latter chapter we see how two Conservative leaders responded differently to the fall of the Hohenzollern monarchy and tried to accommodate the unfamiliar practices of parliamentary democracy in the new republic. In other chapters too, Germans – and not only conservative Germans – enter a forest of political challenges, whose dimensions were daunting even to those whose sight was not blinkered. At a number of points I stress that the paths *out* of that forest were many and crooked: none of them led directly to Hitler, Nazism, or the Holocaust.

In the final section, the kaleidoscope of German history is twisted once again. My dual aim is to reappraise historical portraits of an authoritarian polity and to discern pathways – including rites of passage – that connect past scholarship with historical practice today. Evoking the look and feel of a German election (in chapter 8) provides one means to reassess the planting of democracy in stony soil. The same goal is pursued in chapter 9, where I reconsider how Imperial Germany's "political mass market" emerged and functioned. Here and in chapter 10, I invite readers to grapple with something less than "democracy" per se – a notoriously complex and febrile subject best left to another study. Instead my focus falls on "democratization," characterized as a combination of processes whose effects were felt strongly and at many points – from the North Sea to the Alps, from the moment the Second Reich was forged until after its fate was sealed.

Chapter 10 – the shortest in this collection and also the most speculative – suggests that the portrait of an undemocratic, illiberal Germany painted by the sociologist Ralf Dahrendorf in the 1960s deserves another look. Like Dahrendorf, I consider continuities in German history stretching from the nineteenth century to the collapse of German democracy, signified by Adolf Hitler's appointment as Reich chancellor on 30 January 1933. John Breuilly once remarked that hindsight is an advantage historians should not discard too quickly. There is no looking past signposts in the pre-1918 period that pointed toward antisocialist, anti-liberal, antisemitic, and anti-democratic outcomes even before Hitler was in the picture.[1] It is no accident that this book's last chapter appears where it does, for it tries to dissuade readers from the notion that democratization was unstoppable. It could be stopped, and even reversed, though only in the right circumstances and not on an all-embracing scale.

In an ongoing attempt to appraise the merits and deficiencies of a view that posited Germany's "special path" (*Sonderweg*) to modernity, I concede my own ambivalence about how best to consider Germany's political modernization with a post-*Sonderweg* paradigm. The once-orthodox position premised on Germany's "exceptionalism" has been dethroned, but no alternative consensus has emerged to fill the vacuum. Although the pendulum of historical interpretation will continue to swing – and not just between two poles – while writing this book I have felt a growing sense that its arc is off-kilter, skewed toward a more positive appraisal of the Second Reich than the historical evidence warrants. However robust bourgeois civil society and its public sphere may have been, broad historical narratives of Imperial Germany too often shy away from acknowledging that universal manhood suffrage was not necessarily conducive to democratization, let alone parliamentarization, and that mass politics served authoritarian aims as much as it did liberal aspirations. The Second Reich remained a semi-parliamentary constitutional monarchy with mercurial leaders and executive bodies that were never responsible to the people. It also had a strong, powerful, ambitious bourgeoisie (*Bürgertum*). That bourgeoisie valorized achievement, education, and cultural pluralism. But it was riven by deep cleavages of wealth, rank, power, and ideology. Moreover, large sections of the German bourgeoisie paid no heed to the ideals of social equality or political inclusiveness. It showed little willingness to question the constitutional status quo, even though the pace of social, economic, and cultural change could hardly have been more dramatic.

---

1 I agree with many scholars that the hyphen should be discarded from the common term "anti-Semitism" and "antisemitism" be used instead. For a succinct explanation of why, see Shmuel Almog, "What's in a Hyphen?" *SICSA Report: Newsletter of the Vidal Sassoon International Center for the Study of Antisemitism* 2 (Summer 1989): 1–2; online at http://sicsa.huji.ac.il/hyphen.htm.

How do we reconcile these conflicting images of Imperial Germany and the divergent paths that were all part of its possible future? These chapters provide at best partial answers; they make no claim to solve historical dilemmas or epistemological quandaries of an overarching kind. I have consciously tried to avoid a stance of agnosticism, of sitting on fences; but neither do I imagine I can offer a full-throated resolution of Imperial Germany's historical contradictions and historiographical debates. Such a resolution, if it is possible at all, would require a book quite unlike what I offer here.

Master narratives have fallen into such disrepute that we will not soon find a scholar to match the brilliant works on Imperial Germany published in the years around 1990. Master narratives deserve the opprobrium heaped upon them when they become so large or inflexible that they lose relevancy for younger historians, who are usually the ones closest to the archives. But counting just the multi-authored collections that have appeared in the last half-decade or so, we now have a good handful that cover the whole range of Imperial German history from up-to-date perspectives. I doubt that one more will bring any surprises in the near future. A large synthesis written by a single author – not me – seems more likely to give the interpretive wheel the next turn it needs.

I hope the present volume nevertheless proves illuminating for those who want to gaze on Germany's Second Reich through new windows. They may gaze inward, on the country that Germans and others thought they knew. They may also gaze outward, on a Germany whose historical trajectory was unknowable and whose "national mission" was contentious from the outset. During the imperial era, political choices and attitudinal shifts pushed Germans toward a course that allowed others, later, to steer them away from the ideals of liberty and democracy. As we read in daily headlines, liberals and democrats still struggle to be heard. That struggle is no longer unfolding principally in Germany: it is found in every corner of the globe. But wherever pluralism is under attack, a kaleidoscopic view of history can contribute to revealing the truth and to reconciling opposing groups who mistakenly believe they are embarked on incompatible paths to a better future. For my children I hope such a world will exist long after this book has been superseded by the work of a new generation of scholars.

Toronto
3 October 2014

Other Titles by the Same Author

Red Saxony: Election Battles and the Spectre of Democracy in Germany, 1860–1918, forthcoming.

Decades of Reconstruction: Postwar Societies, State-Building, and International Relations, from the Seven Years' War to the Cold War, ed. with Ute Planert, forthcoming.

Imperial Germany 1871–1918. The Short Oxford History of Germany, ed.

Localism, Landscape, and the Ambiguities of Place: German-Speaking Central Europe, 1860–1930, ed. with David Blackbourn.

Forging an Empire: Bismarckian Germany (1866–1890), vol. 4 of *German History in Documents and Images*, ed. (online).

The German Right, 1860–1920: Political Limits of the Authoritarian Imagination.

Wilhelminism and Its Legacies: German Modernities, Imperialism, and the Meanings of Reform, 1890–1930, ed. with Geoff Eley.

Zwischen Markt und Staat. Stifter und Stiftungen im transatlantischen Vergleich, ed. with Thomas Adam.

Saxony in German History: Culture, Society, and Politics, 1830–1933, ed.

Sachsen in Deutschland. Politik, Kultur und Gesellschaft 1830–1918, ed.

Saxon Signposts, ed.

Germany in the Age of Kaiser Wilhelm II.

Modernisierung und Region im wilhelminischen Deutschland: Wahlen, Wahlrecht und Politische Kultur, ed. with Simone Lässig and Karl Heinrich Pohl.

Between Reform, Reaction, and Resistance: Studies in the History of German Conservatism from 1789 to 1945, ed. with Larry Eugene Jones.

Elections, Mass Politics, and Social Change in Modern Germany: New Perspectives, ed. with Larry Eugene Jones.

Notables of the Right: The Conservative Party and Political Mobilization in Germany, 1876–1918.

PAN

1 Forging an Empire: Economy, Society, Culture, and Politics, 1866–1890

Overview

When compared with the revolutionary excitement of 1848–9 or the horrors of trench warfare in 1914–18, the era dominated by Otto von Bismarck can seem drab – an age of equipoise when conformity and compliance were the first duty of the citizen. Certainly, Bismarck scored stunning military and diplomatic victories between 1866 and 1871, but his later years in office have been characterized as a period of "fortification" – not a terribly exciting interpretive key either. To look beneath the surface calm of Bismarckian Germany, however, is to see quite a different picture, one shot through with contradictions, conflicts, and crises.

Contradictions resulted from attempts both to entrench and to extend the international and constitutional agreements achieved at the time of unification. Conflict was inevitable when the effects of rapid economic, social, cultural, and political change became self-reinforcing and as a younger generation of Germans sought new challenges to match the great deeds of their fathers. Crises arose whenever Bismarck felt his authority in jeopardy.

How do we assess the causes, consequences, and historical significance of all this turmoil? A preliminary hypothesis is that the German Empire was forged in ways that embedded features of a modernizing economy, society, and culture within the framework of an authoritarian polity. This is not a new proposition. Moreover, it is easy to be too categorical in applying the labels "modern" and "authoritarian" so that everything before 1866 is deemed unmodern and everything after 1890 hypermodern. Many features of German politics after 1866 were more democratic than those in other European nations at the time. Conversely, traditional elements are easily discernable in social relations, the arts, and certain sectors of the industrial economy. Nevertheless, the anvil of tradition and the hammer of modernity allowed Bismarck and other reformist conservatives to mould German authoritarianism into new and durable forms.

As a consequence of decisions made (or skirted) in the late 1860s and early 1870s, Imperial Germany encountered hurdles to political reform that would make it more difficult to avoid a German fascism in the twentieth century. Despite the ascendancy of bourgeois codes of conduct and even while industrial capitalism was expanding rapidly, Socialists, Catholics, Poles, Jews, and other out-groups were subjected to social discrimination or overt persecution by the state. Science and technology were harnessed to the interests of military firepower, colonial expansion, and the domination of world markets. Women's demands for equal rights found virtually no resonance. And one charismatic leader, Bismarck, exercised near-dictatorial control over his ministerial colleagues, party leaders, and the entire system of state.

If these portents of a calamitous future tempt us to read history backwards, we should pause for a moment and attune ourselves to the views of contemporary Germans who did not know how the story would end. Germans who found themselves on the right side of class, confessional, and gender boundaries tended to view life in the 1870s and 1880s as stable and predictable. Their pronouncements on the mood of the times are often self-satisfied, and we see them striking complacent poses in the official iconography of the day. For other Germans, though, life was brutal, rigidly controlled, and patently unfair. They, too, took the pulse of the times – in their diaries, autobiographies, letters, party manifestos, and parliamentary speeches. How do we differentiate one group from another, and how do we place Germans who do not fit neatly into either group? One way to address these questions is to consider the sociologist Max Weber's three hierarchies of status, wealth, and power; but it is still difficult to match up Germans' objective places within these hierarchies with their subjective reactions to movement up or down the ladder.

To make a start in this direction, this chapter has been divided into seven sections: 1. Demographic and Economic Development; 2. Society; 3. Culture; 4. Religion, Education, and Social Welfare; 5. Politics I: Forging an Empire; 6. Military and International Relations; and 7. Politics

II: Parties and Political Mobilization. The organization of these materials into discrete sections should not prevent the reader from approaching the text as a single narrative – the story of Germany's early development as a newly unified nation-state. Four themes run through this chapter like threads through a fabric.

The first theme has to do with conflicting preferences felt by Germans in Bismarck's day. Some of them preferred the status quo because it suited their interests or tastes; others were determined to reform the existing order in fundamental ways. Although most Germans fell somewhere between these extremes, it is difficult to say how these differing attitudes towards change actually determined the developments we want to learn about. Which economic structures, social relationships, cultural motifs, and political institutions from 1871 remained in place in 1890 – or, for that matter, in 1918? In each of these areas, what were Germans' subjective reactions to stasis and upheaval in their personal and public lives?

The second theme overlaps with the first. It concerns the tension between authority and protest. Was the principle of authority on display every 2 September (Sedan Day) when Germans celebrated the origins of their empire in the crucible of war? Was revolution the clarion call that inspired a wave of strikes, lockouts, and other labour disputes in the final years of Bismarck's chancellorship? We find that representatives of the authoritarian German state – emboldened by the support of élites and others who feared that the pace of change was getting out of hand – were able to erect many barriers to a more equitable distribution of wealth, privilege, and power. But we also know that a surprising number of Germans were challenging and seeking to overturn such barriers, questioning traditional assumptions about how authority should be legitimated and deployed. These Germans devised or resurrected forms of political, social, and cultural protest that we typically associate with earlier or later periods of German history – with the age of Romanticism, for example, with the revolutions of 1848–9, or with Expressionism, Pan-Germanism, and anarchism in the early years of the twentieth century. In this chapter, however, we grapple with the paradox that authoritarianism actually fostered and radicalized expressions of protest in Bismarck's Germany, too.

The third theme concerns Germany's remarkable regional diversity. This diversity cannot be reduced to a centre–periphery polarity. To be sure, we often encounter the sceptical views of Germans who felt distant from the new imperial capital, Berlin, and alienated by social, cultural, and political developments there. But we must not neglect the extreme geographical unevenness of industrial development, religious affiliation, and regional political cultures across the federal states and provinces of Germany. Only if we abandon the perspective of the political leaders in Berlin and explore the backroads of German history can we properly apprehend the interconnectedness of local, regional, and national affairs. And only then can we appreciate the diversity of outlooks among taxpayers, churchgoers, conscripts, employees, newspaper readers, and others who saw themselves as Leipzigers, Rhinelanders, or Bavarians first and as Germans only secondarily.

Fourth and lastly, unanticipated crises remind us that Germans' hopes and fears for the fate of the new German nation did not diminish between 1871 and 1890. The history of Bismarckian Germany should be read as a book whose ending, because it was unknown, fostered a deep sense of unease among contemporaries. Much of this anxiety first became apparent or was radicalized in the Wilhelmine period – the "age of nervousness." Yet when Germans looked back from the *fin de siècle* on the previous quarter century, they were astounded how much the face of German society had changed – and how rapidly. The new urgency of addressing a national electorate in the age of universal manhood suffrage, the increased tempo of work, travel, and communication, the accelerating pace of artistic experimentation, the sudden appearance of threats on the international horizon: these features of life in Bismarck's Reich contributed to one of the hallmarks of modernity – the sense that life was changing at an ever-faster pace and that the future was becoming less predictable with each passing day.

A final point that should not fall from view is that historical scholarship on Bismarckian Germany has moved in exciting new directions over the past forty years. Compared to historical interpretations that held sway in the early 1970s, more recent accounts emphasize the diversity, dynamism, and paradoxes of German development under Bismarck – without losing sight, however, of what remained from the Reich's founding era. Readers should therefore see the Bismarckian epoch as a transitional one, when Germans were exploring how best to reconcile tradition and change, *and* as a period worth studying in its own right. To emphasize the importance and complementarity of these approaches, a list of suggestions for further reading appears at the end of this chapter, organized according to the section headings below.

1. Demographic and Economic Development

We confront a paradox as soon as we try to assess why material conditions were improving for many Germans even while life was becoming less secure. Although economic opportunities were increasing and the hardware of modern technology was infiltrating workplaces and homes alike, such changes often brought unwelcome consequences: forced migration from the countryside to unfamiliar cities, job insecurity as different occupational sectors experienced booms and busts, a rising cost of living despite increases in nominal wages, and the loss of traditional roots associated in one way or another with smallness of scale. Germany was urbanizing rapidly in the pre- and post-Bismarckian eras, too. But the growth of cities and the concomitant decline in the number of Germans living in rural communities – designated as those with fewer than two thousand inhabitants – was especially pronounced during the 1870s and 1880s. Almost two-thirds of the population lived in such rural communities in 1871; less than half still did so in 1895. In this regard, the extreme disparities in population shifts and urban growth rates across Germany must not be overlooked. Without continuing emigration to America and other destinations, population growth would have been even more dramatic. Even so, it seemed momentous at the time. As the problem of pauperism from the 1840s evolved into the "social question" of the 1860s, overcrowding in Berlin and in other large cities resulted in squalid "tenement barracks" that epitomized the downside of freedom of movement.

Scholars used to contend that most of the Bismarckian period was afflicted by a Great Depression (1873–96). This has now been exposed as a myth. The 1870s and 1880s included shorter periods of boom and bust; some historians use the term "great deflation" to describe the cumulative impact of the latter. Also, some sectors suffered more severe downturns than others, and the German economy as a whole continued to expand. However, that long-term expansion was barely visible to Germans living through these tumultuous decades. Even a brief downturn in a particular occupational branch or local workplace could have devastating effects on families, especially when compounded by the illness or death of a primary earner or the reduced income that came with temporary unemployment or strikes. We can identify periods when the general economy did well: the years 1866 to 1873 and the early 1880s were two such times, and there was a strong upswing during the "founding years" (*Gründerzeit*) beginning in 1871. That upswing, however, was followed by a downturn after 1873, which convinced many Germans that the capitalist system was dysfunctional. Hans Rosenberg advanced the thesis in the 1940s that socio-economic dislocation and anxiety shaped the radical political movements that came to the fore in the period 1873 to 1896. In stark contrast with the 1850s and 1860s, on the one hand, and the period of broader and more sustained prosperity between 1896 and 1913, on the other, Germans *sensed* that they were living through unprecedented hard times in the 1870s and 1880s. That sense of hardship contributed to their growing dissatisfaction with the status quo in the second half of Bismarck's time in office.

After the mid-1870s, German agriculture experienced increased competition from foreign producers. For example, grain from Australia, Russia, and the Canadian prairies could now reach German markets at prices that pushed the owners of large estates in the Prussian east into debt or over the brink of bankruptcy. Yet technological innovations such as the introduction of steam-powered threshing machines in the countryside contributed to overall increases in the productivity of German agriculture. To be sure, growth rates in mining, industry, and commerce outstripped those of German agriculture, especially after the mid-1870s. But we should be careful not to exaggerate the speed of Germany's transition from an agrarian to an industrial state (the tipping point is generally regarded as c. 1900). It makes more sense to speak of a gradual change from an agrarian state with a strong industrial sector (especially during the Bismarckian era) to an industrial state with a strong agrarian sector after the turn of the century.

In the first decade covered by this chapter, the engine of German industrialization was still fuelled by railway construction and by the large-scale mining, iron-rolling, and other industries that sustained it. Small workshops had not disappeared, even though the exclusive rights of the guilds had been breached in most German states in the early 1860s through freedom of occupation legislation. The huge factories we associate with the era of high capitalism were still rare in the 1870s. In 1882 more than half of all heavy industrial enterprises employed five workers or fewer. By the 1880s, however, technological innovations were changing the face of industry: precision machinery, steel, tool-making, and – somewhat later – petrochemical and electrical industries were shifting the German economy onto new paths. Commerce and banking also expanded greatly in these years, and further changes were wrought by the introduction of gas motors, advances in construction technology,

Figure 1.1 The Krupp enterprise was founded by Friedrich Krupp, whose oldest son Alfred Krupp took over sole proprietorship in 1848. Krupp's principal products were machinery and machine components made of high-quality cast steel: equipment for Germany's expanding network of railways (especially the seamless wheels); artillery for the Prussian military; and later, armoured plating for the German navy. At the time of Alfred Krupp's death in 1887, his firm employed more than 20,000 workers. "Gußstahlfabrik von Friedrich Krupp, Essen," after a woodcut by Emil Limmer, appeared with the caption "Aus der Werkstätte für Lafettenbau" ("From the workshop for carriage construction") in Leipzig's *Illustrirte Zeitung*, no. 2471 (8 November 1890): 496–7, bpk, Berlin/Art Resource, NY.

the transition from horse-drawn to electric trolleys, and the increased use of electric light, telephones, and automobiles.

This progress in transportation and urban infrastructure contributed to the remarkable growth of cities: workers were able to live farther from city centres, travelling to and from their shifts by public transport. Urban growth in turn fuelled a recognizable consumer culture that drew the worlds of industry, commerce, and everyday life closer together. By the late 1880s, advertisers were trumpeting modern conveniences; poets were writing paeans to technological progress; and scientists, inventors, and explorers were contending that the age of discovery was being realized through German know-how.

2. Society

Like "German agriculture," the "German countryside" is an abstraction that does not hold water analytically. The lifestyle of a Junker landlord or a day labourer on one of the vast grain-growing estates in eastern Prussia bore little resemblance to that of a poor livestock farmer or a vintner trying to eke out a living from a tiny plot of land in the southwestern state of Baden. These groups benefited to different degrees and in different ways from the rationalization of German agriculture, which included the introduction of new farming techniques, synthetic fertilizers, and mechanization. So historians should emphasize the increasing *diversity* of rural society, not its uniformity. That diversity helps explain why Germans from some regions voted with their feet and left unsatisfying rural lives to move to the big cities. It also coloured the personal reflections written during and after such migrations. Those reflections can be augmented by statistics drawn from an increasing number of social scientific studies of rural and urban life, which suggest a high degree of interpenetration of city and country. The urbanization of what had once been a tiny village near Lübeck, for example, can illustrate the disorienting effect that mobility, machines, and markets had on rural Germany.

One way to appreciate the impact of this interpenetration of city and countryside is by considering the new ways in which time and space were measured. In rural areas, the rhythms of the sun and the seasons still largely determined productive and social activities. But farmers and innkeepers needed to be aware of train schedules and shift times if they were to serve clients who now lived beyond the horizons of the village. Marriage customs and burial rites in the countryside still appeared to unfold according to an ancient time clock – one that ran too slowly for young city dwellers rushing to a dance hall or an international art exhibition. The simple meals and spartan interiors of rural cottages seemed worlds apart from the full larders and ornate decor of middle-class households in the cities. But for the latter, keeping up appearances required social strategies that were not only fluid and ill-defined but also subject to intervention by "outside" forces in both countryside and city: the state in its local, regional, and national guises; lawyers, politicians, and social theorists; and entrepreneurs, consumers, and others for whom the cash nexus was paramount. As parents hoped their children would prosper from their own sacrifices, and as the new significance of wealth gradually erased the boundaries between social "estates" (*Stände*), the contours of a new class society gradually came into view.

Wistfulness over the disappearance of social estates and mixed feelings about the new class relations were characteristic responses to such changes, as the distances of time and space shrank between, say, itinerant labourers in Thuringia out for a Sunday afternoon stroll and upper-middle-class burghers enjoying Dresden's famed Brühlsche Terrasse (the "balcony of Europe"). Satirical journals poked fun at the new pretensions that became evident as these class divisions narrowed or widened. They noted, for instance, that claims to represent "the people" were often put forward by social élites that were as narrow as they were privileged. The hunt for decorations and titles continued to animate burghers eager to rub shoulders with courtiers and the very rich. And successful industrialists such as Alfred Krupp and Carl von Stumm did their best to inject hierarchies of status and authority into workplace relations on the shop floor. Bankers, lawyers, professors, and other members of the propertied and educated bourgeoisie added to the clamour for social prestige. This newly acquisitive society horrified such novelists as Theodor Fontane and Heinrich Mann in the 1890s: they both remarked on the paradox that the ubiquity of status seeking and one-upmanship actually had a levelling effect on society as a whole.

Other levelling influences included near-universal literacy (estimated at 95 per cent in 1890), the rise of the advertisement-driven mass press, increasing access for middle-class youths to secondary schools, universities, and institutes of technology, the pervasiveness of consumer culture, and the general rise in the proportion of family incomes available for discretionary expenditures (i.e., after paying for food, clothing, and housing). For the working classes, this portion rose from about 40 per cent of family incomes in the 1870s to 55 per cent in the 1890s. Among these levelling influences, education (*Bildung*) came to be seen as the most important means for overcoming barriers to advancement. Over time and with great variations among regions, the social and institutional constraints that had made life harsh, painful, and short for most Germans before 1866 loosened or disappeared. The levels of geographical and social mobility achieved in the 1870s indicated that there was no turning back from a dynamic society that had still seemed distant to the revolutionaries of 1848–9.

The capitalist mode of production changed fundamentally in the 1870s and 1880s. On the one hand, artisans and other members of the lower middle classes (*Mittelstand*) were hard-pressed to retain even the vestiges of the "golden age" that they claimed, erroneously, had characterized their working conditions and lifestyles before national unification. On the other hand, the advance of industrialization and the expansion of commercial and consumer cultures produced new opportunities for social groups such as retail clerks. Both groups' reflections remind us that there are always winners and losers in industrialization. The accounts of flax cultivators on the Lüneburg Heath and of farm workers in Mecklenburg or Pomerania, not unlike those that describe working-class hierarchies in a steel factory in Hamburg, suggest that even within apparently monolithic occupations a complicated layering of workplace responsibilities and social ranks was discernable. Such layering sometimes baffled social scientists who were trying to discover why the expenditures and lifestyles of working-class or lower-middle-class Germans varied to such a large extent, despite universal pressure to provide the essentials of life to growing families while saving a few pennies to cope with injury, unemployment, old age, and various calamities. Their studies often yielded ambiguous answers or perpetuated myths about workers' unhealthy or "irrational" lifestyles. Yet as historians we can be pleased that survey takers and photographers crossed the threshold of so many homes: their work offers us a view into the interior lives of Germans who left no other record of their daily affairs.

After promising starts in 1848–9 and the mid-1860s, the bourgeois and working-class women's movements made little headway during the 1870s and 1880s. The growth of the Social Democratic Party in the 1890s and the questioning of bourgeois values that accompanied the philosophical and artistic movements of the *fin de siècle* fostered more successful demands for women's rights. But the Bismarckian period

Forging an Empire, 1866–1890 13

Figure 1.2 This photograph shows Oswald Langrock and Frieda Langrock, née Helas, in Dresden (1901). SLUB Dresden/Deutsche Fotothek/Photograph: Max Helas.

was anything but devoid of commentaries on the double standard that characterized gender relations at the time. Not only literary scholars, artists, and photographers, but also activists and social scientists with widely divergent agendas, provided any number of analyses of the "woman question." Those analyses documented women's sexual exploitation inside and outside the workplace, the social origins of parents of illegitimate or fatherless children, the state regulation of prostitutes, and the many restrictions placed on women's ability to protect their property in marriage, to secure other legal rights inside or outside the family, and to participate in associational life and politics.

Gender-specific roles characterized almost every workplace environment, from street cleaning in Munich to domestic service in Berlin to factory labour in the Ruhr district. Gradually the campaign to increase educational opportunities for women gathered steam, through vocational schools for women and lobbying efforts to overcome conservative views about which occupations "suited" their abilities. In this campaign Hedwig Dohm stands out as having provided cogent and forceful arguments not only for more employment opportunities for women but also for the female vote. At a time when Germany's Social Democratic Party (SPD) was suffering state repression, Clara Zetkin and August Bebel wrote pioneering and no less passionate critiques of gender inequality. These writings and ideas were taken up in bourgeois reading circles and discussion groups and in meetings organized by female members of the SPD. Other accounts describe the supposed sexual morals of working-class women, the effect of socialist activities on working-class marriages, and, further up the social scale, the types of family roles and leisure pursuits that were considered appropriate for bourgeois or aristocratic women.

3. Culture

When the Nazis looked back at fifteen years of Weimar culture (1918–33), their verdict seethed contempt: "a wasteland." Hermann Muthesius, an early pioneer of German architectural modernism, once referred to the nineteenth century as the "inartistic century." It may be true that German Realism produced fewer creative breakthroughs than Romanticism in the first half of the century or Expressionism in the Wilhelmine period. Realist painting often drew on *Biedermeier* conventionality rather than Romantic rebellion. But let it be added that Germany's cultural institutions remained regionally dispersed and resistant to top-down control. Artists sought but never found a distinctive, coherent form of "German" art that would reflect the political "unity" of the post-1871 nation-state.

Germany's federal states and municipalities set their own cultural policies to express and protect what they defined as public taste. These policies became more important after 1890, when a rise in artistic production that took sex, crime, and adventure as its themes summoned into existence a moral purity movement – something that had hardly been necessary in Bismarckian Germany. Unlike France, where Paris was the undisputed cultural capital, late nineteenth-century Germany had many centres of artistic production, not a single definitive one. Dresden and Munich took the lead, but Berlin, the new political capital, was gradually making a name for itself as a cultural centre too. This lack of an artistic centre hindered the development of a cohesive German style, but it also allowed for a diversity that accommodated the personal idiosyncrasies of creative artists. Some artists abandoned the multitude of artistic centres and developed a lighter, "open air" (*plein air*) style of landscape painting. Others followed peasants into tiny rural cottages and rustic taverns in order to paint them in their daily environments. Such ventures into the countryside often revealed land ravaged by open-pit mining, belching smokestacks, and ill-considered attempts to shape the natural environment.

The gradual development of a national art market, the rapid rise in the circulation of journals and popular newspapers, the increasing numbers of illustrated books, book series, and lending libraries, new efforts to make museums and concert halls more accessible to the bourgeois public, the staging of national and international art exhibitions – these developments all had a homogenizing effect on German culture. But it remained impossible to discern, much less impose, identifiably "national" standards for what constituted good German art. Long before 1890, German artists were searching for new ways to express the deeper cultural significance of political unification, industrial capitalism, and alienation from bourgeois conventions. These issues were tackled in every artistic genre but were particularly evident in the novels of Imperial Berlin.

Thus it would be incorrect to say that either complacency or conformism characterized the creativity of individuals who, like Adolph Menzel and Friedrich Nietzsche, followed the beat of a different drummer throughout their career, or who, like Max Liebermann and Gerhart Hauptmann, expropriated the "celebratory" kernel of official court culture even while they embraced new subjects and developed new styles. Artists such as Fritz von Uhde, Hans Marées, Wilhelm Leibl, and Arnold Böcklin laid the groundwork for the Secession movements that developed in Dresden and Munich after 1890. As we see when we compare reactions to two German unifications (1870–1 and 1989–90), cultural anxiety about the durability of fundamental social values was expressed in print, on canvas, and on the stage, even as victorious Prussian troops marched through the Brandenburg Gate in 1866. (The analogous moment in October 1989 might be the now-famous kiss that Mikhail Gorbachev delivered on the cheek of Erich Honecker when they celebrated the fortieth anniversary of East Germany's founding, even as the GDR's popular legitimacy was crumbling.)

The birth of the German Empire was anticipated by a monumental work by Johannes Brahms, *Ein Deutsches Requiem* (Opus 45), completed in 1868. In adopting lines from 1 Corinthians 15, it seemed to anticipate the great national events to come: "We shall not all sleep, but we shall all be changed. In a moment, in the twinkling of any eye, at the last trumpet: for the trumpet shall sound, and the dead shall be raised imperishable, and we shall be changed." In contrast to August Heinrich Hoffmann von Fallersleben's *Founding Songs*, which ridiculed the pretensions of speculators in the early 1870s, the Brahms Requiem provided a deep resonance, a broad reflection on the accomplishment of unity – deeper and broader, certainly, than the verses of *The Watch on the Rhine*, sung by German soldiers marching to the front in the summer of 1870. Likewise, *Parsifal*, the last of Richard Wagner's grand operas, can hardly be said to have lacked resonance. Wagner's Ring Cycle, first performed at Bayreuth in 1876, was the culmination of the composer's search for a "total work of art" (*Gesamtkunstwerk*) sufficiently grand and unique to measure up to the Germany of both ancient and modern times. For better or worse, German music was never the same again.

Few writers of poetry and prose in this era made a lasting mark on German literature. The most significant exception is the giant of German Realist literature, Theodor Fontane, whose novel *Der Stechlin* did three things at once: it captured the spirit and tone of other literature of this era, it depicted with wry humour the unfolding of a local election campaign in backwoods Prussia, and it conveyed Fontane's characteristic mix of admiration for Prussia's rich heritage and his anxiety that German society had lost its moral compass. The same anxiety can be found in other sources that offer contrasting viewpoints – in celebratory poems and satirical cartoons, allegorical murals and children's board games, monumental architecture and kitschy pageants. We can also read pronouncements on the mood of the times from beyond Germany's borders, as well as studies celebrating the accomplishments of the *avant-garde*. It is difficult to overemphasize the diversity of ways in which German cultural production in these years reflected both pride in national achievement and misgivings about the future it would bring about. The opening of the National Gallery in Berlin in 1876 may not have provided the hoped-for opportunity to gather within one temple the variety of cultural expression under Bismarck. But the gallery's very first acquisition, Adolph Menzel's *Iron Rolling Mill*, illustrates the folly of attaching the label "inartistic" to the new Germany.

4. Religion, Education, Social Welfare

Historians were once prone to argue that religious allegiances inevitably wane in the face of modernizing trends such as population explosion, urbanization, industrialization, the rise of a self-conscious working class, the deification of technology and science, and cultural despair. Similarly, when historians observe that modernization had overcome the traditional *Kirchturmhorizont* – literally, the horizon as seen from the local church steeple – they are implying that religion had been superseded by other structuring categories such as class, gender, and ideology. But religion did not become irrelevant during the German Empire. Quite the reverse: religion continued to condition the outlook of Germans as it had for centuries, while also providing the impetus for important new departures on a national scale.

Of these, the *Kulturkampf* ("cultural struggle") between the German state and the Catholic Church was the most important. The *Kulturkampf* was not conjured out of nowhere by Bismarck; it drew on the determination of Protestant liberals to break what they saw as the archaic and dangerous influence of the Roman Catholic hierarchy in general, and the authority of the Pope specifically. Because the Pope, Catholic priests, and the political party leaders who defended the rights of Catholics were defined by Bismarck and the liberals as "enemies of the Empire" (*Reichsfeinde*), they are discussed in Section 7, where other state-sponsored campaigns to discriminate against minority groups are considered. Yet this conflict *was* a cultural one: it cannot be reduced to its purely confessional or party-political dimensions. Based on the tremendous growth of popular piety in the middle decades of the nineteenth century, religion continued to provide a filter through which the overwhelming majority of Germans viewed the material circumstances of their lives and the "Christian state" to which they looked for guidance. Thus religion helped shape discourses about the role of women in society, practices of charity, the scope of social reform, and the legitimate bounds of censorship.

Jews as well as Catholics were the target of nationalists obsessed with the need to define and defend a confessionally homogenous nation-state. The 1870s was not only the decade in which associational life expanded rapidly in support of Protestant and Catholic confessional goals; it was also the decade in which an alleged Jewish threat to the young German nation mobilized antisemites of word and deed. One impetus for the explosion of political antisemitism was the perception that Jews were benefiting disproportionately from the scandals associated with the founding era. The propaganda that carried the antisemites' message to every corner of the land drew on centuries-old stereotypes and falsehoods about the Jews – for example, their alleged propensity for usury and the blood libel myth. But another source of antipathy towards the Jews can be discerned in Germans' uncertainty about whether the boundaries of their nation were sufficiently well-defined to meet the challenges of a precarious geographic position in Europe and the global reach of commercial and cultural networks. In this context it became easy for anxious nationalists to claim that Germany would never be truly unified until the Jewish "inner enemy" had been vanquished.

In obvious contrast to the radical antisemitism that followed defeat in 1918 and the state-sponsored murder of six million Jews after 1933, antisemitism in the Bismarckian era did not attract enough support to lead to widespread violence against Jews. Nor did it destroy the Jews' confidence that Germany would provide a more congenial home as modernization continued. Even so, to further the Jews' integration into German society required great effort, as suggested by Emil Lehmann's campaign for Jewish rights in Saxony and the public advocacy of notables during the "Berlin Antisemitic Dispute" of 1879–81. It is easy to find chilling examples of the radicalism and plainness of language used, even in Bismarck's day, by antisemitic leaders and publicists. They spoke of ostracizing the Jews, destroying their "dominant" position in German business, culture, and the press, stripping them of civil and political rights, banishing them from German territory, even unleashing physical violence against them.

German education was recognized throughout the world for its high standards, relative accessibility, and outstanding contributions to science. No one could ignore the unprecedented growth in the number of primary, secondary, and university-level students studying in Germany and in the number of educators and institutions that taught them. In assessing this success story it is crucial to keep in mind how many educational opportunities were closed to German girls and women. Nor must we forget the confessional and class divisions that made a mockery of claims that German education was universally accessible or based on intellectual merit alone. According to first-hand accounts written by children and university students, corroborated by the recollections of their teachers, there was a decrease over time in the number of children kept from school because they were needed in the fields at harvest time or as messengers for small businesses. At the same time, the pressure to instil "state-supporting" values in students' minds increased markedly. The hypernationalism exhibited in Leipzig by members of the Association of German Students in the early 1880s followed the grain of Kaiser Wilhelm II's later panegyrics about the role of school curricula in combatting the "revolutionary threat" of Social Democracy. German youth were seen as the fount of national regeneration at a time when the "untested" nation faced confessional, class, and gender threats.

Religious piety fuelled charitable efforts to relieve the suffering of the rural and urban poor. After unification, however, as Social Democracy drew attention to the plight of society's most afflicted members, Germans redoubled their efforts to solve the "social question." When Kaiser Wilhelm I's throne speech of November 1881 announced the government's intention to inaugurate a comprehensive system of state-supported insurance for sickness, accidents, and old age, few contemporaries failed to recognize this impressive program as the carrot that went with the stick that Bismarck had been applying to the Social Democratic movement since the early 1870s. Poor-relief doctors and bourgeois social reformers documented the undernourishment and other hardships that afflicted millions of working-class families. Journalists, satirists, artists, and Social Democrats likewise ensured that problems of poor health, premature death, and gaps in the social safety net moved to the forefront of public awareness.

An unbridgeable ideological gulf separated Karl Marx's analysis of 1867, *Das Kapital*, from Kaiser Wilhelm II's pronouncement on the "workers' question" in February 1890. Quite a different justification for workers' compensation was offered by Bismarck in the 1880s. At that time the chancellor was still struggling to wring the building blocks of his program of social legislation from a reluctant, cost-conscious Reichstag. Meanwhile, critics of organized capitalism responded with panic to social crisis, often blaming capitalism's "dysfunctions" on the Jews. Earnest reformers and reactionary doomsayers disagreed fundamentally in their prognostications – so much so that their solutions to the "epidemic" of capitalism made existing problems seem even more poisonous.

5. Politics I: Forging an Empire

Military matters and international relations after 1871 will be dealt with in the next section. This one underscores the interpenetration of domestic and foreign policy in the forging of German unity between 1866 and 1871. If we include the war against Denmark in 1864, these years saw three successful wars bestow immense prestige and power on Bismarck, King Wilhelm I, and the Prussian army. We should reflect, however, on the contingent and contested nature of the political, diplomatic, and constitutional developments that led to the proclamation of the new German Reich in January 1871. Presenting these developments through the eyes of foreign diplomats, the man on the street, and commentators stationed far from Berlin, readily available sources demonstrate that almost every aspect of "imperial" power had to be negotiated. We can read about the deals Bismarck struck with his own king and Germany's federal princes, who were determined to preserve their traditions and autonomy as much as they could at each stage of the unification process; with liberals in Prussia, who were forced to reassess whether it was possible to pursue the twin goals of unity and freedom together; with Helmuth von Moltke, Chief of the Prussian General Staff, who wanted to use the military's battlefield triumphs as a springboard for domestic political influence; and with foreign powers, including France, Britain, and Russia, who worried that Prussia now posed a threat to international peace. These deals made Bismarck the most hated man in Germany at one moment and the most popular the next.

Such sources help us draw back the curtain on discussions that led up to two of the most compelling moments in the unification process. The first was Bismarck's decision to edit the Ems Dispatch on 13 July 1870. Famous both in its original version and in its revised form, the dispatch enabled Bismarck to goad the French into declaring war on Prussia. The second event was the "Hail!" to the new Kaiser in the Hall of Mirrors at the Palace of Versailles on 18 January 1871 – a scene that was famously painted by Anton von Werner in three versions, each with its own distinct perspective and intent. French and German satirical journals offered illuminating assessments of resistance to Prussian hegemony in Central Europe, from depictions of "Wilhelm the Butcher" to countless variations on the Prussian eagle and spiked helmet (*Pickelhaube*). Contemporary drawings and photographs also depicted the opposite sentiment, epitomized by Prussian victory parades through the streets of Paris and Berlin and sentimental paintings telling the story of Prussia's "inevitable" rise. But they do not allow us to forget the dead and wounded whose sacrifices made those victories possible.

Battlefield victories and "Hails!" to the Kaiser were not enough to forge a working constitutional state. The same kinds of political negotiations that led to the imperial proclamation continued afterwards – in parliament, in the press, in the slow process of legal codification, and in the critical reflections of liberals, who still hoped that national unity would foster greater civil and constitutional liberties. By examining the impassioned defence of German federalism written by one Württemberg Democrat (Ludwig Pfau) in the mid-1860s – which he updated in subtle ways in the mid-1890s – we can glean how Bismarck and the liberals found common ground on a broad platform of economic, legal, and constitutional reforms. The particularly fruitful legislative periods of 1866–7 and 1871–4 are worth highlighting in this regard. Where, one wonders, should the emphasis be put when describing this legislative agenda as "reformist conservatism" – on the adjective or the noun? The same question is prompted by the theory and reality of "constitutional monarchy," which can be assessed through Reichstag debates and iconography. Even the new German federal state (*Bundesstaat*) was contentious: the term was meant to suggest that central authority now rested with the imperial state (in the singular) rather than with the confederation of states (*Staatenbund*) that had existed until 1866.

In the 1870s, German leftists, drawn from both the socialist and liberal camps, cast their own light on possible paths to ongoing constitutional reform, even under Bismarck's increasingly autocratic governance. The liberals were now split between left-liberal and National Liberal factions. Their many accomplishments in these years cannot be dismissed. From 1874 onward, though, we see a narrowing of opportunities to realize the dream of a liberal constitutional state with parliamentary control over the executive branch. By the mid-1880s, liberal disunity, the perceived threat of socialism, and Bismarck's unassailable ascendancy in the Prussian state seemed to offer little hope for the future.

For a time it seemed possible that the coming reign of Kaiser Friedrich III might break Bismarck's omnipotence in domestic politics and revive liberal fortunes. More and more Germans had concluded that Bismarck was "a despot" – as Theodor Fontane and others claimed – and that he was also dispensable. However, the opposition parties in the Reichstag were unable to form an anti-Bismarckian coalition. The penetration of imperial institutions – and the *idea* of empire – into the dynastic states provided further impetus for the concentration of power in the office of the imperial chancellor and in the symbol of Kaiserdom. But Friedrich was terminally ill with throat cancer when he ascended the throne, and his reign in 1888 lasted only ninety-nine days. On his death, liberals realized that his son, Kaiser Wilhelm II, would not endorse a return to the "liberal era" of the 1870s.

6. Military and International Relations

The Nikolsburg agreement of 26 July 1866 effectively ended the centuries-old contest between Prussia and Austria for supremacy in German-speaking Central Europe. Four years later, the Germans' victory over the French was described by Britain's future prime minister Benjamin Disraeli as constituting a revolution in Europe whose consequences would affect every other Great Power. For the next two decades, Bismarck's policy would be marked by caution and the consolidation of German power, both internally and externally. That policy was guided by four core principles from which the chancellor never wavered. First, Europe and the world must be reassured that Germany was a "satiated" nation, dedicated to peace. Second, France must be isolated diplomatically to ensure that the "nightmare of coalitions" – two or more Great Powers allying themselves against Germany – would never come to pass. To that end Bismarck encouraged France to redirect its feelings of *revanche* over the loss of Alsace and Lorräine into colonial expansion. Third, Russia must be kept friendly to Germany, or at least friendly enough that it would not join an opposing alliance. Fourth, Germany must consistently prop up the power and prestige of the Austro-Hungarian Empire, to which end it concluded a formal alliance in 1879.

With the benefit of hindsight, students are tempted to conclude that Bismarck's track record – his successful wars of unification and his mastery of *Realpolitik* – made him a genius. This ascription also seems warranted when we compare his accomplishments to the zigzag policies pursued by the German Foreign Office after 1890; when we consider the transformation of the Anglo-German rivalry into estrangement and animosity following Kaiser Wilhelm II's decision to station a battle fleet in the North Sea; and when we consider that the unwinnable two-front war Germany faced in 1914 was the single greatest threat that Bismarck managed to avoid during his term of office. It may be true that Bismarck offered the world forty years of peace and was a gifted diplomatic tactician – for example, when he played the honest broker at the Congress of Berlin in 1878. Such hindsight, however, is not twenty-twenty. It ignores the aggressive expansionism and fearsome loss of life that were instrumental to his *Realpolitik* between 1862 and 1871.

At the end of his time in office, too, we can legitimately question both Bismarck's genius and his long-term goals. He underestimated the power of nationalism both at home and abroad, which not only undermined the diplomatic and military value of his single steadfast ally, Austria-Hungary, but also fuelled restless aggression among a younger generation drawn to Pan-Germanism. Bismarck's own policies contributed to the German public's rapturous reception of the most stirring line in his last major Reichstag speech of February 1888 – "We Germans fear God and nothing else in the world!" – and their utter neglect of his peaceful intentions voiced elsewhere in his speech. By 1889, Bismarck was ready to take previously unacceptable leaps in the dark to preserve his own authority in domestic and foreign affairs. Hence readers should consider both the virtues and the flaws of Bismarck's foreign policy over the *longue durée*. They should pay special attention to the widely divergent assessments of Bismarck voiced by contemporaries who basked in his aura or had to swallow his venomous rebukes.

In the process of forging an empire, the sword of victory was wielded by the Prussian army. Among today's historians, the role of the military in Imperial Germany has become a contentious issue. Exactly what linkage should we draw, for example, between the Prussian victory over Austria in July 1866 and Bismarck's successful whipping through parliament, just two months later, of a bill "indemnifying" him for disregarding the liberal opposition? The heavy symbolism that accompanied the proclamation of the Reich in the palace of Louis XIV in January 1871 was not accidental. At that event, the trappings of military power overwhelmed everything else: when Anton von Werner, commissioned to paint the scene, entered the Hall of Mirrors in Versailles, one Prussian officer exclaimed, "What is that *civilian* doing in here?" But did the annual Sedan Day festivities commemorating the defeat of France reflect a new chauvinism among the German populace? Or were they just occasions for local communities to celebrate the social and cultural ties that bound them together? Was the same bonding experience evident when veterans of the Wars of Unification and others who had been conscripted after 1871 gathered at the "regulars' table" (*Stammtisch*) in the local tavern to discuss their real or imagined memories of wartime service?

Even more open to debate is the degree to which the social ethos of the Prussian officer corps infused German society. This debate revolves around the meaning of the term "social militarism," which has eluded clear definition. Kaiser Wilhelm I and his grandson both placed great importance on the social ethos of Prussian officers. By the time Wilhelm II ascended the throne in 1888, it was clear that the ancient Prussian nobility could no longer supply the number of socially privileged and politically "reliable" recruits needed by a modern army. The young Kaiser made a virtue of necessity. He decreed that a new "nobility of spirit" would ensure the continued respect shown to the officer corps by German society. Although historians no longer believe that popular acceptance of the military's elevated status in society signified the "feudalization" of the bourgeoisie, this issue still elicits debate.

Germany's brief flurry of colonizing activity in the mid-1880s represented the single most important exception to Bismarck's policy of maintaining the status quo in foreign affairs after 1871. Fortifying Germany's position in Europe and insulating it from potential shocks from the international alliance system remained Bismarck's priorities – this was where his map of Africa lay, as he once put it. Some Germans believed otherwise, including Friedrich Fabri, Director of the Barmen Rhine Missionary Society. Fabri was convinced that his 1879 pamphlet *Does Germany Need Colonies?* was instrumental in unleashing the public clamour for overseas colonies. Whatever the merits of that claim, the early 1880s saw the rise of noisy colonial lobby groups and the reorganization or expansion of some older societies promoting emigration, geographic exploration, or the export trade. Fabri's pamphlet and the agitation of these societies captured the public mood of Germans who worried about how to reinvigorate the economy, provide a safety valve to (perceived) over-population through emigration, and secure raw materials and markets for German industry.

Between 1884 and 1886, action followed words, initially through the bold claims to South-West Africa staked by the adventurer Carl Peters and subsequently through the establishment of German protectorates in Cameroon, Togo, German East Africa, and a number of islands in the South Pacific. Bismarck acceded to this land grab even though he had previously refused to consider colonial acquisitions. The chancellor may have been trying to use colonial possessions as pawns in his chess game of international diplomacy. He was not averse to stirring up tension with Britain as a means to undermine the influence of Crown Prince Friedrich Wilhelm and his English wife, the daughter of Queen Victoria. And at least for a short time he recognized the electoral appeal of colonies. His brief, tentative ride on the colonial bandwagon was supported by members of the right-wing National Liberal and Free Conservative parties, whose candidates in 1884 recouped some of the seats they had lost to the left liberals in the Reichstag elections of 1881. None of these explanations makes sense, however, unless we discard the idea that Bismarck conjured up the colonial movement to serve his Machiavellian plans. Instead we should recognize that colonies in the 1880s represented a genuinely powerful expression of nationalist feelings among a significant number of middle-class Germans.

The allure of colonies had its limits. The National Liberal Friedrich Kapp, the Social Democrat August Bebel, and others offered cogent criticisms of colonial chauvinism. Over time many Germans came to share these critics' assessment. They also realized that Bismarck had been correct to worry that Germany would benefit only marginally, if at all, from even a "pragmatic" approach whereby economic control of overseas territories relied on the activity of chartered companies rather than state initiative ("the flag follows trade"). The often brutal treatment of native Africans provided the Social Democrats with plenty of ammunition to denounce Germany's territorial expansion overseas. Satirical magazines also ridiculed claims that colonial conquests represented a "civilizing mission" on behalf of all mankind. Nevertheless, Carl Peters and others were indefatigable in answering such criticism with further claims – as vehement as they were unsupportable – about the economic, national, and cultural benefits of colonies. Sometimes they pointed to the danger of giving socialist critics of colonialism a hearing at all. Whether opposing colonies or calling for more overseas expansion, such pronouncements in favour of colonies expressed a growing sense of unease among nationalists that Germany's mission in the world remained unrealizable within the constraints imposed by Bismarck's system and style of governance.

7. Politics II: Parties and Political Mobilization

In an age of rapid social and economic change, when the new Empire's political culture was still in flux, the tactic of labelling certain outgroups "enemies of the Reich" seemed to offer Bismarck the opportunity to create an alliance of state-supporting parties in the Prussian Landtag and the national Reichstag. Among such "enemies" Bismarck focused his attacks on German Catholics from 1871 onward, on Social Democrats after 1878, on left liberals in the early- and mid-1880s, and on the Poles of eastern Prussia starting in 1885. The first two groups deserve special attention because they most clearly demonstrated that this strategy was prone to backfire on the chancellor. It created or strengthened the common identity of members of the victimized groups where such solidarities had previously been less apparent. Earlier scholars approached the *Kulturkampf* against the Catholic Church and the Anti-Socialist Law of 1878–90 as evidence of Bismarck's manipulation of public opinion to safeguard his fragile Reich. Now historians stress the degree to which both anti-Catholic and anti-Socialist campaigns accorded with the wishes of large segments of the Protestant middle classes. Both struggles also contributed to the destabilization and loss of authority of the Bismarckian state, not its fortification.

The *Kulturkampf* was Bismarck's boldest and most ill-conceived gamble. It was heralded by a gradual escalation in tensions between state authorities and the Catholic hierarchy in the second half of the 1860s in Baden, Prussia, and other German states. Shortly after unification Bismarck and Culture Minister Adalbert Falk inaugurated a series of legislative initiatives designed to undermine the Catholic Church's autonomy in Germany, to reduce its financial independence, to lessen its influence in the schools, and to banish the Jesuit Order from German lands. Left liberals and National Liberals enthusiastically supported this initiative. Some of them agonized over the discrepancy between liberalism's commitment to civil liberties and the obvious fact that Bismarck was targeting a specific group for repression. Most, however, hoped that the struggle against the Catholic Church would achieve three aims: reduce the influence of groups on the Empire's borderlands (Prussian Poland, Bavaria, the Rhineland, and Alsace-Lorraine) who might be tempted to ally with their coreligionists in France or Austria; drive back the forces of "obscurantism" that had allegedly remained ascendant in the Catholic Church since medieval times; and ensure that the liberal parties remained indispensable to Bismarck, thus allowing the expansion of constitutional and economic liberties in the future.

The May Laws of 1873 constituted the centerpiece of *Kulturkampf* legislation. Tensions between Bismarck and the Pope worsened over the next two years. By the end of the decade, however, Bismarck had recognized that counter-efforts by Catholic clergy and their congregations had largely frustrated his plans. The insufficiency of state institutions to combat roughly one-third of the Empire's population had been strikingly revealed. By 1878 the chancellor had many reasons to welcome back into the government fold the principal political representative of Catholic interests, the German Centre Party (*Zentrum*), which drew on a wide variety of ecclesiastical and lay organizations. The Centre Party commanded a large caucus of Reichstag deputies representing Catholic constituencies. In such regions it was often a foregone conclusion that the Centre candidate would emerge victorious on election day, not only due to the clustering of Catholics in specific regions of Germany but also because deep-seated social antagonisms divided Protestants and Catholics and contributed to the latter's feelings of discrimination. Between 1878 and the mid-1880s, the *Kulturkampf* was slowly wound down. Bismarck, however, never publicly admitted defeat, and confessional peace remained fragile in the Wilhelmine era.

Bismarck gradually escalated repressive measures against the allegedly "revolutionary" threat of Social Democracy during the 1870s. Two assassination attempts on Kaiser Wilhelm I led to passage of the Anti-Socialist Law in October 1878. The campaign to outlaw Social Democratic activities was even more popular among bourgeois Germans than the *Kulturkampf*, and its failure proved to be another blow to the authority of the Bismarckian state. The two campaigns shared many features. They both raised hopes among middle-class liberals that a campaign against "enemies of the Empire" would consolidate the strength and inner unity of the new nation-state, either by reasserting the authority of the state over followers of the Pope or by defending private property and the established social order against the forces of revolution. Both led to liberal self-recrimination and second thoughts about the wisdom of designating any single political movement as "beyond the pale." Both demonstrated that the police, the courts, and state administrators lacked the means or were insufficiently committed to combat a political ideology representing such a large portion of the population. And both contributed directly to strong feelings of solidarity among the targeted group, increasing their electoral success and parliamentary influence.

Few German workers had even heard of Karl Marx in the early 1870s or knew anything about his theories of class struggle and revolution. Of those who did, many still followed the teachings of another (already deceased) socialist leader, Ferdinand Lassalle. During the period of the Anti-Socialist Law, Social Democrats developed a comprehensive network of underground agents, couriers, propagandists, and election workers. Due in part to the practical work of August Bebel, Wilhelm Liebknecht, and other Social Democratic leaders in the Reichstag, the Saxon Landtag, and other state parliaments, more and more workers came to believe that tight party organization, an autonomous network of cultural associations, political protest, and the principle of "every man on deck" on election day were the best way to combat a state that had labelled them outlaws. As a result, between 1878 and 1890 the membership of the Social Democratic Party rose, as did the number of deputies in its parliamentary caucuses. Whereas only about 350,000 votes had been cast for Social Democratic candidates in the Reichstag elections of 1874, 1.4 million ballots were cast for the party in February 1890 – almost 20 per cent of the popular vote. This stunning victory contributed to Kaiser Wilhelm II's decision to dispense with Bismarck a month later and it anticipated the party's even more dramatic growth in the 1890s.

Universal male suffrage was introduced in 1867, first for elections to the Reichstag of the North German Confederation and then, in 1871, for the new Empire. In these years the party landscape in Germany assumed patterns that persisted up to 1918 and beyond. Historians disagree about whether the main political parties represented stable socio-moral "milieus," as postulated by M. Rainer Lepsius. Milieu theory fails to accommodate the dynamic nature and opportunities for shifting alliances within Imperial Germany's political system. Yet the durability of the main party groupings and their original party platforms suggests that the genesis of modern mass politics is best located in the Bismarckian, not the Wilhelmine, era. It was in 1866–7 that both the conservative and liberal movements split. The Social Democrats also organized in these years, first in the regional and then the national arenas. In the early 1870s the Catholic Centre Party was consolidated in response to the *Kulturkampf*, and in 1875 the Marxist and Lassallean wings of Social Democracy forged a fragile unity on the basis of the

Gotha Program. The 1880s saw the older left-liberal and newer antisemitic parties split, reunite, or otherwise reconstitute themselves.

These parties' programs and election manifestos illustrate the interdependence of social, economic, and political issues in their respective ideologies. They also reveal opportunities for coalition-building between parties as well as the obstacles to cooperation that have led some historians to speak of the "pillarization" of the party-political system. Satirical cartoons and carefully posed photographs of party leaders in the foyer of the Reichstag suggest that the main parties shared more common values than historians sometimes suppose, even though party alliances seemed arbitrary at one moment and dependent on Bismarck's favour at another.

The emergence of new political parties and party groupings was not the only important feature of the emerging mass politics in Bismarckian Germany. An increasingly powerful mass press brought questions of public policy into the homes of ordinary Germans. As voters came to accept the act of casting a ballot as a natural patriotic duty or as the best means of expressing social solidarities, the turnout for Reichstag elections rose dramatically – again, much more dramatically than the better-studied elections after 1890. In the Reichstag elections of 1874, about 5.2 million Germans cast ballots, resulting in a turnout rate of 61.2 per cent. In the Reichstag elections of 1887, about 7.6 million Germans trooped to the polls. This equated to a turnout rate of 77.5 per cent, which remained unmatched until 1907. One reason for this increase in voter commitment was the effort made by Reichstag deputies to ensure the secrecy of the act of voting.

Such protection was far from ironclad. Whether the principle of secret balloting was respected or undermined depended very much on where a voter lived, who his employer was, and whether the government took a direct interest in the outcome of a particular local campaign. Little wonder that artists of the day depicted the unresolved questions that afflicted "philistine" voters in this era. Voters also became the target of irresponsible promises and appeals from radical parties. The antisemites of the late 1870s and 1880s contributed most to the brutalization of public opinion: they had a high appreciation for the average voter's gullibility. Yet all parties were forced to reckon with the masses, whether or not they wanted to. As one Conservative put it, universal manhood suffrage had grown "too hot under their feet" to allow them to rely any longer on the older and more exclusive politics of notables (*Honoratiorenpolitik*).

A scholarly wag once remarked that a book titled *The Unification of Germany by Kaiser Wilhelm I* should have been titled *"despite* Wilhelm I." Before his death in March 1888, Wilhelm I himself observed wryly that it was not easy to serve as Kaiser under the reign of a chancellor like Bismarck. For his part, Bismarck was consistent and sincere when he argued that he served at the pleasure of his king. During the short reign of Kaiser Friedrich III in the spring of 1888, relations between Bismarck and the royal palace were formally cordial but, below the surface, strained and dishonest. To the surprise of most insiders, a better relationship between chancellor and emperor re-emerged initially when Kaiser Wilhelm II ascended the throne in June 1888. By the end of the "Year of Three Kaisers," though, storm clouds had appeared on the horizon, eventually leading to Wilhelm II's dismissal of Bismarck in March 1890. Even earlier than that, contemporaries had been debating the historical significance and consequences of Bismarck's long term of office. Where next for Germany? This debate would continue for months and years after Bismarck's resignation. A Bismarck cult had already assumed immense proportions before the former chancellor's death in July 1898.

The German Empire had been forged on the anvil of military victory, monarchism, and Prussianism. It had developed into an economic power of the first order, able to dominate industrial markets in any number of sectors. It boasted schools, scientific laboratories, an art scene, and electoral freedoms that were the envy of Europe and the world. And the principle of federalism, so powerful in earlier epochs, had not been sacrificed even as the empire's central political institutions grew in number and importance. Even protection for the rights of Jews seemed secure, or more secure than in other parts of Europe. Nevertheless, the question of whether the authoritarian or the modern features of Germany's Second Reich would come to the fore in the new century remained tantalizingly open. In fact both features persisted and continued to evolve.

On 29 March 1890, Bismarck's train left the Lehrter Station in Berlin to deliver him into retirement on his estate in Friedrichsruh (near Hamburg). That leave-taking provided Germans with an opportunity to look back over twenty-five years of unprecedented change and achievement in the economic, social, and cultural realms. In the process of forging and fortifying their empire, Germans had diminished themselves. They had done so by making existing cleavages of wealth and rank

Figure 1.3 In 1885, Gottlieb Daimler, together with his partner Wilhelm Maybach, adapted an early model of the internal combustion engine and patented what is generally recognized as the prototype of the modern gas engine. On 8 March 1886, Daimler took a stagecoach (made by Wilhelm Wimpff & Son) and adapted it to hold his engine. In the process, he ended up designing the world's first four-wheeled automobile. bpk, Berlin/Art Resource, NY.

even deeper, by attacking the rights of minority groups, by driving a wedge between the working classes and the rest of society, by compromising the prerogatives of parliament, and by following the lead of an increasingly out-of-touch statesman. Such actions and attitudes encumbered later German history in ways that placed barriers in the path of parliamentarization, democratization, and the tolerance of diversity. This interpretation of Bismarckian Germany and its legacy has been downplayed or challenged in most history books published in the past twenty years. However, history must remain open to multiple readings and critical reflection.

SUGGESTIONS FOR FURTHER READING

Overviews

Lynn Abrams, *Bismarck and the German Empire, 1871–1918*, 2nd rev. ed., London and New York, 2006 (orig. 1995).
Volker R. Berghahn, *Imperial Germany, 1871–1914: Economy, Society, Culture and Politics*, 2nd rev. ed., Oxford and New York, 2005 (orig. 1994).
David Blackbourn, *History of Germany, 1780–1918: The Long Nineteenth Century*, 2nd rev. ed., London, 2003 (orig. 1997).
Roger Chickering, ed., *Imperial Germany: A Historiographical Companion*, Westport, CT, 1996.
Ewald Frie, *Das Deutsche Kaiserreich*, Darmstadt, 2004, 2nd rev. ed. 2013.
Lothar Gall, *Bismarck: The White Revolutionary*, 2 vols., Boston, 1986 (orig. German ed. 1980).
Dieter Hertz-Eichenrode, *Deutsche Geschichte 1871–1890*, Stuttgart, 1992.
Matthew Jefferies, ed., *The Ashgate Research Companion to Imperial Germany*, Farnham, 2015.
Matthew Jefferies, *Contesting the German Empire, 1871–1918*, Oxford, 2007.
Katharine Anne Lerman, *Bismarck*, Harlow, 2004.
Wilfried Loth, *Das Kaiserreich. Obrigkeitsstaat und politische Mobilisierung*, Munich, 1996.
Wolfgang J. Mommsen, *Imperial Germany 1867–1918: Politics, Culture, and Society in an Authoritarian State*, London and New York, 1995 (orig. German ed. 1990).
Wolfgang J. Mommsen, *Das Ringen um den nationalen Staat*, pt 1, *Die Gründung und der innere Ausbau des Deutschen Reiches unter Otto von Bismarck 1850 bis 1890*, Berlin, 1993.
Sven Oliver Müller and Cornelius Torp, eds., *Imperial Germany Revisited: Continuing Debates and New Perspectives*, Oxford and New York, 2011 (orig. German ed. 2009).
Thomas Nipperdey, *Deutsche Geschichte 1866–1918*, 2 vols., Munich, 1990–2.
Thomas Nipperdey, *Gesellschaft, Kultur, Theorie. Gesammelte Aufsätze zur neueren Geschichte*, Göttingen, 1976.
Thomas Nipperdey, *Nachdenken über die Deutsche Geschichte. Essays*, Munich, 1986.
Otto Pflanze, *Bismarck and the Development of Germany*, 3 vols., Princeton, 1990.
James Retallack, ed., *Imperial Germany 1871–1918. The Short Oxford History of Germany*, Oxford and New York, 2008.

Matthew S. Seligmann and Roderick R. McLean, *Germany from Reich to Republic, 1871–1918*, New York, 2000.
James J. Sheehan, ed., *Imperial Germany*, New York, 1976.
Helmut Walser Smith, ed., *The Oxford Handbook of Modern German History* (Part III), Oxford and New York, 2011.
Jonathan Steinberg, *Bismarck: A Life*, Oxford, 2011.
Volker Ulrich, *Die nervöse Großmacht 1871–1918. Aufstieg und Untergang des Kaiserreichs*, Frankfurt a.M., 1997.
Hans-Ulrich Wehler, *Deutsche Gesellschaftsgeschichte*, vol. 3, *Von der "Deutschen Doppelrevolution" bis zum Beginn des Ersten Weltkrieges 1849–1914*, Munich, 1995.
Hans-Ulrich Wehler, *The German Empire, 1871–1918*, Oxford and New York, 1997 (orig. German ed. 1973).
Hans-Ulrich Wehler, *Krisenherde des Kaiserreichs 1871–1918. Studien zur deutschen Sozial- und Verfassungsgeschichte*, 2nd ed., Göttingen, 1979.

Many works listed above also provide an introduction to the Wilhelmine period (1890–1918), which this chapter does not address directly. The following works can be added either because they offer insight into that later era or because they have changed the way historians interpret the Second Reich as a whole.

David Blackbourn, *Populists and Patricians*, London, 1987.
Roger Chickering, *Imperial Germany and the Great War, 1914–1918*, Cambridge, 1998.
Roger Chickering, *We Men Who Feel Most German: A Cultural Study of the Pan-German League, 1886–1914*, Boston, 1984.
Christopher Clark, *Kaiser Wilhelm II*, Harlow, 2000.
Christopher Clark, *The Sleepwalkers: How Europe Went to War in 1914*, London, 2012.
Ralf Dahrendorf, *Society and Democracy in Germany*, New York, 1967 (orig. German ed. 1965).
Edward Ross Dickinson, *Sex, Freedom, and Power in Imperial Germany, 1880–1914*, Cambridge, 2014.
Geoff Eley, *From Unification to Nazism*, London, 1986.
Geoff Eley, *Reshaping the German Right: Radical Nationalism and Political Change after Bismarck*, New Haven, CT, 1980.
Geoff Eley and James Retallack, eds., *Wilhelminism and Its Legacies: German Modernities, Imperialism, and the Meanings of Reform, 1890–1930*, Oxford and New York, 2003.

Richard J. Evans, ed., *Society and Politics in Wilhelmine Germany*, London, 1978.
Richard J. Evans, *Rethinking German History*, London, 1987.
Fritz Fischer, *Germany's Aims in the First World War*, London, 1967 (orig. German ed. 1961).
Isabel V. Hull, *Absolute Destruction: Military Culture and the Practices of War in Imperial Germany*, Ithaca, 2006.
Konrad H. Jarausch, *The Enigmatic Chancellor: Bethmann Hollweg and the Hubris of Imperial Germany*, New Haven, CT, 1973.
Peter Jelavich, *Munich and Theatrical Modernism: Politics, Playwriting, and Performance, 1890–1914*, Cambridge, MA, 1985.
Journal of Contemporary History 48, no. 2 (April 2013), Special Issue: "The Fischer Controversy After 50 Years."
Jürgen Kocka, *Facing Total War: German Society, 1914–1918*, Leamington Spa, 1984 (orig. German ed. 1973).
Alan Kramer, *Dynamic of Destruction: Culture and Mass Killing in the First World War*, Oxford, 2007.
Katharine A. Lerman, *The Chancellor as Courtier: Bernhard von Bülow and the Governance of Germany, 1900–1909*, Cambridge, 1990.
J. Alden Nichols, *Germany after Bismarck: The Caprivi Era, 1890–1894*, Cambridge, MA, 1958.
Ute Planert, *Antifeminismus im Kaiserreich*, Frankfurt a.M., 1998.
Kevin Repp, *Reformers, Critics, and the Paths of German Modernity: Anti-Politics and the Search for Alternatives, 1890–1914*, Cambridge, 2000.
James Retallack, *Germany in the Age of Kaiser Wilhelm II*, Basingstoke and New York, 1996.
John C.G. Röhl, *Germany without Bismarck: The Crisis of Government in the Second Reich, 1890–1900*, London, 1967.
John C.G. Röhl, *Wilhelm II*, 3 vols. Cambridge, 1998–2014 (orig. German ed. 1993–2009).
Helmut Walser Smith, *The Continuities of German History: Nation, Religion, and Race across the Long Nineteenth Century*, Cambridge, 2008.

1. Demographic and Economic Development

Klaus Bade, ed., *Auswanderer – Wanderarbeiter – Gastarbeiter. Bevölkerung, Arbeitsmarkt und Wanderung in Deutschland seit der Mitte des 19. Jahrhunderts*, 2 vols., Ostfildern, 1984.
Klaus Bade, ed., *Population, Labour, and Migration in 19th and 20th-Century Germany*, Leamington Spa and New York, 1987.

Helmut Böhme, *Deutschlands Weg zur Großmacht. Studien zum Verhältnis von Wirtschaft und Staat während der Reichsgründungszeit 1848–1881*, Cologne and Berlin, 1966.
David Crew, *Town in the Ruhr: A Social History of Bochum, 1860–1914*, New York, 1979.
Oliver Grant, *Migration and Inequality in Germany, 1870–1913*, Oxford, 2005.
Hans Werner Hahn, *Die Industrielle Revolution in Deutschland*, Munich, 1998.
William O. Henderson, *The Rise of German Industrial Power, 1834–1914*, London, 1975.
Martin Kitchen, *The Political Economy of Germany, 1815–1914*, London, 1978.
Jürgen Kocka, *Industrial Culture and Bourgeois Society: Business, Labor, and Bureaucracy in Modern Germany*, Oxford and New York, 1999.
Sheilagh Ogilvie and Richard Overy, eds., *Germany: A New Social and Economic History*, vol. 3, *Since 1800*, London and New York, 2003.
Tony Pierenkemper and Richard Tilly, *The German Economy during the Nineteenth Century*, New York, 2004.
Jürgen Reulecke, *Geschichte der Urbanisierung in Deutschland*, Frankfurt a.M., 1985.
Hans Rosenberg, *Große Depression und Bismarckzeit. Wirtschaftsablauf, Gesellschaft und Politik in Mitteleuropa*, Berlin, 1967.
Hans Rosenberg, *Machteliten und Wirtschaftskonjunkturen. Studien zur neueren deutschen Sozial- und Wirtschaftsgeschichte*, Göttingen, 1978.
Frank B. Tipton, *Regional Variations in the Economic Development of Germany during the Nineteenth Century*, Middletown, CT, 1976.
Cornelius Torp, *The Challenges of Globalization: Economy and Politics in Germany, 1860–1914*, Oxford and New York, 2014 (orig. German ed. 2005).
Ingeborg Weber-Kellermann, *Landleben im 19. Jahrhundert*, Munich, 2nd ed. 1988.
Frieda Wunderlich, *Farm Labor in Germany, 1810–1945*, Princeton, 1961.

2. Society

Celia Applegate, *A Nation of Provincials: The German Idea of Heimat*, Berkeley, 1990.
David Blackbourn and Geoff Eley, *The Peculiarities of German History: Bourgeois Society and Politics in Nineteenth-Century Germany*, Oxford and New York, 1984.
David Blackbourn and Richard J. Evans, eds., *The German Bourgeoisie*, London, 1991.

Richard Blanke, *Prussian Poland in the German Empire (1871–1900)*, Boulder, CO, and New York, 1981.
Kathleen Canning, *Languages of Labor and Gender: Female Factory Work in Germany, 1850–1914*, Ithaca, 1996.
Barbara Franzoi, *At the Very Least She Pays the Rent: Women and German Industrialization*, Westport, CT, 1985.
Ute Frevert, *Women in German History: From Bourgeois Emancipation to Sexual Liberation*, Oxford and Washington, DC, 1990.
Lothar Gall, *Bürgertum, liberale Bewegung und Nation. Ausgewählte Aufsätze*, Munich, 1996.
Karen Hagemann and Jean H. Quataert, eds., *Gendering Modern German History: Theories – Debates – Revisions*, Oxford and New York, 2007.
Marion A. Kaplan, *The Making of the Jewish Middle Class: Women, Family, and Identity in Imperial Germany*, Oxford and New York, 1991.
Jürgen Kocka with Ute Frevert, ed., *Bürgertum im 19. Jahrhundert. Deutschland im europäischen Vergleich*, 3 vols., Munich, 1988.
Jürgen Kocka and Alan Mitchell, eds., *Bourgeois Society in Nineteenth-Century Europe*, Oxford and Providence, RI, 1993.
Brian Ladd, *Urban Planning and Civic Order in Germany, 1860–1914*, Cambridge, MA, 1990.
Andrew Lees, *Cities, Sin, and Social Reform in Imperial Germany*, Ann Arbor, 2002.
Heinz Reif, ed., *Adel und Bürgertum in Deutschland*, Bd. 1, *Entwicklungslinien und Wendepunkte im 19. Jahrhundert*, Berlin, 2000.
Gerhard A. Ritter and Klaus Tenfelde, *Arbeiter im Deutschen Kaiserreich 1871 bis 1914*, Bonn, 1992.
Angelika Schaser, *Frauenbewegung in Deutschland 1848–1933*, Darmstadt, 2006.
Shulamit Volkov, *The Rise of Popular Antimodernism in Germany: The Urban Master Artisans, 1873–1896*, Princeton, 1978.

3. Culture

Klaus Amann and Karl Wagner, eds., *Literatur und Nation. Die Gründung des Deutschen Reiches 1871 in der deutschsprachigen Literatur*, Cologne, Weimar, and Vienna, 1996.
David Blackbourn, *Marpingen: Apparitions of the Virgin Mary in Nineteenth-Century Germany*, New York, 1994.
David Blackbourn and James Retallack, eds., *Localism, Landscape, and the Ambiguities of Place: German-Speaking Central Europe, 1860–1930*, Toronto, 2007.

Curtis Cate, *Friedrich Nietzsche*, London, 2002.
W.A. Coupe, *German Political Satires from the Reformation to the Second World War*, 6 vols., pt 2, vols. 3–4, *1849–1918*, White Plains, NY, 1987.
Gordon A. Craig, *Theodor Fontane: Literature and History in the Bismarck Reich*, Oxford and New York, 1999.
Götz Czymmek and Christian Lenz, eds., *Wilhelm Leibl. Zum 150. Geburtstag*, Heidelberg, 1994.
Andreas Dorpalen, *Heinrich von Treitschke*, New Haven, CT, 1957.
Françoise Forster-Hahn et al., *Spirit of an Age: Nineteenth-Century Paintings from the Nationalgalerie, Berlin*, London, 2001.
Thomas W. Gaehtgens, *Anton von Werner: Die Proklamierung des Deutschen Kaiserreiches. Ein Historienbild im Wandel preussischer Politik*, Frankfurt a.M., 1990.
R. J. Hollingdale, *Nietzsche: The Man and His Philosophy*, 2nd rev. ed., New York, 1999 (orig. 1965).
Matthew Jefferies, *Imperial Culture in Germany, 1871–1918*, Basingstoke and New York, 2003.
Claude Keisch, Marie Ursula Riemann-Reyher, eds., *Adolph Menzel, 1815–1905: Between Romanticism and Impressionism*, New Haven, CT, and London, 1996.
Clayton Koelb and Eric Downing, eds., *German Literature of the Nineteenth Century, 1832–1899*, Rochester, 2005 (Camden House History of Germany, vol. 9).
Joachim Köhler, *Richard Wagner: The Last of the Titans*, trans. Stewart Spencer, New Haven, CT, 2004.
Robin J. Lenman, *Artists and Society in Germany, 1850–1914*, Manchester, 1997 (orig. German ed. 1994).
Beth Irwin Lewis, *Art for All? The Collision of Modern Art and the Public in Late Nineteenth-Century Germany*, Princeton, 2003.
Vernon Lidtke, *The Alternative Culture: Socialist Labor in Imperial Germany*, Oxford and New York, 1985.
Walter Pape, ed., *1870/71–1989/90: German Unifications and the Change of Literary Discourse*, Berlin and New York, 1993.
Peter Paret, *Art as History: Episodes in the Culture and Politics of Nineteenth-Century Germany*, Princeton, 1988.
Joachim Remak, *The Gentle Critic: Theodor Fontane and German Politics, 1848–1898*, Syracuse, 1964.
Katherine Roper, *German Encounters with Modernity: Novels of Imperial Berlin*, Atlantic Highlands, NJ, 1991.
Ronald Speirs and John Breuilly, eds., *Germany's Two Unifications: Anticipations, Experiences, Responses*, Basingstoke, 2005.

George S. Williamson, *The Longing for Myth in Germany: Religion and Aesthetic Culture from Romanticism to Nietzsche*, Chicago, 2004.

4. Religion, Education, Social Welfare

James C. Albisetti, *Schooling German Girls and Women: Secondary and Higher Education in the Nineteenth Century*, Princeton, 1988.

James C. Albisetti, *Secondary School Reform in Imperial Germany*, Princeton, 1983.

Wolfgang Ayass, Florian Tennstedt, and Heidi Winter, eds., *Von der Kaiserlichen Sozialbotschaft bis zu den Februarerlassen Wilhelms II. (1881–1890)*, vol. 1, *Grundfragen der Sozialpolitik. Die Diskussion der Arbeiterfrage auf Regierungsseite und in der Öffentlichkeit*, Darmstadt, 2003.

Olaf Blaschke and Frank-Michael Kuhlemann, eds., *Religion im Kaiserreich. Milieus – Mentalitäten – Krisen*, Gütersloh, 1996.

Walter Boehlich, *Der Berliner Antisemitismusstreit*, Frankfurt a.M., 1965.

Raymond H. Dominick, *The Environmental Movement in Germany: Prophets and Pioneers, 1871–1971*, Bloomington, IN, 1992.

Michael B. Gross, *The War against Catholicism: Liberalism and the Anti-Catholic Imagination in Nineteenth-Century Germany*, Ann Arbor, 2004.

Barnet Hartston, *Sensationalizing the Jewish Question: Anti-Semitic Trials and the Press in the Early German Empire*, Leiden and Boston, 2005.

Heinz-Gerhard Haupt and Dieter Langewiesche, eds., *Nation und Religion in der deutschen Geschichte*, Frankfurt a.M. and New York, 2001.

Róisín Healy, *The Jesuit Specter in Imperial Germany*, Boston, 2003.

Konrad H. Jarausch, *Students, Society, and Politics in Imperial Germany: The Rise of Academic Illiberalism*, Princeton, 1982.

Uffa Jensen, *Gebildete Doppelgänger. Bürgerliche Juden und Protestanten im 19. Jahrhundert*, Göttingen, 2005.

Karsten Krieger, ed., *Der Berliner Antisemitismusstreit 1879–1881*, 2 vols., Munich, 2004.

Marjorie Lamberti, *State, Society, and the Elementary School in Imperial Germany*, Oxford and New York, 1989.

Simone Lässig, *Jüdische Wege ins Bürgertum. Kulturelles Kapital und sozialer Aufstieg im 19. Jahrhundert*, Göttingen, 2004.

Thomas M. Lekan, *Imagining the Nation in Nature: Landscape Preservation and German Identity, 1885–1945*, Cambridge, MA, 2004.

Charles McClelland, *State, Society, and University in Germany, 1700–1914*, Cambridge, MA, 1980.

Michael A. Meyer with Michael Brenner, eds., *German-Jewish History in Modern Times*, vol. 3, *Integration in Dispute, 1871–1918*, edited by Stephen M. Lowenstein et al., New York, 1996.

Thomas Nipperdey, *Religion im Umbruch. Deutschland 1870–1918*, Munich, 1988.

Peter G.J. Pulzer, *The Rise of Political Antisemitism in Germany and Austria*, rev. ed., Cambridge, MA, 1988 (orig. 1964).

Gerhard A. Ritter, *Social Welfare in Germany and Britain: Origins and Development*, Leamington Spa and Dover, NH, 1986 (orig. German ed. 1983).

Ronald J. Ross, *The Failure of Bismarck's Kulturkampf: Catholicism and State Power in Imperial Germany, 1871–1887*, Washington, DC, 1998.

Helmut Walser Smith, *German Nationalism and Religious Conflict: Culture, Ideology, Politics, 1870–1914*, Princeton, 1995.

Helmut Walser Smith, ed., *Protestants, Catholics, and Jews in Germany, 1800–1914*, Oxford and New York, 2001.

Jonathan Sperber, *Popular Catholicism in Nineteenth-Century Germany*, Princeton, 1984.

Florian Tennstedt, *Sozialgeschichte der Sozialpolitik in Deutschland. Vom 18. Jahrhundert bis zum Ersten Weltkrieg*, Göttingen, 1981.

Shulamit Volkov, *Germans, Jews, and Antisemites: Trials in Emancipation*, Cambridge, 2006.

Paul Weindling, *Health, Race, and German Politics between National Unification and Nazism, 1870–1945*, Cambridge and New York, 1989.

Massimo Ferrari Zumbini, *Die Wurzeln des Bösen. Gründerjahre des Antisemitismus von der Bismarckzeit zu Hitler*, Frankfurt a.M., 2003.

5. Politics I: Forging an Empire

Horst Bartel and Ernst Engelberg, eds., *Die großpreußisch-militaristische Reichsgründung 1871. Voraussetzungen und Folgen*, 2 vols., Berlin-GDR, 1971.

Otto Becker, *Bismarcks Ringen um Deutschlands Gestaltung*, Heidelberg, 1958.

Otto von Bismarck, *Werke im Auswahl*, 8 vols. in 9, Darmstadt, 2001.

Arden Bucholz, *Moltke and the German Wars, 1864–1871*, Basingstoke, 2001.

William Carr, *The Origins of the Wars of German Unification*, London and New York, 1991.

Gordon A. Craig, *The Battle of Königgrätz: Prussia's Victory over Austria, 1866*, Philadelphia, 1964.

Michael B. Klein, *Zwischen Reich und Region. Identitätsstrukturen im Deutschen Kaiserreich (1871–1918)*, Stuttgart, 2005.

Dieter Langewiesche, *Nation, Nationalismus, Nationalstaat in Deutschland und Europa*, Munich, 2000.

Werner E. Mosse, *The European Powers and the German Question, 1848–1871*, Cambridge, 1958.
Ludwig Pfau, "Centralisation oder Föderation?", in Pfau, *Politisches und Polemisches aus den nachgelassenen Schriften*, Stuttgart, 1895, 151–74.
Klaus Erich Pollmann, *Parlamentarismus im Norddeutschen Bund 1867–1870*, Düsseldorf, 1985.
James Retallack, ed., *Saxony in German History: Culture, Society, and Politics, 1830–1933*, Ann Arbor, 2000.
Theodor Schieder, *Das Kaiserreich von 1871 als Nationalstaat*, Cologne and Opladen, 1961.
Theodor Schieder and Ernst Deuerlein, eds., *Reichsgründung, 1870/71. Tatsachen – Kontroversen – Interpretationen*, Stuttgart, 1970.
Dennis Showalter, *Railroads and Rifles: Soldiers, Technology, and the Unification of Germany*, Hamden, CT, 1975.
Dennis Showalter, *The Wars of German Unification*, London, 2004.
Dan P. Silverman, *Reluctant Union: Alsace-Lorraine and Imperial Germany, 1871–1918*, Harrisburg, PA, 1972.
Fritz Stern, *Gold and Iron: Bismarck, Bleichröder, and the Building of the German Empire*, London, 1977.
Karina Urbach, *Bismarck's Favourite Englishman: Lord Odo Russell's Mission to Berlin*, London, 1999.
Geoffrey Wawro, *The Austro-Prussian War: Austria's War with Prussia and Italy in 1866*, Cambridge and New York, 1996.
Geoffrey Wawro, *The Franco-Prussian War: The German Conquest of France in 1870–1871*, Cambridge and New York, 2003.
Siegfried Weichlein, *Region und Nation. Integrationsprozesse im Bismarckreich*, Düsseldorf, 2002.
George C. Windell, *The Catholics and German Unity, 1866–1871*, Minneapolis, MN, 1954.

6. Military and International Relations

Klaus Bade, *Friedrich Fabri und der Imperialismus in der Bismarckzeit. Revolution – Depression – Expansion*, Freiburg i.Br. and Zurich, 1975.
Konrad Canis, *Bismarcks Außenpolitik 1870–1890. Aufstieg und Gefährdung*, Paderborn, 2004.
Sebastian Conrad, *German Colonialism: A Short History*, Cambridge, 2012.
Sebastian Conrad, *Globalization and the Nation in Imperial Germany*, Cambridge, 2010 (orig. German ed. 2006).

Sebastian Conrad and Jürgen Osterhammel, eds., *Das Kaiserreich transnational. Deutschland in der Welt 1871–1914*, Göttingen, 2004.
Stig Förster and Jörg Nagler, eds., *On the Road to Total War: The American Civil War and the German Wars of Unification, 1861–1871*, Cambridge and New York, 1997.
Sara Friedrichsmeyer, Sara Lennox, and Susanne Zantop, eds., *The Imperialist Imagination: German Colonialism and Its Legacy*, Ann Arbor, 1998.
Imanuel Geiss, *German Foreign Policy, 1871–1914*, London, 1976.
Horst Gründer, *Geschichte der deutschen Kolonien*, 2nd ed., Paderborn, 1991.
William O. Henderson, *The German Colonial Empire, 1884–1919*, London, 1993.
Klaus Hildebrand, *Deutsche Außenpolitik 1871–1918*, Munich, 1989, 2nd ed. 1994.
Paul M. Kennedy, *The Rise of the Anglo-German Antagonism, 1860–1914*, London, 1980.
Birthe Kundrus, *Moderne Imperialisten. Das Kaiserreich im Spiegel seiner Kolonien*, Cologne, Weimar, and Vienna, 2003.
Wolfgang J. Mommsen, *Großmachtstellung und Weltpolitik. Die Außenpolitik des Deutschen Reiches 1870–1914*, Frankfurt a.M. and Berlin, 1993.
Arne Perras, *Carl Peters and German Imperialism, 1856–1918: A Political Biography*, Oxford, 2004.
Michal Pesek, *Koloniale Herrschaft in Deutsch-Ostafrika. Expeditionen, Militär und Verwaltung seit 1880*, Frankfurt a.M., 2005.
Gerhard Ritter, *The Sword and the Scepter: The Problem of Militarism in German History*, 4 vols., Coral Gables, FL, 1969–88 (orig. German ed. 1956–68).
Andreas Rose, *Deutsche Außenpolitik in der Ära Bismarck (1862–1890)*, Darmstadt, 2013.
Woodruff D. Smith, *The German Colonial Empire*, Chapel Hill, NC, 1978.
George Steinmetz, *The Devil's Handwriting: Precoloniality and the German Colonial State in Qingdao, Samoa, and Southwest Africa*, Chicago, 2007.
Bruce Waller, *Bismarck at the Crossroads: The Reorientation of German Foreign Policy after the Congress of Berlin, 1878–1880*, London, 1974.
Hans-Ulrich Wehler, *Bismarck und der Imperialismus*, Cologne, 1969, 2nd ed. 1985.
Lora Wildenthal, *German Women for Empire, 1884–1945*, Durham, NC, 2001.
Heinz Wolter, *Bismarcks Außenpolitik 1871–1881. Aussenpolitische Grundlinien von der Reichsgründung bis zum Dreikaiserbündnis*, Berlin, 1983.

7. Politics II: Parties and Political Mobilization

Margaret Lavinia Anderson, *Practicing Democracy: Elections and Political Culture in Imperial Germany*, Princeton, 2000.

Margaret Lavinia Anderson, *Windthorst: A Political Biography*, Oxford and New York, 1981.

Andreas Biefang, *Bismarcks Reichstag. Das Parlament in der Leipziger Straße*, Düsseldorf, 2002.

Andreas Biefang, *Die andere Seite der Macht. Reichstag und Öffentlichkeit im "System Bismarck" 1871–1890*, Düsseldorf, 2009.

Matthew P. Fitzpatrick, *Purging the Empire: Mass Expulsions in Germany, 1871–1914*, Oxford, 2015.

Dieter Fricke et al., eds., *Lexikon zur Parteiengeschichte. Die bürgerlichen und kleinbürgerlichen Parteien und Verbände in Deutschland (1780–1945)*, 4 vols., Leipzig, 1983–6.

Lothar Gall, ed., *Otto von Bismarck und die Parteien*, Paderborn, 2001.

Lothar Gall, ed., *Regierung, Parlament und Öffentlichkeit im Zeitalter Bismarcks. Politikstil im Wandel*, Paderborn, 2003.

Lothar Gall and Dieter Langewiesche, eds., *Liberalismus und Region. Zur Geschichte des deutschen Liberalismus im 19. Jahrhundert (Historische Zeitschrift, Beiheft 19)*, Munich, 1995.

Hans-Peter Goldberg, *Bismarck und seine Gegner. Die politische Rhetorik im kaiserlichen Reichstag*, Düsseldorf, 1998.

Winfrid Halder, *Innenpolitik im Kaiserreich 1871–1914*, Darmstadt, 2003.

Larry Eugene Jones and James Retallack, eds., *Elections, Mass Politics, and Social Change in Modern Germany*, Cambridge and New York, 1992.

Thomas Kühne, *Dreiklassenwahlrecht und Wahlkultur in Preussen 1867–1914. Landtagswahlen zwischen korporativer Tradition und politischem Massenmarkt*, Düsseldorf, 1994.

Dieter Langewiesche, *Liberalism in Germany*, trans. Christiane Banerji, Basingstoke, 2000 (orig. German ed. 1988).

Vernon L. Lidtke, *The Outlawed Party: Social Democracy in Germany, 1878–1890*, Princeton, 1966.

J. Alden Nichols, *The Year of the Three Kaisers: Bismarck and the German Succession, 1887–1888*, Urbana, IL, 1987.

Thomas Nipperdey, *Die Organisation der deutschen Parteien vor 1918*, Düsseldorf, 1961.

Otto Pflanze with Elizabeth Müller-Luckner, eds., *Innenpolitische Probleme des Bismarckreiches*, Munich, 1983.

James Retallack, *The German Right, 1860–1920: Political Limits of the Authoritarian Imagination*, Toronto, 2006.

James Retallack, *Notables of the Right: The Conservative Party and Political Mobilization in Germany, 1876–1918*, London and Boston, 1988.

Gerhard A. Ritter, *Die deutschen Parteien 1830–1914*, Göttingen, 1985.

Gerhard A. Ritter, ed., *Der Aufstieg der deutschen Arbeiterbewegung. Sozialdemokratie und Freie Gewerkschaften im Parteisystem und Sozialmilieu des Kaiserreichs*, Munich, 1990.

Gerhard A. Ritter, ed., *Wahlen und Wahlkämpfe in Deutschland. Von den Anfängen im 19. Jahrhundert bis zur Bundesrepublik*, Düsseldorf, 1997.

Gerhard A. Ritter with Merith Niehuss, *Wahlgeschichtliches Arbeitsbuch. Materialien zur Statistik des Kaiserreichs 1871–1918*, Munich, 1980.

Karl Rohe, *Wahlen und Wählertraditionen in Deutschland*, Frankfurt a.M., 1992.

James J. Sheehan, *German Liberalism in the Nineteenth Century*, Chicago, 1978.

Jonathan Sperber, *The Kaiser's Voters: Electors and Elections in Imperial Germany*, Cambridge and New York, 1997.

Volker Stalmann, *Die Partei Bismarcks: Die Deutsche Reichs- und Freikonservative Partei 1866–1890*, Düsseldorf, 2000.

Peter Steinbach, *Die Zähmung des politischen Massenmarktes. Wahlen und Wahlkämpfe im Bismarckreich im Spiegel der Hauptstadt- und Gesinnungspresse*, 3 vols., Passau, 1990.

Lech Trzeciakowski, *The Kulturkampf in Prussian Poland*, New York, 1990.

Hans-Peter Ullmann, *Politik im Deutschen Kaiserreich 1871–1918*, Munich, 1999.

Dan S. White, *The Splintered Party: National Liberalism in Hessen and the Reich*, Cambridge, MA, 1976.

2 British Views of Germany, 1815–1914

Introduction

In the late 1990s, when the idea of publishing a collection of British diplomatic reports about nineteenth-century Germany was conceived, a half-dozen historiographical trends made for an auspicious launch to the project.[1]

I. A decade after Germany's (re)unification in 1990, scholars and laymen were debating – as they still are today – the historical significance of an economic and political powerhouse in the centre of Europe. The "rush to unification" in 1989–90 provided tantalizing contrasts to the longer and more agonized processes that produced Germany's Second Reich in 1871. A volume on *Germany's Two Unifications*, whose contributors included historians, political scientists, and students of German language and literature, compared and contrasted these events. How were they anticipated, lived through, reflected upon?[2] Was the "epoch of territoriality" over?[3] What determined whether new unions were legitimate? How did writers and others develop a national consciousness out of disparate (or starkly opposing) parts? Two years later another collaborative effort asked how Germans coped with "the ambiguities of place" as heartlands and borderlands were understood, transformed, and contested in new ways. As "the borders of Germany moved in and out like a concertina" from the eighteenth century to the 1990s, Germans were repeatedly forced to explore their feelings of belonging and markers of identity: "Divided, united, divided again, united again, no European nation state has been more chameleon-like."[4] What did Germany's neighbours think of this? What did British diplomats imagine they were seeing when Metternich or Bismarck hit the reset button – as former US Secretary of State Hillary Clinton claimed to do with Russia in the spring of 2009? These questions suggest why the British found the German Confederation (*Deutscher Bund*, 1815–66) so enigmatic and why foundational moments remain intriguing to us today.

II. Even before 2000, "culture" and "diplomacy" had begun to provide a double optic through which to view historical processes that were rooted in, but transcended, high politics. Johannes Paulmann's *Pomp und Politik* accelerated the trend.[5] So did two other collaborative volumes on different aspects of the same problem, both sponsored by the German Historical Institute (GHI) London.[6] Of course previous work had gone below decks to the "engine room of international relations," that is, the world in which ambassadors and less high-ranking diplomats – consuls, chargés d'affaires, ministers resident, military plenipotentiaries, and others – actually toiled.[7] Zara Steiner's work on the British Foreign Office and Raymond Jones's study of the British diplomatic service highlighted the inner motivations of Foreign Office officials and the changing social profile of the diplomatic service in the wake of mid-century reforms.[8] The many new dimensions of nineteenth-century diplomacy included the introduction of competitive civil service exams, the stationing of diplomats in unfamiliar cultures, the need for new kinds of information, and the advent of the mass press. As the editors of *The Diplomats' World* asserted, the ideals and values that put the "culture" in diplomatic culture "can be reduced neither to the diplomats' private dispositions nor to their official functions. They thus transcend the divide between the individual and institutional sphere of diplomats."[9]

III. Diplomats must interest themselves in matters of war and peace. But they need to advance their own careers too. As Andreas Gestrich, Director of the GHI London, once noted of nineteenth-century diplomacy, the most interesting details about diplomats' experiences had rarely found their way into older books about international relations: "the nuances of diplomatic etiquette and the operating norms of the diplomatic services, the social encounters and the personal experiences of the diplomats, and the local contexts of their foreign missions that characterized diplomatic life so strongly, disappeared when the hard facts of political decision-making entered the printed narratives compiled by historians, with the exception of the occasional anecdote or flowery illustration."[10] The personal reflections that regularly appeared in nineteenth-century travellers' accounts may be grossly inferior in wit and wisdom to Mark Twain's *Innocents Abroad*. But diplomatic reportage was not always dry as dust – "what one clerk said to another"[11] – and even when it was, scholars have long striven to decode the underlying story: "Nowadays," Raymond Jones has written, "no self-respecting diplomatic historian attempts a simple *explication de texte*."[12] Readers want to know about the diplomats' training, prior appointments, and local connections within each capital city's diplomatic corps. From such information we can often tease out why a particular envoy's reports might lurch between optimism and pessimism as a crisis approaches. Consider the case of Count Hugo Lerchenfeld-Köfering, Bavaria's long-time envoy to Prussia. Lerchenfeld's closest ally in Berlin was Saxony's envoy, Count Wilhelm von Hohenthal und Bergen. Lerchenfeld's own boss – Count Georg von Hertling – understood the importance of this personal connection. As Hertling remarked after some uncomfortable incident in Dresden, "the relationship between Bavaria and Saxony remained on a normal footing only as long as Count Hohenthal took breakfast every day in the Bavarian embassy in Berlin."[13]

IV. The first dozen years of the twenty-first century produced socio-economic upheavals, booms and busts, that mirrored the insecurities of life in pre-1848 Europe. Consider the dot.com and housing bubbles in the United States, the sovereign debt crisis in Europe (which pit Europe's "core" against its periphery), and the worldwide recession that began in 2008. These calamities prompted reflections of the sort that had once been penned by British diplomats trying to come to grips with the new diplomatic realities created by the French and Industrial Revolutions. They faced a trading bloc in Central Europe after 1834, the consolidation of disparate sovereignties into powerful nations in a short period of time (Italy and Germany, 1859–71), and the beginnings of globalization. The latter development compelled Foreign Offices and Boards of Trade to consider questions of political economy with an eye to the New World, Russia, and Japan.

German historiography until 1989–90 had neglected the long arc of these historical developments, although the German Confederation was being rehabilitated by the time the Berlin Wall fell. In the 1980s, West Germany had gradually reconciled itself to a division of the German nation-state. In both a political and a scholarly context, the provisional, fractious German Confederation seemed more interesting and "normal" than it had before.[14] The *Wende* ("turn") of 1989–90 brought with it a historiographical realignment. Since 1990, writing on German history has focused on the East German dictatorship, on new ways to explain the crimes of the Third Reich, and on the era from 1890 to the 1920s, described by some as the period of Germany's transition to "classical modernity."[15] The lure of the twentieth century is unmistakable in dissertation proposals and conference programs. But because scholarly attention falls less and less often on the nineteenth century (let alone the first two-thirds of it), this editorial project reminds readers how hotly Germans and Britons debated ways to foster reform without fomenting revolution. The reactions of the British Foreign Office to events in Central Europe between 1848 and 1866 now seem eerily familiar to anyone who looked on as the Arab Spring of 2011 unfolded (and who still wonders how it will all turn out). One of Britain's most astute diplomats, Robert Morier, struck a note that resonates today when he recalled a *tête-à-tête* with the later Tory prime minister, Lord Salisbury, at his estate in Hertfordshire shortly before the German Civil War broke out in June 1866.[16] At that time Morier had described – apparently at some length – his "notions of a German future." Morier foresaw the emergence of a nation-state that would be "worthy of the soul of ... Goethe, Schiller, and Kant." Writing to Lady Salisbury from Vienna only four days after the Battle of Königgrätz (3 July 1866) effectively decided the German Question in Prussia's favour, Morier rued his earlier ramblings. Lord Salisbury had interrupted him with a sobering reminder: "'But, Mr. Morier, this is revolution!'"[17] As Salisbury's remark suggests, it is not only in the rear-view mirror that unexpected developments, whether cultural or diplomatic, can appear revolutionary in nature.

V. The 1990s and early 2000s were a heady time for scholars venturing into newly accessible archives in central and eastern Europe. Historians of Germany travelled to the former German Democratic Republic and the former Soviet Union, where they made remarkable discoveries. Meanwhile, historians of Britain's diplomatic service were finally allowed to use digital cameras in the Public Record Office, Kew – now The National Archives (TNA). Digital photography proved to be a two-edged sword. It made a larger number of reports accessible to individual scholars, but it also eliminated some of the imponderables that have characterized archival research for centuries: hurried visits, slow delivery of documents, sloppy transcription. It also made archival research less fun.

VI. The internationalization of scholarship in the internet age is helping compensate for the diminishing institutional support that many faculty members and graduate students receive when they apply for funds to visit archives overseas. Internet users have access to more online sources for German history after 1871 than they do for the era of the German Confederation. But thorny questions remain about how the intended audiences actually use these primary sources. The age of the hyperlink has reduced the authority of editors and transformed the way their work is received. Narratives have become less linear and less cohesive – perhaps a welcome development. But custodianship of editorial projects such as those that chronicle British views of Germany cannot be discounted or taken lightly. This point was made at a 2002 workshop held at the GHI London, devoted to Editing Documents in the Age of Technology.[18] It was made more recently by the editors of the ten-volume *German History in Documents and Images* project, sponsored by the GHI Washington, DC.[19] Open questions about digital history anthologies remain – about the users to be targeted, the viability of editorial principles, translation problems, and the optimal degree of commentary and annotation. Scholars also disagree about the most effective way to use different media (print, DVDs, internet) to reach cost-conscious customers in different parts of the world, now and in the future. Given the speed at which communication technologies change, such differences of opinion can hardly be a bad thing.

Taking Stock

Existing monographs based on diplomatic reports from Germany are surprisingly sparse. Works by Agatha Ramm, Ilse Neumann, and Scott R. Murray have enlightened us about the career of Sir Robert Morier, of whom Queen Victoria's daughter once said that *"no one* understood Germany as he did."[20] Karina Urbach provided an indelible portrait of Lord Odo Russell, "Bismarck's favourite Englishman."[21] John R. Davis illuminated Britain's reaction to the German *Zollverein* (Customs Union), relying in part on the highly regarded reports sent by the British Consul-General in Leipzig, John Ward.[22] Frank Lorenz Müller explored *Britain and the German Question* more comprehensively, though only up to 1863; Günter Hollenberg pursued the same question up to 1914.[23] John McDermott examined the important consular service that supplemented Britain's team of ambassadors and envoys,[24] while John R. Davis recently contributed *The Victorians and Germany*. Jan Rüger, Patrick Major, and Andreas Fahrmeir have offered *tours d'horizon* of new scholarship on Anglo-German relations, though it is unlikely any of them would claim to supersede Paul Kennedy's *The Rise of the Anglo-German Antagonism*.[25] With their own articles and books, the editors of

British Envoys to Germany have shown in practice what these reports can tell us.[26]

Despite the high quality of such work, I contend that British reports from Germany will eventually cast more light on Germans' quest for liberty, equality, and fraternity at home than on either Germany's or Britain's role in Europe's international system.[27] After 1815 Germans appraised their new place in the world with excitement and pride. But they were disinclined to abandon familiar touchstones of economic, social, political, and cultural ways of life. Such touchstones were pre-national and sub-national. Germans measured their progress through the nineteenth century in relation to their neighbours – far and near – but the principles of the French Revolution provided no trustworthy yardstick. After 1871 – a period to be covered by the last two volumes in the *British Envoys to Germany* series – Germans sought new means to liberate themselves from internal and external constraints. They tried to prove themselves equal or superior to other nations and "races." And they cultivated fraternal bonds that would permit them to redefine Germany's global role. On each count, their successes conjured up dark clouds for the future.

British observers reversed themselves many times when they wrote about the future shape of a united Germany and its supposed historical mission. Britain's Envoy Extraordinary and Minister Plenipotentiary to the Federal Diet, writing to Lord Palmerston from Frankfurt am Main in June 1851, expressed relief that "the vessel of the Confederation is then once more afloat."[28] Until the beginning of the reactionary 1850s in Germany – which recent scholarship has proved were not so reactionary after all[29] – the alternatives to the *Deutscher Bund* appeared unsavoury to British eyes. Thereafter a growing consensus recognized that a Prussian-led unification held many advantages for Britain. Not the least of these was Germany's continuing role as a bulwark against expansionist aims entertained by France and Russia. On 9 February 1871, after the Franco-German war had effectively been decided, Britain's future prime minister Benjamin Disraeli famously told the House of Commons that "this war represents the German revolution, a greater political event than the French revolution of last century."[30] Yet at almost the same moment, Bismarck the "White Revolutionary" could not see how the social and political ramifications of universal manhood suffrage would conspire against his best-laid plans.[31]

British envoys often sympathized with those German liberals – mainly members of the National Association (*Nationalverein*) or the National

Liberal Party – who hoped that Germany could be unified and liberalized together. Early studies by James J. Sheehan and Dieter Langewiesche demonstrated that careful attention to sub-national variants of German liberalism reveals successes that previously went unacknowledged.[32] Recent scholars have gone further, for example, by drawing attention to German liberals' achievements in the 1870s and claiming that the German bourgeoisie exercised a kind of hegemony in the social, economic, and cultural spheres. Ever since David Blackbourn and Geoff Eley's pioneering work, *The Peculiarities of German History*, appeared in 1984, one of the easiest ways to debunk the concept of a German special path to modernity (*Sonderweg*) has been to chronicle all the good reasons why liberals decided to stand shoulder to shoulder with Bismarck in the 1860s and 1870s and why bourgeois Germans did not have a bad conscience about living in an authoritarian regime.[33] Today, the *topos* of German liberalism's "failure" demands less respect than it did when Langewiesche and Sheehan first inveighed against it.

One can expect that proponents of a more liberal, more reformist, more flexible Kaiserreich will find evidence for their arguments in the forthcoming volumes of *British Envoys to Germany* covering the years 1871 to 1897. One expects, further, that liberal achievements and bourgeois confidence will be chronicled most conspicuously in reports emanating *not* from Berlin but from the capitals of middle-sized German states. This second expectation will be proven wrong. Once we leave Germany's southwestern corner, where liberal traditions dating from the time of Napoleon persisted into the Wilhelmine era, things begin to look different. In central and eastern Germany – not to mention the two Mecklenburgs in the north, where no British envoys were posted – liberalism was not hegemonic, even in societies where Junkers and priests had little power. In Protestant, industrialized Saxony, the Landtag was described around 1900 as the most conservative parliament in Germany. Conservative deputies held a two-thirds majority in the lower chamber, and most of them had impeccable bourgeois credentials. If British observers failed to untangle the many ties that linked Germany's liberal and nationalist movements, perhaps that failure was due to differing conceptions of politics among the two countries' middle classes. In the less-studied regions of Germany, two variants of German nationalism – chauvinism in foreign policy and the struggle against democracy at home – were mentioned often in reports sent to London's Foreign Office. The relationship between these two variants of nationalism was rarely explained in those reports. But the ways in which Germany's *Bürgertum* contributed to both were even harder to decipher.

Consider one report from 1890, written by Britain's envoy to Saxony. George Strachey wrote that Dresden's leading newspaper "has always been the Exponent of the most malignant type of Anglophobia. In yesterday's leader, that journal surpassed itself in virulence and misrepresentation."[34] With a nod to Gilbert and Sullivan, Strachey repeatedly referred to Saxons' and Germans' desire to subordinate themselves to a (modern) Major General.[35] As we shall see, this was among Strachey's milder condemnations of the new Germany he saw emerging. The larger point is that Strachey was not under the sway of political opinion in Berlin as he observed and reported on German attempts to balance an authoritarian political system against the effects of modernizing social and economic developments. Regional parochialism and radical nationalism, he understood, fit hand in glove. Some British envoys continued to hope that Germany as a whole would eventually adopt a liberal parliamentary system. Strachey was not one of them. His trepidation about anti-British feeling – and the anti-liberalism that underpinned it – grew by leaps and bounds, from the time of the Anti-Socialist Law of 1878 and continuing until he retired in 1897, just when things were about to get worse.

Reporting for Duty

British Foreign Secretaries were better informed about Germany between 1816 and 1866 than about any other country in the world. France, Russia, and Sweden hosted only one British diplomatic mission each. The states of German-speaking Europe hosted no fewer than eight of the twenty-two legations and embassies Britain maintained at midcentury. The diplomats themselves, who worried about their salaries down to the shilling, knew the precise pecking order among German and non-German missions. Those missions were headed by ambassadors (first class: France, Austria, Turkey); envoys extraordinary and ministers plenipotentiary (second class: including Russia, Spain, Prussia, and other non-German missions; and third class: including, from the German Confederation, Bavaria, Hanover, Frankfurt am Main, Württemberg, and Saxony); and consuls general and chargés d'affaires (fourth class).[36] British envoys in Germany, moreover, were normally accredited at more than one royal court. This had the advantage of offering them a wider view of German affairs. Sometimes, however, it meant they were travelling to lesser capitals when events of great importance occurred in their principal place of accreditation (*Residenzstadt*).[37]

How should we treat Raymond Jones's assertion that sometimes the diplomatic service was the tail that wagged the Foreign Office dog? With a grain of salt, certainly, but not a whole shaker. To cite just one example: In the spring of 1866, when it appeared inevitable that Austria and Prussia would soon be at war, the Foreign Office had come to regard Prussia's victory as the most advantageous outcome for British interests. Frank Lorenz Müller has explained why this viewpoint gained ascendancy.[38] However, this alleged consensus is not easy to reconcile with Foreign Office instructions sent to a British envoy in May 1866, after both powers had begun partial mobilization.[39] From London, Britain's strategic interests were explained thus:

> To Her Majesty's government the course that Prussia has taken ... appears calculated above all things to light upon civil war and so far from leading to the Constitutional reform which Prussia has proposed for the consideration of the Confederate states, to tend to the dissolution of that Confederacy, and to a general re-arrangement of the states of Germany that will preclude the possibility of that union which was at the period of the general peace held to be an essential element of the balance of power in Europe.

Two months earlier, Foreign Secretary Lord Clarendon had written to Britain's ambassador in Berlin: "In the name of all that is rational, decent, and humane, what can be the justification of war on the part of Prussia?"[40]

The envoys rarely amended their reports once the fair copy had been prepared. However, the first drafts of their reports can tell us a great deal about the envoys' real opinions, unfiltered by the necessities of diplomatic circumspection. This is an important (though unresolved) issue debated by specialists in the field: Did diplomats include their most candid reflections in their official reports? Or is real candour to be found instead in the private correspondence that circumvented the hierarchy of communication leading to the foreign secretary or prime minister?[41] Among British diplomats who published memoirs that revealed unfamiliar aspects of their service, some of the most prominent and influential were Lord Augustus Loftus, Robert Morier, John Ward, and Joseph Archer Crowe.[42] Ward wrote in the preface to his memoirs that he had been encouraged to put pen to paper after his retirement when a friend told him that his *personal* recollections held special value: "If any one would only be satisfied with stating exactly what he has seen, without preparation, without ornament, without trying to shine," argued Ward's friend, "he would have more readers than the best authors."[43] Here Ward added: "As to my opinions, they may be deemed right or wrong; but none have been expressed without serious reflection, and a deep sense of the duty of speaking plainly where one speaks at all."

A fourth, related point needs to be made, about the usefulness of comparing draft reports to the final product. At an early stage of my own research on the Kingdom of Saxony, I worked my way through what I mistakenly believed were the only extant copies of George Strachey's (and others') reports from Dresden (in the Public Record Office collection FO 215). Of course these turned out to be merely drafts for the final reports found in FO 68. I had only myself to blame for not finding the latter collection first. However, I learned a good deal about Strachey's personal opinions by comparing the drafts with the final versions. As illustrated by one of his reports from 1874, Strachey considered Saxons' deficiencies to be *German* deficiencies. These included "worship of authority" and impatience with "any teaching wh[ich] is not completely dogmatical."[44] But the force of Strachey's critique is found in passages he deleted from his draft. On one occasion he wrote about "the indisposition of the Germans/peculiarities of/the nature of the German mind, wh[ich] is content to remain uninformed about minorities until the moment comes for trying to thrash them."[45]

Fifth and lastly, readers of such reports can rarely navigate the sea of information under their keel without key biographical information about individual envoys and the connections to which they owed their career advancement. Karina Urbach's study of Odo Russell illustrates how these factors determined when Russell would be sent abroad, and where. Among many other things, we learn that Foreign Office officials held Augustus Loftus's reporting from Berlin in low esteem,[46] that Russell was eager in July 1870 to see the French "beaten to paste, in the interest of culture and progress,"[47] and that Russell's conviviality during his stay at German headquarters in Versailles contributed to his later acceptance in Berlin's social circles. Reinforcing the argument of those who claim that official dispatches only reveal (and perhaps obscure) the tip of the iceberg of international relations, Urbach notes that Lord Derby dedicated a great deal of space in his diary to one of Russell's Versailles anecdotes. The incident Russell related is not the main point: it revolved around German officers' contempt for the French, illustrated when a French general and his staff arrived in Versailles so hopelessly drunk that, "when the soup came round [the general] began to wash his hands in it, smiling benignly."[48] More important is the degree to which Russell's observation provided a hint of what Friedrich Nietzsche identified as a peculiarly German ability to confuse military prowess with cultural superiority.[49] "Even this little story," writes Urbach, "was used by Odo to show his listeners the extent to which German self-confidence, this newly acquired feeling of superiority, would change the continent in the future."[50]

Britain and Germany

British perceptions of the German Confederation before 1863 were generally negative; but they were not uniformly damning. There was no *one* British view of Germany. Part of the reason was sheer ignorance, or disinterest – among British statesmen and the public alike. The *Times* of London reported in 1832 that "more is known in England respecting South America than of the true state of Germany."[51] In July 1862, after Bismarck met with Lord Palmerston and Lord Russell in London, he remarked that these experienced ministers "know less about Prussia than about Japan and Mongolia."[52] A decade later, the British ambassador to Germany claimed that in England, "continental talk bores everyone to death."[53]

Nevertheless, British envoys fed so much valuable information to London that historians have to ask themselves why it had so little impact on British foreign policy. One answer suggests that British ministers found Germany useful as a kind of "think tank." Their envoys' reports helped them consider Britain's own domestic problems from unfamiliar perspectives. According to this hypothesis, Foreign Office secretaries and ministers used German examples of discrimination against Catholics and Jews to think through the implications of Catholic emancipation and Irish opposition at home.[54] They saw the Carlsbad Decrees and the Six Articles of 1832 in the context of Peterloo and the First Reform Act. They expressed first horror, then relief, that the revolutions of 1848–9 on the continent exceeded Chartism in both immediate and long-term effect. Perhaps most important of all – still following this line of argument – after 1860 they assimilated discrepant opinions about the prospects of liberalism, constitutionalism, and nationalism in the individual federal states as confirmation that British non-interference in

German affairs was the best policy.⁵⁵ The "think tank" hypothesis, however, stands on shaky ground.

There is scant evidence that *any* element of British foreign policy – besides non-intervention – can be linked to specific information the Foreign Office received from its German envoys. Lord Odo Russell frequently joked (or half-joked) to Robert Morier and his other friends that the Foreign Office was indifferent to his dispatches.⁵⁶ From Dresden, George Strachey felt obliged to preface a long report on the early Social Democratic movement by writing that "my [dispatch] will, I fear, be long & dry, but Y[our] L[ordship] will probably find a detailed local study of this important subject more satisfactory and suggestive than a collection of agreeable generalizations."⁵⁷ Other ambassadors and envoys to Germany felt the same way – about their need to feel appreciated and about the advantages of specificity in their reporting. Nevertheless, it cannot have escaped their attention that permanent undersecretaries in the Foreign Office were far more important in policy formation than envoys stationed abroad.

Scott Murray has demonstrated that foreign secretaries in London could hardly be expected to keep up with their own envoys' see-sawing opinions about the prospects of German liberalism. As two of the most astute observers of the constitutional conflict between the liberal Prussian Landtag (state parliament) and King Wilhelm I's government in the early 1860s, Robert Morier and Joseph Crowe lurched between optimism and pessimism. Would the two sides resolve their differences on the basis of an English-style constitutional monarchy? Both men were friendly with and willing to assist the Progressive Party, which led the Landtag's resistance to Wilhelm's army reforms. That Morier and Crowe also had the ear of Prince Albert, Queen Victoria, and the Prussian crown princess made them impact players in this struggle between parliament and monarchy. In 1864 Morier wrote from Berlin that "I am firmly convinced that the law of nationality which has asserted itself so triumphantly in Italy is a *natural* law that cannot in the long run be resisted & will assert itself in Germany as well as in Scandinavia."⁵⁸ But by 1867 both men had abandoned hope that German liberals would prevail. Morier was so disheartened that he turned his attention to writing long reports comparing commercial policies and local self-government in Germany and England.

Had he "gone native" in succumbing to the lure of unity over liberty, as older accounts of German liberalism claim? Apparently so. "Between Königgrätz and Sedan ... Robert Morier shelved his dreams of

Germany's liberalization – once thought to be close at hand – in the belief that progress on this front would follow the settlement of the national question."⁵⁹ Writing from Leipzig, Joseph Crowe doubted whether Prussia's appetite for swallowing up smaller states in northern Germany would be resisted by the new Reichstag, regardless of particularists' worries on that score: "The German people, it must be recollected, is not fully alive to the enjoyment of constitutional liberty; and I should be very loth [sic] to predict that the national parliament will not be led by some subterfuge to grant what public opinion now rejects."⁶⁰ By December 1870, when British and American sentiment towards Germany had already soured as a result of the bombardment of Paris, Crowe would probably have agreed with Morier (and Nietzsche) that the annexation of Alsace and Lorraine did not bode well for the future. "The lust for *gloire*," wrote Morier, "kindled as it is within [Germany], will burn with a much more terrible fierceness than it did in the *grande nation*."⁶¹

The diversity of reports from Germany could hardly have produced a cohesive picture of Germany in the Foreign Office, let alone one that illuminated Britain's own domestic challenges. Some of the most interesting reading in those reports concerns the attempts of envoys stationed in Stuttgart and Berlin to *refute* Crowe's early claims that national sentiment for a Prussian-led "smaller Germany" (*Kleindeutschland*) was irresistible. Those envoys pulled no punches in describing Crowe's blinkered enthusiasm for Prussia.⁶² Britain's envoy to Württemberg referred to the "flimsy structure" of evidence upon which Crowe's dispatches had been built. Thus, as Karina Urbach has written, the reports of British envoys to Germany "offer a kaleidoscope of images, some written on a sunny and some on a grey day, and one wonders whether the recipients of these letters were actually capable of decoding this great mixture and finally coming to a useful conclusion about German affairs."⁶³

Why else did envoys' reports have so little influence on British foreign policy? British statesmen from 1816 to 1866 – and beyond – saw Germany less through a kaleidoscope than through the filter of the threat of revolution. British attention was piqued at times when Germany seemed on the brink of succumbing to mob rule – the "wrong" kind of democracy, that is, which had been inaugurated by the French Revolution, carried abroad in the backpacks of Napoleon's *Grande Armée*, and consolidated in the plebiscitary regime of Napoleon III. To be sure, other German "threats" came to the fore regularly. But some "threats" that have become clichés in the scholarly literature – for example, British fears about the impact of the German Customs Union on British trade – were not really considered threats at all.⁶⁴

Moreover, British uncertainty as to whether Germany would play a stabilizing role in Europe after the Congress of Vienna was always coupled with the question of whether German dynasts would succumb to calls for democratic reform from their own people. Article 2 of the Federal Act of 1815 had obligated the German Confederation to preserve the security of Germany between the Great Powers of France and Russia and to maintain the independence and legitimacy of the individual German states (and their ruling dynasties). Thus British reportage became more dense as German constitutions were granted and withdrawn after 1815. But it also reflected a diversity of views among individual envoys regarding what security and independence really meant. In 1820 the theology student Karl Sand was publicly executed in Mannheim for the murder of the playwright August von Kotzebue. That murder gave Austrian Foreign Minister Clemens von Metternich, the "coachman of Europe," the opportunity to impose the Carlsbad Decrees, which dissolved the *Burschenschaften* (student fraternities) and cracked down on the liberal press and German universities. Britain's envoy in Frankfurt was outraged by the "lamentations" of Sand's supporters, and he was pleased that the "scaffold" had put to rest the "pernicious notion that the Government did not dare to execute him."⁶⁵ George H. Rose, writing from Berlin in his typical overheated prose, wrote that "the [German] people is now apprized of the nature of the danger, of the object of the conspirations, & of the detestable means, by which they strive to attain it; It must, as thus enlightened, feel the call to repose confidence in the Government."⁶⁶ By contrast, the British envoy in Dresden, John Philip Morier, was much calmer – so calm that he famously wrote a brief history of Saxony after 1806 when he had nothing else to do.⁶⁷ Writing in 1819, Morier conceded the possibility that some sort of loose conspiracy might exist among "desperados," "demagogues," and "madmen" like Sand. But "fortunately the number of these men is small, they are well known, and the poison of their principles is of slow action in a country subdivided into so many states, many of rival interests, and the people of which, are of a calm and dispassionate nature." The "abstract principle" of reform, he added, "pervades generally the minds of all men."⁶⁸

Such diversity of opinion was not merely the result of British envoys' personal proclivities: it reflected a German reality. As Morier pointed out, revolutionary "mischief" was made possible by lack of unanimity among the various federal states and even within them. As "proof" of contradictory policies that were pursued within a single state, Morier reported that at the same moment Württemberg's representative was signing the Carlsbad Protocol of 1819, imposing severe restrictions on the press, a "new constitution was promulgated at Stutgard [sic] giving unlimited freedom to it." Frederick Lamb in Frankfurt saw little hope of "tranquillity and satisfaction" in the member states of the German Confederation as long as some of them had representative parliaments and others did not.

British attention to the fate of reform and revolution in Germany was piqued at later moments too: when Germany (and Europe) faced rebellions in 1830; when Germany (and Europe) experienced full-blown revolutions in 1848–9; and when Prussia's Prince Regent Wilhelm set out on a collision course with the Prussian Landtag after 1859 by demanding funds for a major army increase.[69] In June 1860, Crowe forwarded to Morier a memorandum prepared by Wilhelm (which Morier translated and forwarded to Lord Russell). The Prince Regent likened the "art of government" to "regulating the bed of a river, in which the banks must not be too close together, as in Hanover and Hessen, or too far apart, as in England."[70]

After Bismarck was appointed Prussian minister president in September 1862, all bets were off. His radical departure from the preferred path of slow, steady reform was no less worrisome to the British Foreign Office than it was to German liberals – with whom many (perhaps most) British diplomats sympathized. A national parliament elected on the basis of universal manhood suffrage was part of Bismarck's strategy to out-manoeuvre Vienna and Dresden (the latter being the heart of the "absurd trias" idea).[71] London was aware of its international implications. Yet when Foreign Secretary Lord John Russell wrote to the British ambassador to Prussia in September 1863, fear of democratic (not international) revolution was his central concern. It conjured up images of France's Reign of Terror. "The first question to be asked," wrote Russell, is 'What is to be the franchise?'" He continued: "If high it will not satisfy the great liberal party of Germany. If low it will be pretty sure to lead to a revolution by which the hereditary sovereigns of Germany would be reduced to insignificance ... In short the liberals of Germany would probably follow closely the footsteps of the liberals of France in 1791."[72] This fear was not immediately mitigated by the creation of the German Reichstag. However, it gradually declined during the Bismarckian and Wilhelmine eras. By the last decade before the

Figure 2.1 This cartoon appeared not long after the Second Moroccan Crisis of 1911 and was drawn by one of the Second Reich's most famous satirical artists. The "Prize Question" asks: "How does it happen that the English diplomats have so much success and the Germans so little?" The "answer" is provided at the bottom: "The English diplomat looks like this … and the German like this." "That would explain it." "Preisfrage," by Eduard Thöny, *Simplicissimus* 16, no. 38 (18 December 1911): 684. Klassik Stiftung Weimar.

First World War, it was Prussia's *refusal* to compromise with democracy – epitomized by resolute defence of the Prussian three-class suffrage – that elicited British calls for action to pre-empt revolution.

Interior Germany

It is difficult to overemphasize the variety of local and regional concerns that were discussed, often at great length, in dispatches from German capitals. British envoys were instructed to report on the local conditions, temperament, and ambitions of the people among whom they lived. Joseph Crowe remembered that the first step – though *only* the first – towards learning about such things was to participate in the "real enjoyment and the pleasures of intimate society." In Berlin, "it was not till ten o'clock [p.m.] ... [that] the *attaché* forgot his red tape, the Prussian minister or secretary forgot that he had a uniform and a stiff collar ... and men, who during the daytime only had leisure for a bow, unbent, physically and morally."[73] The second necessity for an envoy was to organize his day to have time to write dispatches to London. When Robert Morier's father David was appointed minister plenipotentiary to the Swiss Confederation in 1832, he addressed a humorous letter to his "darling Mother." His goal was to defend himself against charges of having become "either a fine gentleman or a lazy dog." Morier's indignation was only semi-feigned when he answered a question his mother had not posed: Why had he "not found time for a letter to A.B.C. ... to Z ..."?

> First – Because I have been plenipotising. Do you think that I have nothing to learn, nothing to talk, nothing to read, nothing to meditate, nothing to write about my twenty-two sovereign independent ____ [here appears a picture of two waddling ducks]? Have I not to study German in order to understand the forty-six newspapers of this enlightened many puzzled-headed confederation? Have not I to talk politics with ... Landammans, avoyers, "Great Raths," and "Little Raths," and to look wise all the time ... *Secundo* – Because I have a wife and five children ... *Tertio* – Because I have lots of other things to do, etc.[74]

Between 1815 and 1865, British envoys reported on awakening patriotism in the German and Polish student movements and the expanding influence of a liberal press even in the face of Metternich's repression. Other aspects of internal German affairs that received considerable attention included German postal systems, trade fairs, urban crime, crop failures, and industrial expansion. To many such reports the envoys appended lengthy statistical studies. After 1866, British envoys to Germany continued to report on the interior life of a nation that now represented a very different diplomatic challenge to Britain. This is not to say that cabinet decisions and parliamentary debates in the individual states did not figure largely in these reports. The British envoy to Saxony, J. Hume Burnley, was not only premature but incorrect when he reported in 1868 that "the debates in the Saxon Chambers have lost a good deal of their interest now that their sphere of action is confined to local and, if I may so term it, parish work."[75] Yet it is also true that British ambassadors and envoys in Germany fought tooth and nail to resist the commissions of a House of Commons that wanted a less expensive diplomatic service, which was to be achieved by closing German missions of secondary rank. British envoys were supported in this effort by their foreign secretaries and prime ministers in London.[76]

In a letter to his friend William Cartwright – a charming Liberal member of parliament who was so eccentric his friends called him "Cartwrong" – Odo Russell provided an emphatic rationale for maintaining envoys in the lesser German states.[77] The Foreign Office, Russell observed, would never be able to understand the direction of future German policy unless it realized that such policy was not made in a vacuum in Berlin but depended on the cabinets of the other confederate German states. It was important for the Foreign Office to get "reliable information as to the tendencies & manner of seeing of those other Cabinets – information which Berlin would be absolutely unable to supply, or I would even say which would be obtained anywhere *rather* than of Berlin." Because of local jealousies and suspicions between Berlin and the other German capitals, Russell continued, it was "absurd" to suppose "that a British Ambassador at Berlin ... wd. be able alone & of himself to *démeler* the ins & outs of German policy, to form for instance a perfectly clear idea of the direction Germany was going in in regard to Austria & Russia, unless he had independent eyes working at Munich & Stuttgart & Dresden or at all events one hand in the old Nord Bund & another in the South."[78]

British envoys continued to be stationed in lesser German capitals from 1871 until the First World War, and instead of reporting only on "the ins & outs of German policy" they continued to interpret their mandate broadly.[79] A sample drawn from just the reports of British envoys to Saxony suggests the range of topics covered that had little or nothing to do with international relations. In April 1868, J. Hume Burnley explained to the British Foreign Office why the Saxon Landtag had just abolished capital punishment. Saxony's King Johann was a strong advocate of this reform because of the shock he had received in December 1866, when his pardon for a prisoner about to be executed arrived with just minutes to spare. A year later Burnley reported on public reaction to a huge explosion in the mines of Baron Carl von Burgk-Roßthal, southwest of Dresden, when upwards of 240 miners were killed.[80] In 1870, Burnley sent London one of his longest reports (fifty-two pages), on the topic of land tenure. In it he provided a detailed, systematic analysis of the size of Saxon landholdings, crops and yields, the different wages paid to male and female agricultural day labourers, and evictions in the countryside.

Burnley, however, missed the mark when he began reporting on the Social Democratic movement in Saxony. In January 1871 he wrote that August Bebel and Wilhelm Liebknecht were making progress with their agitation among Saxon workers due mainly to foreign influences preaching revolution or the "utopian" ideals of the workers themselves. "The arrest of the two Saxon Deputies ... is a stern proof that a German Government knows how to put down what may become a disturbing element unless firmly taken in hand ... As the German workman enjoys a greater amount of well being & many more opportunities of rationally passing his time at places of amusement to which both rich and poor may resort in the greatest goodfellowship and harmony, I do not think the labouring classes have much to complain of."[81]

Suffice it to say that Burnley's successor, George Strachey, saw things differently. Between 1874 and 1889 his reports about the wrongheadedness of Bismarck's Anti-Socialist Law, about the legitimate grievances of workers, and about the witch-hunts that put their leaders on trial became more scathing with each passing year. Strachey also criticized the Reich Press Law of 1874, revisions to the German Criminal Code in 1875, celebrations of Sedan Day, visits to Saxony by Kaiser Wilhelm (I and II), the caste mentality of German civil servants, and the arrival of racial antisemitism in Dresden in December 1879.[82]

Strachey frequently contrasted German inadequacies of policy and temperament with British virtues of good governance and common sense. Consider his reaction when Saxony's minister of the interior explained why he had always considered Bismarck's *Kulturkampf* a mistake. Reporting his side of the conversation with Baron Hermann von Nostitz-Wallwitz, Strachey wrote: "I observed [to Nostitz-Wallwitz] that the Prince's [Bismarck's] church legislation appeared to me to be the most gigantic political failure of our time." Strachey was incredulous when Nostitz-Wallwitz explained that a new bill (1880) dismantling the most onerous of the anti-Catholic laws "was to a great extent a concession to the wishes of the Emperor William who was exceedingly anxious that a religious peace should be arranged before he died – the Emperor was an old man, he had set his heart on a ceremonial of contrived architectural imagination and religious revival to be transacted in the autumn in Cologne Cathedral (which is now verging on completion), and the 'Master's' wishes were of decisive weight with Pr. Bismarck." Strachey could not resist ending his conversation, and his report, with a bitter rejoinder:

> I said [to Nostitz-Wallwitz] that if the explanation was true, then the political condition of Prussia was a sad one. It was namely an absurd state of things for the year 1880 if a system established only yesterday with such deliberation was to be knocked down today, not because it was bad, but because it vexed a sovereign who happened to be old, and who desired to see a picturesque display of Romish ritual in a particular Church.

Nostitz-Wallwitz replied that he could not deny his interlocutor's claim, adding laconically that "the absurd always played a considerable part in human affairs."[83]

The Anglo-German antagonism, which we can already read about in reports dating from the Berlin Conference (1884–5) and Kaiser Friedrich III's brief reign (1888), grew poisonous under Kaiser Wilhelm II and Chancellor Bernhard von Bülow (1900–9). The same is true of German government efforts, at every tier of politics, to meet the challenge of the Social Democratic movement, which the German establishment insisted on labelling "revolutionary." Related to the "red threat" were the efforts of less doctrinaire German state ministers to implement meaningful reforms in a democratic direction. Both before and after 1905, the suffrage reform movements in Hamburg, Württemberg, Bavaria, Saxony, and Prussia drew considerable attention from British envoys. Lastly, Germany's industrial might in a global age, its international position in a Europe divided into opposing armed camps, and its determination to build a fleet of battleships against Britain all figured centrally in envoys' reports after 1890. The Second Reich's "fortification" was not restricted to the period of Bismarck's chancellorship alone.[84] Albeit on a very different footing, that process continued after 1890.

Historical Triangulation

British reports on Germany may act as a resource and a spur to future research because a larger puzzle comes into focus when we employ a kind of historical "triangulation." British envoys were not the only diplomats accredited to the courts of Germany's federal states. In 1907, some fourteen envoys were stationed in Dresden alone.[85] Moreover, Britons who described their rambles in Central Europe – for example, Henry Mayhew, Sidney Whitman, and Cicely Sidgwick[86] – rubbed cheeks with John Lothrop Motley, Mark Twain, and W.E.B. Du Bois from America, not to mention hundreds of others from less distant lands.[87] What does this mosaic of impressions look like when we pull back and view it from different perspectives?

Let us begin with diplomacy narrowly defined and with another English-speaking power, the United States of America.[88] American diplomats may have been unique in their ability to misjudge German affairs. Just before the German Civil War of 1866 broke out, US Ambassador Joseph A. Wright tried to analyse the Austro-Prussian "difficulty." He pronounced: "There will be no fighting ... [and] the present contest will end, in my opinion, with the retirement of Count Bismarck."[89] By 1867 the historian George Bancroft had taken over as US ambassador to the North German Confederation. His assessment of Germany's future contained as much wishful thinking as any report sent to the British Foreign Office. "The present union of German states," wrote Bancroft,

> is the ripened fruit of nineteen generations of continued sufferings and struggles,[90] and is so completely in harmony with *natural laws* and so thoroughly the concurrent act of government and people, that it is certain to endure ... This wonderful result has a special interest for America, because it has sprung from the application of *the principles which guided the framers of the constitution of our United States*. The constitution of North Germany corresponds in so many things with ours that *it must have been formed after the closest study of our system* ... [and] the discovery and application of similar political principles ... The president of the German United States is the king of Prussia. *His powers are very much like those of our president* only they are for life and are hereditary.[91]

Bancroft was not the first American diplomat to overestimate his country's influence on Germany. A year earlier, while German soldiers and diplomats were still mopping up after the German Civil War, the

US representative in Brussels, H.S. Sanford, wrote a private letter to Secretary of State William Seward. "You see how the democratic wave in Europe has grown in breadth and strength," Sanford exclaimed. "The influence of our victory [in the US Civil War] upon Europe's fate is immeasurable. Prussia with its king 'by divine right' is in favour of universal suffrage. It sweeps away a half-dozen small dynasties by the grace of God in order to put itself at the head of this irresistible development and to lead it ... England must follow – whether by peaceful means or under compulsion depends on its aristocracy."[92]

Just as remarkable is the forbearance towards German authoritarianism voiced by Bayard Taylor, who served in the legation in Berlin in 1878 after extensive travels in Germany.[93] Immediately after Bismarck's Anti-Socialist Law was passed in the autumn of 1878, Taylor reported to Secretary of State William M. Evarts that the Reichstag majority that had passed this bill included "the most prudent, conscientious and patriotic members of the legislative body." Bayard added that "the suppression measures would be enforced in a liberal and charitable spirit."[94] Some American diplomats doubted the fairness or efficacy of this anti-socialist legislation, but H. Sidney Everett was not among them. In a report of 15 February 1879, Everett wrote that "it is difficult to criticise impartially the measures of self preservation adopted by the monarchical governments of Europe in face of the recent universal socialistic demonstrations and excesses."[95] Further examples would only confirm the degree to which American observers welcomed Germany's stern response to the "red" (socialist) and "black" (Catholic) threats.[96]

The middle-sized and small German states, having struggled to retain their independence in the Holy Roman Empire and the German Confederation, tried to maintain the fiction of their autonomy within the new empire by stationing their own envoys in other German capitals between 1866 and 1918.[97] Because the reports these envoys sent back to their Foreign Offices are preserved in European archives, scholars can assess whether their views of "interior Germany" were as insightful or blinkered as the Anglo-American views cited so far.

I can provide one example of how this intra-German reportage permits a kind of historical triangulation. It is drawn from my own study of Saxon politicians' attempts to stem the "red tide." In essays published in the early 1990s, drafted before my first visit to the Saxon Central State Archive in Dresden, I cited the reports of the Prussian envoy to Saxony to illustrate the mindset of ministers attempting to meet these dual threats by manipulating the local suffrage in an anti-democratic direction.⁹⁸ From the *Catalogue of Files and Microfilms of the German Foreign Ministry Archives, 1867–1920*, I had discovered that Prussian envoys filled hundreds of volumes with their reports from Dresden on every conceivable aspect of Saxon politics during the Second Reich.⁹⁹ I consulted some of these files in the Political Archive of the German Foreign Office, then in Bonn (now Berlin); but most of them were read in Toronto from microfilms borrowed from the Center for Research Libraries, Chicago. Soon other scholars working on Saxon Social Democracy were using the same reports, supplementing them with similar ones written by the Austrian and Bavarian envoys.¹⁰⁰ Following in their footsteps, I am exploring Saxon and German political culture by triangulating – rather as a professional surveyor might – the different angles these non-Saxon diplomats provided.¹⁰¹

"Foreign" envoys stationed in German capitals served two functions of historical importance. First, they acted as sounding boards for party politicians and government leaders who wanted to explain, excuse, or simply test the impact of their own decisions. Envoys were able to convince their interlocutors to speak candidly about their own political philosophies and future plans. Despite the certainty that such conversations would be reproduced almost verbatim in reports sent back to one or the other Foreign Office, many politicians obviously welcomed the opportunity to unburden their political conscience to these nominal outsiders (thus the special value of British reports). Second, these envoys became integral parts of the political community to which they had been appointed. As such, they had an impact on the events they were asked to chronicle, as we shall see presently.¹⁰²

Whether they reported back to Berlin, Vienna, or Munich, these German envoys were able to penetrate beneath the highly formalized language of diplomacy exchanged by the respective governments, based on personal relationships of trust and understanding. While parliament was in session, the more diligent among them met virtually every day with state ministers and party leaders. They attended important sessions of the Landtag and sometimes even functioned as ersatz caucus whips when deputies in the Reichstag had to be nudged towards consensus. Apart from their ability to parse the nuances of the German language, as few Britons or Americans could, Prussian, Austrian, and Bavarian envoys generally held high social and diplomatic rank. This also set them apart from their Anglo-American counterparts, especially once British civil service reforms provided opportunities for commoners to advance to the level of chargé d'affaires, minister resident, or

British Views of Germany, 1815–1914   67

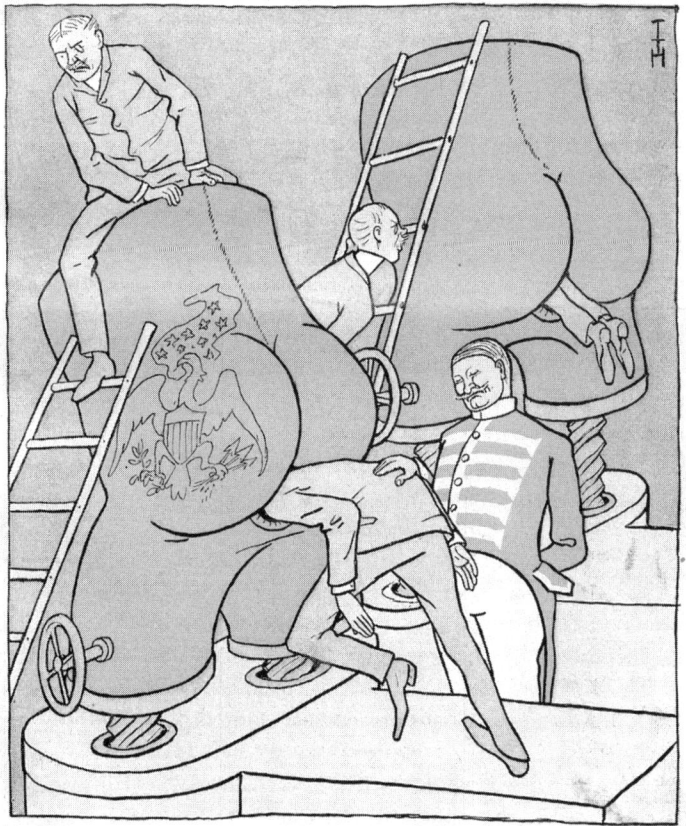

Figure 2.2 "Gesandten-Erziehung" by Thomas Theodor Heine, *Simplicissimus* 8, no. 6 (5 May 1903): 41. © Estate of Thomas Theodor Heine/SODRAC (2015). The text reads: "It is probably not generally known that there is an institute in Berlin that devotes itself exclusively to the training of young diplomats. Only those who have successfully completed this school have the abilities that are absolutely necessary to hold an embassy post in a foreign country. Through systematic schooling, the last traces of Bismarck's dilettantism have been successfully erased from our foreign policy." The uniformed figure at right is an obvious caricature of Chancellor Bernhard von Bülow.

ambassador in the diplomatic service. Thus a sample of reports written by different envoys in one German capital can help us analyse the interplay among national stereotypes, cultural transfers, and the quotidian affairs of everyday life (which were as "thick" as the analysis envoys gave them). In this sense a historical methodology based on multiple reports from envoys to Germany is neither stereoscopic nor merely an exercise in triangulation. Instead it provides a multi-level, multivariate view of German affairs that directly informs and complements accounts told by social, cultural, and intellectual historians.

A Case in Point

My example demonstrates how differently Prussian, Austrian, Bavarian, Saxon, Baden, and other governments viewed Bismarck's Anti-Socialist Law of 1878 and the Minor State of Siege (§28) that was subsequently imposed on Berlin and Hamburg and, in 1881, on Leipzig. The government of Baden did everything in its power to render Bismarck's antisocialist legislation less repressive. The Bavarian government adopted a position roughly between those of Baden and Prussia. But Bavaria's envoy in Dresden reflected (stereo)typical Bavarian sentiments when he reacted to the assassination attempts on Kaiser Wilhelm I. He blamed the crimes on Germany's loss of spirituality, its accelerating industrialization, and the advancement of the Jews, whom he accused of hollowing out the lower middle classes, or *Mittelstand*. Police measures alone, he noted, could never contain Social Democracy: "family, church, school, community, and the state must help each other to ensure that dissolution is never tolerated."[103] The Austrian envoy reported back to Vienna in almost identical terms. For the first assassination attempt he blamed freedom of speech, "licentiousness" and "de-Christianization." New laws against press offences and against freedom of assembly would be mere palliatives, and likely unsuccessful, unless state governments also undertook a more comprehensive "reform of legislation in the areas of religious and social life."[104]

Saxony, the cradle of the German Social Democratic movement, was initially happy to see Prussia take the lead in cracking down on the socialist threat. On 9 September 1878 the Reichstag was sent a proposal for a "Law Against the Publicly Dangerous Endeavors of Social Democracy." After seeing the draft bill, Saxony's military plenipotentiary in Berlin wrote that "my expectations have been *very far* exceeded; in truth it deserves its characterization as draconian."[105] Yet the self-proclaimed defenders of state and society held more ambivalent views than historians have generally acknowledged. Even socialism's most determined foes in Saxony conceded that they could not curtail socialist agitation, keep the movement's leaders in jail, stifle its propaganda, or convince the "parties of order" (*Ordnungsparteien*) to set aside their differences. Recognizing these failures, the British envoy Strachey could not fathom why Saxon statesmen continued to believe throughout the 1880s that repression was the right answer to Social Democracy: it simply drove socialists underground and fuelled their determination to fight on. He was even more appalled by the "war-whoops of exultation" when the right-wing parties in Bismarck's *Kartell* rallied together to prevent even one Social Democrat being elected from Saxony to the 1887 Reichstag. Jubilation on the part of the *Kartell* parties, he wrote, had now attained "that maximum of ferocity to political opponents, that alacrity in trampling on the defeated, which is so characteristic of the new Germany."[106]

It is only thanks to British and Prussian envoys' reports that we now understand the complex mix of motives – including self-congratulation and resentment – that characterized the reaction of Saxon Interior Minister Hermann von Nostitz-Wallwitz in 1881 when Prussia insisted that Saxon authorities repress Social Democrats more severely than they had since 1878. In assessing Nostitz's remarks to foreign envoys, we must appreciate that he tended to stress his humanitarian outlook to the British envoy and his repressive instincts to those representing Prussia and Austria. Strachey once wrote that Nostitz was "painfully reserved and monosyllabic" – he "always answers questions, as far as possible, in tangents."[107] Yet Nostitz appears to have been genuinely unsure how best to meet the socialist threat. Barely a fortnight after the Anti-Socialist Law took effect, Strachey reported Nostitz's "personal opinion [that] if the *Vorwärts*[108] turned over a new leaf, [it] ought not to be suppressed just to spite the editor and [his staff]." With mixed regret and frustration, Nostitz noted that even he, as minister of the interior, was subject to the whims of reactionary civil servants, despite the fact that they answered directly to him. "The regional governor in Leipzig," Nostitz told Strachey, "will take his own view of such questions, to which the ordinary conceptions of justice and injustice do not apply."

There had been warning signs that the Prussians' patience with Saxony was nearly exhausted.[109] Berlin Police President Guido von Madai had long had his eye on the "nest" of Social Democratic agitators in Saxony. "Sooner or later" the Minor State of Siege would have to be considered for Leipzig.[110] Each report that reached Berlin brought discouraging news: Socialists banned from Berlin and Hamburg were being welcomed by their party comrades in Leipzig and provided with 10 Marks per week until they found work. *Der Sozialdemokrat* was being read in Leipzig watering holes as openly as "La Marseillaise" was being sung in the tailors' hostel near the Catholic church. Madai corresponded regularly with police and district governors in Leipzig, Chemnitz, and Dresden.[111] But he did not trust them: Social Democrats always seemed to know beforehand when house searches were about to be undertaken.[112]

Madai, Bismarck, and Prussia's new minister of the interior, Robert von Puttkamer, each contributed a piece to the puzzle that finally came together in June 1881 with the imposition of the Minor State of Siege on Leipzig. Bismarck sent a long memorandum to his envoy in Dresden, Carl von Dönhoff, instructing him to inform the Saxons that they could expect no sympathy from Berlin if their future looked black – or red. According to Bismarck, Saxony had only itself to blame.[113] The best remedy was for the Saxon authorities to take the lead in finding a "common operational basis" for what Dönhoff had begun to label the "*so-called* parties of order."[114] Another turn of the screw came barely a fortnight later when Interior Minister Puttkamer addressed the Reichstag. Responding to "provocations" from the SPD speaker Ignaz Auer, Puttkamer was anything but subtle in alluding to developments growing more dangerous "day by day" in Leipzig.[115] As August Bebel noted in his memoirs, "it was not possible to exceed the effrontery with which the minister of one government dropped a broad hint to another [minister] of what was expected of him. And in Dresden the hint was understood."[116]

Nostitz-Wallwitz deeply resented being blindsided this way by the Prussians. In the next few days he did his best to explain why his government did not feel there was any need to invoke §28 for Leipzig. But he did not back down immediately either. In his view the only advantage the Minor State of Siege offered over the current situation was its expulsion clause, which allowed local authorities to banish individual Social Democrats from their jurisdiction to another region of Germany. The Prussian envoy Dönhoff reported that Nostitz was obviously sensitive about the issue, even embarrassed.[117] But to the British envoy Strachey, Nostitz declared that Puttkamer's statement in the Reichstag had been "as ~~amazing~~ surprising to him as it was to the public."[118] (Once again, the terms Strachey struck from his draft reports are revealing.) Falling back on sarcasm to belittle the haughty Prussians, Nostitz underscored the gulf that separated Saxon appraisals of the socialist threat from those entertained in Berlin:

If the Prussian government ... knew of danger hatching in Leipzig, they were better informed than he was: Bebel and nine or ten other socialist leaders were settled there, and the old, chronic, evil was not, of course, eradicated, but nothing new and acute ~~had happened~~ was happening. These people must live somewhere, and they were not doing any ~~particular~~ extraordinary harm where they were, so as to justify the discovery that their presence constituted ~~any actual~~ a danger. If it did, the "minor" state of siege would be a useless remedy. He [Nostitz] should then have the right to order Bebel and his associates to leave Leipzig, whereupon they would go somewhere else. On the whole, said Herr von Nostitz, I think we may leave our socialists alone for the present. But this, he added ~~discourteously~~ sarcastically, is subject to the superior lights which they may have in Berlin.[119]

This example prompts two observations. The diplomatic reports of envoys stationed in Germany reveal that the anti-Prussian and inter-state tensions recorded by British envoys before 1866 persisted after that date with only slightly diminished intensity (now under the name of "particularism"). Comparing different envoys' reports on such significant domestic affairs as the rise of Social Democracy and the progress of suffrage reform underscores the importance of understanding what federalism actually meant to populations and their governments in different parts of Germany. The role of British and other non-German envoys is especially important here: it is difficult (though not impossible) to imagine Nostitz criticizing Puttkamer so angrily and forthrightly if he were speaking to a fellow German minister. Second, these reports complement more familiar sources that chronicle government policy in different ways. Diplomatic reports have an analytical value beyond the realm of international relations in the narrow sense. Exaggerating only somewhat, the reports of Prussian, Austrian, Bavarian, Saxon, and other states' envoys are treasures waiting to be discovered by historians of German domestic politics.

Conclusion

The hell of life, said French film director Jean Renoir, is that everyone has his or her reasons. British views of Germany confirm Renoir's *mot*. In their reports to London, British envoys captured the nuance and ambivalence they heard every day in their conversations with powerful players in the worlds of German politics. They penetrated beneath the sneers and crotchets that ricocheted among Germans themselves to discern the more tangible prospects that lay hidden from view. As a result, and without recourse to the notion of an unbridgeable Anglo-German antagonism – which appeared later – we can now better understand the myriad reasons, including hellish ones, for such intense British interest in Germany during the nineteenth century.

Central Europe held a fascination for the British because it was embroiled in multidimensional struggles to avoid, to reverse, or – in Bismarck's case – to foment a "national" revolution. Seen from inside, seen from afar, pre-unification Germany now looks quite different than it did only a few years ago. British diplomats discerned little evidence that Prussia would emerge victorious from the power struggles that shook the continent. Scholars have been working long and hard to dispel the last remnants of Borussian triumphalism (à la Heinrich von Treitschke) and its attendant teleologies. But we can now add another nail to the coffin of the original *Sonderweg* theory. Germany was "special." Indeed. But so were its constituent parts. Despite the unique ways in which the French and Industrial Revolutions shaped its history, Germany was not following a single path towards modernity. The British were uncovering new dimensions of "German" history before Germany existed. To them, the *Sonderweg* concept would have seemed ridiculous.

NOTES

1 See *British Envoys to Germany, 1816–1866* (Camden Fifth Series, vols. 15, 21, 28, 37). Cambridge: Cambridge University Press for the Royal Historical Society in Association with the German Historical Institute London. Vol. 1: *1816–1829*, edited by Sabine Freitag and Peter Wende, 2000. Vol. 2: *1830–1847*, edited by Markus Mösslang, Sabine Freitag, and Peter Wende, 2002. Vol. 3: *1848–1850*, edited by Markus Mösslang, Torsten Riotte, and Hagen Schulze, 2006. Vol. 4: *1851–1866*, edited by Markus Mösslang, Chris Manias, and Torsten Riotte, 2010. Historical interest has not waned: see the many collaborative activities undertaken in conjunction with the research project headed by Richard J. Evans, "Germany and the World: Cultural Exchanges and Mutual Perceptions": http://www.hist.cam.ac.uk/research/research-projects/modern-european/germany-globalization.
2 Ronald Speirs and John Breuilly, eds., *Germany's Two Unifications: Anticipations, Experiences, Responses* (Basingstoke, 2005).
3 Charles S. Maier, "Consigning the Twentieth Century to History: Alternative Narratives for the Modern Era," *American Historical Review* 105, no. 3 (2000): 807–31.

4 David Blackbourn and James Retallack, "Introduction," in *Localism, Landscape, and the Ambiguities of Place: German-Speaking Central Europe, 1860–1930*, edited by Blackbourn and Retallack (Toronto, 2007), 3–4.
5 Johannes Paulmann, *Pomp und Politik. Monarchenbegegnungen in Europa zwischen Ancien Régime und Erstem Weltkrieg* (Stuttgart, 2000).
6 Dominik Geppert and Robert Gerwarth, eds., *Wilhelmine Germany and Edwardian Britain: Essays on Cultural Affinity* (Oxford, New York, 2008); Markus Mösslang and Torsten Riotte, eds., *The Diplomats' World. A Cultural History of Diplomacy, 1815–1914* (Oxford, New York, 2008).
7 In German, an ambassador was a *Botschafter*, whereas *Gesandter* subsumed a diversity of ranks; in this chapter I use the generic term "envoy" except when more specificity is needed. On the "official" and "unofficial" daily duties of German diplomats, see Donata Maria Krethlow-Benziger, *Glanz und Elend der Diplomatie. Kontinuität und Wandel im Alltag des deutschen Diplomaten auf seinen Auslandsposten im Spiegel der Memoiren 1871–1914* (Bern, 2001).
8 Zara S. Steiner, *The Foreign Office and Foreign Policy, 1898–1914* (Cambridge, 1969); Raymond A. Jones, *The British Diplomatic Service 1815–1914* (Gerrards Cross, 1983).
9 Mösslang and Riotte, *The Diplomats' World*, 8. See also the discussion of Paulmann's work and the first volume of *British Envoys to Germany* in Karina Urbach, "Diplomatic History since the Cultural Turn," *Historical Journal* 46, no. 4 (2003): 991–7.
10 Andreas Gestrich, "Foreword," in Mösslang and Riotte, eds., *The Diplomats' World*, v.
11 G.M. Young, cited in Scott W. Murray, *Liberal Diplomacy and German Unification: The Early Career of Robert Morier* (Westport, CT, and London, 2000), xii.
12 Jones, *The British Diplomatic Service*, 9.
13 Hugo Graf Lerchenfeld-Köfering, *Erinnerungen und Denkwürdigkeiten*, 2nd ed. (Berlin, 1935), 197. Both men spent decades reporting from Berlin; representing the Reich's second and third largest federal states, they were highly respected and influential not only because of their longevity.
14 See *inter alia* Wolf D. Gruner, *Die deutsche Frage. Ein Problem der europäischen Geschichte seit 1800* (Munich, 1985).
15 Detlev Peukert, *Die Weimarer Republik. Krisenjahre der Klassischen Moderne* (Frankfurt a.M., 1987).
16 Also known as the Austro-Prussian War. Robert Cecil, 3rd Marquess of Salisbury after 1868, was three times British prime minister and four times foreign secretary. In July 1866, early in his career, he began a brief period as secretary of state for India.

17 Robert Morier, Vienna, to Lady Salisbury, 7 July 1866, in [Robert Morier], *Memoirs and Letters of the Right Hon. Sir Robert Morier, G.C.B. from 1826 to 1876*, edited by Rosslyn Wemyss, 2 vols. (London, 1911), 1: 83.
18 Markus Mösslang, "Conference Report: Editing Documents in the Age of Technology: Principles and Problems," *Bulletin of the German Historical Institute London* 24, no. 2 (November 2002): 106–16.
19 At http://www.germanhistorydocs.ghi-dc.org. See also ch. 3 in this volume.
20 Agatha Ramm, *Sir Robert Morier: Envoy and Ambassador in the Age of Imperialism, 1876–1893* (Oxford, 1973); Ilse Neumann, *Die Geschichte der deutschen Reichsgründung. Nach den Memoiren von Sir Robert Morier* (Vaduz, 1965); Murray, *Liberal Diplomacy*; [Morier], *Memoirs and Letters*, esp. vol. 1.
21 Karina Urbach, *Bismarck's Favourite Englishman: Lord Odo Russell's Mission to Berlin* (London and New York, 1999).
22 John R. Davis, *Britain and the German Zollverein, 1848–66* (New York, 1997); but also see John Ward, *Experiences of a Diplomatist ... 1840–1870* (London, 1872), esp. chs. 4–7 on Leipzig and later chapters after Ward's appointment to the Hansa cities.
23 Frank Lorenz Müller, *Britain and the German Question: Perceptions of Nationalism and Political Reform, 1830–1863* (Basingstoke and New York, 2002); Anselm Doering-Manteuffel, *Vom Wiener Kongreß zur Pariser Konferenz. England, die deutsche Frage und das Mächtesystem 1815–1856* (Göttingen, 1991); Günter Hollenberg, *Englisches Interesse am Kaiserreich. Die Attraktivität Preussen-Deutschlands für konservative und liberale Kreise in Grossbritannien 1860–1914* (Wiesbaden, 1974); John R. Davis, *The Victorians and Germany* (Bern, 2007). On the same theme of reform or revolution, cf. Günther Heydemann, *Konstitution gegen Revolution. Die britische Deutschland- und Italienpolitik 1815–1848* (Göttingen, 1995), and selected essays in Wolfgang J. Mommsen, ed., *Die ungleichen Partner. Deutsch-britische Beziehungen im 19. und 20. Jahrhundert* (Stuttgart, 1999).
24 John McDermott, "The British Foreign Office and Its German Consuls Before 1914," *Journal of Modern History* 50, no. 1 (March 1978), online ed. D1001-D1034. The British Foreign Office (hereafter FO) was always under pressure to legitimate the expense of new and existing consulates in Germany. Consider (D1003) Lord Dufferin's response to a request that a consulate be established in Koblenz: "We cannot have a Consular Officer in every continental town in which an English governess may happen from time to time to be stranded." Cited from a minute of 17 July 1913 by Dufferin in TNA, FO 369/584.
25 Jan Rüger, "Revisiting the Anglo-German Antagonism," *Journal of Modern History* 83 (2011): 579–617; see also Patrick Major, "Britain and Germany:

A Love-Hate Relationship?," Andreas Fahrmeir, "New Perspectives in Anglo-German Comparative History," and other contributions to a special issue of this journal devoted to "Imagining Germany from Abroad": *German History* 26, no. 4 (2008): 457–68, 553–62, and passim; Paul Kennedy, *The Rise of the Anglo-German Antagonism, 1860–1914* (London, 1980).

26 See Markus Mösslang, "Gestaltungsraum und lokale Lebenswelt: Britische Diplomaten an ihren deutschen Standorten, 1815–1914," and other essays on the culture of diplomacy, in *Akteure der Außenbeziehungen. Netzwerke und Interkulturalität im historischen Wandel*, edited by Hillard von Thiessen and Christian Windler (Cologne, Weimar, Vienna, 2010), 199–215; Mösslang, "'Side by Side with Sound Commercial Principles.' Deutscher Zollverein und deutsche Nation in der Wahrnehmung britischer Diplomaten," in *Der Deutsche Zollverein. Ökonomie und Nation im 19. Jahrhundert*, edited by Hans-Werner Hahn and Marko Kreutzmann (Cologne, Weimar, Vienna, 2012), 229–54; Sabine Freitag, "'The narrow limits of this Kingdom.' Sachsen im Spiegel britischer Gesandtschaftsberichte aus dem Vormärz," and other essays in the thematic issue "Großbritannien und Sachsen – Erfahrungen gemeinsamer Kultur," *Dresdner Hefte* 20, no. 70 (2002): 27–37 and passim; Torsten Riotte, *Hannover in der britischen Politik (1792–1815)* (Münster, 2005); Philip Mansel and Torsten Riotte, eds., *Monarchy and Exile: The Politics of Legitimacy from Marie de Médici to Wilhelm II* (Basingstoke, 2011).

27 I am grateful to Markus Mößlang for allowing me to see pre-publication versions of documents and transcriptions to appear in the two volumes covering 1871–83 and 1884–97, of which the first should appear in 2016.

28 Henry Richard Charles Wellesley, 2nd Baron Cowley, to Lord Palmerston, 9 June 1851, *British Envoys*, IV, 29.

29 See Christopher Clark, "After 1848: The European Revolution in Government," *Transactions of the Royal Historical Society* 22 (2012): 171–97; also see Wolfram Siemann, *Gesellschaft im Aufbruch. Deutschland 1849–1871* (Frankfurt a.M., 1990); Abigail Green, *Fatherlands: State-Building and Nationhood in Nineteenth-Century Germany* (Cambridge, New York, 2001).

30 Hansard, *Parliamentary Debates*, Ser. III, vol. cciv, February–March 1871, speech of 9 February 1871, 81.

31 See *inter alia* Andreas Biefang, "Modernität wider Willen. Bemerkungen zur Entstehung des demokratischen Wahlrechts des Kaiserreichs," in *Gestaltungskraft des Politischen. Festschrift für Eberhard Kolb*, edited by Wolfram Pyta and Ludwig Richter (Berlin, 1998), 239–59; Richard Augst, *Bismarcks Stellung zum parlamentarischen Wahlrecht* (Leipzig, 1917); more comparatively, see Markus Mattmüller, "Die Durchsetzung des allgemeinen Wahlrechts als gesamteuropäischer Vorgang," in *Geschichte und*

politische Wissenschaft. Festschrift für Erich Gruner zum 60. Geburtstag, edited by Beat Junker, Peter Gilg, and Richard Reich (Bern, 1975), 213–36.

32 James J. Sheehan, *German Liberalism in the Nineteenth Century* (Chicago, 1978); Sheehan, "Liberalism and the City in Nineteenth-Century Germany," *Past and Present* 51 (May 1971): 116–37; Dieter Langewiesche, *Liberalism in Germany*, trans. Christiane Banerji (orig. 1988) (Basingstoke, 2000); Langewiesche, ed., *Liberalismus und Region. Zur Geschichte des deutschen Liberalismus im 19. Jahrhundert* (Munich, 1995).

33 David Blackbourn and Geoff Eley, *The Peculiarities of German History: Bourgeois Society and Politics in Nineteenth-Century Germany* (Oxford and New York, 1984). Cf. David Blackbourn, "New Legislatures: Germany, 1871–1914," *Historical Research* 65, no. 157 (June 1992): 201–14.

34 George Strachey, Dresden, to British FO (draft), 7 February 1890, TNA, FO 215/40.

35 Writing of Chancellor Leo von Caprivi, an army general, Strachey reported: "Most of the maxims which our own public philosophy affirms are repudiated here. In Germany, it is thought natural that the highest political functions should be entrusted to persons without political knowledge – to a 'Major-General,' a desk-official, an Ambassador. Parliamentary experience, and popular influence, are not reckoned among the qualifications which should be exacted [i.e., expected] from a Prime Minister." Strachey to British FO, 26 March 1892, TNA, FO 68/177.

36 Jones, *The British Diplomatic Service*, 69.

37 After Strachey retired, Sir Condie Stephen was among the most slothful British envoys posted to Dresden (1897–1901). He reported from Gotha and the other Saxon principalities almost as often, or as seldom, as he did from Dresden; see, e.g., TNA, FO 68/301. His successor, 3rd Viscount Hugh Gough (1901–07), was not much better. For *German* diplomats, most contemporaries considered a posting in Dresden to be a plum because of the city's cultural riches and the beauty of its surrounding countryside: Willy Real, *Karl Friedrich von Savigny 1814–1875* (Berlin, 1990), 177.

38 Müller, *Britain and the German Question*, passim.

39 FO to Charles Augustus Murray, Dresden, 1 May 1866, TNA, FO 215/20.

40 George Villiers, 4th Earl of Clarendon, to Lord Augustus Loftus (Britain's ambassador in Berlin), 7 March 1866, cited in Augustus Loftus, *The Diplomatic Reminiscences of Lord Augustus Loftus, 1862–1879*, Second Series, 2 vols. (London, 1894), 1: 43. Loftus recalled that when he left his post in Bavaria to take up his appointment to Prussia in mid-February 1866, "I found on my arrival at Berlin the political atmosphere very 'loaded' – '*Il sentait la poudre*,' as a Frenchman would say." When Loftus conveyed

London's desire to see Prussia and Austria reconcile their differences, Bismarck quoted the words of Richelieu to his discarded mistress: *"Nous ne sommes pas ennemis: mais nous ne nous aimons plus."* 1: 39, 45.

41 As argued by Owain James Wright in his review of *British Envoys*, vol. I, in *European History Quarterly* 33, no. 2 (2003): 271–2, and in Wolfgang Elz's review, cited previously, 474.

42 Joseph Crowe was a long-time consul in the Saxon city of Leipzig, a friend of German liberals, and the father of Eyre Crowe, who as a senior clerk in the Foreign Office wrote a famous memorandum in 1907 warning of Germany's aggressive foreign policy. Kennedy, *The Rise of the Anglo-German Antagonism*, 136f., notes that only J.A. Crowe rivalled Morier's knowledge of German politics. See also Odo Russell to Lord Granville, 22 May and 12 July 1880, in *Letters from the Berlin Embassy ... 1871–1874, 1880–1885*, edited by Paul Knaplund, 3 vols. (Washington, DC, 1942), 2: 143, 153–4.

43 Ward, *Experiences of a Diplomatist*, v–vi. Ward's preface was dated 31 December 1871.

44 Cf. Julian Hawthorne, *Saxon Studies* (Boston, 1876), 50–1, referring to the Saxons' "habit of following authority and precedent in all concerns of life ... They swim everywhere in the cork-jacket of Law; and, should it fail them, flounder and sink." See ch. 5 in this book.

45 Strachey to British FO (draft), 21 October 1874, TNA, FO 215/34, final version in FO 68/158. Only a few months earlier, Strachey had written that "tolerance of dissident opinions is not a German virtue, or ideal ... No one with a tolerable knowledge of Germans ... can be unaware of their ... infirmity of temper, of their impatience of ridicule, sarcasm, and contradiction ... They easily sympathize with systems that punish energetic criticism of public mew and measures, and make minorities mute." Strachey to British FO, 21 March 1874, TNA, FO 68/158.

46 See Loftus, *The Diplomatic Reminiscences*, Series 1 and 2.

47 Odo Russell to his brother Arthur, July 1870, TNA, FO 918/84 (Ampthill Papers), cited in Urbach, *Bismarck's Favourite Englishman*, 47. In this case the usual translation of *Geist* as "spirit" seems out of place.

48 Diary of Lord Derby, 78 (11 March 1871), cited in Urbach, *Bismarck's Favourite Englishman*, 74.

49 Friedrich Nietzsche, "David Strauss, the Confessor and the Writer," in Nietzsche, *Untimely Meditations*, edited by Daniel Breazeale, translated by R.J. Hollingdale (Cambridge, 1997), 3–6.

50 Urbach, *Bismarck's Favourite Englishman*, 74.

51 The *Times*, 15 September 1832, cited in Müller, *Britain and the German Question*, 4.

52 Bismarck to his wife Johanna, 5 July 1862, cited in Lothar Gall, *Bismarck: The White Revolutionary*, translated by J.A. Underwood, 2 vols. (London and Boston, 1986), 1: 181.
53 Cited in Urbach, "Diplomatic History," 995.
54 See Keith Robbins, *Protestant Germany through British Eyes: A Complex Victorian Encounter*, Annual Lecture of the German Historical Institute London (London, 1993).
55 Klaus Hildebrand, *No intervention. Die Pax Britannica und Preußen 1865/66–1869/70* (Munich, 1997).
56 Urbach, *Bismarck's Favourite Englishman*, 110.
57 Strachey to British FO, 3 December 1874, TNA, FO 68/158.
58 Morier, Berlin, to Odo Russell, 1 February 1864, TNA, FO 918/55, original emphasis.
59 Murray, *Liberal Diplomacy*, 71. For Morier's earlier views on German nationalism, see ch. 4 of Murray.
60 Crowe to British FO, 11 January 1867, TNA, FO 68/147. Crowe also disparaged Bismarck's draft constitution for the North German Confederation, which he submitted to a conference of ministers from the federal German states in late 1866: the White Paper had been circulated "under the name of a constitution." FO 68/147.
61 Morier to Ernst von Stockmar, 15 December 1870, Morier Papers, Balliol College, Oxford, box 5, cited in Murray, *Liberal Diplomacy*, 82. Cf. Arthur Russell to Robert Morier, 16 February 1871, Morier Papers, box 5/2, cited in Urbach, *Bismarck's Favourite Englishman*, 110.
62 George John Robert Gordon, Stuttgart, to Lord Russell, 28 May 1861, TNA, FO 82/99, in *British Envoys*, IV, 365–9 at 367; Charles Augustus Murray, Dresden, to Russell, 18 December 1863, TNA, FO 68/127, in *British Envoys*, IV, 324.
63 Urbach, "Diplomatic History," 994.
64 See Mösslang, "Side by Side."
65 Frederick Lamb, Frankfurt, to Viscount Castlereagh, 25 May 1820, TNA, FO 30/20, in *British Envoys*, I, 25.
66 George H. Rose, Berlin, to Castlereagh, 15 July 1819, TNA, FO 64/119, in *British Envoys*, I, 101–2.
67 John Philip Morier, Dresden, to Castlereagh, 9 March, 20 and 27 April, 6 and 11 May 1819, TNA, FO 68/22, not included in *British Envoys*. I am grateful to Markus Mößlang for providing me with copies of these reports.
68 John Philip Morier, Dresden, to Castlereagh, 20 May and 19 September 1819, TNA, FO 68/22, in *British Envoys*, I, 401–3. Morier ascribed the "most

glaring defects" of German universities to "the non-existence of separate colleges." Morier to Castlereagh, 16 March 1819, in *British Envoys*, I, 400.

69 After the wars of Italian unification, Crowe recalled: "Austria, Prussia, and the Confederation seemed alike helpless: Austria because she had lost her game, Prussia because she had missed her mark, the Confederation because its framework had been loosened. The Prince Regent [later Prussian King Wilhelm I] was in despair, the German people divided." Joseph Archer Crowe, *Reminiscences of Thirty-Five Years of My Life*, 2nd ed. (London, 1895), 384.

70 TNA, Russell Papers, 30/22/63, cited by Murray, *Liberal Diplomacy*, 36.

71 The reference here is to the failed political conception of Saxony's government leader, Count Friedrich Ferdinand von Beust; see his memoir, *Aus drei Viertel-Jahrhunderten. Erinnerungen und Aufzeichnungen*, 2 vols. (Stuttgart, 1887); Jonas Flöter, *Beust und die Reform des Deutschen Bundes 1850–1866* (Cologne, Weimar, Vienna, 2001).

72 Russell to Sir Andrew Buchanan (draft), 30 September 1863, TNA, FO 64/537, cited in Müller, *Britain and the German Question*, 199 (and 200 for the following). Russell added a month later: "I fear he [Bismarck] is going to bring upon us a democratic revolution in Germany."

73 Crowe, *Reminiscences*, 1: 414.

74 Letter dated Berne, February 1833, in [Morier], *Memoirs and Letters*, 1: 6–7. On Robert Morier's estimate of the excessive work imposed on British diplomats, see his comments before a Select Committee on the Diplomatic and Consular Services in 1870, cited in Murray, *Liberal Diplomacy*, xiii: "The actual amount of knowledge which a diplomatist has to master before he can fit himself for the work is so great, because the peculiar feature of the day is the way in which political questions, and social questions, and religious questions, and scientific questions, are all dovetailed the one into the other, that the time of a man who really wishes to fit himself for this work is more than filled."

75 Burnley, Dresden, to British FO, 10 February 1868, TNA, FO 68/148.

76 Details in Jones, The *British Diplomatic Service*, ch. 6.

77 Urbach, *Bismarck's Favourite Englishman*, 19.

78 Russell to Cartwright, 25 March 1870, TNA, FO 918/55, emphasis added.

79 The following is based on my systematic reading of reports from envoys and consuls stationed in Dresden, 1866–1905, TNA, FO 68/142 to 68/323; FO 215 (drafts), passim; and select FO files from other German capitals.

80 Cf. Stadtarchiv Dresden, 16.1.1, PA II, Nachlaß Burgk, Nr. 85.

81 Burnley to British FO, 31 January 1871, TNA, FO 68/153.

82 See Strachey to British FO (draft), 20 December 1879, TNA, FO 215/34, reporting on a speech the radical antisemitic leader Wilhelm Marr delivered in Dresden, outlining his demands of the Jews: "For instance – Jews are not to serve in the Army, but to pay a blood tax for wh[ich] the Judenthum in the aggregate is to be responsible. The 'Mosaic Man' to be removed from all official posts of every description. Bills owing to Jews to be paid [in] ready money, so that dealings with them may not fall under commercial legislation. Jew[ish] newspapers not to publish articles on the religion & political affairs of ††ians. Jews not to hold land unless for cultivation of Hebrew laborers ..."

[Strachey continued:] "These ideas are perhaps less amazing than the fact that in 1879, in the so-called 'Elbe-Florence' a large and intelligent audience listened to them with patience, and, apparently, without astonishment. The leading journal of Dresden reproduced them with seeming approbation and approval and again denounced with appropriate insults [Eduard] Lasker, [Gerson von] Bleichröder, the 'Golden International', Monometallism & Free Trade."

[Strachey concluded:] "It is characteristic of German statesmanship that [Minister of the Interior] Fr[ei]herr [Hermann] von Nostitz-Wallwitz avowed a certain sympathy with this sentiment. He spoke with regret of the good old 'Ghetto' principle maintained here in full vigor until the year 1867 wh[ich] prohibited the residence of Jews in Saxony except in Dresden & Leipzig. This, said [Nostitz-Wallwitz] was an Excellent rule, for it prevented those acquisitions of property [by] Jewish owners which had been found so mischievous elsewhere."

83 Strachey, Dresden, to British FO (draft), 25 June 1880, TNA, FO 215/34.

84 See Otto Pflanze, *Bismarck and the Development of Germany*, 3 vols. (Princeton, 1990), vol. 3, *The Period of Fortification, 1880-1898*.

85 Representing Bavaria, Belgium, Greece, Great Britain, Italy, the Netherlands, Austria-Hungary, Persia, Portugal, Prussia, Russia, Sweden, Spain, and Württemberg; *Staatshandbuch für das Königreich Sachsen auf das Jahr 1907* (Dresden, n.d.), 405ff.

86 Henry Mayhew, *German Life and Manners As Seen in Saxony at the Present Day*, 2 vols. (London, 1864); Sidney Whitman, *Imperial Germany: A Critical Study of Fact and Character* (Leipzig, 1890); Whitman, *German Memories* (London, 1912); Mrs Alfred Sidgwick, *Home Life in Germany*, orig. 1856, 2nd ed. (London, 1908). See Heinz-Joachim Müllenbrock, "Trugbilder: Zum Dilemma imagologischer Forschung am Beispiel des englischen Deutschlandbildes 1870–1914," *Anglia* 113, no. 3 (1995): 303–29, and ch. 6 in the present volume.

87 Mark Twain, *The Innocents Abroad*, orig. 1869 (New York, 1996); Kenneth Barkin resurrected Du Bois's writings from Berlin in "W.E.B. Du Bois, "The Present Condition of German Politics (1893)," *Central European History* 31, no. 3 (1998): 171–88. For an earlier period, see Michael Maurer, "Außenwahrnehmung Deutschland und die Deutschen im Spiegel ausländischer Reiseberichte (1500–1800)," in *Föderative Nation. Deutschlandkonzepte von der Reformation bis zum Ersten Weltkrieg*, edited by Dieter Langewiesche and Georg Schmidt (Munich, 2000), 309–25; Johann Georg, Herzog zu Sachsen, ed., *Briefwechsel König Johanns von Sachsen mit George Ticknor* (Leipzig and Berlin, 1920); Thomas Adam, "Germany Seen Through American Eyes: George and Anna Eliot Ticknor's German Travel Logs," in *Transatlantic Cultural Contexts: Essays in Honor of Eberhard Brüning*, edited by Hartmut Keil (Tübingen, 2005), 151–63; Anna Ticknor, *Two Boston Brahmins in Goethe's Germany: The Travel Journals of Anna and George Ticknor*, edited by Thomas Adam and Gisele Mettele (Lanham, 2009); Eberhard Brüning, "Sachsen mit amerikanischen Augen gesehen. Das Sachsenbild amerikanischer Globetrotter im 19. Jahrhundert," *Neues Archiv für sächsische Geschichte* 67 (1996): 109–31.

88 For Saxony alone, the United States maintained consulates in Dresden, Leipzig, Chemnitz, Glauchau, Plauen, and Zittau; National Archives and Records Administration (NARA), College Park, Maryland, Record Group 59, T-series. See Eberhard Brüning, *Der Konsulat der Vereinigten Staaten von Amerika zu Leipzig* (Berlin, 1994); Michael Löffler, *Preußens und Sachsens Beziehungen zu den USA während des Sezessionskrieges 1860–1865* (Münster, 1999), which distinguishes between the views of German consuls stationed in the north and south; Price Collier, *Germany and the Germans from an American Point of View* (Toronto, 1913); and Otto Graf zu Stolberg-Wernigerode, *Deutschland und die Vereinigten Staaten von Amerika im Zeitalter Bismarcks* (Berlin and Leipzig, 1933).

89 Joseph A. Wright, Berlin, to US Secretary of State William Seward, Washington, DC, 11 April 1866; NARA, Record Group 59, M44, reel 13. Wright had previously served as US envoy extraordinary and minister plenipotentiary to Prussia from 1857 to 1861.

90 Cf. John Whiteclay Chambers II, "American Views of Conscription and the German Nation in Arms in the Franco-Prussian War," in *The People in Arms*, edited by Daniel Moran and Arthur Waldron (Cambridge and New York, 2003), 75–99; Jörn Leonhard, "Die Nationalisierung des Krieges und der Bellizismus der Nation: Die Diskussion um *Volks-* und *Nationalkrieg* in Deutschland, Großbritannien und den Vereinigten Staaten seit den 1860er Jahren," in *Der Bürger als Soldat*, edited by Christian Jansen (Essen, 2004),

83–105; Frank Lorenz Müller, "The Spectre of a People in Arms: The Prussian Government and the Militarisation of German Nationalism, 1859–1864," *English Historical Review* 122, no. 495 (2007): 82–104.

91 George Bancroft, Berlin, to US Secretary of State William Seward, 1 November 1867, NARA, Record Group 59, M44, reel 14, emphasis added. American diplomacy vis-à-vis Vienna cannot be overlooked; see, e.g., Erwin Matsch, *Wien–Washington. Ein Journal diplomatischer Beziehungen 1838–1917* (Cologne, Weimar, Vienna, 1990). Margaret Sterne, "The Presidents of the United States in the Eyes of Austro-Hungarian Diplomats: 1901–1913," *Austrian History Yearbook* 2 (1966): 143–71, makes for fascinating reading.

92 Letter of 31 August 1866, cited (in German) in Stolberg-Wernigerode, *Deutschland und die Vereinigten Staaten*, 77–8. I have not been able to locate the original English version of this letter.

93 Bayard Taylor, *Views A-Foot or Europe Seen with Knapsack and Staff*, orig. 1846, rev. ed. (New York and London, 1892).

94 Bayard Taylor to US Secretary of State, 8 November 1878, NARA, Record Group 59, M44, reel 42.

95 H. Sidney Everett to US Secretary of State, 15 February 1879, NARA, Record Group 59, M44, reel 42.

96 See, e.g., Andrew D. White to US Secretary of State, 15 August 1879, NARA, Record Group 59, M44, reel 43.

97 An exemplary edition of one such set of diplomatic reports is found in Hans-Jürgen Kremer, *Das Grossherzogtum Baden in der politischen Berichterstattung der preussischen Gesandten, 1871–1918*, 2 pts (Stuttgart, 1990–2). On German–German diplomatic reportage, see *inter alia* Hans-Joachim Schreckenbach, "Innerdeutsche Gesandtschaften 1867–1945," in *Archivar und Historiker* (Berlin-GDR, 1956), 404–28; Otto Esch, *Das Gesandtschaftsrechte der deutschen Einzelstaaten* (Bonn, 1911); Hellmut Kretzschmar and Horst Schlechte, eds, *Französische und Sächsische Gesandtschaftsberichte aus Dresden und Paris 1848–1849* (Berlin-GDR, 1956); Hans Philippi, *Das Königreich Württemberg im Spiegel der preußischen Gesandtschaftsberichte, 1871–1914* (Stuttgart, 1972); Anton Chroust, *Gesandtschaftsberichte aus München, 1814–1848*, 15 vols. (Munich, 1935–51); Konrad Reiser, *Bayerische Gesandte bei deutschen und ausländischen Regierungen 1871–1918* (Munich, 1968); August Bach, ed., *Deutsche Gesandtschaftsberichte zum Kriegsausbruch 1914* (Berlin, 1937); and Paul Marcus, "Die Preußische Gesandtschaft Dresden im 19. und 20. Jahrhundert und ihre Überlieferung im Geheimen Staatsarchiv Preußischer Kulturbesitz," *Archivalische Zeitschrift* 81 (1998): 112–37.

98 James Retallack, "'What Is to Be Done?' The Red Specter, Franchise Questions, and the Crisis of Conservative Hegemony in Saxony, 1896–1909," *Central European History* 23 (1990): 271–312; Retallack, "Anti-Socialism and Electoral Politics in Regional Perspective: the Kingdom of Saxony," in *Elections, Mass Politics, and Social Change in Modern Germany*, edited by Larry Eugene Jones and James Retallack (Cambridge, 1992), 49–91.

99 Politisches Archiv, Auswärtiges Amt, Abteilung A, Bonn (now Berlin) (hereafter PAAAB), esp. collections I.A.A.b (Deutschland), and I.A.A.m (Sachsen [Königreich]), Nrn. 39–62.

100 Simone Lässig, *Wahlrechtskampf und Wahlreform in Sachsen (1895–1909)* (Cologne, Weimar, Vienna, 1996); Lässig, *Reichstagswahlen im Königreich Sachsen 1871–1912. Beiheft zur Karte D IV 2, Atlas zur Geschichte und Landeskunde von Sachsen* (Leipzig and Dresden, 1998); Wolfgang Schröder's introductory essay to Elvira Döscher and Wolfgang Schröder, eds, *Sächsische Parlamentarier 1869–1918* (Düsseldorf, 2001); Schröder, *Landtagswahlen im Königreich Sachsen 1869 bis 1896/1896. Beiheft zur Karte D IV 3, Atlas zur Geschichte und Landeskunde von Sachsen* (Leipzig and Dresden, 2004); Gerhard A. Ritter, "Wahlen und Wahlpolitik im Königreich Sachsen 1867–1914," in *Sachsen im Kaiserreich*, edited by Simone Lässig and Karl Heinrich Pohl (Dresden, 1997), 29–86.

101 My recent rereading of Konrad H. Jarausch's *The Enigmatic Chancellor: Bethmann Hollweg and the Hubris of Imperial Germany* (New Haven, CT, and London, 1973), provided a humbling reminder of how such triangulation illuminated German high politics decades ago. Among an extraordinarily rich source base Jarausch included reports from envoys representing Prussia, Bavaria, Saxony, Baden, Württemberg, Austria, and the United States. The only noteworthy gap is the lack of reports from the Public Record Office, Kew.

102 Count von Bernstorff, ambassador to Britain (1903–6) and the United States (1908–17), disagreed: "Bismarck maintained the missions to the German courts to please the princes. These missions were actually only appendages to the courts, a kind of flag that was hung out to demonstrate that the individual states still existed. For the chief [of mission] these posts – with the exception of Munich – signified almost nothing more than an old-age benefit; for the secretary of mission they nonetheless offered the advantage that one came back to Germany again and saw it from another point of view." Bernstorff's claims – for example, that Dresden in the mid-1890s had good theatre but "no politics whatsoever" – should not be accepted uncritically. Johann Heinrich Graf von

Bernstorff, *Erinnerungen und Briefe*, orig. 1936 (Hamburg, 2013), 28; *NDB*, 2 (1955): 141–2.

103 Baron Rudolf von Gasser, Dresden, to Bavarian FO, 5 June 1878, Bayerisches Hauptstaatsarchiv, Abteilung II, Geheimes Staatsarchiv, Munich, Ministerium des Äußern, III, Bd. 2849.

104 Baron Karl von und zu Franckenstein, Dresden, to Austrian FO, 18 May 1878; Österreichisches Staatsarchiv, Haus-, Hof- und Staatsarchiv, Vienna (hereafter HHStAV), Ministerium des Äussern, Politisches Archiv (PA), V (Sachsen), Nr. 42.

105 Major Paul Edler von der Planitz, Berlin, to Saxon War Ministry, 13 August 1878 (original emphasis); Sächsisches Hauptstaatsarchiv, Sächsisches Kriegsarchiv, Dresden, 2.1, Nr. 4490.

106 Strachey to British FO, 4 March 1887, TNA, FO 68/171.

107 Strachey to British FO, 22 January 1879, TNA, FO 68/163.

108 The Social Democrats' leading national newspaper.

109 See Heinzpeter Thümmler, *Sozialistengesetz §28. Ausweisungen und Ausgewiesene 1878–1890* (Vaduz, 1979), 74–88; cf. Horst Thieme, "Die Verhängung des kleinen Belagerungszustandes über Leipzig und Umgebung am 29. Juni 1881 – Vorgeschichte und erste Auswirkungen," *Sächsische Heimatblätter* 9, no. 6 (1963): 78; and Fritz Staude, *Sie waren stärker. Der Kampf der Leipziger Sozialdemokratie in der Zeit des Sozialistengesetzes 1878–1890* (Leipzig, 1969), esp. 73–82.

110 Madai to Prussian Minister of the Interior Botho zu Eulenburg, 25 November 1879, Brandenburgisches Landeshauptarchiv, Potsdam (hereafter BLHAP), Nr. 12844.

111 BLHAP, Nr. 12844; Madai's "Uebersicht" (31.12.80), Bundesarchiv, Abteilungen Potsdam (now Berlin) (hereafter BAP), Reichskanzlei, Nr. 646/6; Dieter Fricke, *Bismarcks Prätorianer. Die Berliner politische Polizei im Kampf gegen die deutsche Arbeiterbewegung (1871–1898)* (Berlin-GDR, 1962), 102.

112 Unsigned reports, 23 and 26 April 1880, probably from Madai's spies in Saxony; BLHAP, Nr. 12844.

113 Bismarck to Dönhoff (draft), 18.3.81, PAAAB, Deutschland 102, Vol. 3. Cf. Bismarck to Puttkamer (draft), 24 March 1881, BAP, Reichskanzlei, Nr. 646/6.

114 Emphasis added.

115 *Stenographische Berichte über die Verhandlungen des Deutschen Reichstags* (Berlin, 1881), 30 March 1881, 638.

116 August Bebel, *Aus meinem Leben*, 3 pts in 1, 3rd ed. (Berlin-GDR, 1961), 753.

117 Dönhoff to Prussian FO, 4 June 1881, PAAAB, Sachsen 48, Bd. 5.

118 Strachey to British FO, 9 April 1881, TNA, FO 215/34 (draft), FO 68/165 (final).
119 Yet, a few months later, an unnamed Saxon minister – most likely Nostitz-Wallwitz again – endorsed Prussian arguments about the need for more severe repression. After the Saxon government had failed to invalidate Bebel's election to the Landtag, despite the Minor State of Siege, this minister complained to the interim Austrian envoy in Dresden that "the Socialist Party, whose assemblies have been dissolved [*gesprengt*] and whose press has been rendered silent, finds an opportunity to continue its rabble-rousing [*Hetzereien*] from the podium of the Landtag through the word of its most important leader." Acting envoy S[igismund] von Rosty, Dresden, to Austrian FO, 13 August 1881, HHStAV, PA V, Nr. 43.

3 Digital History Anthologies on the Web

ORIGINALLY CO-AUTHORED WITH
KELLY McCULLOUGH
GERMAN HISTORICAL INSTITUTE, WASHINGTON, DC

This chapter charts unfamiliar paths into the Second Reich and through it.[1] It is intended principally for readers whose appetite for working with primary sources may have been whetted by chapter 1 but who are willing to wait for the chance to focus on the Second Reich through the eyes of individuals such as Otto von Bismarck. This chapter emphasizes the diverse ways we can pan across the long sweep of German history. This is especially true of the chapter's final section, which deals with editorial authority. How are the histories we write (or "choose") actually read (or "consumed") by scholars, students, and lay audiences around the globe who access them via the internet? By asking such questions, we may come to appreciate a novel, topsy-turvy world of German history – a world that lies within our reach when chronological linearity is subverted or nudged aside.

This chapter also explores how we might depict ordinary Germans living in the Second Reich if we wanted to look through a microscope and a wide-angle lens at the same time. It suggests that we can view such Germans through the changing filters provided by today's and tomorrow's internet while, at the same time, allowing Germans to put themselves "on view" (e.g., through the genre of autobiography) – so explicitly on view, indeed, that we can no longer look through them or past them. Whether we imagine ourselves doing the work of a laboratory scientist or a studio photographer, this enterprise provides a chance to discover Germans who only at first blush seem to have disappeared into the past. And whether we choose one lens or the other matters little: close-ups, group shots, and panoramas complement one another. The more important point is that digital history allows many familiar facets of the Second Reich to come into clear focus for the first time. By its very nature the internet allows historians, whether professional or lay, to access archival materials previously hidden behind barriers thicker than any firewall; to collaborate and to communicate the fruits of their labour at fibre-optic speeds; and to offer the multiplicity of perspectives that cannot fit between the covers of a book. In a double sense, then, digital history puts a new face on the German Empire. It does so in ways that hardly seemed possible just two decades ago.

Initial public offerings in the dot.com world are not always the darlings they are expected to be. Ask Mark Zuckerberg about Facebook's disappointing IPO in May 2012. But new ventures often defy their founders' expectations and become great successes. As we hope to suggest, *German History in Documents and Images* (GHDI)[2] – a project that has put thousands of primary source texts, drawings, photographs, and maps on the internet, along with hundreds of pages of accompanying commentary – has drawn critical appreciation from specialists and non-specialists alike; but it has also raised thorny questions about authorship, authority, and audience. Those questions concern the writing of history in general and the newer, more specific discipline of "history on the web." Like the project itself, this chapter is the result of a collaboration among the GHDI project staff, which is based at the German Historical Institute, Washington, DC, and the GHDI volume editors, all of whom teach (or taught) German history at colleges and universities in North America. In the following pages, we briefly outline the early goals of the venture, describe the challenges associated with the realization of a large, collaborative history project of this nature – whether in book or digital form – and reflect upon what we perceive as the promise and perils of digital history anthologies.[3]

The origins of the GHDI project date back to 2002, a time not terribly far removed from us – especially when the subject is history and the writing of it. But when viewed in "internet years," 2002 already seems like another lifetime, a moment when the web, as we know it, was relatively new. The first web pages appeared in the early 1990s, but it was only after the introduction of Netscape, in 1994, that "the History Web came into its own."[4] According to Daniel J. Cohen and Roy Rosenzweig, the mid-1990s marked the start of a "fever to bring the primary sources of the past online."[5] It was a fever shared by scholars and teachers but also by amateur enthusiasts with specific interests – sometimes vested interests – in particular historical topics.

German History in Documents and Images was both part of this fever and a response to it. By 2002, the German Historical Institute (GHI) and a group of scholars associated with it had noted the potential of primary source websites to enliven the teaching of German history, but they had glimpsed some attendant dangers as well.[6] They were inspired by early teaching archives, such as Paul Halsall's Internet History Sourcebooks Project, which gave students greater access to quality historical texts in translation, filling a void felt keenly by educators; they were also concerned by the proliferation of other, less academic websites, including ones devoted to military history.[7] Such websites sometimes reflected an undue fascination with the Nazi war machine. The initiators of GHDI were particularly dismayed to see that student term papers were making increasing – and wholly uncritical – use of homegrown websites that advocated particular agendas, well-intentioned or not.

In the spring of 2002, Christof Mauch, then director of the GHI, consulted with two board members of the Friends of the GHI, Roger Chickering and Konrad H. Jarausch. Together, they forged plans to develop a project that would make a large selection of German historical documents available in both German and English on the website of the GHI in Washington, DC. Their goal was twofold. First, and most generally, they wanted to take the lead, as one of them recalled, in putting "responsible historical content" on the web. Second, as they explained in a broadly sketched grant application, they aimed to use primary source documents "to revitalize the study of German history and culture in the United States and beyond."

By the end of 2002, funding had been secured and the project's steering committee was in place. The committee decided that each volume would have a separate editor (or team of editors), that each would include documents in both English and German and a selection of images, and that each editor would write a brief but comprehensive introduction to the history of the period in question. To prevent an overemphasis on political history and to ensure that more recent topics of historical inquiry, such as gender and popular culture, were well represented in the project, the committee devised a list of subject headings for the editors to consider in selecting their materials.[8] This decision was made with an eye towards enhancing the pedagogical value of the site. "After all," as one committee member observed, the goal of the website was "to provide sources for classroom purposes as well as historical research."[9]

With these guidelines in place, the GHDI steering committee began the first phase of its work and set about finding editors for the volumes.

To start, three committee members (Chickering, Jarausch, and Gerald Feldman) agreed to sign up as editors themselves.[10] The GHDI project staff meanwhile began brainstorming about the nature of the website that would display all of the materials. From the start, there were two core requirements. First and foremost, the site would endorse the principle of open access. Second, the site would be self-contained: it would not link to content – primary source texts, images, commentary – on other websites. The staff then began meeting with web designers, who posed questions such as, "Which three adjectives would best describe your ideal website?" Words such as "transparent," "straightforward," and "trustworthy" came up again and again. But one word, whether explicitly mentioned or not, informed the design of the site like no other: "book-like." Although the project was "born digital," it was never a web project per se so much as a primary source reader in digital form – a point that becomes clearer as the site gets older. Reports of the death of "the book" have been greatly exaggerated. Many users of *German History in Documents and Images* appreciate its straightforward division into volumes, which are then divided into chapters, sections, and so on. In short, they like its familiar feel.[11]

Images occupied an important place in the project from the outset. The emphasis on images was a reflection of the steering committee's appreciation of the internet's visual nature. But it was also an acknowledgment of the increasingly important role of visual studies in general and an attempt to reach a younger generation of students. As one committee member put it in 2003, the project had to be "more now." The visual emphasis was also an effort to expand the corpus of free, high-resolution digital images available to teachers of German history. The committee believed that the selection of historical images on the web was too limited and too homogeneous – too many reproductions of the same famous scenes that could already be found in countless textbooks. The images were to be understood not merely as "illustrations" or accompaniments to the documents, but rather as historical sources on a par with them. This was made clear from the start by the name of the project and the structure of the website.[12]

Whereas *German History in Documents and Images* was principally envisioned as a primary source website, the steering committee recognized the need to include explanatory material as well. That each editor would write an introduction to his or her volume was clear from the beginning. But over time other forms of editorial guidance began to assume greater importance, and, for better or worse, greater length.

This material included abstracts that introduced each document, captions for the images, and, less frequently, footnotes explaining obscure people, places, or events in the texts. The decision to include all of this editorial material in German as well as English represented a major turning point for the project. At that moment, GHDI went from being an English-language website that included primary source documents in both the original German and English translation to a completely bilingual website where every page appeared in parallel form in two languages. This decision – we have no doubt it was a good one – had far-reaching implications, not least with respect to the project's target audience.

By November 2003, the entire GHDI editorial team was in place, and the volume editors were invited to Washington, DC, to meet with the GHDI steering committee and project staff. The agenda included a range of topics: the basic parameters of the project and its component volumes, practical matters such as deadlines and document delivery, and administrative concerns (such as copyright procurement and publicity). Tellingly, it was not these issues, but rather larger ones regarding periodization, categorization, interpretation, and uniformity, that dominated the conversation that Saturday afternoon. The chronological division of the volumes, especially those devoted to Germany after 1945, was a point of particular interest. But the liveliest discussion was sparked by the question of categorization.

Did the editors want to adhere to the steering committee's proposed categories? Did they prefer to come up with their own? And did *any* uniform categorization suggest that the editors were overstepping their epistemological and pedagogical mandate? Some editors argued that the very act of dividing the materials into categories put too much weight on the editorial commentaries, insofar as editors would be compelled to explain why a document or image was assigned to one category and not another. Others emphasized the project's role as a teaching aid, arguing that grouping the documents and images into categories was best left to classroom instructors. In the end, it seemed clear that there was a practical need to organize the materials in some way, even if doing so imposed a level of interpretation unwanted by some.[13] At the end of the meeting, the volume editors, the GHDI steering committee, and the project staff promised to meet again as a group (though they ultimately never did).

The conversation did continue on a smaller scale, however, as the work progressed. In late 2009 and early 2010, two conference panels were dedicated to *German History in Documents and Images*. After these two panels, we, the authors of this article, put together a short survey and sent it to each GHDI editor. While our survey was no substitute for that second meeting that never took place, the editors' thoughtful responses did represent a continuation of that conversation. We posed the following questions: How and why did you select certain documents and images over others? Did you try to "tell a story" as you shaped your volume? Have you used this resource in your own teaching? Why did you choose to organize your volume as you did? Did you try to strike a balance between social, economic, political, cultural, and international history? The editors' replies offered a host of wide-ranging reflections on the novelty and scope of the enterprise and on the broader questions it raised about "doing" history in the twenty-first century. How do historians imagine they are using these documents and images to communicate with other scholarly researchers, with students in classrooms, and with the lay public in far-flung corners of the world? And how are they *actually* communicating with these groups?

The replies we received to our questions varied tremendously. No surprise there: the editors' teaching institutions, career paths, and research agendas provided no common denominator. One note of consistency was nonetheless apparent. In selecting the texts and images in his or her volume, each editor intentionally mixed well-known and unfamiliar materials to fire the imagination of readers and viewers. In this regard, the editors wanted to track down new images even more than they wanted to present non-canonical texts. Helga Welsh, co-editor of volumes 9 and 10, put it this way: "The images should make the reader curious to learn more about particular topics and to help visualize broader themes; familiar images were complemented by less accessible ones." Welsh's statement is borne out by the images she and Konrad Jarausch chose for volume 9. These include iconic images, such as the photograph of Peter Fechter dying at the Berlin Wall, along with less familiar but provocative scenes of generational rebellion.

William W. Hagen, the editor of volume 2 (1648–1815), articulated a methodological note sounded by others, namely, that unfamiliar images should, like unfamiliar texts, work against the grain of German historiography as presented in older textbooks or on the History Channel. Hagen wanted to present the "immediate" and "inartful" experiences of a range of historical actors. His volume, like all the others, had to provide "coverage" of the high (and low) points of German history, lest the selection become wilfully idiosyncratic. At the same time, Hagen was aware that, for the early-modern period in particular, readers and viewers would be rewarded if the editor shone a light on less well researched areas of German life. The editors whose volumes covered more contemporary periods faced a similar challenge. Eric Weitz observed that the "highly contested nature of *everything* during the Weimar period" made it important to "get many voices" into the collection. Insiders and outsiders in the Weimar Republic had to be found in unfamiliar places: in foreign relations, in the world of learning, and in many realms of politics and economics that have been neglected in prior treatments of Germany's "failed experiment in democracy."

This quest for diversity reflected scholarly, pedagogical, and pragmatic motives among the team of editors. Richard Breitman, the editor of volume 7 on Nazi Germany (1933–45), was intent on appealing to many different types of audiences, some of which came to his volume with the images and slogans invented or perpetrated by the Nazis themselves. Jarausch and Welsh faced a different challenge in their two volumes. A general familiarity with the canonical texts of German history since 1961 could be assumed among older readers, whereas images were especially important for two reasons: the thirty-year rule for releasing German archival documents, and the ubiquity of newspaper, television, and film images from these years. Jarausch and Welsh thus sought out non-official documents and made a virtue of easy access to memoirs, newspapers, and magazines. Unfamiliar sources were also chosen, wrote Jarausch, because they are "more experiential and communicate a feeling for a certain situation" in a way that treaties and speeches cannot.

The same approach characterized volume 8 (1945–61), which was co-edited by Volker Berghahn and Uta Poiger. They paid tribute to recent scholarship that had led them to important documents about under-researched topics not yet anthologized in any language – for example, returning German prisoners of war, the "Americanization" of German society, and "mixed race" children in postwar Germany. For Berghahn and Poiger, collaboration was crucial to the success of their volume. The two settled upon a division of labour that allowed them to draw on their expertise in particular subfields: Berghahn in politics and economics, Poiger in culture, society, and gender. Jarausch and Welsh also made use of the collaborative approach – to similarly good effect – in volumes 9 and 10. That some of the editors, namely Berghahn and Welsh, have either a strong interest or an actual background in political science, helps explain why the social science approach was well represented in the project.

Whereas none of the editors presumed to offer a master narrative even for their particular volume, they provided a number of reasons for trying to tell a coherent story. More than one editor was working on a general account of his or her time period while serving as editor of a GHDI volume. For example, Chickering remarked that his organizational schema for volume 5 reflected the same conclusions he had reached in writing a "total history" of the First World War in *The Great War and Urban Life in Germany: Freiburg 1914–1918* (2007). The "whole story" of Wilhelmine Germany, including the origins of the war, was to be presented in "the most effective and elegant way" possible. Thus, in both works, Chickering stressed the "reactions to the great social dislocations and dynamism of the high-industrial era" and the politics of mobilization. The balance between these aspects of Wilhelmine history complicated Chickering's task because he "had two stories to tell." Therefore, in his GHDI volume, he changed course between chapters 1 through 6, which culminated in the outbreak of war, and chapters 7 through 10, in which military events and the materials used in his monograph necessarily figured more prominently. In a similar way Eric Weitz structured volume 6 along the lines of his survey, *Weimar Germany: Promise and Tragedy* (2007). Weitz wanted to emphasize that although every move to realize the promise of Weimar was, "needless to say, deeply contested," he refused to read the ultimate triumph of the National Socialists back into the fourteen years of the republic.

Even more important than the books the editors were writing at the time was the influence of their teaching on the shape of their volumes. Most editors were conscious of how their volume might be used in curricula offered in North American universities versus those in Germany, Great Britain, and elsewhere. Nowhere is teaching with documents particularly easy, but Jarausch noted that his American students had to be weaned off "predigested Pablum." They had to be pointed towards key phrases and subtexts in the primary sources. He and others stressed the importance of providing historical context for these sources without feeding students the answers too quickly. Instead, they needed to be encouraged to research more deeply the historical contexts in which these documents and images were embedded.

Like all historians, the editors wanted their narratives to show both continuity and change. Most also emphasized that students should be exposed to the varieties of behaviour in the past. In this regard, Hagen's reflections were programmatic. In dealing with the period "From Absolutism to Napoleon," one had to offset "the accustomed and by now not-so-interesting representations of bewigged and bejeweled baroque elites and the worlds they moved in." Equally important, he continued, was the need to avoid "clichéd representations of the common people, in the patronizing style of contemporary bourgeois art." In other words, the "positively valorized liberal Whig account" of Germany's (and other nations') transition to "a modern bourgeois-liberal/democratic-rationalist-capitalist-industrial society" needed redress. Reflecting conclusions he had reached in *Ordinary Prussians: Brandenburg Junkers and Villagers, 1500–1840* (2002), Hagen sought out documents and images that emphasized the "heightened articulation of self among women and ordinary people," changes in rural society, and the many paths of capitalist development.

Once the sources were selected, translations from German into English presented another challenge. Hagen, for example, wanted translations "that avoided replication of eighteenth- or nineteenth-century upper-class English, or other forms of archaicism." In this respect, the "stories" told in these ten volumes benefited in crucial ways from the talented team of translators that was mustered for this project. This was certainly true of volume 1 (1500–1648), the only volume whose editors did much of the translating themselves.[14] Like Hagen, Brady and Glebe sought to include the voices of women and ordinary people. Their first section, "Eyewitnesses," includes accounts by a lady-in-waiting, an Augsburg burgher, a goatherd turned teacher of Greek, and a Swabian cobbler-farmer – ordinary people who emerge as anything but.

Reflecting on the organizational choices he made, Jonathan Sperber reported that he was eager to have his readers do what he asks of his own students: "investigate several different sides of a question, then compare and evaluate them." Sperber's section on the emancipation of the Jews, for example, offers Jewish, Gentile, and state perspectives on particular topics. Likewise, his section on economics offers alternative views, pro and con, about the impact of free markets on land, labour, and capital. This technique was replicated in Retallack's volume 4 (1866–90), which presents contrasting views of "provincial" and "national" Germany and asks readers to consider how those views were accepted or resisted by certain groups of Germans. For later periods of German history it was possible to emphasize to students the multifaceted nature of the available material, even while acknowledging that contemporaries often faced binary choices. Volker Berghahn and Uta Poiger noted that such binaries included the two Germanies in the aftermath of National Socialism and war, and the impact of Cold War divisions on the place of Germany in the world.

To a certain degree, Sperber's approach provided a template: any narrative that might emerge from a GHDI volume, or a discussion based upon it, would be inherently Socratic. But the editors did not want to not stop there. Helga Welsh observed that in volume 9 (1961–89) she and Konrad Jarausch had to write a history of two countries that would not marginalize East German history. Therefore, rather than emphasizing the "success story" of West Germany, they asked students to consider shared experiences during the period of transition and consolidation of the two states, as well as the challenges they shared, such as adjusting to a changing international order, the energy crisis, and post-industrial relations. Richard Breitman was conscious of the limited ability of undergraduate students to absorb a great deal of information at one time. Like others, he published the most compelling excerpts from documents that were sometimes dozens or even hundreds of pages long. Breitman conceded that the rubrics laid down for the editors "precluded any single or simple story." Within each section of his volume, however, he did try to construct a narrative (a "story within a story," as Welsh put it), albeit with due attention to continuity, change, and variations of behaviour and experience. As he observed, the balance adopted by any given editor is always a matter of judgment. In fact conformity across ten volumes was never imagined as attainable, or even desirable, either at the outset of the project or thereafter.

At the start of the project, few participants anticipated the breadth or diversity of the global audiences who now use these documents and images on a daily basis. Web logs monitored by the GHDI project staff report the number of "unique visitors" to the website each day. But they tell us much more: the visitors' countries of origin, for example, and the websites, search engines, and keywords that referred them to the site. Much of this data confirms the original expectations of the GHDI steering committee and staff. For instance, the fact that the site registers approximately 20 per cent more traffic during the North American academic year than during the summer months suggests that GHDI is reaching its original target audience of undergraduate students and faculty. More surprising is the extent to which K–12 teachers are also making use of the website.[15] This information comes not only from web logs, which record visitor IP addresses that are registered to public school systems, but also from the many e-mails written to the project staff by secondary school teachers in North America and Europe.

At the editors' meeting in 2003, there was a general assumption that the site "would be used in English mostly." The record has been more complicated. Germany and the United States always occupy the top two spots on the list of referring countries, but the first-place position alternates between them. On average, Google.de seems to drive more traffic to the website than Google.com, and the list of referring URLs is almost always topped by http://www.google.de/imghp. The popularity of the website among Germans validates the steering committee's decision to create a totally bilingual website. But while this move was beneficial in expanding the project's audience, it also complicated matters – and not just from the perspective of cost or labour. Posting all of the content in German meant that the site was, in effect, pitching itself to a German (or at least a German-speaking) audience. This represents something different from offering content in English that can also be read by Germans who know the language. For the most part, however, the site was not geared towards German readers: most of the didactic texts, image captions, and other editorial aids were written in English, with North American students in mind, and then simply translated into German.[16] In some instances, this approach proved problematic. For example, compared to a North American reader, a German brings a different background and perspective to an image such as Willy Brandt's *Warschauer Kniefall*.[17] A "one size fits all" caption is impossible to write.

The popularity of the images is overwhelming, particularly among instructors. University faculty write enthusiastically about "popping" images into PowerPoint presentations "twenty minutes before lectures." A cursory survey of online syllabi from North American and British universities confirms the ease with which images are captured from the GHDI website and incorporated into other teaching tools. Less clear is the extent to which the editors' introductory essays, document abstracts, and image captions are serviceable for front-line teachers. One line of argument is that the editors put so much effort into writing detailed abstracts that they provided a disincentive to teachers and students to read the documents or interpret the images on their own terms. In other words, they provided *too much* context. Some historians in the field have suggested that the abstracts and captions are good but perhaps unnecessary, since the "documents and images speak for themselves." Others suggest that such an assumption is naive – perhaps dangerously so. Here, it is important to note that the website is used not only by historians of Germany but also by non-specialists who have to cover German history in the context of broader European

History and Western Civilization survey courses. Many of these nonspecialists seem grateful for a point of orientation. One hopes that individual instructors will choose carefully how much of this editorial material to serve up to their students. In the end, the project aims to present new materials without constraining anyone in their use.

On a different front, GHDI has given graduate students an important research tool. Those with the requisite language skills can read the texts in the original German, while others can rely on the translations. Some editors indicated that they were initially more comfortable using the primary sources in graduate seminars, less so in undergraduate tutorials. Others have taken the opposite tack, revising undergraduate lecture courses (where tutorials are not offered) in order to incorporate brief discussions of relevant documents and thereby break up the lecture. It remains to be seen how quickly or deeply these new primary sources will be embedded in cutting-edge scholarship by advanced researchers. URLs and active hyperlinks to these sources are appearing in the footnotes and bibliographies of standard works, though less frequently than some editors anticipated. In the future, it may prove easier than it is today to incorporate active hyperlinks into the increasingly prominent electronic versions of scholarly monographs.

Among the GHDI editors, Roger Chickering has offered the most provocative reflections (so far) about the way these sources are *actually* being consumed. He has noted that some of the editors – most conspicuously Berghahn and Poiger – were willing, perhaps even eager, to liberate their interpretive, introductory essay from the documents, meaning that their essay makes no explicit reference to the documents included in their volume. Others took the opposite approach, either mentioning individual documents and images by name or providing links to them. Jarausch and Welsh opted for a third path: like Berghahn and Poiger, they authored a stand-alone general introduction that makes no reference to the documents, but they also wrote shorter introductions (or "overviews") to each of the subsections included in their two volumes. These overviews make explicit reference to the chosen documents, and readers thus have the option of viewing the primary source materials through a particular interpretive lens.

Given these different editorial choices, Chickering's question is germane: How much does this guidance really matter? On the one hand, he suggests, Berghahn and Poiger were simply being realistic in assuming that users are happy to sever the editors' introductory essay from the body of documents. This approach is consistent with the nature of the internet and the way it is used by older and younger generations alike. "The hypertext format frees documents from their narrative moorings and whatever interpretive claims the editors may seek to make. Readers are free to establish their own narratives with the click of a mouse, as the hyperlink subverts editorial privilege ... Readers are now free to pick and choose in a vast sea of documents. The stories are theirs to construct." Here, one could add that the pilots (teachers) who navigate this "vast sea" are also free to embrace non-linear modes of instruction. The technical equivalent would be the internet "node" from which an instructor could set off in any direction, choosing hyperlinks that correspond to the particular needs and dynamic of a unique classroom situation. The by-now "traditional" PowerPoint presentation, in other words, could well become the dodo bird of twenty-first-century instruction thanks to the GHDI and other digital history anthologies.

On the other hand, Chickering's observations did not dismiss the possible survival of the narrative. He noted that established interpretive claims, which persist in the GHDI collection, may prove more robust than we imagine. The editors have been far from powerless. "The documentary sea may be vast, but the editors have created it." Moreover, the hyperlink itself possesses narrative powers that cannot be ignored. Mindful of these powers, the steering committee originally envisioned the site as "a network of links" that would allow users to "pull together information that is closely linked thematically but appears in different volumes."[18] And today there are a number of links that do exactly that.

While the hyperlink has the power to "pull" information together, it can also create narratives, intended or not. Consider the caption to the photograph "Krupp Smokestacks in Essen (1867)," the first of many references to Krupp in the project.[19] The photograph appears in Retallack's volume on Bismarckian Germany, where it is grouped with other industrial scenes. The caption includes two links to materials in the same volume: a letter from Alfred Krupp in 1867 "on the charm of belching smokestacks,"[20] and a speech to his employees in 1877.[21] The speech, an example of *Herr-im-Haus* paternalism, is then linked to a woodcut of the Krupp steel factory in Essen in 1890.[22] The hyperlink narrative ends here, but it did not have to. Retallack's caption to the 1890 scene mentions Krupp's role as a producer of Prussian artillery, offering an implicit invitation to jump forward to a 1910 Krupp factory scene in the Wilhelmine volume, where the theme of militarism and armaments production emerges more clearly.[23] And from there, it would have been just as easy to insert a link to a photograph of a

Digital History Anthologies on the Web 99

Figure 3.1 The impact of air pollution on a modern, industrial scale becomes alarmingly clear in this depiction of the Burbach Smelting Works near Saarbrücken. This woodcut (1876) is based on a drawing by Georg Ludwig Wilhelm Arnould. bpk, Berlin/Art Resource, NY.

grenade exploding in Verdun, then to a photograph of members of the Nazi military-industrial complex, and finally to two pictures of the demolished Krupp factory in Essen in 1947.[24]

This story of industrialism and militarism, which follows a narrative arc, is just one of the hyperlink narratives that could, by design or not, have found its origins in "Krupp Smokestacks in Essen (1867)."[25] A different and shorter narrative could have emerged as well. Retallack's caption, which interprets the scene through the lens of the environment, provides readymade opportunities for links to any number of materials in Jarausch and Welsh's section on "The Green Movement" (volume 9, 1961–89).[26] By this route, the reader would have bypassed two world wars and landed squarely in the ecological movement of the 1970s and 1980s.

Figure 3.2 A NSDAP rally at the *Sportpalast* in Berlin (15 August 1935). The two banners on the rear wall read: "The Jews are our Misfortune" (*Die Juden sind unser Unglück*) and "Women and girls, the Jews are out to debauch you" (*Frauen und Mädchen, die Juden sind Euer Verderben*). The first phrase had been coined by the nationalist historian Heinrich von Treitschke in the *Preußische Jahrbücher* in November 1879, in effect launching the "Berlin Antisemitic Dispute" (*Berliner Antisemitismusstreit*) of 1879–81. bpk, Berlin/Art Resource, NY.

As these examples suggest, questions of narrative and authority in historical writing, which are difficult in any medium, are further complicated by the internet. Is it a good thing that the caption to a portrait of Heinrich Heine (volume 3, 1815–66)[27] mentions that his books were banned and burned by the Nazis in 1933? Would it be dangerous – would we be implicitly endorsing the dubious proposition that Germans embraced an "eliminationist" antisemitic mentality[28] even before the First World War – if we chose to link Heinrich von Treitschke's infamous pronouncement from 1879, "*Die Juden sind unser Unglück!*" (volume 4, 1866–90),[29] to the NSDAP mass rally in Berlin's *Sportpalast* on 15 August 1935 (volume 7, 1933–45), where the same phrase was emblazoned in a huge banner in the hall?[30]

Rather than attempting to answer these questions, the editors and the project staff continue to interrogate their own intentions and question the epistemological ramifications of this resource. If this chapter encourages further reflection about the organizational, interpretive, and pedagogical issues raised in a project of this scope, and if more scholars prove willing to navigate the same uncharted seas we have, the teaching of German history and its relevance to global audiences will become more interesting and important objects of research in their own right.

NOTES

1 I must go beyond the usual duty of relieving my co-author of responsibility for any errors of fact or judgment in what follows, by pointing out that this opening section was written solely for the present volume.
2 *German History in Documents and Images* (GHDI) is an initiative of the German Historical Institute, Washington, DC. It was made possible by the generous support of the Max Kade Foundation and the ZEIT-Stiftung Ebelin und Gerd Bucerius, and was undertaken in cooperation with the Friends of the German Historical Institute, Washington, DC. The authors would like to thank GHI directors Christof Mauch and Hartmut Berghoff for their support of the project. The site can be viewed at http://www.germanhistorydocs.ghi-dc.org.
3 We have not attempted to integrate into our analysis other websites that present documents on German history. They differ fundamentally from GHDI in format and purpose, and the term "anthology" does not describe them well. See *inter alia* three such sites: 1. *Lebendiges virtuelles Museum Online (LeMO)*, https://www.dhm.de/lemo; 2. *PMS-Data*, http://www.zum.de/psm/lv/germany.php3; 3. *Protokolle des Preussischen Staatsministerium (1817–1934/38)*, http://preussenprotokolle.bbaw.de/editionsbaende-im-Internet.
4 Daniel J. Cohen and Roy Rosenzweig, *Digital History: A Guide to Gathering, Preserving, and Presenting the Past on the Web* (Philadelphia, 2006), 20. In chapter 1, "Exploring the History Web," Cohen and Rosenzweig provide an excellent overview of the history of digital history. Their book, which also contains much helpful information gleaned from their hands-on

experience at the Center for History and New Media at George Mason University, is an indispensable resource for historians who are interested in developing their own web-based history projects. The entire book is available online at http://chnm.gmu.edu/digitalhistory.

5 Cohen and Rosenzweig, *Digital History*, 29.
6 See also Markus Mösslang, "Conference Report: Editing Documents in the Age of Technology: Principles and Problems," *Bulletin of the German Historical Institute London* 24, no. 2 (2002): 106–16.
7 See http://legacy.fordham.edu/halsall/index.asp. In addition to primary source websites, the originators of GHDI were also impressed with websites such as H-German and H-Soz-und-Kult, which had already emerged as powerful resources for members of the profession in general.
8 These categories were Government and Administration; Parties and Organizations; Military and War; Economy and Labor; Gender, Family, and Generation; Region, City, and Countryside; Nature and Environment; Religion; Literature, Art, and Music; Elite and Popular Culture; and Science and Education.
9 Dirk Schumann, minutes of the GHDI steering committee meeting, 21 November 2002.
10 A list of the entire editorial team follows: Thomas A. Brady, Jr., and Ellen Yutzy Glebe, editors of volume 1, *From the Reformation to the Thirty Years' War, 1500–1649*; William W. Hagen, editor of volume 2, *From Absolutism to Napoleon, 1648–1815*; Jonathan Sperber, editor of volume 3, *From Vormärz to Prussian Dominance, 1815–1866*; James Retallack, editor of volume 4, *Forging an Empire: Bismarckian Germany, 1866–1890*; Roger Chickering and Steven Chase Gummer, editors of volume 5, *Wilhelmine Germany and the First World War, 1890–1918*; Eric D. Weitz and Eric S. Roubinek, editors of volume 6, *Weimar Germany, 1918/19–1933*; Richard Breitman, editor of volume 7, *Nazi Germany, 1933–1945*; Volker Berghahn and Uta Poiger, editors of volume 8, *Occupation and the Emergence of Two States, 1945–1961*; and Konrad H. Jarausch and Helga A. Welsh, editors of volumes 9 and 10, *Two Germanies, 1961–1989*, and *One Germany in Europe, 1989–2009*.
11 Here, the staff was mindful of the recommendations given in Patrick Lynch and Sarah Horton, *Web Style Guide: Basic Design Principles for Creating Web Sites* (New Haven, CT, and London, 1999), 59–61, 99–100.
12 The GHI is extremely grateful for its partnership with the Bildarchiv Preussischer Kulturbesitz (bpk, Berlin), which has supplied more than 1,000 images from its collection and thus played a crucial role in the development of GHDI.
13 Notes by Kelly McCullough, GHDI editors' meeting, 22 November 2003.

14 Editors Thomas Brady and Ellen Yutzy Glebe were assisted by Heidi Bate, Katherine G. Brady, Jeanne Grant, and Julie Tanaka.
15 This is true of many historical websites. Cohen and Rosenzweig, for example, describe the unforeseen popularity of the Library of Congress's "American Memory" project among K–12 teachers and students. Cohen and Rosenzweig, *Digital History*, 26.
16 Because all of the GHDI editors teach (or taught) at North American universities, American and Canadian students were the primary target audience. There was always a strong awareness, however, that the website would be used by students in other English-speaking countries, especially the United Kingdom and Ireland.
17 http://germanhistorydocs.ghi-dc.org/sub_image.cfm?image_id=161.
18 The word "networks" is perhaps too strong. To date, the links that appear in GHDI have been entered sporadically and unsystematically. It is difficult and time-consuming to add links on a piecemeal basis as a project develops.
19 http://germanhistorydocs.ghi-dc.org/sub_image.cfm?image_id=1332.
20 http://germanhistorydocs.ghi-dc.org/sub_document.cfm?document_id=1790. See Figure 3.1 on page 99.
21 http://germanhistorydocs.ghi-dc.org/sub_document.cfm?document_id=492.
22 http://www.germanhistorydocs.ghi-dc.org/sub_image.cfm?image_id=1279&language=english. See Figure 1.1 on page 9.
23 http://germanhistorydocs.ghi-dc.org/sub_image.cfm?image_id=1602.
24 http://germanhistorydocs.ghi-dc.org/sub_image.cfm?image_id=2530.
25 The website's keyword search function can also create unintentional narratives or stories within stories. To stay with the present example, a keyword search on "Krupp" returns fifteen documents and nine images, which are listed in chronological order. In effect, the story of industrialism and militarism is created by the search results themselves.
26 http://germanhistorydocs.ghi-dc.org/sub_doclist.cfm?sub_id=39&section_id=15.
27 http://germanhistorydocs.ghi-dc.org/sub_image.cfm?image_id=272.
28 On "eliminationist" antisemitism, see Daniel J. Goldhagen, *Hitler's Willing Executioners: Ordinary Germans and the Holocaust* (New York, 1996).
29 http://germanhistorydocs.ghi-dc.org/sub_document.cfm?document_id=1799.
30 http://germanhistorydocs.ghi-dc.org/sub_image.cfm?image_id=1901.

FOCUS

4 King Johann of Saxony and the German Civil War of 1866

[An] important question for many countries in the second half of the nineteenth century was how the administrative integration of large territorial nation-states or empires was to be achieved … A focus on the respective peripheries rather than the national centers makes more apparent the obstacles and limits of state-led centralization. It is therefore worth considering the founding of the German Reich from the point of view of a small component state, or Meiji unification from that of a *han* turned into a prefecture, or the political history of late Imperial China from that of an individual province.

Jürgen Osterhammel, *The Transformation of the World: A Global History of the Nineteenth Century*[1]

How did the Kingdom of Saxony and its Wettin dynasty so narrowly avoid extinction in 1866 – not only in the crucible of war but under duress from rapacious occupiers and unforgiving peace-makers? When Saxony's ruling house escaped the worst, did it rise from the ashes of Germany's fratricidal war as a phoenix, "reborn" as a loyal member of the emerging Reich? Or was it now a timid, domesticated breed – one that paid homage to the ascendant Prussian eagle with transparently artificial and increasingly ludicrous displays of power? Did Saxony's defeat in 1866 signify a morality tale, a retelling of *Paradise Lost* perhaps?[2] For King Johann and his court in exile, these open questions required the creation of new myths. In the struggle to define who was a "loyal liegeman," a "true Saxon," and a "good German," Johann and his entourage were not idle bystanders. As we shall see, distinctions between "patriots" and "turncoats" lay in the eye of the beholder. And such distinctions offered more than one path into the new empire.

King Johann and the Wettin Court

"Modest" and "supportive" – these terms have been used to describe Saxony's monarchs after 1815.³ They exerted far less influence on the political life of their kingdom than did Prussia's rulers in Berlin. Long gone was the era when August the Strong made Dresden one of Europe's most important centres of Baroque architecture and art. The dynasty's conversion to Catholicism, which had permitted August's elevation to King of Poland in 1697, had not been reversed. But gone was the pretence of great power status that had led Saxony into the Seven Years' War, when defeat and occupation at the hands of the Prussians virtually bankrupted the state. The *Rétablissement* of 1762–3 laid the basis for enlightened reforms and early industrialization.⁴ But hardly forgotten were the series of diplomatic reversals that led first to Napoleon's granting Saxony the status of a kingdom in 1806 and then to the humiliations suffered by King Friedrich August I. The king's tardiness in switching his allegiance to the Allies forced Saxony to share France's defeat at the Battle of Nations near Leipzig in October 1813. Thereafter the state was partitioned and occupied by first Russian and then Prussian administrators, until the king regained his throne in June 1815. Popular rebellion in 1830 forced the six-year co-regency of King Anton and his nephew, Friedrich August II. The latter survived the revolution of 1848 and the Dresden Uprising of May 1849, though only with the help of Prussian troops. But he suffered a fatal accident during a trip to the Tyrolean Alps in August 1854. Dying childless, he was succeeded by his brother Johann.

King Johann (1801–1873) appears in history books as Johann the Truth-Loving (*der Wahrhaftige*) – a dowdy appellation confirmed by contemporary portraits but belied by the hagiographic treatments of his life still pouring out of Saxon publishing houses.⁵ Any scholarly assessment of this monarch's historical role must be mixed. In the 1830s and 1840s, Johann's writings and opinions reflected both progressive and reactionary tendencies. His Catholic prejudices and lack of sensitivity contributed to a bloody encounter between soldiers and a throng of protesters in Leipzig in 1845. Writing to an American friend about the incident, Johann defended himself by noting that the "mob" would have been fired upon by American soldiers, too.⁶ At that time Johann was principally a scholar. In Schloss Weesenstein he translated and annotated Dante's *Divine Comedy* under the pseudonym "Philalethes –

Friend of Truth." After ascending the throne he developed more political acumen: in 1863, Bismarck referred to Johann as "the cleverest of all diplomats."[7] But like his predecessors he unwisely took up arms against Prussia and almost lost his kingdom. During the German Civil War of 1866 – also known as the Austro-Prussian War – he had to flee to Bohemia to escape Prussian troops.[8] He is said to have sobbed as he crossed the border, "We will be revenged for these tears, so help me God."[9] Yet shortly thereafter, he was reputedly ready to abandon his throne for the sum of 20 million Thaler or exchange it for the crown of Bohemia.[10]

In 1900 the Saxon court numbered just 619 persons, roughly half of what it had been in 1819. Funds available for the Saxon king's civil list had shrunk proportionately, from 10 per cent of the total state budget in 1833 to about 5 per cent in 1862 and less than 2 per cent in 1890–1. In both cases the trend in Prussia was in the opposite direction, particularly under Kaiser Wilhelm II. Thus the Saxon king's civil list in 1890–1 (2.94 million Marks) was less than one-fifth that of the Prussian king in 1888.[11] Tellingly, when an American visitor – Nathaniel Hawthorne's son Julian – had the opportunity to observe the celebrations attending King Johann's golden wedding anniversary in Dresden in 1872, he was scornful in describing the king's passage across the historical stage. Amid the "dangers, turmoils, and revolutions of the nineteenth century," wrote Hawthorne, Johann and his wife had been "living their royal little lives, doing their formal little duties, making their stiff little visits, enjoying their sober little glories, suffering their unimportant little misfortunes, [and] worshipping according to the tenets of their bigoted old religion."[12]

We may be thankful that Saxon kings left many tasks undone and intervened rarely in policy-making. Affairs of state in Saxony were subject to "no court camarilla, no *éminences grises*, no shadow cabinet behind the scenes, no circle of favorites."[13] This created political space that did not exist in Prussia, and it was filled by a larger-than-life diplomat, Count Friedrich Ferdinand von Beust, de facto government leader from 1849 to 1866. As would-be leader of the "third Germany," Beust was also Bismarck's arch-rival. The suppression of civil liberties, the partial emasculation of Saxony's Landtag, economic prosperity at home, a Greater German (*großdeutsch*) policy abroad – these issues were inseparable in Beust's attempt to rally support in 1866 for a war against Prussia. Such a war was purportedly to defend the German Confederation against Prussian aggression.[14] Characteristically, on 13 June, when a liberal deputy in the Landtag asked Beust whether a decision had been made to mobilize against Prussia, the Saxon leader was reduced to a barefaced lie to defend his pro-Austrian policy.[15] Three weeks later, on 3 July 1866, the German Question (*Deutsche Frage*), which had simmered since 1815 in the form of a Prussian-Austrian dualism, was decided at the Battle of Königgrätz. There, Prussian forces routed not only the Austrian army but also its Saxon allies, who defended its left flank valiantly enough to permit a semi-orderly retreat. However, the task of bringing Saxony into Prussia's orbit and embedding it in an emerging Germany was not decided on the field of battle or dispatched in a single day. Even after Königgrätz it required hard-nosed diplomatic negotiations, an odious Prussian occupation, and the appointment of a new ministry of state to determine whether Saxony would survive at all.

Saxony's Occupation

Late in the evening of Friday, 15 June 1866, the British ambassador to Prussia, Lord Augustus Loftus, was sitting with Prussian Minister President Otto von Bismarck in his garden in Berlin. To Loftus's astonishment, when the midnight hour struck Bismarck took out his pocket watch and said, in French, "At this moment our troops have entered Hanover, Saxony, and Hesse-Cassel." He added, "The struggle will be severe. Prussia may lose, but she will, at all events, have fought bravely and honorably." In Dresden, Beust also knew that war could no longer be avoided: "Le vin est tiré, il faut le boire."[16]

By twentieth-century standards the Saxon population suffered relatively little during the German Civil War of 1866. No fighting took place on Saxon soil after war was declared on 15 June: the movement of Saxon troops southward into Bohemia began immediately. The Saxon army received deserved praise for its courageous fight in a lost cause at the Battle of Königgrätz on 3 July. The preliminary peace accord agreed upon at Nikolsburg on 26 July promised to respect Saxony's geographical integrity (although, as we shall see, the question lay in some doubt for three more months).[17] And the final peace treaty between Prussia and Saxony, signed on 21 October 1866, allowed King Johann to return to Dresden and reclaim the Saxon throne.[18] Saxony was forced to enter the North German Confederation (1867–71) under Prussian domination and to amalgamate its military with the new federal army under Prussian command; but these peace terms were considered relatively lenient and, thus, auspicious for Germany's progress towards unity.

Lord Loftus reflected this viewpoint in a letter he wrote barely a week after the Nikolsburg accord was signed. "I may observe that Count Bismarck has passed through with wonderful success one phase of his ambitious undertaking – namely, that of 'Demolition.' The second phase is about to commence – namely, the work of Reconstruction. In carrying out this latter phase, Count Bismarck will encounter great difficulties – difficulties, however, which his energy and iron will may succeed in overcoming."[19] This picture drawn by Loftus takes on a different hue when we consider how Saxons reacted to the combined psychological blows of military defeat, foreign occupation, escalating political conflict, and rumours emanating from King Johann's court.[20]

Austria's unwillingness to support even token resistance in Saxony had an enormous moral effect on both Saxon and international opinion, exactly as Prussian Chief of Staff Helmuth von Moltke hoped. According to Moltke's prewar calculations, a quick occupation of Saxony by Prussia's Army of the Elbe – numbering about 46,000 men – would prevent the Austrians from using Saxony to impede the Prussian advance southwards, as they had against Frederick the Great in the Seven Years' War. It would also encourage Bavaria and other south-German states allied with Austria to rethink their commitment to move their own troops against Prussia. "If we could occupy Dresden before the Austrians and establish ourselves there," wrote Moltke, "we could compel the Saxons to go with us. If that didn't work, then the Saxon army would have either to withdraw to Bohemia or to barricade itself in a secure position at Pirna. In either case, we would make ourselves masters of the rich resources of the country."[21] Moltke's plan was realized because of Austria's slow mobilization, the tactical difficulty of defending Dresden, and Saxony's determination to keep its fighting force intact for a showdown in Bohemia.

Moltke was not the only one who was initially unsure what military role the Saxons would play. At a diplomatic *soirée* in London hosted by the Prince of Wales, the Saxon envoy to Britain was ridiculed by an English general and other guests. Handing the Saxon envoy a clutch of telegrams reporting that the Prussians had taken Dresden, the Prince of Wales exclaimed: "Read it for yourself. You're no longer a minister!"[22] The envoy politely replied that he had not yet been recalled from service by his government. He added that Saxon troops were holding the mountain passes between Saxony and Austria (they were not). But later he remarked acidly that the British "are not very talented when it comes to German geography." Because they had expected the Austrians to be in Berlin within a week, "it has to make a bad impression when they read in the newspapers that the Prussians have conquered two kingdoms in two days."[23] In his memoirs Lord Loftus recalled general disappointment that Austria had chosen not to defend Saxony: "On this occasion the Austrians were, as usual, too late."[24]

This brings us to "the strange survival of monarchical Saxony."[25] Early on the morning of Monday, 18 June, Beust was summoned from his bed to a royal audience in the Dresden palace. Because the Saxons had temporarily slowed the Prussian advance from the north by destroying the Elbe bridges at Riesa and Meißen, King Johann had unexpectedly been able to spend one more night in the royal bedchamber. But he had slept little, he told Beust, and had "thought everything through again." He hoped Saxony's army would prove victorious: in that case he might have to consider whether Saxony should repossess the significant territories the Prussians had taken from it in 1815 ("our old land"). "But I do not wish it," the king told Beust. "It would revive and perpetuate old animosities, giving us only disaffected subjects in return." In his reply Beust saw no reason to upset the king's "calm and easy conscience" by telling him that the impending military showdown could very possibly have a different outcome (by this point the Saxons were already aware of the Austrians' slow and disorganized military mobilization). As Beust put it laconically, "What I thought privately to myself was that it would not be anytime soon before this matter would again force me to get up so early!"[26]

The Saxon population, likewise expecting an Austrian victory, was initially more intrigued than enraged by the Prussian occupiers. The British envoy stationed in Dresden, soon to be packing his bags for London, emphasized how congenial the whole affair seemed when the Prussians entered the Saxon capital shortly after noon on 18 June.[27] This event was captured on a large canvas by Carl von Behrenberg. It depicts Prussian soldiers marching through Dresden's *Postplatz* near the royal palace. Curious civilians are running to catch a glimpse of them.[28] Some have turned their backs on the martial display: they are reading the first flyer distributed by the Prussians, which proclaims no animosity towards the Saxon people and calls for calm.[29] A few children hide fearfully behind their mothers' skirts. But the overall impression is one of ambivalent edginess. As one eyewitness observed a few days later, Dresdeners were "down-hearted and excited" at the same time.[30]

Figure 4.1 Prussian troops march into Dresden's *Postplatz* on 18 June 1866 and occupy the Saxon capital without a shot being fired. *Einmarsch preußischer Truppen am 18. Juni 1866,* by Carl von Behrenberg (n.d). Städtische Galerie Dresden – Kunstsammlung, Museen der Stadt Dresden. Photograph: Frank Zadnicek.

By the night of 18 June, King Johann and Crown Prince Albert had fled their kingdom. They led the Saxon army, about 28,000 active soldiers, across the border into Bohemia.[31] Five days later the Prussian Army of the Elbe crossed the same border in pursuit. In the process the Prussians outstripped their supply lines: by the time they debouched from the mountain passes on the Austrian side of the *Erzgebirge* (Ore Mountains) they were already desperate for whatever provisions could be requisitioned in occupied Saxony and sent on to them.[32] Trouble began in Dresden on 20 June. Rumours had it that advance units of the Austrian army were on the outskirts of Dresden and were about to bombard it. "The alarm of an immediate attack was spread through the town, and the panic thereby occasioned was increased by the preparations made by the Prussians who commenced cutting down shrubs and trees in the public gardens, digging trenches, and turning all the lodgers and proprietors out of their houses."[33] Soon the Prussian occupiers were engaged in a battle of wits with a Provisional Government (*Landeskommission*) headed by Saxony's finance minister and Beust's eventual successor as government leader (1866–76), Baron Richard von Friesen.

The transition from Beust to Friesen represented the triumph of probity over panache. Carl von Weber, a senior civil servant and de facto secretary to the Provisional Government, joined others in making sport of Friesen's celibate lifestyle and ascetic devotion to duty. He likened Friesen's bald spot to a tonsure and described him as a "helpless cleric."[34] In any case, members of this Provisional Government remained in Dresden to ensure that a kernel of Saxony's sovereignty would survive the occupation intact. On 18 June they opened negotiations with the Prussian commander, General Karl Herwarth von Bittenfeld, who headed a military *Generalgouvernement*. But within a few days Bittenfeld had departed for Bohemia, beginning a succession of Prussian generals in the same post.[35] The Provisional Government dealt mainly with Civil Commissar Lothar von Wurmb, a forty-two-year-old Prussian civil servant (and army major) who knew Saxony well and who would serve as Berlin's police president from 1867 to 1872.[36]

When they met for the first time on 19 June, Wurmb opened the "negotiations" with Friesen and his colleagues by telling them they would be summarily shot if they did not provide him with reliable information or fulfil their promises to cooperate. This grotesque situation was quickly defused with a little Saxon humour. But Wurmb's demands during the next three months made little distinction between military and political objectives. They included the provision and quartering of Prussian troops,[37] the dismissal of Dresden's police director (Beust's "creature" and *"persona ingratissima"* in Berlin),[38] tight control of travel into and out of the city, the shutting down or censorship of anti-Prussian newspapers,[39] and – most egregious of all – the erection of massive defensive earthworks in and around Dresden.[40] Throughout the summer, these fortifications enraged the Dresden population. They appeared frequently in Leipzig's *Illustrirte Zeitung* and were cited in complaints from the Provisional Government and Dresden's own Committee of Emergency.[41] The fortifications were allegedly necessary to defend Dresden against a Bavarian attack. But the Bavarians' unwillingness to leave their native soil made it clear that the fortifications were being maintained to intimidate and demoralize Dresdeners until a peace treaty was signed.[42] Asserting that the Prussian king had personally ordered the construction of the fortifications, Wurmb claimed that Dresdeners were meant to see what misery the policies of King Johann had brought them. If the tide of war turned and the Saxon king tried to retake his capital with foreign help, he would soon realize "that every Saxon bullet fired at the earthworks must strike his own city of Dresden and bring ruin to its inhabitants."[43]

In some realms of everyday life, passive resistance was the order of the day. None of the usual summer concerts were held in Dresden in 1866. Women from the middle and upper classes were seen in the streets either not at all or in mourning. Prussian soldiers were snubbed at every turn in Dresden society. At a court ball the following winter, Prussian officers had to seek their dance partners exclusively among a small group of foreigners – even among Americans, one eyewitness reported with some dismay – for fear of being turned down and humiliated by the Saxon women.[44] For enlisted men, the drawn-out peace negotiations prevented timely reunions with their families. This situation was made more onerous when the Prussian occupiers decreed that any reservist who tried to return from Bohemia while Prussia and Saxony were still officially on a war footing would be sent to a prisoner-of-war camp or executed as a spy.[45]

Complacency and a faulty estimation of the military strength of Saxony's and Austria's armies characterized one side of Saxony's response to invasion. But not even Friesen's self-serving memoirs can obscure the practical steps he took to preserve Saxon statehood at a time when most European diplomats expected Johann's kingdom to be swallowed up by the Prussians.[46] Friesen's efforts were crucial in dissuading Bismarck from a course that might, as the inverse of Johann's fantasy, have given Prussia disaffected new citizens through the total absorption of Saxon territory into the Hohenzollern kingdom.[47]

In his role as finance minister Friesen implemented an elaborate series of measures to make sure that Saxony would not suffer financial collapse when the Prussians invaded. In June, in an extraordinary session that ended the day before war was declared, he and Beust made sure the Landtag approved a massive war credits bill. Friesen also arranged for all state debts and the king's civil list to be paid off; and he ordered that monies owed to Saxony's towns and cities be disbursed without delay. In a cloak-and-dagger operation he arranged for about 35 million Thaler in banknotes to be dispatched to safety in Munich; another 450,000 Thaler in silver was secured in the Königstein fortress southeast of Dresden.[48] After the Prussians spent much of their time from 15 to 21 June marching into city halls across Saxony and confiscating municipal treasuries, Friesen agreed to Wurmb's proposal, approved by Bismarck, that Saxony pay Prussian authorities 10,000 Thaler – half in silver, half in paper notes – for every day the occupation lasted. (The Prussians demanded and received three retroactive payments to cover 18–20 June.)[49] When the peace was finally signed in October, the Prussians refused to deduct from the Saxon indemnity of 10 million Thaler either this sum, which by then amounted to 1.25 million Thaler, or the value – double that amount – of materials and services requisitioned during the occupation.

Little was Friesen to know how this war booty would be spent. Gerson von Bleichröder, Bismarck's Jewish banker, used these payments to recruit and pay the leaders of a "Hungarian Legion," which Bismarck hoped would foment subversion or revolution in the Habsburg Empire and undermine Austria's war effort.[50] Closer to home, the Prussians paid 2,998 Thaler during the summer and early autumn of 1866 to pro-annexationist National Liberal editors such as Karl Biedermann in Leipzig: these funds were used for "press and political purposes" and "without receipts."[51] Yet from Friesen's perspective even this arrangement had advantages. It put an end to the lawless confiscation of state funds that had led to such unpleasantness in the first week of the occupation. It restored a measure of predictability to Saxony's economic outlook during the war and after. Most important of all, it preserved the autonomy of Saxony's finances and, hence, a measure of its political sovereignty.[52]

Friesen also had to deal with Wurmb's insistence that the Provisional Government draw up appropriate constituency boundaries for elections leading to a national parliament.[53] Foot-dragging was Friesen's chosen strategy here, and it worked. At the same time he went ahead with plans to hold Saxony's own Landtag elections, scheduled for the autumn of 1866. In this way he ensured that Saxony's representative institutions continued to operate in a way that preserved the logic of Saxony's independent statehood. He was wise to do so. The US ambassador in Berlin believed that Bismarck's proposal of universal manhood suffrage for a national parliament was "so liberal and Democratic" that the middle-sized and smaller states would refuse to hold elections under its provisions. "In this event, Count Bismarck would accomplish what he so much desires, a more perfect and speedy annexation by treaty."[54]

The Dynasty in Jeopardy

Between August and October 1866, Friesen spent much of his time in Berlin negotiating the final peace treaty between Saxony and Prussia. He also attended preliminary talks on the military convention between the same two states, which was finally signed in February 1867.[55] These on-again, off-again negotiations proceeded at a pace guaranteed to cause mounting anxiety, not least because treaties with Austria and other German states were concluded by the end of August and because Bismarck departed for Putbus (Pomerania) at the end of September to recover his nerves.

Brochures and petitions advocating the complete absorption of Saxony into Prussia began to appear in Saxony and raised the stakes on both sides.[56] Prussian King Wilhelm I, Crown Prince Friedrich Wilhelm – who had saved the day with his timely arrival on the battlefield of Königgrätz – and some of their advisers were allegedly outraged that Bismarck had guaranteed the integrity of Saxon territory at Nikolsburg in July. They were soon working towards the de facto annexation of Saxony through indirect means.[57] One such scheme advocated treaty stipulations so draconian that the Saxon king would be induced to abdicate voluntarily and relinquish his kingdom to his fellow monarch Wilhelm. In another variation, Saxony would be ceded to the Grand Duke of Saxe-Weimar-Eisenach, whose family was tied by blood to the Hohenzollerns. Either solution would have put to rest Wilhelm's conviction that Saxony was about to become "a nest of enemy intrigues."[58]

Still another possibility was floated by French Emperor Napoleon III. "Wouldn't it be better," he wrote, "for Prussia to annex Saxe, a Protestant country, and put the king of Saxony [a Catholic] on the left bank of the Rhine, a Catholic country?"[59] Another tactic recognized that after Nikolsburg the Prussians could not *demand* territory from Saxony. This was technically true. France and Austria had lobbied not merely for Saxony's continued existence but for the "present territorial integrity of the Kingdom of Saxony in its existing dimensions," and this clause had been accepted. By September some Prussians in Berlin were suggesting that the Saxons would demonstrate good judgment if they *offered* some territory to the Prussians in return for a more conciliatory stance on other fronts. The Prussian negotiator Karl von Savigny, who had previously served as Prussian envoy in Dresden, stated flatly that this arrangement might reduce Saxony's indemnity. Savigny raised this point quite literally at the eleventh hour, but the Saxon negotiators rejected it, and the peace treaty was signed shortly before midnight on 21 October 1866.[60]

The possibility that Saxony would forfeit its statehood in the autumn of 1866 was very real. In the first week of the occupation, Leipzigers were told that their city would be spared onerous billeting requirements if the occupiers encountered no resistance. Based on the premise that the Prussians wanted to incorporate a prosperous city rather than one drained by rapacious occupiers, pro-Prussian Leipzigers willingly believed that the Prussians planned to seize the prize that had been denied them at the Congress of Vienna in 1815.[61] In both the Prussian court and Saxon political society, other voices suggested that the most obvious course of action was for Prussia to swallow the Saxon kingdom whole, as it had Hanover. On the day the Nikolsburg accord was signed, King Johann wrote to his wife: "Prussia appears to have a good appetite for the north of Germany. The king [Wilhelm I] was absolutely set on having the district of Leipzig and Lusatia; *qu'est ce que nous serait resté*? But on this Austria was firm and Bismarck accommodating. In the meantime one will have to wade in and swim."[62]

One week later, viewing the situation from Berlin, Lord Loftus summed up the situation rather differently. His report to London's Foreign Office suggested just how uncertain Saxony's survival remained:

> The public – grateful for the restoration of peace – appears generally to approve the conditions agreed upon, although by some they are considered to be within the limits of what Prussia had a right to demand; whilst by others – more especially by the Liberal party – not only in Prussia, but in Germany, they are viewed with disappointment and disfavour, as creating a "division" and not the "unity" of Germany. There is also much disappointment that Saxony was not annexed to Prussia, that kingdom being regarded as of vital importance to Prussia, in a political, industrial, and strategic point of view. The annexation is even urged in the interest of Saxony herself, for it is asserted that she would have enjoyed far greater advantages by becoming a component part of Prussia than by remaining in a position of *quasi*-vassalage.[63]

In subsequent negotiations, whenever the Saxons dug in their heels, Prussian negotiators claimed that King Wilhelm was about to revert to his demand for Saxon territory or a change of dynasty. It is not clear to what extent the Saxon negotiators actually believed these bluffs. The

King Johann of Saxony and the German Civil War of 1866   119

Figure 4.2 This caricature by "Cham" – a pseudonym for Count Amédée Charles de Noé – appeared in the French journal *Le Charivari* in September 1866. It expresses both French opinion and anti-Prussian sentiment in Saxony and southern Germany. A soldier wearing the universal symbol of Prussian militarism, the *Pickelhaube*, tries to stitch together the defeated German states of 1866 into a new nation. Hence the title: "It takes a needle …" The caption reads: "It is one thing to know how to use a needle … But it's a skill that should not be abused." The cartoonist is making an oblique reference to the Prussian "needle gun," a breech-loading rifle that gave Prussian infantrymen greater firepower than their Austrian and Saxon opponents at the Battle of Königgrätz. bpk, Berlin/Art Resource, NY.

Saxon envoy in Berlin, Count Karl Adolf von Hohenthal, observed at one point that, after all, "the Saxon king could not return to his monarchy as a kind of Prussian mayor."[64] On another occasion Hohenthal wrote that Bismarck and Wilhelm were playing a "put-up job with assigned roles."[65] For his part, another leading National Liberal in Leipzig, Gustav Freytag, editor of the influential *Grenzboten*, was appalled that Bismarck's "improvised" war was followed by such "impromptu" peace negotiations: "The arbitrary moods of the king, a small predilection on Bismarck's part – these things can now impose a cost of millions onto the people and make so many square miles part of Prussia or part of Oldenburg."[66]

It is true that the Prussians preferred to begin each phase of negotiations with threats and bombast. The king, the crown prince, and their military advisers were also susceptible to fits of pique, for instance when they heard that the Saxon army, though defeated, had paraded through the streets of Vienna. They resented the fact that Saxony continued to seek French and Austrian intervention, and they believed rumours that Beust and King Johann had set up a pro-Austrian "closet government" (*Nebenregierung*) behind the back of the Provisional Government. Unfortunately we know less than we would like about Johann's perigrinations after Königgrätz. Those travels took him to Vienna and then back to Saxony by way of Prague and Teplitz. We are also poorly informed about how closely he kept in touch with leading politicians of the day.[67] But there is no reason to doubt the veracity of Wurmb's assessments sent from Dresden to Berlin during that summer of discontent.

In those reports Wurmb chronicled the many signs of a particularist resurgence in Saxony. For example, he had heard that the leader of the rabidly anti-Prussian Conservatives, Ludwig von Zehmen, was being considered as Saxony's next minister of the interior. Bismarck's reactions to these reports and rumours demonstrate that partial annexation was still an option. When Bismarck read that another leading Conservative had travelled to Vienna to warn King Johann that public opinion at home was growing uncertain, he wrote in the margin of one report, "If Prussia were to get Lusatia and Leipzig, *then* we could relax our demands in military matters."[68] The next time Wurmb wrote, on 23 September, he warned Bismarck not to consider any concession to the Saxons. In doing so he documented his own and other Prussian authorities' failure to sway (or even fully understand) the public mood in Saxony. He also noted the inability of pro-Prussian liberal nationalists to establish a political base there.

Wurmb's assessment was dramatic and candid: "It could be that King Johann and the crown prince, after their recent experiences with Austria, actually want and will strive toward an honourable and genuine cooperation with Prussia; their ministers may, from their understanding of clever statecraft, pretend for a time to want to maintain friendship with Prussia; however, for all the other numerous officials in the Saxon civil service, from the regional governor down to the assistant gendarme, one finds not a trace of sympathy, but rather only fundamental, deep hatred of Prussia. As soon as these officials have power once again in their hands, neither the king nor his state ministry will be able to prevent the mistreatment of Prussians living in Saxony or even of Saxons sympathetic to Prussia."

Wurmb then described the phases through which Saxon public opinion had passed since the Prussian invasion in June: "At the beginning of the Prussian occupation, a period of terror set in, where everything that was demanded happened out of fear; after Königgrätz an oppressive disappointment invaded the public mood; but then, as soon as Saxony's integrity was declared in the Nikolsburg peace negotiations – which were reported with curious speed throughout the country – suddenly Saxon particularism reappeared and grew." Wurmb's frustration with other occupation authorities was obvious. Public disappointment "was cultivated by the mild occupation policy of [Prussia's civil commissar] General von Schack, especially in the most recent period, when the most fantastic rumours about the terms of the peace agreement (which was allegedly already concluded) are being spread from Vienna directly through the organs of the court with such demonstrativeness that one might actually believe oneself to be living in the capital city of the victors and not of the defeated."

Saxon "patriots" were using all means at their disposal to sow discord, reported Wurmb. "Addresses of loyalty, telegrams of congratulation, deputations – these are all being sent to the king [residing] in Vienna; patriotic articles and poems are appearing in the newspapers, especially the local government organs; and a semi-official brochure, *Saxony and the North German Confederation*, currently represents the political creed of all Saxon patriots."[69] Here Wurmb alluded to the longstanding antagonism between Prussia and the Catholic Wettin dynasty. "In a Jesuitical manner [this brochure] turns history around, not only completely to excuse Saxon policy but to vindicate its actions as far as possible and to suggest that it has more privileged status than the other states allied with Prussia in the North German Confederation."

As to Prussia's future course in Saxony, Wurmb was not reticent in advocating a dramatic change of policy. "Prussia had three paths to accomplish its goals in Saxony," he wrote, in order to prevent a return to Beust's policy of trying to lead a "third Germany." "It could have created the necessary safeguards by strengthening and fostering the liberal democratic party, which is overwhelmingly German-Prussian in orientation ... Or Prussia could have thrown Saxony out of the Customs Union and thereby established a following in the land that the Saxon government would not be able to resist even for a year." Prussia's third option Wurmb outlined in the present tense: "it can use the lengthy stationing of a strong Prussian garrison in the 8 or 10 largest cities, particularly in Dresden, to maintain such control over Saxony that it would not be in a position to follow an independent, anti-Prussian policy." Wurmb continued:

> The first two paths were not chosen, and both entailed serious problems anyway. The third path, however, is still open in so far as it offers a means to realize a good part of those safeguards that Prussia actually requires if it is not, despite its victory, to become the laughing stock of the Saxon court nobility and if it is not completely to lose the influence over the Saxon government that it requires as the hegemonic state in northern Germany. I therefore humbly entreat Your Excellency [Bismarck] to use your influence to persuade His Majesty [Prussian King Wilhelm I] not to be too merciful in the peace negotiations, for, if he does, he will receive no real thanks here.

Wurmb's appraisals contributed to the Prussians' determination to protect Prussian sympathizers in the peace accord of 21 October 1866. Article 19 of the treaty was transparent on this score. The same article included a clause that protected Saxon civil servants and the authors of brochures that had slandered Prussia or its monarch. Thus the Saxons were able to protect their own local administrators and police directors who had been disciplined, imprisoned, or banished by the Prussians. These actions confirmed the fears voiced by Wurmb in September. They also revealed that the pro-Prussian historian Heinrich von Treitschke – the son of a Saxon general but now a fierce partisan of Prussian hegemony in Germany – had hit the mark in a pamphlet he published in late July 1866. In that pamphlet he had warned Prussia that it must annex the middle German states. "The Saxon court will return," he wrote, "with its heart full of hatred and revenge; it will politely accommodate itself to the current situation and quietly begin to spin its fine web toward the Hofburg in Vienna ... Then the gendarmes will pull out the lists of those who are friendly to Prussia ...; the most important offices will fall into the hands of those subjects ... [loyal to] King Johann ...; [and] the [Saxon] military's *esprit de corps* will give rise to ... particularistic traditionalism and spitefulness."[70]

Despite evidence that Johann would be unable to wring a "loyal" policy vis-à-vis Prussia from his own civil servants, the Prussians dreaded the thought of Johann's abdication. They feared they would take the blame for driving a respected monarch from his throne.[71] This appraisal hit the mark. So did the comments of insiders who ascribed pro-Saxon influence to Prussian King Wilhelm's wife, Queen Augusta. This Saxon princess allegedly did not want to be "declassed" by the extirpation of her native land.[72] King Wilhelm I and Crown Prince Friedrich Wilhelm received (and replied to) many entreaties from Augusta for Prussian leniency towards Saxony. Just two days after Königgrätz she asked her husband to exert "wisdom" and "moderation" in dealing with Prussia's defeated enemies. He should preserve the Hanoverian and Saxon kingdoms in the interest of building a future Germany through "moral pressure." "The actual occupation of these lands," wrote the queen, "transforms the power of brute force into the power of wise magnanimity."[73] But other factors were more important in Bismarck's calculations. He knew that either full or partial annexation of Saxony might result in the enmity of Austria in the long term, of the southern German states in the medium term, and of France in the short term (because Napoleon III had hinted that agreeing to Saxony's annexation would require "compensation" for France in the form of Prussia's Rhine province or the city of Mainz).[74]

These speculations were hardly confined to the sphere of high politics. As so often happens in wartime, rumours had a tangible effect on the postwar settlement. Leipzig schoolboys were convinced that the French emperor would save their kingdom: clandestine poems said so.[75] In describing the mood in Germany around this time, Lord Loftus recalled what Alexander Pope had written about rumours:

> They, flying rumours, gather'd as they roll'd,
> Scarce any tale was sooner heard than told;
> And all who told it added something new,
> And all who heard it, made enlargements too;

In ev'ry ear it spread, on ev'ry tongue it grew.
Thus flying east and west, and north and south,
News travell'd with increase from mouth to mouth.[76]

Prussian troops from the Rhineland, who constituted a large part of the army occupying Dresden, supposedly had "no heart or enthusiasm" for Germany's fratricidal war because they believed rumours that "their own native provinces would be given up to France."[77]

The National Idea

Upon signing of the peace treaty between Prussia and Saxony on 21 October 1866, foreigners observed that Saxony had retained nothing more than the appearance of a sovereign state. On the day before the treaty was signed, the British envoy, Charles Eden, wrote that "it is not to be presumed that the sovereignty of Saxony will be left sufficiently intact, to suffer her in any way to become an obstacle in the gradual transformation of the new Staaten-Bund [confederation of states] into a Bundes-Staat [federal state]." The US ambassador in Berlin had already reported that Prussia would compel the Saxon army corps to swear the usual military oath of allegiance to the king of Prussia, that it would take possession of Saxony's military forts, and that it would disband all regiments that had fought under Austrian colours at Königgrätz. "Saxony may be ruled for a few years [by King Johann] as a temporary Governor without authority or power," he wrote; but this anomalous situation would soon pass and "the ancient Saxon will become a part of the Prussian Empire." A few days after the peace treaty was signed, both diplomats were more blunt. "The independence left to Saxony is the shadow of a shadow," wrote Murray. The British consul in Leipzig, Joseph Archer Crowe, agreed: "There are very few ... who believe in the restoration of the Saxon monarchy to independence." So did the US ambassador in Berlin: "The Nationality and Sovereignity [sic] of Saxony in the future exist only in name."[78]

What did the Saxon people think about all this? Did they believe that King Johann had gambled his sovereignty in war and lost? And if it had been lost, even in a formal sense, what did this imply for the survival of a distinctive Saxon identity? Here we can draw upon the reports of two British envoys to Saxony because they did not flee with the Saxon court to Vienna, Prague, and Teplitz. Charles Murray and his successor Charles Eden realized that state-building – insofar as it entailed region-building and nation-building too – did not constitute a zero sum game. In the fullness of time it became clear to Saxons, as it has to historians, that Saxony's forced entry into the North German Confederation was not incompatible with its continued existence as a semi-autonomous kingdom. Reporting from war-torn Dresden, foreign envoys displayed remarkable sympathy for the common people embroiled in a civil war they had not wanted, for the lesser German dynasties, and for populations experiencing the disorienting effects of a national election campaign being waged while their territories were still under military occupation.

One such report, written on the eve of Königgrätz, distinguished among the many strands of the German Question. On 28 June, Charles Eden reported to London that

> English readers of the *Times* will of course believe that the Prussians are welcomed here as brothers, and that the Saxons wish no better and could do no better than to become incorporated with Prussia; that the population received the occupying army in a friendly way is perfectly true, for what other course was open to them? Unavailing opposition would only have produced more cruel exaction, and moreover, as regards the individuals composing the mass of the population and the soldiery, there was no hostile feeling, they felt that they were speaking the same language and formed part of the same German People, and scores of the soldiers openly avowed that they abhorred the war and the authors of it; but towards the Prussian Govt. and the military authorities who represent it here it is impossible but that the poor Saxons should feel the most intense hatred.[79]

How did things stand four months later? Eden reported that "many eyes were wet with tears" when close to two thousand Saxon subjects greeted King Johann upon his return to his riverside palace at Pillnitz on 26 October.[80] Eden concluded that the king's promise of loyalty to the new North German Confederation represented a watershed of profound importance: "With the scene of yesterday evening at Pilnitz [sic] the old order of things was closed & Saxony must from today look cheerfully forward to the new." Nevertheless – and this is historically more significant – it was not necessary for either the king or his subjects to abandon their mistrust of Prussia or their pride as Saxons on the way to becoming loyal Germans: "Although there exists no doubt a party in favor of incorporation with Prussia in the large industrial centres, I believe the mass of the rural population to be true Saxons and faithful liegemen."

The acrimonious mood generated by the upcoming Reichstag elections – eventually held on 12 February 1867 – nevertheless reflected the

Figure 4.3 King Johann is shown here disembarking at the waterside palace of Pillnitz on the Elbe, a few miles upriver from Dresden, on 26 October 1866 – five days after the peace treaty with Prussia was signed. *Illustrirte Zeitung* (Leipzig), vol. 47 (July–December 1866): 305 (10 November 1866).

inner turmoil of Saxons. Faced with clear but uncomfortable choices between pro- and anti-Prussian Reichstag candidates (National Liberals and Conservatives, mainly), Saxons were being asked to decide how local, regional, and national allegiances could be reconciled – with one another but also with the need to protect personal interests, livelihoods, and reputations. Thus a darker tone intruded: Charles Eden reported that Saxons were being compelled to engage in the "convenient" act of forgetting when they celebrated their king's return from exile.

A few days before the king's entry into Dresden, scheduled for 3 November 1866, Eden reported that the city "is already a blaze of colours from the countless Saxon and German flags; but the only Prussian banners I have been able to detect are those which still flutter ominously above the earthworks of Prussian creation."[81] One day before the event, the envoy returned to the question of how Saxons might reconcile older "feelings" and newer "interests." On one level, such conflicts could now be more easily accommodated than they had been during the most onerous and uncertain phase of the occupation – that is, the transition period between war and postwar about which Wurmb had written. The celebrations expected to take place the following day, Eden wrote, would "without doubt give rise to the most enthusiastic demonstrations of loyalty." He continued: "Even those few inhabitants of Dresden who forgot for a time their devotion to the Royal family under the pressure of the billeting system" would "find now once more their feelings & their interests in happy & convenient harmony." If we read this report against the grain, we sense that the quality of neither loyalty nor harmony – let alone mercy – was unstrained.[82]

Epilogue

The Saxon denouement to the German Civil War was a long one. It included a royal visit to Berlin by King Johann and Crown Prince Albert in mid-December 1866. The visit was meant to show their loyalty to their new partner, Prussia. A return visit to Dresden by King Wilhelm in February 1867 continued this task. The denouement also included Saxony's good fortune – after the calamitous defeats and occupations of 1756, 1813, and 1866 – in finally choosing the winning side in the summer of 1870 in the Franco-German War. With increasing confidence from the mid-1880s onward, British envoys in Dresden could claim that Saxon particularism was dead.[83]

A more fitting conclusion to this chapter is provided by the retrospective observation of King Albert, who succeeded Johann on the Saxon throne in 1873. Albert had commanded the Saxon forces at Königgrätz; he distinguished himself again on the battlefield in 1870; and as king he followed his father's lead in demonstrating his loyalty to the German Empire. One year after coming to the Saxon throne, King Albert spoke about the strange survival of monarchical Saxony during those fateful months in 1866. His remarks were made in 1874 to the British envoy George Strachey, who reported them to London in the form of a "He said, I said" account.[84]

THE KING [ALBERT] – For me, I am of course very far from being one of those who worship [Bismarck]. But I must say he is the Prussian I like best. In fact I have every personal reason for being grateful to him. *In 1866 we Saxons were within an inch of being swallowed up.* Bismarck was doubtfully inclined at first, but having once sided with us he stuck to us. It is his great merit that he is a man of his word. ... You see Bismarck is not so *Prussian* as most of them! ...

MYSELF [STRACHEY]   Y[our] M[ajesty] concludes that he has got some sincere *German* fibres. –

THE K[ING] – Exactly. That is one of his great merits. We are all comparatively safe with him.

Saved by a feather from extinction, Saxon kings continued to provide adornment to the flock of German monarchs who claimed that the sovereignty of the Second Reich lay with them, not with Prussian victors or the German people. But as well-preserved cutouts in a world they barely understood, after 1866 they were playing it safe – nothing less, nothing more.

NOTES

1 Translated by Patrick Camiller (Princeton, 2014), 613f. (orig. German ed. 2009).
2 The ironies found in a Google search on "King of Saxony" are tantalizing. The King of Saxony measures 8.3 inches or 21 centimetres in length, and up to 50 centimetres if we include his head plumage. He is one of many Birds of Paradise. In German he is known as the *Wimpelträger*; in English, Birds of Paradise are also called "emperor birds." The King of Saxony lives in the mid- to upper montane forests and their edges. So bizarre are the King of Saxony's ornamental head plumes that, when the first specimens left New Guinea in the South Pacific and toured Europe, he was thought to be a fake. Indeed, those two long, scalloped, enamel blue brow plumes, which can be erected at the bird's will, have ensured that the King of Saxony has a devoted human entourage. In both Papua New Guinea and neighbouring Indonesia, the birds bearing them are rumoured to come from the heavenly realm. Hence the brow plumes are proudly displayed as symbols of power, authority, and tradition, on emblems, flags, and currency. The King of Saxony's plumes are even stolen by other birds – for example, Archbold's Bowerbirds – for their own ritual displays. Cut-out

photocopies of the plumes are even sometimes worn by tribesmen in place of the real thing. Thus *Pteridophora alberti* was named for King Johann's son and successor Albert in 1894. According to one still-popular New Guinea myth, a girl placed her brother's lifeless body in a hollow tree; when she struck the tree, the highland Birds of Paradise exploded upward, "symboliz[ing] a birth. They're the origin of the world." Gillian Gillison, cited in Jennifer S. Holland, "Feathers of Seduction," *National Geographic* 212 (2007): 82–101, at 94.

3 Karlheinz Blaschke, "Das Königreich Sachsen 1815–1918," in *Die Regierungen der deutschen Mittel- und Kleinstaaten 1815–1933*, edited by Klaus Schwabe (Boppard a.R., 1983), 81–102 at 82, 285–94.

4 Uwe Schirmer, ed., *Sachsen 1763–1832. Zwischen Rétablissement und bürgerlichen Reformen* (Beucha, 1996); cf. Simone Lässig, "Reformpotential im 'dritten Deutschland'? Überlegungen zum Idealtypus des Aufgeklärten Absolutismus," in *Landesgeschichte in Sachsen. Tradition und Innovation*, edited by Rainer Aurig, Steffen Herzog, and Simone Lässig (Bielefeld, 1997), 187–215; Katrin Keller, "Saxony: *Rétablissement* and Enlightened Absolutism," *German History* 20, no. 3 (2002): 309–31. See also two themed issues of *Dresdner Hefte*: 30, no. 111 (2012), "Sachsen und Preußen. Geschichte eines Dualismus"; and 31, no. 114 (2013), "Sachsen zwischen 1763 und 1813."

5 Including Reiner Groß, *Die Wettiner* (Stuttgart, 2007); Winfried Müller and Martina Schattkowsky, eds., *Zwischen Tradition und Modernität. König Johann von Sachsen 1801–1873* (Leipzig, 2004); Jürgen Helfricht, *Die Wettiner. Sachsens Könige, Herzöge, Kurfürsten und Markgrafen* (Leipzig, 2003); Sächsische Schlösserverwaltung and Staatlicher Schlossbetrieb Schloss Weesenstein, eds., *König Johann von Sachsen. Zwischen zwei Welten* (Halle, 2001). Older works include Hans Philippi, *Die Wettiner in Sachsen und Thüringen* (Limburg, 1989); Reiner Groß, ed., *Sachsen und die Wettiner. Chancen und Realitäten* (special issue of *Dresdner Hefte*) (Dresden, 1990); and Albert, Prinz von Sachsen, Herzog zu Sachsen, *Die Wettiner in Lebensbildern* (Graz, 1995). Useful documentary collections include Josef Matzerath, *Der sächsische König und der Dresdner Maiaufstand. Tagebücher und Aufzeichnungen aus der Revolutionszeit 1848/49* (Cologne, Weimar, Vienna, 1999); Hellmut Kretzschmar, *Die Zeit König Johanns von Sachsen 1854–1873. Mit Briefen und Dokumenten* (Berlin, 1960); and Johann Georg, Herzog zu Sachsen, ed., *Briefwechsel zwischen König Johann von Sachsen und den Königen Friedrich Wilhelm IV. und Wilhelm I. von Preußen* (Leipzig, 1911).

6 Sabine Freitag, "'The narrow limits of this Kingdom.' Sachsen im Spiegel britischer Gesandtschaftsberichte aus dem Vormärz," *Dresdner Hefte* 20,

no. 70 (2002): 27–37, esp. 35f.; Johann Georg, ed., *Briefwechsel*, 20–3; Richard J. Bazillion, "Urban Violence and the Modernization Process in Pre-March Saxony, 1830–31 and 1845," *Historical Reflections* 12, no. 2 (1985): 279–303, esp. 296–301.

7 Throughout this chapter I cite dates in the dd.mm.yy format. Bismarck to his daughter, 24.8.63, cited in Militärgeschichtliches Forschungsamt, ed., *Entscheidung 1866. Der Krieg zwischen Österreich und Preußen* (Stuttgart, 1966), 44.

8 Historians disagree about whether this was an international, fratricidal, or civil war. Although the term *Bürgerkrieg* was rarely used in 1866, *Bruderkrieg* – literally, a war between brothers – was used often in the sense of an *intra-German* conflict and thus can be legitimately translated as civil war. See, for example, King Wilhelm I of Prussia to Queen Augusta of Prussia, 15.6.66: "So yesterday the die was cast in F[rankfurt] a.M., and the good Germans, who have always jammered on about a civil war [*Bruderkrieg*] when it is only a matter of a war between two Great Powers, now offer their hand light-heartedly [*de gaîté de Coeur*] to a real civil war." Wolfgang Steglich, ed., *Quellen zur Geschichte des Weimarer und Berliner Hofes in der Krisen- und Kriegszeit 1865/67*, vol. 2, *Der Berliner Hof* (Frankfurt a.M., 1996), 220. Cf. the titles of works listed in these notes, including Theodor Fontane's two volumes devoted to "the German war."

9 Gustav Adolf Fricke to his wife, 21.6.66, in Fricke, *Aus dem Feldzuge 1866. Briefe aus dem Felde und Predigten und Reden im Felde* (Leipzig, 1891), 12.

10 As reported by the British envoy to Saxony, George Strachey, to British Foreign Office (hereafter FO), 31.12.74 (draft), The National Archives, London (formerly the Public Record Office, Kew, hereafter cited as TNA), FO 215/34; anon., "Ein Beitrag zur Geschichte der Sächsischen Politik," *Preußische Jahrbücher* 34, no. 5 (1874): 550–81; A. Kutschbach, *Jugenderinnerungen eines alten Leipizgers*, edited by Friedrich Schulze (Leipzig, 1926), 152–3.

11 Karlheinz Blaschke, "Hof und Hofgesellschaft im Königreich Sachsen während des 19. Jahrhunderts," in *Hof und Hofgesellschaft in den deutschen Staaten im 19. und beginninden 20. Jahrhundert*, edited by Karl Möckl (Boppard a.R., 1990), 177–206 at 187–204; *Sächsische Politische Nachrichten* 1, no. 12 (21.10.04).

12 "A Golden Wedding in the Best Society," *Appleton's Journal* 9, no. 189 (4 January 1873): 49, cited in Maurice Bassan, *Hawthorne's Son: The Life and Literary Career of Julian Hawthorne* (Columbus, OH, 1970), 70. See also ch. 6 in this book.

13 Blaschke, "Königreich Sachsen," 101.

14 Jonas Flöter, *Beust und die Reform des Deutschen Bundes 1850–1866. Sächsisch-mittelstaatliche Koalitionspolitik im Kontext der deutschen Frage* (Cologne, Weimar, Vienna, 2001), 466f.; Andreas Neemann, *Landtag und Politik in der Reaktionszeit. Sachsen 1849/50–1866* (Düsseldorf, 2000), 430–87.

15 Sachsen, Ständeversammlung, *Mitteilungen über die Verhandlungen des ordentlichen Landtags im Königreich Sachsen*, 1866, II. Kammer, 121f. (13.6.66); cf. Baron Josef von Werner to Austrian FO, 30.5.66, in Heinrich Ritter von Srbik and Oskar Schmid, eds., *Quellen zur deutschen Politik Österreichs 1859–1866*, 5 vols. (Osnabrück, 1967), 5: 812f. On this lie and its awkward repercussions, as well as for descriptions of the Wettin court and its relationship to the Landtag, see Josef Matzerath, "Parlamentseröffnungen im Reich und in den Bundesstaaten," in *Das politische Zeremoniell im Deutschen Kaiserreich 1871–1918*, edited by Andreas Biefang, Michael Epkenhans, and Klaus Tenfelde (Düsseldorf, 2009), 207–32 at 230–1.

16 Bismarck and Beust, cited in Augustus Loftus, *The Diplomatic Reminiscences of Lord Augustus Loftus, 1862–1879*, Second Series, 2 vols. (London, 1894), 1: 60, 69; cf. Heinrich von Poschinger, *Fürst Bismarck und die Diplomaten 1852–1890* (Hamburg, 1900), 209–11.

17 [Prussian General Staff], *Campaign of 1866 in Germany. The War With Austria. Compiled by the Department of Military History of the Prussian Staff*, translated by Colonel von Wright and Captain Henry M. Hozier (orig. London, 1872, rpt. Nashville, 1994), 382–3; Ernst Rudolf Huber, ed., *Dokumente zur deutschen Verfassungsgeschichte*, 4 vols., vol. 2, *Deutsche Verfassungsdokumente 1851–1900*, 3rd rev. ed. (Stuttgart, 1986), 247–9.

18 *Gesetz- und Verordnungsblatt für das Königreich Sachsen*, 21. Stück (1866), no. 199, 211–21; Huber, *Dokumente*, 2: 262–4.

19 Loftus to Foreign Secretary Lord Stanley, 4.8.66, in Loftus, *The Diplomatic Reminiscences*, Second Series, 1: 107.

20 For official chronicles, see *Der Antheil des Königlich Sächsischen Armeecorps am Feldzuge 1866 in Oesterreich. Bearbeitet nach den Feldakten des Generalstabes*, 2nd ed. (Dresden, 1869); [Prussian General Staff], *Campaign*; Theodor Fontane, *Der deutsche Krieg von 1866*, 2 vols. (orig. Berlin, 1870–1, rpt. Cologne and Düsseldorf, 1979), vol. 1, *Der Feldzug in Böhmen und Mähren*; Gordon A. Craig, *The Battle of Königgrätz: Prussia's Victory over Austria, 1866* (Philadelphia and New York, 1964); Gerd Fesser, *Der Weg nach Königgrätz 1866* (Berlin, 1978); Georg Fesser, *1866, Königgrätz – Sadowa. Bismarcks Sieg über Österreich* (Berlin, 1994); Wilhelm von Voß, *Illustrierte Geschichte der deutschen Einigungskriege 1864–1866* (Stuttgart, Berlin, Leipzig, n.d.); Sir Henry Montague Hozier, *The Seven Weeks' War: Its Antecedents and Its Incidents* (London, 1867), esp. 166ff.; Konrad

Sturmhoefel, *Illustrierte Geschichte des Albertinischen Sachsen. Von 1815 bis 1904* (Leipzig, n.d.), 424–42; Max Dittrich, *König Albert und seine Sachsen im Felde 1849, 1866, 1870–71* (Berlin, 1898), ch. 5; Paul Hassel, *Aus dem Leben des Königs Albert von Sachsen*, 2 pts (Berlin, Leipzig, 1898–1900), pt 2, *König Albert als Kronprinz*, 261–306 and, on the peace talks, 307–42. Especially important on the occupation is Richard Dietrich, "Preußen als Besatzungsmacht im Königreich Sachsen 1866–1868," *Jahrbuch für die Geschichte Mittel- und Ostdeutschlands* 5 (1956): 273–93. Eyewitness and anecdotal accounts of war and occupation include Fricke, *Aus dem Feldzuge 1866*; Gustav Billig, *Deutschlands verhängnißvolles Jahr 1866* (Dresden, n.d.); Moritz Busch, *Tagebuchblätter*, 3 vols. (Berlin, 1892), 3: 452–558; Gustav Freytag's reportage for *Die Grenzboten* in 1866, in Freytag, *Gesammelte Werke*. Neue Wohlfeile Ausgabe, Erste Serie, vol. 7, *Politische Aufsätze* (Leipzig, n.d. [1900]), 184–9, 289–300, 305–8, 319–29; Hans Blum, *Lebenserinnerungen*, 2 vols. (Berlin, 1907), 1: 260–3; Alfred Hahn, "Der Deutsche Bruderkrieg von 1866," in Hahn, *Dresden im Wandel der Zeiten*, 2 vols. (Dresden, 1937), 2: 120–5; Richard von Friesen, *Erinnerungen aus meinem Leben*, 3 vols. (Berlin, 1880–1910), 2: 153–358; Friedrich Boettcher, *Eduard Stephani* (Leipzig, 1887), 63–81; Kutschbach, *Jugenderinnerungen*, 135–71. On peace talks, Richard Dietrich, "Der Preußisch-sächsische Friedensschluß vom 21. Oktober 1866. (Ein Kapitel aus der Vorgeschichte der Norddeutschen Bundesverfassung)," *Jahrbuch für die Geschichte Mittel- und Ostdeutschlands* 4 (1955): 109–56; and Fritz Dickmann, *Militärpolitische Beziehungen zwischen Preußen und Sachsen 1866 bis 1870* (Munich, 1929).

21 Cited in Craig, *The Battle of Königgrätz*, 28–9; cf. Dennis Showalter, *The Wars of German Unification* (London and New York, 2004), 143; [Prussian General Staff], *Campaign*, 29–30, 59–61; and the report of the British envoy temporarily stationed in Dresden, Charles A. Murray, to British FO, 28.6.66, TNA, FO 68/142.
22 Letter of 19.6.66 in Karl Friedrich Vitzthum von Eckstädt, *London, Gastein und Sadowa, 1864–1866. Denkwürdigkeiten* (Stuttgart, 1889), 218–19.
23 Hanover and Saxony.
24 Loftus, *The Diplomatic Reminiscences*, Second Series, 1: 76.
25 My allusion is to George Dangerfield, *The Strange Death of Liberal England*, orig. 1935 (New York, 1961).
26 Sturmhoefel, *Illustrierte Geschicht*, 390; Friedrich Ferdinand Graf von Beust, *Memoirs, Written by Himself*, 2 vols. (London, 1887), 1: 300; see also Josef Matzerath, "Sachsen zwischen Preußen und Österreich 1866," in *Sächsisch-böhmische Beziehungen im Wandel der Zeit*, edited by

Kristina Kaiserová and Walter Schmitz (Dresden, 2013), 43–60, esp. 53–7.
27 See Charles Murray (19.6.66) and Charles Eden (12.7.66) to British FO, TNA, FO 68/142; [Prussian General Staff], *Campaign*, 60; Hozier, *Seven Weeks' War*, 169–70.
28 Carl von Behrenberg, *Einmarsch preußischer Truppen am 18. Juni 1866* (n.d.), Stadtmuseum Dresden; woodcuts of similar scenes in Billig, *Deutschlands verhängnißvolles Jahr 1866*, 78f., and James Retallack, ed., *Forging an Empire: Bismarckian Germany (1866–1890), German History in Documents and Images* (hereafter *GHDI*), vol. 4, sec. 5, http://german historydocs.ghi-dc.org/sub_image.cfm?image_id=1380.
29 Friesen, *Erinnerungen*, 2: 199.
30 Baron Anton von Gablenz to Bismarck, 25.6.66, Geheimes Staatsarchiv Preußischer Kulturbesitz Berlin (hereafter GStAB), III. Haupt-Abteilung, 2.4.1. I, Ministerium des Auswärtigen Angelegenheiten (hereafter HA III, MdAA), Nr. 765. For much of the following, ibid. Nrn. 766–8. Cf. letters from Dresden, 23.6.66 and 26.7.66, in Vitzthum von Eckstädt, *London*, 225–7, 253.
31 King Johann's manifesto, "An Meine treuen Sachsen!" (16.6.66), *Dresdner Nachrichten*, 17.6.66. Other materials in Sächsisches Hauptstaatsarchiv Dresden (hereafter SHStAD), Hausarchiv Albert, König, Nr. 33, esp. on the military campaign. Saxon "losses" (dead, wounded, taken prisoner) on 3.7.66 were reported as 1,500 men.
32 From 16 to 25.6.66, Prussian soldiers marched 115 miles from Torgau to Gabel, the last portion through very mountainous terrain; [Prussian General Staff], *Campaign*, 64; Prussian routes of march described in Hozier, *The Seven Weeks' War*, 166–205 (with map, 195).
33 Murray to British FO, 23.6.66, TNA, FO 68/142; *Constitutionelle Zeitung*, 21.6.66.
34 Diary entry of 18.6.61 (and others), SHStAD, Nachlaß Carl von Weber, Bde. III–IV.
35 Bittenfeld's successor, General von der Mülbe, left Dresden in the second week of July to join Prussian troops in Bohemia; he was succeeded by Generals Hans von Schack (died 25.9.66) and Ludwig Karl von Tümpling.
36 Wurmb later sat in the Reichstag and in both houses of Prussia's *Landtag*.
37 *Protokolle der Stadtverordneten zu Dresden* (1865–66), Stadtarchiv Dresden (hereafter StAD), esp. 153ff. and 186ff.; StAD, 2.1.6., G.XXXII, including individual files listed below.

38 Karl August Schwauß was Dresden Police Director (later Police President) from 1863 to 1893.
39 Full details in GStAB, HA III, MdAA 3.6, Nr. 9156 (Die Presse in Sachsen, Vol. VII, August 1866 bis December 1867).
40 Wurmb to Bismarck (draft), 21.1.66, 2.7.66, 7.7.66; Wurmb to Landeskommission, 28.6.66. Cf. other correspondence in GStAB, HA III MdAA, Nr. 766, and in SHStAD, Landeskommission 1866; the latter contains (Nrn. 14–16) a daily register of the Provisional Government's activity, while Nr. 13 lists printed matter seized or banned by the Prussians. The fortifications are pictured in Billig, *Deutschlands verhängnißvolles Jahr 1866*, 264f., and in the *Illustrirte Zeitung* (Leipzig), Bd. 47 (Jul. –Dec. 1866), 329 (17.11.66). Some of the following details are drawn from SHStAD, MdAA, Nrn. 1012–14, and from StAD, 2.1.6., G.XXXII, Nr. 127z.
41 StAD, 2.1.6., G.XXXII, Nr. 128, vols. I–II.
42 [Prussian General Staff], *Campaign*, 60–1; reports of 27.8.66, 8.9.66, SHStAD, MdAA, Nr. 1012.
43 Wurmb cited (n.d.) in Friesen, *Erinnerungen*, 2: 202.
44 See the report of the Bavarian envoy to Saxony, Maximilian von Gise, to Bavarian FO, 17.2.67, Bayerisches Hauptstaatsarchiv Munich (hereafter BHStAM), Abteilung II, Geheimes Staatsarchiv, Ministerium des Äußern, MA III, Nr. 2841.
45 Friesen, *Erinnerungen*, 2: 228, 312–3; Saxon General Staff, *Antheil*, 390ff. and Anlage XIII.
46 Friesen, *Erinnerungen*, esp. 2: 162ff.; cf. Theodor Flathe, "Die Memoiren des Herrn von Friesen," *Historische Zeitschrift* 46 (1881): 1–47.
47 Cf. GStAB, HA III, MdAA, Nrn. 766–7; SHStAD, Landeskommission 1866, Nrn. 14–16; StAD, 2.1.6., G.XXXII; Dietrich, "Preußen als Besatzungsmacht."
48 See Sturmhoefel, *Illustrierte Geschichte*, 375–7; Dietrich, "Friedensschluß," 126.
49 Wurmb to Bismarck, 21.6.66, GStAB, HA III, MdAA, Nr. 766; Fricke, *Aus dem Feldzuge 1866*, 9–14.
50 Bleichröder to Bismarck, 8.7.66, cited in Fritz Stern, *Gold and Iron: Bismarck, Bleichröder, and the Building of the German Empire* (New York, 1977), 90.
51 [Wirkl. Geheimrat Hermann] von Thile, MdAA, to King Wilhelm I, 11.6.68, and reply (copy), 17.6.68, GStAB, HA I, Rep. 89, Nr. 13189.
52 See materials in GStAB, HA III, MdAA, Nr. 768, and Wurmb to Bismarck (draft), 29.11.66, ibid., Nr. 767.

53 Wurmb to Landeskommission, 25.6.66, 25.7.66; replies, 26.6.66, 27.7.66, and Bismarck to Wurmb, 10.7.66; ibid. Nrn. 766–7; *Constitutionelle Zeitung*, 22.7.66.
54 Joseph A. Wright to US State Department, 24.9.66, US National Archives and Records Administration, College Park, Maryland (hereafter NARA), Record Group 59, M44, microfilm reel 13.
55 SHStAD, MdAA, Nr. 1014; SHStAD, Hauptarchiv Albert, Nr. 19. Cf. SHStAD, Gesamtministerium, Loc. 17, Nrn. 6 and 8; Dietrich, "Preußisch-sächsische Friedensschluß."
56 Savigny to Wurmb, 29.8.66, GStAB, HA III, MdAA, Nr. 767; Falkenstein to Friesen, 13.9.66, in Friesen, *Erinnerungen*, 2: 277–8; Friesen to Johann, 18.9.66, 4.10.66, SHStAD, MdAA, Nr. 1014.
57 Friesen, *Erinnerungen*, 2: 248ff.; Gustav Freytag to Salomon Hirzel, 30.9.66, in *Gustav Freytags Briefe an die Verlegerfamilie Hirzel*, edited by Margarete Galler and Jürgen Matoni, 2 pts (Berlin, 1994), 2: 48; cf. Friedrich Thimme, "Wilhelm I., Bismarck und der Ursprung des Annexionsgedankens 1866," *Historische Zeitschrift* 89, no. 2 (1902): 401–56.
58 Cited in Frank Zimmer, *Bismarcks Kampf gegen Kaiser Franz Joseph. Königgrätz und seine Folgen* (Graz, Vienna, Cologne, 1996), 155.
59 Napoleon III's handwritten letter, 26.8.66, cited in Vitzthum, *London*, 288.
60 Friesen, *Erinnerungen*, 2: 324–6; Willy Real, *Karl Friedrich von Savigny 1814–1875* (Berlin, 1990), 210–19, 232.
61 Busch, *Tagebuchblätter*, 3: 462, 464 (entries for 19.6.66 and 20.6.66).
62 Johann Georg, Herzog zu Sachsen, "König Johann von Sachsen im Jahre 1866," *Neues Archiv für sächsische Geschichte* 47 (1926): 295–328, esp. 314. See also 318, for King Johann to King Wilhelm I, 2.8.66.
63 Loftus to British FO, 4.8.66, in Loftus, *The Diplomatic Reminiscences*, Second Series, 1: 105.
64 Reinhard Freiherr Dalwigk zu Lichtenfels, *Die Tagebücher des Freiherrn Reinhard v. Dalwigk zu Lichtenfels aus den Jahren 1860–71*, edited by Wilhelm Schüßler (Osnabrück, 1967), 263 (entry for 4.9.66). Cf. Charles Eden to British FO, 4.9.66, TNA, FO 68/142.
65 Vitzthum, *London*, 324, 339. Cf. Friesen's reports to Johann in SHStAD, MdAA, Nr. 1012.
66 Freytag to Count and Countess Baudissen, 13 and 14.9.66, cited in Peter Sprengel, "Der Liberalismus auf dem Weg ins 'neue Reich': Gustav Freytag und die Seinen 1866–1871," in *Literatur und Nation. Die Gründung des Deutschen Reiches 1871 in der deutschsprachigen Literatur*, edited by Klaus Amann and Karl Wagner (Cologne, Weimar, Vienna, 1996), 163.

67 I am grateful to Gavin Wiens for scanning pages from the daily register of the Landeskommission (June to October 1866), SHStAD, Landeskommission 1866 (now Bestand 10696), Nrn. 14–16.
68 The following paragraphs draw on reports from Wurmb to Bismarck (13./25.8.66, 23.9.66, 7.10.66) and from Schack to Bismarck (19.7.66, 27.8.66, 8.9.66), GStAB, III. HA, MdAA, Nr. 765.
69 Anon. [Cäsar Dietrich von Witzleben], *Sachsen und der norddeutsche Bund* (Leipzig, 1866). Witzleben was the government's representative with the semi-official *Leipziger Zeitung* and was known for his anti-Prussian sentiments.
70 Heinrich von Treitschke, *Die Zukunft der norddeutsche Mittelstaaten*, 2nd ed. (Berlin, 1866), 22f.
71 Friesen's and Fabrice's reports to Johann in SHStAD, MdAA, Nr. 1014.
72 Albrecht von Stosch to Freytag, 29.10.66, and reply, 1.11.66, both cited in Freytag, *Gustav Freytags Briefe*, 51.
73 Prussian Queen Augusta to Prussian King Wilhelm I, [6.7.66], Anlage 1, "Zur Situation am 5. Juli 1866," in Steglich, *Quellen*, 2: 254–5, contrasting "die Macht der Gewalt" with "die Macht weiser Großmut"; see generally 2: 216–81.
74 Bismarck to Prussian Crown Prince Friedrich Wilhelm, 3.2.67, in *Die auswärtige Politik Preußens 1858–1871. Diplomatische Aktenstücke*, ed. Historische Reichskommission et al., 10 vols. (Oldenburg and Berlin, 1933), 8: 359f.; Friesen, *Erinnerungen*, 2: 229f.; Poschinger, *Fürst Bismarck*, 214.
75 Kutschbach, *Jugenerinnerungen*, 150.
76 Loftus, *The Diplomatic Reminiscences*, Second Series, 1: 164; the citation here, more accurate than Loftus's, is from "The Temple of Fame" in *The Works of Alexander Pope ... in Ten Volumes* (London, 1824), 2: 291.
77 Charles Murray to British FO, 19.6.66, TNA, FO 68/142.
78 Charles Eden to British FO, 20 and 26.10.66, TNA, FO 68/142 (drafts of Eden's reports are in TNA, FO 215/20); Crowe to British FO, 5.11.66, TNA, FO 68/144; Joseph Wright to US State Department, 3.9.66, 1.11.66, NARA, 59, M44, reel 13.
79 Charles Eden to British FO, 28.6.66, TNA, FO 68/142.
80 Charles Eden to British FO, 4.9.66, 27.10.66, TNA, FO 68/142; cf. Crowe to British FO, 29.10.66, 5.11.66, TNA, FO 68/144. Festivities chronicled in SHStAD, Kreishauptmannschaft Dresden, Nr. 267.
81 *Illustrirte Zeitung* (1866), 325 (17.11.66), showing Johann's entry into Dresden on 3.11.66.
82 Charles Eden to British FO, 2.11.66, TNA, FO 68/142. Cf. Crowe to British FO, 29.10.66, TNA, FO 68/144; Loftus to British FO, 17.11.66, in *Die*

King Johann of Saxony and the German Civil War of 1866   137

auswärtige Politik Preußens 1858–1871, edited by Historische Reichskommission et al., 8: 147–8. A useful comparison is provided by Sir Henry Francis Howard (Britain's envoy to Bavaria) to British FO, 3.12.66, TNA, FO 9/177, in Retallack, ed., *Forging an Empire*, GHDI, http://germanhistorydocs.ghi-dc.org/sub_document.cfm?document_id=1817. Howard summed up the mood in the annexed territories and in the southern German states: Prussia's hegemony was proving difficult to swallow by those who had fought on the losing side in 1866.

83 The Franco-German War of 1870-1 is commonly (but misleadingly) known as the Franco-Prussian War. On waning Saxon particularism see e.g. George Strachey to British FO, 1.1.85 (draft), 2.7.88, and 3.9.95, in TNA, FO 215/37, FO 68/173, and FO 68/180, respectively. Cf. Miloš Řeznik, "Königgrätz als sächsischer Erinnerungsort. Denkmäler des Krieges von 1866 in Ostböhmen," *Dresdner Hefte* 30, no. 111 (2012): 34–41; and Lord Gough to British FO, 14.5.07, on the occasion of Kaiser Wilhelm II's visit to Dresden in 1907. Wilhelm II regarded the Saxon king "with great favour, as animated by a wholehearted devotion to the historic idea of German Unity, there being no trace of particularism to be found in King Friedrich August. This absence of particularism does not prevent His Majesty [Friedrich August III] being extremely Saxon in every respect." TNA, FO 371/260.

84 Strachey to British FO, 20.1.74 (draft), TNA, FO 215/34; original emphasis.

5 Julian Hawthorne's *Saxon Studies*

Introduction

Fated to stand in the shadow of his gifted father Nathaniel Hawthorne (1804–1864), Julian Hawthorne (1846–1934) might be forgiven for imagining he knew better. When fortune took Julian to Dresden, capital city of the Kingdom of Saxony, his effort to go native led him astray. Hawthorne wrote a misanthropic tome titled *Saxon Studies*.[1] First published serially in the *Contemporary Review* in 1874–5, the book weighed in at 452 pages when it appeared in 1876. It may well have contributed to Hawthorne's British and American publishers going bankrupt a few weeks later: the only copies that exist today are those sent out for review purposes. Hawthorne remarked that the book "was murdered simultaneously on both sides of the Atlantic" and "vanished like a ghost at cock-crow."[2]

Hawthorne claimed that he set out to write an objective, candid appraisal of Saxon society. But if this was a "warts and all" study, the face of Saxony quickly morphed into caricature. Soon one saw nothing *but* warts. *Saxon Studies* fits into no literary or scholarly genre: it is part autobiography, part travelogue, part social anthropology *avant la lettre*, part *Heimattümelei* stood on its head. Hawthorne did not seem to acquire much self-knowledge during his time abroad or even enlighten his readers about the local society in which he had, with some initial enthusiasm, immersed himself. Or did he?

To address this tantalizing question, in this chapter I explore three related ones: Where did Hawthorne think he was coming from, so to speak, when he set himself up as an authority on Saxon society? Where did the reviewers of his book imagine that his Dresden sojourn had taken him? And why did the self-awareness that Hawthorne cultivated in examining Saxons' "national" character contribute only marginally to his own self-knowledge?

Dresden became known as the Valley of the Clueless (*Tal der Ahnungslosen*) under the East German regime, principally because West German television and radio signals could not penetrate the city's surrounding hills. Saxony belongs to the Wild East of German history, not the Wild West. How can we travel to this faraway land? The *Wanderlust* that took Julian Hawthorne to Dresden, the road that forked when *Saxon Studies* was cut to pieces by Henry James, the detour that dragged the author's reputation through the Saxon mud, and, finally, the literary *Sonderweg* that ran parallel with other nineteenth-century travel accounts – these are the paths I hope to chart.

Judged purely as literature, Hawthorne's book stinks. Julian did not inherit his father's universalizing vision. To cite a money line from US presidential debates, everyone in America knew his father, and Julian Hawthorne was no Nathaniel. No wonder contemporary reviewers panned *Saxon Studies*. In Hawthorne's text, local colour is presented with little of the wit or craft that made Mark Twain's impish *Innocents Abroad* (1869) the first and best exemplar of the not-so-innocents-abroad genre. In Hawthorne's not-so-nimble hands, Twain's wry twists and self-deprecation seem to become twists of the knife and ugly-American haughtiness.

Nevertheless, I will argue that reviewers did not fully understand the hybrid identities that shaped Julian's lived experience in Dresden. Personally and in his authorial voice, Hawthorne had more ironies in the fire than his critics knew. His self-doubts about why he was writing the book in the first place, and his self-distancing from the local society he depicts, may have gone over their heads. Hawthorne's American pretensions are actually less sniffy than many contributions to the genre, and there is little of the greasy self-aggrandizement or national hubris one finds in similar works. In fact *Saxon Studies* is of considerable value to historians interested in hybrid identities, cultural transfers, and the kinds of literary cross-fertilizations that either incubate or break down essentialist national stereotypes. Therefore, lest we close the book on young Hawthorne too quickly, let us join the author and the little American colony in Dresden with an open mind.

Saxon Studies

It is impossible to follow Julian Hawthorne on all his rambles to expose the foibles of Saxon peasants, servants,[3] husbands, professors, students, architects, duellists, listeners of music, soldiers,[4] policemen, noblemen, and dynastic rulers.[5] But three aspects of Hawthorne's analysis set it apart from more positive accounts of travel in nineteenth-century Saxony: his special interest in interiors and exteriors, reflecting a determination not to confuse reality with illusion (*Sein* with *Schein*); the frequency with which Hawthorne pauses – both literally and figuratively – to contemplate Saxony's hills and valleys, its forests and lakes, its large cities and its tiny villages; and the way Hawthorne forces modern and not-modern aspects of Saxon life into close proximity.

Hawthorne's portrait has been aptly described as "dissonance abroad."[6] Just as Mordecai Richler enjoyed citing early passages from Twain's *Innocents Abroad* because they were "a tad broad, proffering more burlesque than inspired satire," it is not inappropriate to cite exemplary passages from *Saxon Studies* with a nose for effect: after all, readers quickly tire of landscapes viewed with an unremittingly jaundiced eye or served up as a rhetorical screed. Attention to rhetorical effect is important for another reason. Julian Hawthorne in 1874, like Mark Twain in 1869, was on the threshold of his first major success: his authorial voice was just starting to emerge. Hawthorne's voice never gathered the assurance or force of Twain's. It never insinuated itself, as Twain's has, into how Americans spoke in the late nineteenth century and still speak today. It may be coincidence, but more than one critic has ascribed this difference to the question of forebears and upbringing. Do Twain and Hawthorne exemplify the difference between mature and immature empathy? If the answer is yes, the obvious follow-up is to ask whether the hand of a famous father was at play. "At least for an American writer," Roy Blount, Jr, has written, it is impossible "to parody Mark Twain. It would be like doing an impression of your father or mother: he or she is already there in your voice." Sometimes a dissonance is just a dissonance. Yet as Freud once wrote, "analogies decide nothing, that is true, but they can make one feel more at home."[7]

Julian Hawthorne's *Saxon Studies* begins and ends in Dresden. Yet the very first lines of chapter 1 provide a self-imposed, pre-emptive leave-taking from the city. As Hawthorne sets out for Dresden's environs, the city's charm "lurks" behind him only in the towers of its churches and palaces.[8] "The capital of Saxony," Hawthorne writes, "although not devoid of some pleasant interior features, improves, like the Past as we walk away from it; until, seen from a certain distance, it acquires a smack of Florence.[9] But cross this line in either direction, and the charm begins to wane. Here erects itself a moral barrier, which the temperate traveler should not transgress" (11). As Hawthorne climbs farther out of the valley, his mood initially brightens. Like the nineteenth-century sociologist Wilhelm Heinrich Riehl before him, he has laced up stout walking shoes and is determined to hike and hike and hike.[10] "From the summit of this grassy upland," life looks good to Hawthorne. "We turn our backs on the city," he writes, "and ramble country-wards for to-day. We may walk as leisurely as we like, pausing whenever the humor takes us. For my own part, I refuse at the outset to be hurried, or to stick to the main road when the by-path looks more inviting" (15).

Soon, though, those by-paths have trapped Hawthorne in a riff on modernization – again not unlike Riehl. Hawthorne reads the contrast between modernity and traditionalism on the landscape and on the piteous faces of the first peasants he meets. The physicality of it all sets the tone for the rest of his book:

> As the sun of planets, so is Dresden centre of a spattering of villages. It is observable, that, although the central body is greatly larger, and presumably older than its satellites, yet the latter are more antique in aspect and conservative in character. Like the smallest babies, they have the oldest faces, and are farthest behind the age ... Dresden is, at present, not very far behind the age in some respects: it knows something about velocipedes, tram-ways, and expensive living. But the villages are still early in their eighteenth century. (15–16)
>
> Barriers against civilization are rather physical than moral, – a matter of good or bad roads ... Time sleeps beneath immemorial ruins at one spot, while he mounts the telegraph-pole at another.
>
> The Nineteenth Century, accordingly, while it ambles easily down the current of the Elbe, and along the high-roads and railways, seldom exerts itself to climb a hill or wind its way into a sequestered valley. There are retreats but a few miles from Dresden, where still lingers the light of centuries sunk beneath the general horizon. (19)

Venom soon infects Hawthorne's analysis of rural society: perhaps he is still under the influence of the "thin brown mist" and "indolent breeze" that followed him from Dresden. "The ignorance of the average Saxon peasant is petrifying – all the more in view of the fact that, of late years, he has begun to learn reading and writing. Such acquirements appear to be a poor gauge of intelligence. Of the march of events – the news of the day – of all such knowledges as the American infant sucks in with the milk from his feeding-bottle – your Saxon peasant has no inkling" (15–16).[11] Almost as quickly the analysis broadens out to include Saxons in general: "The Saxon mind is capacious of an indefinite amount of information; but its digestion is out of proportion weak. There is not power to work up the meal of knowledge into the flesh and blood of wisdom. I have observed in the faces of the learned an expression of mental dyspepsia, – bulbous foreheads and dull pale eyes" (16–17).

So far my citations have been taken from only the book's first twenty pages. A few representative examples must suffice to convey the overall tone of Hawthorne's study. In chapter 2, some fifty pages are required to squeeze every drop of meaning from the genre's mandatory examination of German drinking customs. Dresden is a lake of beer, "of which the breweries are the head-waters ... The fishes are the Dresdeners themselves, who, instead of swimming in the lake, allow it to swim in them" (89). The national song, writes Hawthorne, should not be the sentimental "Wacht am Rhein" but rather "'Lieber Land! kannst ruhig sein;/Fest steht und treu' – das Bier-Verein" (75). One suspects that Hawthorne enjoyed a pint as much as the next fellow. He writes at one point: "The genius of beer is peaceful ... The effect upon thoughts is peculiar and grateful. It gently anoints them, so that they move more noiselessly and sleekly, getting over much ground with little jar." Indeed, it is impossible to overlook the blurry banality of lines possibly written in an introspective stupor: "With what profound speculation do we mark the course of yonder leaf earthwards floating from its twig, overweighted by the consideration we have bestowed on it" (79–80).

It is at table that exteriors and interiors begin to meet: "[The beer] draws a transparent screen between us and our mental processes," we read, "as a window shuts out the noise of the street without obstructing our view of what is going on there." Soon Hawthorne and his Saxon drinking comrades are engorged with feelings of superiority and complacency. We see them as foreigner and native, but they view each other across facing pages of *Saxon Studies*: on one side is Hawthorne, sitting "full-orbed and complete," regarding his "fellow-men with the sweet-tempered contempt of superiority"; and there, on the next page, we survey the rest of the room. "Who calls the Saxon cold?" asks Hawthorne.

Figure 5.1 A poor family in central Germany eating together. *Am Tagelöhnertisch*, by Otto Günther (1875). bpk, Berlin/Museum Wiesbaden/Photograph by Rainer Maria Schopp/Art Resource, NY.

"I like to hear him call for his beer – as though he had been wrongfully separated from it, and claimed it as his Saxon birthright. There is a certain half-concealed complacency in his tone, too; arising partly from pleasurable anticipation, partly from patriotic pride that there is so good a thing to call for. Having got it, he never shows to such advantage as with it in his hand ... It seems a pity, then, that he should ever strive to be aught sublimer than a beer-drinker" (80–2).

For Hawthorne, there's the rub: the Saxon imagines that he has a higher purpose in life, for instance by imagining that he is above the sameness of the national drink.[12] With enough drink in him, and "with a crown to back him," the Saxon "will sling his mug at anybody; and it is instructive to observe, when once his victory is secure, how voluble, excited, and indignant he becomes." These are not exactly Friedrich Nietzsche's *Untimely Meditations* (1873). Yet the chronological fit is a little uncanny. Hawthorne was not alone in seeing the German philistine, drunk with victory, becoming "implacable and over-bearing towards his foe." In Hawthorne's study we encounter "the same Saxon in his beer-saloon as at Sedan!" (88).[13]

Subsequently the theme of hybridity is developed under such chapter titles as "Stone and Plaster" and "Types Civil and Uncivil." These chapters provide the inevitable treatises on German scholarship, German music, and German love of authority. In each case Hawthorne is bound to demonstrate that if German professors, shopkeepers, and students are a bad lot generally, they are nowhere worse than in Saxony. The section on music is typical. "The Saxons have a less correct ear for music than any people with which I am acquainted," Hawthorne blares. The problem is not that good music does not exist in Saxony, he concedes, but rather that the average Saxon orchestra and the typical group of young students singing together are alike in one respect: "they are exhaustively and indefatigably trained. Bismarck and Wagner are at the bottom of it" (116). The ubiquitous beer tent is also to blame. The Saxon "is continually doing things false in harmony … Who but he can sit through a symphony of Beethoven's, applauding its majestic movements with the hand which has just carried to his lips a mug of beer, and anon returns thither with a slice of sausage. It seems as if no length of practice could marry this gross, everlasting feeding, to any profound appreciation of music" (55).

The training of Saxon philistines begins early. "A Saxon baby has but little cry in him and no persistent noisiness. In infancy he is stiffened out in swaddling-clothes, and lives between two feather pillows, like an oyster in his shell … moving only his pale bluish eyes and pasty little fingers[14] … I am credibly informed, that they must be dashed with cold water in order to bring their lungs into action. A dash of cold water would be apt to produce a spasm in a Saxon of whatever age" (49–50). And so the "habit of following authority and precedent in all concerns of life grows with them … They swim everywhere in the cork-jacket of Law; and, should it fail them, flounder and sink; or even lose their heads and are betrayed into some folly which helps them to the bottom" (50–1).[15]

The airless, swaddling culture and the ingrained respect for authority stifle all independent thinking. The Saxon dreads nothing more than a drought of fresh air, Hawthorne notes: "I fancy their coffins must be more air-tight than other people's … Why windows in Saxony were made to open, is a mystery" (51). Deficient initiative and lack of humour compound lessons learned early and well. Hawthorne declares with authority that Saxons "are so accustomed to walking through life with the policeman's hand on their coat-collar, that when his grasp is relaxed they stray without helm or compass" (142). Thus petit bourgeois shopkeepers "look at the pictures in *Kladderadatsch*" – Germany's leading satirical journal – "but they do not understand the political allusions" (211). Even Saxon scholars are incapable of critical, independent thought. "They are wood of a straight, close grain, – displaying none of the knots and eccentric veins which make a polished surface attractive" (102).

"False Images" of Nineteenth-Century Germany

Hawthorne's book provided sufficient kindling to light a fire of protest under every group of Saxons who might have rallied in the name of political correctness. What Mordecai Richler said of Twain's *Innocents Abroad* also applies to Hawthorne's *Saxon Studies*: were it to be released today, it would probably "be banned in schools, the author condemned as a racist, and possibly, just possibly, [he would find] himself the subject of a *fatwa*."[16]

In trying to embed Hawthorne's book in primary and secondary literatures about American and British views of nineteenth-century Germany, one can also draw upon accounts by diplomatic envoys stationed in Dresden. Literary, scholarly, and diplomatic sources offer wildly fluctuating assessments of German culture. Extremely positive and extremely negative appraisals are found in each genre, often within the covers of a single book or consular report. A growing scepticism towards Germany can be noted among British observers from the 1870s onward; American doubts intrude rather later. It is impossible to separate idealists from realists within these camps, and it is rather too easy to say that Americans fell prey to a Manichaean trap in their stance towards Germany.[17]

This lack of consensus has not been sufficiently appreciated by historians who rely on nineteenth-century American accounts of travel in Saxony. Bolstered by an arsenal of quotations from some of the most famous American travellers of the century, these accounts tended to praise almost everything about Saxon life and letters.[18] Such travellers almost never forgot – as Hawthorne did – to "accentuate the positive."[19] They emphasized how well the Germans were practising democracy, or they focused on the Germans' military might, expert civil service, state support for the arts, local self-government, social welfare schemes, and accomplishments in higher education (particularly in science and technology).[20]

At the time Hawthorne was writing in the 1870s, Americans still appreciated German (especially Protestant) support for the Union cause during the American Civil War. Having barely held their own nation together in the 1860s, Americans praised German unification in 1871.[21] But because memories of the Civil War were still painful, American commentators of the 1870s underplayed the whole issue of states' rights, federalism, and the preservation of local customs – indeed, such matters were almost taboo.[22] Americans believed they had good reason to side with a strong German state and a strong executive authority.[23] They did so not to repudiate Germans' own efforts to achieve greater individual liberty, still less to slow down the Germans' advance towards American ideals of Western civilization. They did so, rather, because a strong, unitary, "modern" constitution was viewed as the only framework within which individual liberty could flourish.[24] "The emperor is the point of union" – this was how American constitutional experts affirmed that a unified and militarily secure state precluded the "despotism" of parliament, of the masses, or any secessionist threat.[25] Thus Julian Hawthorne, writing less than ten years after the end of the Civil War, wanted to explain what was progressive and what was retrograde about Saxon society; but he paid almost no attention to Saxony's role within Germany's federal system.

Since 1815, Americans had been invading Göttingen, Heidelberg, Leipzig, and other German university cities to study, tramp about, and hang out. This well-heeled élite, disproportionately from New England, was inclined to praise Germany as the embodiment of academic ideals and high culture. American journals such as *The Nation*[26] and US diplomats such as George Bancroft[27] enthused both before and after 1871 about how well Germans understood the separation of powers and other features of American republicanism. But if we expand the social range of our chosen writers, we find that foreign admiration for German styles of governance was less pronounced.[28] In both England and America, a tendency to lump Saxons, Prussians, and other Germans together into a unitary "drilled nation on furlough"[29] had already begun by the time Hawthorne wrote *Saxon Studies*. We can date the genesis of this trend to the German encirclement, bombardment, and attempted starvation of Paris in the autumn of 1870.[30] By the time the Second Reich was proclaimed in January 1871, Walt Whitman spoke for many: "As the case now stands, I find myself now far more for the

French than I ever was for the Prussians." A growing number of critics believed the Germans "had dreamed of freedom, but had not dreamed of the way to secure it."[31]

Rarely did such observers inject into their accounts any ironic or critical self-distancing.[32] In most positive appraisals written by foreign travellers in Germany one finds neither the accidental nor the intentional "false images" (*Trugbilder*) that constitute part of the excitement for scholars trying to distinguish between image and reality.[33] What do we mean by unintentional false images? One might cite the German middle-class manager in David Lodge's novel *Nice Work* (1988), who clicks his heels in a way no bourgeois of his day would do. Or the middle-ranking German official, "Herr Rat," in Katherine Mansfield's short story "Germans at Meat" (from *In a German Pension*, 1911), who supposedly – but implausibly – "fixed his cold blue eyes upon me with an expression which suggested a thousand premeditated invasions." These false images are as intriguing as they are perplexing because their multiple alterities can leave us in a "wilderness of mirrors." So the question arises: What does this interpretive landscape offer to historians seeking reliable description and insight, not voluntary submission to existing national stereotypes or polarizing rants?[34]

The field of imagology first gained currency among French scholars after the Second World War when they tackled the topic of "how one nation sees the other."[35] Such scholars were concerned not only with the origins and meanings of supposed national characteristics, but also with the "motivations and the effects of our habit of thinking, speaking, and writing in the form of prejudices, stereotypes and clichés." Since the 1980s, under the influence of cultural, postcolonial, and other studies, imagology has helped scholars explain how "thinking, judging, writing in the form of images reflects fundamental conditions of perception, imagination, and representation."[36] But lest we imagine that only "pure" literature and not other kinds of historical documents open a window on these subjects, consider the following 1885 report by a high-ranking British diplomat who had arrived in Berlin less than a fortnight earlier:

> Since my arrival here 10 days ago I have seen a great many people of all sects & classes ... The Germans *like ourselves* are a vain people, & like the French are a very touchy people – but touchy not like the French because they are an arrogant & blustering nation, but because they are a young

nation suddenly hoisted on the highest pinnacle of military strength in Europe ... The whole matter lies in a nutshell ... Germany [is] generally represented by us allegorically as a student drinking beer ... [However,] far from being as rough in her feelings as she appears outwardly when represented drinking & smoking, she in reality has all the delicate little vanities of a woman, & the Englishman who deals with the German should be a veritable Don Juan in his delightful & insinuating manner, & in irresistable [sic] powers of persuasion.[37]

Merely listing the symbolic investments that are made in exemplary national figures (e.g., the German *Michel* but also John Bull, Uncle Sam, William Tell, and Don Quixote) would explode the bounds of this chapter. However, a list of keywords central to the field of imagology suggests why a work like Hawthorne's *Saxon Studies* might help us better understand how notions of "national character" can become the main discursive rationalization for cultural difference. Those keywords (in alphabetical order) include alterity/identity, anthropology, caricature, centre/periphery, cliché, cosmopolitanism, discourse, East–West, ethnocentrism, exoticism, geography/topography, hetero-stereotype, homeland, hybridity, irony, memory, nationalism, North–South, perspective, savage/barbarian, sexuality, social types, temperament/climate, topography (again), travel writing, triviality, and xenophobia.[38] These categories provide useful touchstones as we try to determine how Julian Hawthorne attempted to sum up a complex set of attitudes and attributes that together constituted "Saxonness." They help us interrogate Hawthorne himself as much as his subject. Did *he* see Saxonness as something fixed – as expressing itself in the same way from generation to generation or village to village? Or did it appear to him more protean and malleable than that? Was Hawthorne claiming to reveal eternal truths about Saxony, Germany, America, or the human condition? Or was he satisfied to provide only glimpses of personal and societal behaviours?

Keith Robbins once suggested that the best way to address questions about why people construct national stereotypes may be to steer a path between extreme simplicity and extreme sophistication.[39] Before we turn to contemporary reviews of *Saxon Studies*, we might adopt the simple approach long enough to make the point that Hawthorne's caustic dismissal of Saxon localism does not stand as far outside the mainstream of the genre as both contemporary reviewers and recent historians have suggested. An instructive example is provided by Henry

Mayhew's *German Life and Manners as Seen in Saxony*, which appeared in 1864 and was compared with Hawthorne's book as soon as the latter was published. Mayhew signals in his Preface that he has not gone looking for sophistication:

> It has long appeared to the author, who has passed several years of his life abroad, that travelling southward from England is like going backward in time – every ten degrees of latitude corresponding to about a hundred years in our own history; for, as in France we see society in the same corrupt and comfortless state as prevailed in our nation at the beginning of the present century, so in Germany we find the people, at the very least, a century behind us in all the refinements of civilization and the social and domestic improvements of progress.

One dares not repeat what Mayhew goes on to say about Spain, Russia, and Central Africa. And lest we believe that Julian Hawthorne took out a patent on rhetorical excess, one line from Mayhew's conclusion sets the record straight: "Never was such a lanthorn-jawed, sallow-faced, hollow-eyed, herring-gutted, spindle-shanked, gôitre-necked, sore-mouthed, sad-looking, half-clad, tatter-demalion race of people, as the working population of Saxony, seen in any other part of the civilized world."[40]

Henry James Puts the Knife In

Henry James's review of *Saxon Studies* is a thing of beauty: concise and cutting, a slap where a slap is needed.[41] The opening line sets the tone: "Mr. Hawthorne is decidedly disappointing." The second line states the obvious: the son is not up to the father's craft. Julian Hawthorne, we read, writes with "vigor and vivacity" and even some charm, "but he perpetually suggests more than he performs, and leaves the reader waiting for something that never comes." Hawthorne's approach to his subject is "masculine" and exhibits "conscious cleverness," but it is "not characterized by a high degree of wisdom." Thus "the reader's last impression is of a strange immaturity of thought." Nathaniel's figure looms over the review. James writes that *Saxon Studies* contains "a good deal of light, rambling talk about nothing in particular." But "the promise is never justified, ... the story is never told."

Henry James identified three principal flaws in *Saxon Studies*. Hawthorne's depiction of Saxon society, first, is criticized as mean-spirited.

The lack of generosity towards a foreign people strikes James as unfair: Hawthorne seems to have been motivated by "the simple desire ... to pour forth his aversion to a city in which, for several years, he had not been able to guard himself against being regrettably irritable and uncomfortable." As a result, *Saxon Studies* is "unduly trivial and even rather puerile." It takes for granted "in an off-hand, allusive manner" that the Saxon people are "an ignoble and abominable race." Hence Hawthorne's humour is "acrid and stingy." His "reveries are ill-natured." His "ingenuity is all vituperative."

Second, James objects to the method of the book. "It gives us the feeling," he writes, "that the author has nursed his dislikes and irritations in a dark closet, that he has never put them forth into the open air, never discussed and compared and intelligently verified them." James continues the thought: "This – and not at all the fact that they *are* dislikes – is the weak point of Mr. Hawthorne's volume." According to James, Hawthorne's readers will look in vain for specific examples of Saxon sloth or turpitude: "Mr. Hawthorne," given "more to fancy than to observation," is "always sweeping and always vague." He "spins his thread out of his own fancy," James writes, "and at the touch of reality it would very soon snap." James concedes that he would still have found fault with the spirit of Hawthorne's study even if the author had "made the Saxon vices much more vivid, and his irritation much more intelligible." But his main point is clear: Hawthorne had every right to detest the Saxons, and James has no reason to defend them. His objections to Hawthorne's book, thus, are purely in defence of "good literature."

Third, James feels that Hawthorne "has quite violated" the canon. Exactly *what* canon, we are not told. One can surmise, however, that such a canon would comfortably have included Mark Twain. James writes that Hawthorne "had a perfect right, of course, to produce a fanciful book about Dresden; but such a book ... is more than usually bound to justify itself. It must have a graceful, agreeable, and pliable spirit to reward us for the extra steps we take." Instead, Hawthorne did not understand "why the tone in which he has chosen to talk about the worthy inhabitants of Dresden is not a rational, or a profitable, or a philosophic, or a really amusing one." Thus Hawthorne "has written a *brooding* book, with all the defects and none of the charms of the type."

James hints at the kinds of questions that imagologists might have posed to Hawthorne if they had the chance. He first quotes one of Hawthorne's bolder assertions – about the "cold, profound selfishness which forms the foundation and framework of the national and individual character in every walk of life, the wretched chill of which must ultimately annul the warmth of the most fervent German eulogist." James believes that this is "a sweeping but an interesting charge." The reader, he continues, would have profited if the author had gone a little "into the psychology of the matter." But instead Hawthorne pulls up short in every chapter: "he gives us no report of his social observations proper, of his impressions of private manners and morals; no examples of sentiments, opinions, conversations, ways of living and thinking."

What else constitutes part of the canon to which James refers? Knowledge of a foreign country's theatre, literature, press, and the arts: on all these subjects, "Mr. Hawthorne is entirely dumb." Moreover, Hawthorne has wilfully refused to make the kinds of literary allusions the genre demands. The only such allusion, James writes, is Hawthorne's observation that the relation of Schiller and Goethe to the Saxons he met in the 1870s is best described as "sublimity reflected in mud-puddles." Implying that Julian's father would not have missed the same opportunity, James concludes that the son has failed to write a book that sees the large things and ignores the very small things. Bringing the theme of disappointment full circle, James observes that *Saxon Studies* is the kind of book that a very young man might write "in a season of combined ill-humor and conscious cleverness; but it is a book which most young men would very soon afterwards be sorry to have written."

Was Julian Hawthorne sorry he wrote *Saxon Studies*? We return to that question in this chapter's conclusion. His publishers and other reviewers of the book were certainly sorry. None of them put the knife in quite so delicately as Henry James; but many compared *Saxon Studies* with Ralph Waldo Emerson's *English Traits* (1856) and Mayhew's *German Life and Manners* (1864). The latter, it was said, provided a more mature, a more compelling, and a less capricious picture of Saxon society: it was "factual," not impressionistic. Be that as it may, Mayhew and Hawthorne tackled many identical topics – for example, the question of absurd place names, the mendacity of Saxon servants and journalists, army and police regulations, and Saxon men who worked their women harder than horses and cows.[42] Hawthorne's "lively spirit of observation" drew praise from some reviewers. But his method was described as thorough and mechanical rather than insightful or allusive. Most reviewers echoed James in asking why Hawthorne seemed so "unaccountably angry"? Why had he allowed his book to become so infected with the spirit of gratuitous denunciation and petulance? No one knew.

Opinion was more divided as to whether Hawthorne had caught any sense of the Saxon people's "characteristic" and "national" traits.[43] Most agreed he had not. One reviewer warned readers of *The Academy* not to accept Hawthorne's descriptions of German life and manners, his denigration of Saxon taste, and his description of their abject willingness to submit to authority. Although the book contained "certain picturesque passages," no reader could commune with nature in Saxony or be inspired by Dresden's architecture without being caught in the downdraft of Hawthorne's peevishness and his "misleading" conclusions. For this reviewer, the caricatures Hawthorne had drawn were so unlike the real inhabitants of Dresden that the work might as easily have been titled *Siberian Studies*.

Germans were sorry too.[44] A particularly rancorous reception greeted Hawthorne's book in the review columns of the *Dresdner Nachrichten*.[45] It is important to know that this newspaper represented the far Right in Saxony: its snobbish, antisemitic, and chauvinistic rhetoric perfectly mirrored the views of Dresden's conservative elite.[46] Thus the two anonymous reviews of *Saxon Studies* that appeared in the first week of February 1876 fairly "crackled with resentment."[47] The second review was more devastating than the first, suggesting that the anonymous critic needed four days to think of all the things he should have said initially. But the first was damning enough.

The *Dresdner Nachrichten*'s reviewer was determined to transcend geographical and class boundaries in condemning Hawthorne's "take" on Saxony. Hawthorne of Boston, we read, "has perpetrated an outrageous libel on Dresden." Thus the narrowness of the American's horizons was condemned at the outset. But the calumnies being hurled by this "bumptious American," this "snobbish blockhead," this "clownish upstart," were seen to be aimed at Leipzig, Saxony, and the whole of Germany. Although Hawthorne's unkind remarks centre on Dresden and Leipzig, the *Nachrichten*'s reviewer observed that "it would really be hard to name any spot in Germany which would not appear … in a much more perverse light." Did Hawthorne actually expect, the reviewer asked incredulously, that all Saxons should live "in the same style as wealthy people on Fifth Avenue in New York"? In this regard, the German response to *Saxon Studies* exactly mirrored that of American critics, who questioned Hawthorne's preoccupation with the dullest, most brutish Saxons he could find: low-ranking businessmen, women pulling carts, peasants who were more like their geese than their poets, students who had nothing to do but *Schlagen* and *Saufen*, and soldiers-automatons.

Most of the initial review in the *Dresdner Nachrichten* is actually an extended quotation from a newspaper cited as the *Newyorker Staatszeitung* of 12 January 1876. This "honored newspaper," we read, has offered "admirable remarks" and a "vigorous defense of Germany" – a defence upon which the *Nachrichten*'s reviewer can apparently improve only in details. Still, he adds a footnote: numerous Americans live in Saxony as "our beloved and honored guests," and these Americans disagree with their "self-conceited fellow-countryman." Four days later, however, the reviewer has unleashed his own diatribe against "the Yankees who proffer in bombastic phrases a refuge to all the oppressed of the world, but who, with sovereign scorn, look down on all foreign-born whom they have seduced to immigration in order to exploit their labor and savings. Having enticed them to immigrate they then try to represent them unworthy of freedom and equality." To drive this argument home, the *Nachrichten*'s reviewer hits Julian Hawthorne where he thinks it will hurt most: by citing his father. He quotes the lines from Nathaniel's *English Notebooks* that read, "Nothing is so absolutely odious as the sense of freedom and equality pertaining to an American grafted on the mind of a native of any other country in the world. A naturalized citizen is HATEFUL. Nobody has the right to our ideas, unless born to them."[48] Here the reviewer adds: "Certainly one can expect no just estimate of Dresden, Saxony, and the Germans from a son who has learned from his father that freedom and equality are a monopoly of Americans." But family ties alone are not responsible for the younger Hawthorne's vitriol. On the contrary: the Dresden reviewer claims that Hawthorne's book fits a larger pattern of American barbarism and atrocity.

Lastly, the reviewer takes umbrage at Julian Hawthorne's emphasis on the *least* cultured and *least* attractive elements of Saxon society. Such emphasis, he believes, was the natural result of Hawthorne's having failed to gain admission to high society in Dresden – or even the higher ranks of the American colony in its midst. Now, it may be true that there is no more disgruntled outsider than the uninvited American.[49] But the *Nachrichten*'s reviewer is too confident he knows the score on this point:

Because [Hawthorne] was unable to gain admittance to the respectable society of Dresden and Leipzig, and found himself confined to association with the masses, he revenged himself by describing the habits and customs of the lowest orders as if they were those of the whole people: as when, for example, he asserts that [the] only way the dance-loving Saxons dance is for the man to grasp the woman round the waist with both hands. Were a European traveler to take a fancy to make studies of society in New York after such a fashion as this, what a distorted picture of American life he might paint: and yet he would not find it necessary to sin half as much against truth as the author of this book has done, in order to produce no less repulsive an effect.

How can we test the validity of this charge – found in both American and German reviews – that Hawthorne had cobbled together accumulated personal irritations and frustrated social climbing into a superficial, transparently self-serving polemic? Let us try, first, by examining Hawthorne's own circumstances during his years in Dresden, and second, by following clues he provides in the opening and closing pages of *Saxon Studies*.

Mr Hawthorne Sees It Through

Our task is not to sleuth out disguised literary merit or to save Hawthorne's book from historical oblivion. But still we would like to know what Hawthorne was really up to in Dresden. What axe did he have to grind? Was his father the only family member to provide the chip that rested not so lightly on his shoulder? If Mark Twain's *Innocents Abroad* is the classic "*American* coming-of-cultural-age book, the first major offering of a great writer," can we shoehorn the younger Hawthorne into an upbeat *personal* coming-of-age story, one that stands in contrast to Henry James's insistence on the book's brooding tone and the author's immaturity?[50] Can we find for Hawthorne a place in the historical and literary contexts of the late 1860s? This was a decade when, as Stephen Leacock once noted, "of American literature there was much doubt in Europe; of American honesty, much more; of American manners, more still."[51]

When Julian Hawthorne first visited Dresden in 1869, he was hardly a stranger to foreign travel.[52] At the age of seven, in 1853, he had accompanied his parents to Italy and France. One wonders what early lessons Julian learned on that trip from his father, a very shy man though self-possessed. Nathaniel Hawthorne habitually lived within himself, and seemed – Julian once said – to find no better society. Ten years after that trip Julian entered Harvard. But he spent more time on rowing and other athletics than in the classroom. Eventually, in the same year (1866) that the Saxons met their match at the hands of Prussia in the Battle of

Königgrätz, Julian met his too: he was expelled from Harvard.[53] Two years later he began the study of civil engineering at the Lawrence Scientific School in Cambridge, Massachusetts. James Russell Lowell – Nathaniel's old friend, a Harvard professor, and a seasoned travel writer himself – was induced to give young Hawthorne "a little preliminary insight into German" by tutoring him in his study two or three evenings a week. Lowell obligingly undertook what Julian described as "the mollifying of my barbarism."[54] However, Julian's subsequent stays in Saxony were hampered by an inadequate preparation in the German language, rendering him unable to mimic Twain's joyful grapplings with German nomenclature:[55] "He [Lowell] would assign me a passage from [*Faust*]," wrote Hawthorne. Lowell would "courteously assume at our next meeting that I had mastered it, and would then proceed to read-out and construe it himself ... Ostensibly, we read Goethe's 'Faust' together – in reality he read and I listened."[56] Hawthorne later admitted that "it wasn't until I had been in Dresden nearly two years that I awoke one morning and found that I could say what I wanted to and understand what was said to me well enough to get along."[57]

Julian seems to have preferred close encounters of another sort when he set out for Germany with his mother and sisters in October 1868. During that Atlantic crossing he confided to his journal that every once in a while "I captured a young lady, and eloped with her to the bows, or behind the Pilot-House."[58] After disembarking at Bremen, the family made its way through Magdeburg and Leipzig to Dresden. On this arduous trek, Julian's first impressions were uniformly positive.[59] He remarked on the pleasant German cafés and their "most excellent Bier" served "in very large glass tankards, with covers." "Everything is absurdly cheap" – an almost universal accolade offered by American visitors of the day. Less typically, Hawthorne observed that everything, not just the prices, was "much better than in America."[60]

The first winter in Dresden was a mainly happy one, spent visiting galleries and frequenting "hospitable kellers and breweries." Julian rhapsodized at length about Raphael's "divine" *Madonna and Child* in Dresden's portrait gallery (*Gemäldegalerie*).[61] Indeed, when he made comparisons with his unpleasant boyhood visits to other national galleries, he expressed surprise that he could find "so much beauty in the old pictures." In other words, more than a half-decade before *Saxon Studies* was published and Henry James's wrath invoked, Julian would have dismissed the notion that his account of life in Saxony was unschooled or superficial.

His critics also missed the mark when they surmised that he had never visited Dresden's *Semperoper* or attended high society masked balls during the "season." For almost a year after his arrival in 1869, Hawthorne put off actually taking up formal studies at Dresden's *Realschule* – "famous as the best in the world for training civil engineers."[62] He certainly had the time and the opportunity to indulge in a congenial mix of socializing and observation. A German tutor was engaged to expand Julian's vocabulary beyond *Faust*, and it was decided that Julian should attend a few lectures at the *Realschule* to prepare himself for the technical terms he would be encountering in the lecture hall. However, the "unhealthy and hopeless looking creatures" he found upon his "debut among the German schoolboys" appalled the young American, as did his tutor: "an elderly man, with a rusty gray schock-head of hair, rusty clothes, [and] a deficiency of front teeth." By the time he could formally be admitted to the *Realschule*, in October 1869, Julian confided to his journal that he wanted above all to "get through by next fall and go home." His mother and his sisters seem to have enjoyed the experience even less. Hawthorne's older sister Una found the language unfathomable, and she felt that "these stolid, dirty Germans" "disenchant one of all ideas of beauty." As for Rose Hawthorne, still a teenager, Julian was concerned that she was mixing in social circles that were beneath her.

If Julian was to be frustrated in his goal of getting a German degree, other longings were left unsatisfied too, at least for a time. Following upon brief romances in Concord and while crossing the Atlantic, he claimed to have fallen deeply in love with a Miss Sherman, a beautiful member of the American colony in Dresden. But according to Hawthorne, Miss Sherman was "alarmingly correct in all her ideas." Echoing one his father's favourite literary themes, Julian thought it would enhance Miss Sherman's intellectual development if "she could be turned to evil courses." Meanwhile Julian amused himself with his male American friends:

> [We] drank beer out of glass schoppen with porcelain covers; we smoked pipes and Laferme cigarettes, we attended open-air concerts in the Grosser Garten, the Bruehlsche Terrace, the Waldschlösschen; we fought schläger [fencing] duels, and wore high boots, black velveteen jackets, and caps four inches in diameter; we went to masked balls, where neither we nor anybody else behaved quite properly; we went to other dances in queer places; we thought we owned the earth and the fullness thereof; and we talked metaphysics.

This life changed when Hawthorne met Miss May Albertina Amelung – known to everyone as "Minne" – in February 1869. Minne was living with her family in Dresden for the same reason Hawthorne was, to save money. Hawthorne's journal recorded long intellectual conversations that reveal earnest but ambivalent affections. These entries mirror *Saxon Studies* insofar as they balance muted admiration with explicit criticism: a first, positive impression is belied by further study.[63] An entry dated 15 April 1869 illustrates this trope:

> Miss A is a very singular young lady ... Her eyes are gray, and shaped differently from each other – the left eyelid sometimes sinks a little over the eye ... Her cheek bones are high, and give her whole expression an air of experience and "hardness"; but the impression wears off a good deal after a while. She is twenty, but ... looks two or three years older ... She wishes to make herself out an ordinary fast American girl ... [but] I am pretty sure, if she ever met an individual who she feared and respected ... she would be true as steel.

On his twenty-third birthday (22 June 1869) Hawthorne confided to his journal that Minne was the birthday present most likely "to elevate and purify my life." But then he immediately distanced his affection and undercut his commitment with the tag line: "Have I met more than my match?" The uncertainty was real. On 3 June, Hawthorne had proposed marriage and Minne had accepted, but within a week they had quarrelled because he had been "fresh" – testing the limits of physical intimacy. "The temptation was strong" not to await the marriage night "and the visible evil little or nothing." They quickly reconciled and spent the afternoon of 19 July "sparking" on a park bench, "to the dismay of passersby."[64]

One day later, Minne left for America. Immediately young Hawthorne distanced himself further from this girl, who, he had earlier written, "will never think of surrender, unless she can freely acknowledge herself quite overmatched and outdone." To encourage that surrender, Julian set about to become what the frail Minne was not – a "marvel of muscle." He worked out regularly with a fifty-pound dumbbell he had acquired for the purpose. By August of the same year he was also busy writing what have been called "conventional but not insincere" love poems – the first literary products he published under his own name. In the historical rather than the literary record these love poems are noteworthy, for they reflect a dissonance between Hawthorne's overheated reveries and a misogynist streak. Later in his career, that unlovely trait would manifest itself in disparagement of almost every woman writer of the nineteenth century.

Minne apparently returned to Europe in 1870. But after a semester or two of unaccomplished attendance at the *Realschule*, Julian followed Minne back to New York. There he was temporarily stranded by the outbreak of the Franco-German War in July 1870. And there he and Minne finally married, in November. Soon he gained employment as a hydrographic engineer under General George B. McClellan in the New York Department of Docks. He began writing more stories and reviews for journals of the day. But new disappointments and new hardships soon intruded. His mother died in February 1871, and the next year he lost his job.

Julian now turned to writing "full time" – as it were. Before long, a sublimated love for Europe pulled him back to Dresden, where he remained from June 1872 until September 1874. While there he published two novels, *Bressant* (1873) and *Idolatry* (1874), which received only marginally more favourable reviews than those we have quoted for *Saxon Studies*. The mixed reception that greeted these novels helps explain why the author never sought to frame his *Saxon Studies* as a work of fiction. As he explained fifteen years later, "In two or three cases I have tried to make portraits of real persons whom I have known; but these persons have always been more lifeless than the others, and most lifeless in precisely those features that most nearly reproduced life." Instead, he sought a style not unlike the one that had served his father well – creating a romantic or even supernatural mood, not a realistic one, based on plausible coincidences that would make the fanciful more accessible to the reader.[65]

Such Gothic tendencies were bolstered by Hawthorne's lifelong fascination with the exotic and the sensual,[66] as demonstrated in lengthy notebook speculations about Salome and, in the late 1890s, his crude notation of sex acts with his mistress.[67] He wrote once that the picaresque was the "true, right form of fiction." But these affinities were theoretical and almost never translated into practice. Hawthorne noted that his novel *Bressant* was "rather morbid, and not crisp and telling." But at this point he had no alternative other than to press ahead, despite his subsequent reaffirmation that *Bressant* was "a good book spoiled": "were it not for the consideration of lucre," he wrote, "I would suppress the edition at once."

Hawthorne gradually became more comfortable with a different method, one he used to observe and record the events in *Saxon Studies*. For example, in a sketch titled "A Golden Wedding in the Best Society,"[68] he described the golden wedding ceremonies of Saxony's King Johann and his wife, which lasted for six days in November 1872 and included a visit to Dresden by Kaiser Wilhelm I and his entourage. In tone and substance this sketch prefigured the sharp, dismissive tone of *Saxon Studies*: it took aim at the "royal little lives" of the Wettin dynasty and their "bigoted old religion." Around the same time that "A Golden Wedding" was written, loutish German officers and other villainous caricatures began to populate Hawthorne's short stories.

Julian Hawthorne's sympathetic biographer Maurice Bassan (1961) granted him a "shrewd perceptiveness": "Hawthorne's eye is a sharp one, and his descriptions as he looks from his study window [and] mingles with the crowds in the streets … betray a keen if not impartial observer."[69] Gary Scharnhorst's biography (2014), based on many hitherto unknown sources, is considerably less generous. Scharnhorst notes that even after installing his father's writing desk in his flat, the younger Hawthorne "composed no great novels and few good ones."[70] In most of Hawthorne's fiction – for example, in "The Real Romance" (1872) – Julian either "compensated for his crude technique with sensational effect" or poked fun at romantic stereotypes.[71] The "fun" we find in *Saxon Studies* is sparing, just as Julian's attempts at fanciful name-play in his fiction have been described as ludicrous and pathetic ("Dr. Hiero Glyphic"). But we should not be deceived that *Saxon Studies* was ever meant to be a reliable travelogue or a faithful chronicle.

What do we know of Hawthorne's material existence while living with his wife and two children on the third floor at Waisenhausstrasse 13 in Dresden for £150 a year?[72] Fragmentary evidence dispels some points of conjecture about why he was so dismissive of Saxons, though it confirms others. He was growing more inclined, temperamentally and artistically, to give free rein to the structural laxness that characterizes *Saxon Studies* and the novels written around the same time. Of *Idolatry*, published not long before *Saxon Studies*, Hawthorne noted retrospectively that, in contrast to previous years in which he had seldom rewritten even a page, this book "was actually rewritten, in whole or in part, no less than seven times … The discipline of 'Idolatry' probably taught me how to clothe an idea in words."[73] An idea, perhaps, but hardly a novel. *Idolatry* has been described as crudely composed and

Figure 5.2 Washerwomen from the suburbs would bring clean laundry to their customers with panniers and carts drawn by various animals, including dogs. Photograph by Rudolf Brauneis, Dresden, c. 1908, in the series *Dresdner Typen*. Stadtmuseum Dresden.

"perhaps the worst book [Hawthorne] ever wrote."[74] What was once said of Bret Harte can be said of Hawthorne's craft: "the long breath was not his."

Physically, the author worked harder. Reliving or trying to revive the athleticism that had drawn admiring looks at Harvard, Hawthorne ran "four or five miles every morning" in Dresden, and he continued working out with that dumbbell. He recorded proudly in March 1873 "that his upper arm measures 14¼ inches, his forearm 11¾ inches, and his chest, inflated, 45 inches."[75] Yet it was symptomatic that although Julian was delighted when he found four Englishmen in May 1873 with whom he could form a rowing crew, he harboured feelings of guilt that their exertions up and down the Elbe usually landed them at a nearby beer garden. Nor could he resist smoking as many as fifteen cigars a day, as he confided to his journal.

Financial room to breathe – that was another concern. In Dresden, Hawthorne never escaped his lifelong flirtation with bankruptcy. "We find our bullion so much decreased," he wrote in 1873, "that we dare not so much as go to the concert."[76] A "brazen system" of theft existed among Dresden tradesman, he claimed: "They can spy a bargain through a stone wall, and a thievish advantage through the lid of a coffin."[77] Neither American nor German reviewers of *Saxon Studies* were correct in assuming that Hawthorne had mixed only with the lowest social classes or that he was perpetually angry with Dresden and its inhabitants. In the winter of 1872–3, for example, the Hawthornes joined happily in the social events that were *de rigueur* during the "season" in Dresden. An American friend who visited in early 1874 found that the Hawthornes lived in "one of the best houses of one of the finest streets in Dresden, amid luxurious surroundings."[78]

Nevertheless, Hawthorne seems to have discovered within himself, and then perhaps consciously nurtured, real doubts about just where he fit in. His longer period of residence was not as carefree as his earlier visit had been in 1869. "Dresden is fast becoming an outpost of American civilization," he wrote – for better and worse. "It has high prices, bad servants, fashionable bonnets, and a Club, not to speak of horse-railroads and rowing regattas."[79] He was twice elected vice-president of the city's American Club, but he pretended to disdain it: "I find [it] absolutely paralyzing & palsying: it is like a stale burial-vault, haunted by the memory of past gentility, which makes it worse."[80] By early 1874, he was again thinking seriously about leaving Dresden – not for America, where *Bressant* was currently gleaning mainly negative reviews, but for England, where the favourable comments of English reviewers had surprised him and reawakened his interest in "lucre." Given that a reviewer in *The Nation* had skewered *Bressant* as containing "a morbid fingering of unclean emotions"[81] and then completely ignored *Idolatry*, perhaps Julian got off lightly with Henry James's review of *Saxon Studies* in the same journal. But these negative reviews help explain why Hawthorne was eager to turn from the racy, pseudo-philosophical, and unappreciated styles he had adopted in those two novels and take up the richer material that a study of contemporary manners in a faraway land might provide.

Hawthorne hoped that the "many disadvantages, both physical and mental," under which *Bressant* had been written would cease to plague him. However, just when he was writing the first sketches that were later fit into *Saxon Studies*, he confided to his diary how heavily his personal and professional fortunes weighed upon him. The famous father, faraway Boston, and the continuing struggle to find both material security for his family and international acclaim for *his* writing are all noted.

On his birthday in June 1873 he wrote that he, like the Saxons he was about to describe, could be both sober and sanguine in the most oppressive circumstances. Yet his claim that he had experienced no sense of restlessness or displacement while living in Saxony rang hollow: "Yesterday 27 years ago I was born in Boston. I had there a father who was a man of genius ... Now I have neither father nor mother; my sister is living alone in London; another sister might be dead for all she is to me ... I am poor and likely long to be so ... I have no sense of loss, of homesickness, of longing: save the ever-present longing to be a man honored by men."[82]

Saxons into Germans

We now know enough about Julian Hawthorne to interpret *Saxon Studies* in a new light.[83] This does not entail reading between the lines so much as sensitizing ourselves to the opportunities for ironic detachment that Hawthorne sought in tackling his subject. It is not difficult to find passages in *Saxon Studies* where the outsider-as-insider-as-outsider speaks to the theme of hybrid identities.

Let's start with geese. Geese, writes Hawthorne, "constitute a goodly proportion of the village population" of any Saxon community – and "they are invariably at home." This Goose-*Gemeinschaft* reveals something important about Saxon social relations, believes Hawthorne. "How happens it, now, that there should be so many geese in Saxon villages? ... I fear there must be an occult vein of sympathy between them and their owners, reaching deeper than the flavor of roast goose ... can justify; some mutual consciousness of similar dispositions" (47). While not overly prideful of their military accomplishments, goose-stepping Saxons, to Hawthorne, reflect a German tendency to over-organize everything and thereby privilege the needs of the community over the rights of the individual.[84] It is a hateful ordering of priorities, he implies, that both delivers and elicits the response so typical of the enraged goose: "There is admirable unanimity in a flock of geese, as though each were magnetically conscious of all his companions' sentiments and emotions. All wish to do the same thing at the same time ... Yet is each goose a kingdom to himself; pride waddles in his gait, and unbounded self-complacency wallows with him in the dirt. You may easily put him to flight; but out of countenance – never! ... There is something very human in their hiss."

Hawthorne is equally disenchanted with the way Saxons manage nature. After visiting the *Bastei* in Saxon Switzerland – a natural rock outcrop that overlooks the Elbe for miles in each direction – he inverts the usual American wonderment at its beauty. For him, it is literally and metaphorically anomalous. Whereas German literature has produced "cloud-capped giants" that give the land its reputation, Hawthorne asks: "Why so flat and tedious, O Saxony?" But the author is not talking just about wastelands and hollow men: he is disappointed that the march of *moral* progress has not yet reached Saxon territory. "Is there any remedy?" he asks. "I see none, short of a general eruption, whereby the whole surface might be broken up in volcanoes, and become a Switzerland indeed. And may the physical upheaval be prophetic of a moral one. It is of significance that mountainous tracts are generally inclined to freedom" (62–3).

Saxon forests, too, are to blame: Hawthorne can't escape them. "I do not like to see my path marked out before me," he writes. "I am kept perpetually in mind of the nearness of mankind." We are not in a position to say precisely what Hawthorne was trying to escape in seeking anonymity and refuge in the dark Saxon woods, or even what sort of artistic inspiration he hoped to find there. But perhaps we can understand his peevishness about German *Ordnung* by parsing his words about the oppressiveness of the Saxon forest:[85]

> It is a noticeable trait of this country – the impossibility of getting beyond every-day limits. There is no seclusion, whereof we may feign ourselves the first invaders, and, as such, secure from pursuit or encounter. There is no profound wildness, even where the surroundings seem least tame. The woods are supervised by foresters ... Who but a hypocrite would pretend to lose himself in a forest, all of whose trees were numbered? ... We may find them set forth in the forester's book thus: "No. 27. Oak. Heinrich the Stout." "No. 28. Elm. Karl the Long-legged." What is to happen to a people who can do such things as this? (57)

We have already remarked that Hawthorne insisted on distinguishing between the exterior and interior sides of life in a foreign land. During his stay in Dresden he would almost certainly have heard natives describe Saxony's place in Germany as Heinrich von Treitschke described it in the summer of 1866: "Dresden is ultimately a large spa, a quiet place for rich and retired people ... From Saxon patriotic lore [continued Treitschke] I have learned that Germany is the heart of Europe, Saxony is the heart of Germany, and Dresden is the heart of Saxony. But ... even a Dresden child realizes that in any Prussian provincial capital, there is more true big-city life than in this deepest ventricle of the world."[86] Hawthorne uses a different metaphor, but his target is the same as Treitschke's. "[Many houses] in Dresden are lifeless shells, or nearly so. They look like empty, ugly, overgrown hotels; no human life and bustle informs them. They would seem to have been born insignificant, and subsequently, for no sufficient reason, to have expanded into gawky giantship. In this respect they might be compared with the Saxon people, who possess no qualities to warrant their rising above pygmydom, but whom an ironic freak of destiny has uplifted to a foremost place among nations. They should be taken down and reconstructed upon a smaller and more economic scale" (135–6).

Yet we would be wrong to suppose that the brush with which Hawthorne tars all Saxons is so broad that it cannot render detail. "When I read of a country unknown or only slightly known," wrote Cicely Sidgwick, the author of *Home Life in Germany* (1912), "I like to be told all the insignificant trifles that make the common round of life."[87] Hawthorne agrees. Indeed, the details of the lived environment become programmatic for him. This helps explain why the "trivialities" that reviewers of *Saxon Studies* dismissed so readily hold value for historians. Thus, in a chapter titled "Sidewalks and Roadways," Hawthorne takes on the mantle of a social anthropologist. He is determined to help us understand the connections between the unique and the universal. Cities, Hawthorne pronounces, represent nothing less than *doctrines*, though they appear as bricks and mortar:

> To the vulgar mind the word city conveys the idea of streets and houses, and nothing more; or at best (if they have read Blackstone), of a town which has or had something to do with a bishop. Strictly speaking, however, these walls and pavements are but the incarnation of the true city, which primarily inheres in the brains and wills of the citizens (127) ... [Let the observer] describe what he will – a paving stone or a door-knob, a window-blind or a church-steeple – he can always rebut the charge of triviality by admonishing the critic of a hidden symbolism contained in the passage, the vital significance of which only ignorance or levity could overlook. And if, in the course of his narrative, he happen upon some hit of personal gossip, some human characteristic, humorous or pathetic, let him admit it without fear of inconsistency ...
>
> In these days of the ballot, and of universal suffrage, some enthusiastic elector may object, that the true representatives of a people's doctrines are, not the cities they live in, but the gentlemen they return to Congress or to Parliament. (128)

> The suggestion is a valuable one ... Every man is a microcosm, but some advance must be made in uniformity of condition and opinion, and in consistency of belief, before it would be possible for him, humanly speaking, to become a micropolis. His incongruities would kill him, in real life; even the creations of modern fiction could scarcely fulfil the exigencies of the position. (129)

If a précis is, by definition, faulty when diversity is being rendered in the ironic mode, Hawthorne is alive to this dilemma and does his best to slip between its horns.

One last example will suffice to illustrate how Hawthorne addresses the problem of portraying both uniqueness and universality within German diversity. In the following passage, Hawthorne examines Germany's fragile unity in the early 1870s with uncharacteristically broad humour – which may explain why it was never cited by contemporary reviewers. Despite his avowed interest in unwrapping "a romantic and poetical enigma," his analogy here is more explicitly political than any other in the book. It turns on the question of where encroachments on local brewing customs might ultimately lead. Hawthorne's logical but intentionally absurd conclusion is that the "life-blood of the country" must remain local, not national. Otherwise, he suggests, the last iota of sub-national identity will disappear into the Black Hole of Bismarck's centralizing tendencies:

> This liquor [German beer] can be neither brewed nor exported beyond the Father-land; nay, a journey of but a few miles from its birthplace impairs its integrity. Why – is a romantic and poetical enigma ...
>
> A profound political truth is symbolized here, if we would but see it; it elucidates the subject of emigration and the effect of locality on temperament ... Now, the Berlin Government seems desirous of proving (what we Americans have already proved to the world's satisfaction, if not to our own), that people living, no matter how far apart and under what different circumstances, may be united in mind, sentiment, and disposition as one man. To this end, what method more effective than to ordain a universal beer, and forbid the brewing or drinking of any other? Condense into one the many inconsiderable principalities of Gambrinus ... Surely Prince Bismarck, who can do so much, will not be beaten by a beverage: the difficulty will be ultimately overcome, if military discipline and legislation be worth anything. Two alternatives suggest themselves at once. The first, to create a uniform climate, soil, and water, throughout the Father-land,

– not an impossibility to German science, I should suppose; the second, to brew the beer nowhere save in Berlin, to be drunk on the premises ... If, as is believed, Germans are Germans by virtue of the beer they drink, if all drank the same beer, of course they all would become the same Germans.

Moreover, if this may be done with the nation, why not apply the principle to the individual? ... If a nation may be concentrated at a single point, as Berlin, why not concentrate the persons composing it into a single individual, as Bismarck? Having swallowed his countrymen, the prince could thereafter legislate to please himself, and might ultimately proceed to swallow himself into a universal atom. (76–8)

Leave-Taking; or, The Death of the German Cousin

We have already determined why Julian Hawthorne was happy to bid goodbye to Dresden in the autumn of 1874. Ultimately, we cannot know whether he went to Dresden as a passionate pilgrim, to escape looming disappointments in New York, or because of the lure of lucre. We have also documented some of the affronts he suffered in the Saxon capital. Hints in the text (23–8, 411–15) suggest that Hawthorne may have become either infatuated or actually involved with a Saxon woman while his wife was pregnant with their third child. From the venomous passage directed against Saxon merchants we can surmise that Hawthorne was cheated by local tradesmen (211–13). He may even have been the unnamed American who bled profusely (but who ultimately bettered his German opponent) in the mandatory duelling scene (308–10). But it is in the Preface to *Saxon Studies*, which so baffled Henry James, and in its final lines, that Hawthorne works the magic that (almost) reveals all.

The Preface announces how Hawthorne will seek the universal in the unique. He writes that "under cover of discussing certain aspects of Dresden life," he "has stolen entrance to a far wider field of observation and remark." He claims "that his interest in Saxony and the Saxons is of the most moderate kind, – certainly not enough to provoke a treatise upon them." But the "plan of his work" has required "some concrete nucleus round which to group such thoughts and fancies as he wished to ventilate." Since Dresden had "chanced" to have been his residence of late, he has "used it, rather than any other place, to serve his turn in this respect." Therefore, he is not in the least worried that a critic might discover nothing essentially Saxon in *Saxon Studies*: on the contrary, he writes, he would "insist upon thinking such a verdict complimentary" (3–4).

Hawthorne has also planned *Saxon Studies* to examine built environments and local customs; but he is not presuming he can improve either. The author proclaims boldly that he has no wish to be seen as a "patcher-up of dilapidated manners and morals" (5). His misanthropic appraisal of Saxon society and his determination "to speak home truths on this subject" are motivated "by reason of the mawkish tendency, very observable of late, to make Germans of all people in the world, and Saxons with them, objects of sentimental hero-worship." He claims that everything he includes in *Saxon Studies* errs on the side of being too mild rather than too severe (4). As historians, we may accept or reject his pronouncements about the backwardness or modernity of Saxon society, about the centralizing or centrifugal tendencies in German politics, about the respect or disrespect paid to policemen and soldiers, and about the accuracy with which he sketches the look and feel of Saxon villages, towns, and cities. However, to dismiss Hawthorne's book as inept caricature is to miss other, richer ways of seeing the local in literature.

Hawthorne's personal disappointments seem to be reflected nowhere more clearly than in the final lines of *Saxon Studies*. As he takes leave of Dresden, he wants us to know that his stay has not been a fleeting one. He has taken the time to learn some hard lessons about Saxon life – and, we are meant to suppose, about life itself. The bookends of Hawthorne's analysis emphasize that the charm with which Dresden envelopes the unwary traveller is deceitful. "[Dresden] charms at first sight – at a distance – or mirrored in the glass of the imagination." There is a "mirage of grace and neatness" about the city that captivates the visitor unawares. Nearer study, he writes, "dispels all illusions: we discover various unlovely traits, intrinsic no less than accidental." The verdict *seems* unequivocal. "The place is in bad hands," the author writes. It is "vulgarly companioned" and "invested with a questionable atmosphere." "It is impossible to enjoy [Dresden's] beauties apart from its defects," he concludes; "the latter are innate, the former purely superficial." Therefore Dresden is all the more disappointing now that it is time to bid it farewell. Its initial promise was great. But that promise, like the author's own, remains unfulfilled. Hawthorne has neither lost himself in anonymity as the innocent abroad nor fully come to terms with the expectations that continue to rest upon his shoulders years after his father's death. "The parting disappointment is the saddest of all," he writes, precisely because "so few and slight regrets attend our last farewell!" (451–2).

But is this *in fact* the final impression Hawthorne wants to convey?

Mr Hawthorne's Secret[88]

To address this question and conclude this chapter, some final musings are in order about Hawthorne's hybrid identities. Two observations on the power of Mark Twain's writing are à propos here.[89] Arthur Miller once wrote that we keep reading Twain because he "wrote much more like a father than a son." Miller continued the thought: "[Twain] doesn't seem to be sitting in class taunting the teacher but standing at the head of it challenging his students to acknowledge their own humanity, that is, their immemorial attraction to the untrue."[90] *Saxon Studies* was condemned because it was so patently untrue – so taunting. But was genuine edification from "the head of the class" what Hawthorne offered his readers? Or was he more interested in the "attraction of the untrue"? The second observation springs from Bobbie Ann Mason's suggestion that Mark Twain "relied on the punch of plain words" to show nineteenth-century American writers how to move beyond the "wordy romantic rubbish" that still predominated in the New World fiction of the day. As Mason put it, Twain was "one of the first writers in America to deflower literary language."[91]

Julian Hawthorne did no such thing. On the contrary: he prized imagination too highly, he scorned "the rush of rational knowledge" and the touchstone of scientific truth too consistently, to embrace plain language as either his medium or his message. He was "the spiritual son" of Coleridge and Emerson: for him, the imaginative process had to begin in nature and refuse to distort it. Art depended not upon literal fact but upon perception of what Hawthorne once called "the underlying truth, of which fact is but the phenomenal and imperfect shadow."[92] The authorial voice towards which Hawthorne was groping in *Saxon Studies* fans out to cover a variety of meanings, but none of them bear any resemblance to Realism, let alone Naturalism.[93] As the reviews of *Saxon Studies* made clear, no evidence of Nathanial Hawthorne's genial humour could be found in his son's writing either.

Some sixty years after *Saxon Studies* was published, Hawthorne reminisced about his *Sturm und Drang* period of the 1870s. Retrospectively he disagreed with Henry James that this was the kind of book a young author would soon regret. He even claimed that *Saxon Studies* "was the best book I ever wrote." Oh dear, we shudder. But Hawthorne's retrospective expression of delight that the *Dresdner Nachrichten*'s reviewer had demolished his book, like his proud claim that "the German emperor was moved to issue an edict forbidding its circulation in his dominions," indicates how ironic the book was meant to be and how playful he still felt about it decades later.[94] To the end of his life he would insist that he had "made fun of the Dresdeners" and "peppered them with sarcasms, though not ill naturedly."[95]

The clues are all there.[96] The 1932 article where he wrote about *Saxon Studies* bore the title "Recalling Heinrich Heine." In it Hawthorne explained that in 1876 he had been moved to have the *Dresdner Nachrichten* review – the "critic's curse" – translated and fixed to the flyleaf of the book. As he put it, the German reviewer had "repaid me for the labor of composition and satisfied me that I had not done amiss." The *Nachrichten*'s rant, *not* his own, was deemed worthy "to put the Anglo-Saxon reader in tune with my little satire." This half-twist of the knife did not have the intended effect when his publishers went bankrupt: "fate was too swift for me," and "the circulation of the 'Studies' was naturally small."[97] But we must not be fooled by smallness *or* fate. Hawthorne, at any rate, was pleased by the little splash made by his little book. Years later, while living in Chicago, he authored a parody of a guidebook, *Humours of the Fair*, which, like *Saxon Studies*, was intentionally "an antidote to the various guidebooks which you will be compelled to buy, or have already bought." Hawthorne on that occasion repeated the warning – or the assurance – that he included in *Saxon Studies*: he had expended "sustained effort to divest its pages of anything that could be construed as Useful Information."[98]

We have reached this conclusion about the need to understand Hawthorne in the satirical mode by combining study of the text and study of the intellectual environment in which it was written. We have not so much retraced Hawthorne's intellectual journey as taken a separate path to the same point of discovery he reached. Identity "is not about one's given place, but about one's chosen position."[99] Hawthorne's identity at the time he wrote *Saxon Studies* was hybrid, but it held at least a kernel of universality within it, in a manner suggested by Walt Whitman in *Song of Myself*:[100]

> Do I contradict myself?
> Very well then I contradict myself,
> (I am large, I contain multitudes.)

Hawthorne's self-image in the mid-1870s was more coherent than it had been in the 1860s, but it was still fragile and in flux, in a manner suggested by the Argentinian writer Jorge Luis Borges when he wrote that, if the visible universe is an illusion, then "mirrors and fatherhood are abominable because they multiply and extend it."[101] Hawthorne's self-awareness was reflective, even though his journey to self-knowledge would continue for many years. He thought Dresden looked best when seen in the nineteenth-century equivalent of a rear-view mirror. Therefore the up-close grubbiness he portrayed was intentionally unattractive. To the extent that he took a realistic approach at all, that realism was narrow and reductive, derivative and strained. But he had discovered, and we along with him, that familiar objects can indeed be larger than they appear in reflection.

At the time *Saxon Studies* was written, Hawthorne probably surprised even himself in the degree to which he transcended, fleetingly, those barriers to artistic creativity that plagued him throughout his life. W.H. Auden once wrote that a poet can hope for no more than "to be, like some valley cheese, local, but prized everywhere."[102] That final leave-taking from Dresden at the end the book *is* more brooding than poetic. But we should not ignore the author's genuine expectation that *Saxon Studies* would be more popular than his novels. More important still, we should not disregard his personal delight that he had successfully disguised his book's hidden ironies.

Can *Saxon Studies* be seen as an "interesting moment in the history of American reaction to Europe"? Does it deserve a place "in the American-abroad genre of jaundiced realism"?[103] The jury is still out. But one suspects that Julian Hawthorne would have agreed with Montreal's own irascibly hybrid Mordecai Richler, who once noted that to become a tramp abroad is to rediscover how even our most jaded senses are heightened by "all things counter, original, spare, [and] strange."[104]

NOTES

1 Julian Hawthorne, *Saxon Studies* (Boston, 1876) (*SS*; hereafter most page numbers from the book are included in the main text). Installments of *Saxon Studies* began appearing in Alexander Strahan's *Contemporary Review* in November 1874 and ended in November 1875. Other contributors to the journal in these months included T.H. Huxley and Matthew Arnold.
2 Cited in Gary Scharnhorst, *Julian Hawthorne: The Life of a Prodigal Son* (Urbana, IL, 2014), 75.
3 On this subject – but not this one alone – Hawthorne's rebukes are mild compared to those of Henry Mayhew in *German Life and Manners As Seen in*

Saxony at the Present Day: With an Account of Village Life – Town Life – Fashionable Life – Domestic Life – Married Life – School and University Life, Etc., of Germany at the Present Time, 2 vols. (London, 1864), 1: 361: "English servants may be plagues, but the German ones are a species of vermin far more troublesome than any which ever tormented poor Moses in Egypt – vermin in their love of dirt, vermin in the loathsomeness of their habits, and vermin in the amount of irritation to which they can subject anyone with the least notion of cleanliness or decency, and who happens to be a shade less thick-skinned than a rhinoceros, or is a degree more civilized than a Cossack."

4 "Saxon soldiers are the best in the world. They can swallow most discipline. They submit to so much stuffing with rules and regulations, great and small, that little of the original creature is left save organic life and uniform. They are a docile sort of Frankensteins ... It would be edifying to contrast Saxon soldiers with other nations, point by point, and so arrive at a practical comprehension of their superiority. Much is signified in the fact that their captains address them as 'children,' while we Americans, and our English friends, try to inspire our warriors by appeals to their 'manhood.' Men, forsooth! Such is the fruit of illogical sentiment. But persist in calling a person child, and treating him so, and presently he will share our view of the matter, and thus become fit for the camp. But my business is not so much with comparisons" (*SS*, 317f.).

5 Sidney Whitman, a well-connected foreigner who was a frequent guest of the Bismarck family and had his portrait painted by Franz Lenbach, provides a valuable barometer of how Saxon life changed in the second half of the century. Whitman entered Dresden's famous Vitzthum Gymnasium in 1859 and then returned in the autumn of 1903 to attend the inauguration of a new school building, now taken over by the city of Dresden. He described the changes in the intervening decades: "The German upper classes are no longer brought up in that spirit of reverence and frugality which was general fifty years ago. Those that I saw appeared to have become fossilized with the bourgeoisie rising upon the débris." Whitman, *German Memories* (London, 1912), 16; see also Whitman, *Imperial Germany: A Critical Study of Fact and Character* (Leipzig, 1890), 73, where among Germany's ruling dynasties only the Hohenzollerns are said to have demonstrated a "freedom from rascality."

6 George Knox, "Dissonance Abroad: Julian Hawthorne's *Saxon Studies*," *Essex Institute Historical Collections* 96 (April 1960): 131–9.

7 Sigmund Freud, *New Introductory Lectures on Psychoanalysis* (1933), cited in *The Oxford Dictionary of Quotations*, edited by Elizabeth Knowles (Oxford, 2001), 324.

8 "Had I a grudge against Dresden, with power to back it, I would overthrow her towers. Had they never been erected, the city would today have been unknown. The traveller, downward-gazing from yonder long-backed hill, and beholding a flattened swarm of mean-featured houses spreading dingily on both sides of a muddy river, would have hastened on to carry fame and fortune elsewhere" (SS, 13).

9 Dresden for centuries has been referred to as "Florence on the Elbe."

10 See Celia Applegate, "The Mediated Nation: Regions, Readers, and the German Past," in *Saxony in German History: Culture, Society, and Politics, 1830–1933*, edited by James Retallack (Ann Arbor, 2000), 33–50, esp. 42–3: "Much of the popular appeal of Riehl's *Naturgeschichte* lay in its capacity to take the reader along on such a journey over the backroads, pausing – as his 'trade secrets' suggest – to make direct inquiries of the 'educated man,' indirect inquiries of the less educated man, and to engage in rambling conversation with the local peasants ... The genius of Riehl's presentation is to suggest just how *ordinary* these 'countless voyages of discovery into the German heartland' actually are, and how *accessible* they are to anyone at any time" (original emphasis).

11 Consider the parallel drawn by Sidney Whitman in *German Memories*, 236, when he called upon the Saxon socialist leader August Bebel in Berlin in the winter of 1890–1: "Bebel reminded me somewhat, by his manner and cast of features, of a type I was familiar with in Saxony, where the mass of the people are largely of Slavonic stock, having something also of the Celt, with some affinity to the type of Keir Hardie."

12 Hawthorne elides Saxon and German opinion on this point: "Only Germans can properly be said to possess a national drink; beer takes with them the place of all other beverages; an American bar, with its myriad eye-openers and stone-walls, would be absurdly out of place here. The Saxon's palate is not tickled with variety; one thing suffices him, which he loves as he loves himself – because it has become a part of him. It fascinates him, not as aught new and strange, which might be potent for a time, but eventually palls. But it is dear to him as are the ruddy drops which visit his sad heart – a steady, perennial, exclusive affection, constant as his very selfishness" (SS, 81).

13 The reference is to the Battle of Sedan (1–2 September 1870) when the army of Emperor Napoleon III was routed in the Franco-German War. In his essays *On the Study of Celtic Literature* (1867), 81–2, Matthew Arnold had identified German coarseness and Saxon phlegm as defining aspects of philistinism. Although Arnold praised familiar German traits (industry, science, etc.), he did not differ much from Hawthorne in painting the

negative side of things: "The universal dead-level of plainness and homeliness, the lack of all beauty and distinction in form and feature, the slowness and clumsiness of the language, the eternal beer, sausages, and bad tobacco, the blank commonness everywhere, pressing at last like a weight on the spirits of the traveller in Northern Germany, and making him impatient to be gone." Cited in Fritz Schultz, *Der Deutsche in der englischen Literatur vom Beginn der Romantik bis zum Ausbruch des Weltkrieges* (Halle, 1939), 106.

14 Here Hawthorne was distinctly unoriginal. See Mayhew, *German Life*, 2: 640–1: "the Government is left to do as it pleases – to treat the people as though they were literally the *children* of the Fatherland: to deal with them, indeed, as the German nurses do with newly-born infants – bind the poor things in no end of swaddling clothes, till they have not the power to move either hand or foot, as if the Almighty had never intended them to have the least liberty, and as if it were better to prevent them going alone as long as possible" (original emphasis).

15 By contrast, see "The Criminal Practice of Saxony," an anonymous American study based on 'some months' attendance, off and on, upon the criminal courts of Dresden," in *American Law Review* 9 (1874–5): 459–68: "The jurisprudence and practice of Saxony are reputed to be the most scientific and complete in the German States ... A little book which can be had for twenty-five cents contains the whole criminal law of Germany ... The general intelligibility and expedition [of this book] ... are in strong contrast to the frequent cumbrousness of our own, and let a stronger light into these sacred mysteries ... The juries are respectable and trustworthy in appearance, evidently drawn from the upper and middle classes ...
In general, their duties are well and carefully performed, with perhaps a leaning towards mercy ... No bullying of witnesses, no tyrannizing over the court, and above all no cross-examination. This last consideration is one that must give us pause ... It is a perversion of justice ... when the issue of a case can be made to depend upon the strength of counsel. That this is notoriously the fact with us [in the USA] need not be urged" (459–61, 465–6).

16 Mordecai Richler, "Introduction," in Mark Twain, *The Innocents Abroad* (orig. 1869), edited by Shelley Fisher Fischkin (Oxford, 1996), xxxvi.

17 Detlef Junker, *The Manichaean Trap: American Perceptions of the German Empire, 1871–1945* (German Historical Institute, Washington, DC, Occasional Paper no. 12) (Washington, 1995).

18 Eberhard Brüning, "'Saxony is a prosperous and happy country': American Views of the Kingdom of Saxony in the Nineteenth Century," in *Traveling*

between Worlds: German–American Encounters, edited by Thomas Adam and Ruth Gross (College Station, TX, 2006), 20–50. This essay is a slightly revised translation of Brüning, "Sachsen mit amerikanischen Augen gesehen. Das Sachsenbild amerikanischer Globetrotter im 19. Jahrhundert," *Neues Archiv für sächsische Geschichte* 67 (1996): 109–31; cf. Thomas Adam, "Germany Seen Through American Eyes: George and Anna Eliot Ticknor's German Travel Logs," in *Transatlantic Cultural Contexts: Essays in Honor of Eberhard Brüning,* edited by Hartmut Keil (Tübingen, 2005), 151–63.

19 For example, Bayard Taylor, *Views A-Foot or Europe Seen with Knapsack and Staff* (orig. 1846), rev. ed. (New York and London, 1892), 204: "As far as I have yet seen, Saxony is a prosperous and happy country. The people are noted all over Germany for their honest social character, which is written on their cheerful, open countenances." Similar works consulted for this section include Charles Loring Brace, *Home-Life in Germany* (orig. 1853) (New York, 1856); Pierre M. Irving, *The Life and Letters of Washington Irving,* 4 vols. (New York, 1863–4); *Autobiography of Andrew Dickson White,* 2 vols. (London, 1905); Wolfgang Drechsler, *Andrew D. White in Deutschland. Der Vertreter der USA in Berlin 1879–1881 und 1897–1902* (Stuttgart, 1989); Johann Georg, Herzog zu Sachsen, ed., *Briefwechsel König Johanns von Sachsen mit George Ticknor* (Leipzig and Berlin, 1920), esp. 135 on Americans' failure to understand Germany; and Price Collier, *Germany and the Germans from an American Point of View* (Toronto, 1913).

20 Among guides to this literature I have found the following most useful: John G. Gazley, *American Opinion of German Unification, 1848–1871* (New York, 1926); Otto Graf zu Stolberg-Wernigerode, *Deutschland und die Vereinigten Staaten von Amerika im Zeitalter Bismarcks* (Berlin and Leipzig, 1933); Peter Krüger, "Die Beurteilung der Reichsgründung und der Reichsverfassung von 1871 in den USA," in *Liberalitas. Festschrift für Erich Angermann,* edited by Norbert Finzsch and Hermann Wellenreuther (Stuttgart, 1992), 263–83; Clara Eve Schieber, *The Transformation of American Sentiment toward Germany, 1870–1914* (New York, 1923, rpt. 1973). See also two essays in David E. Barclay and Elisabeth Glaser-Schmidt, eds., *Transatlantic Images and Perceptions: Germany and America since 1776* (New York and Cambridge, 1997): Hermann Wellenreuther, "'Germans Make Cows and Women Work': American Perceptions of Germans as Reported in American Travel Books, 1800–1840," 41–64; and Jörg Nagler, "From Culture to *Kultur:* Changing American Perceptions of Imperial Germany, 1870–1914," 131–54; as well as Barclay and Glaser-Schmidt, "Introduction," 1–17. See also Konrad H. Jarausch, "Huns, Krauts or Good Germans? The German Image in America, 1800–1980," in *German–American Interrelations:*

Heritage and Challenge, edited by James F. Harris (Tübingen, 1985), 145–59, esp. 147–9; Henry Cord Meyer, *Five Images of Germany: Half a Century of American Views on German History* (Washington, DC, n.d. [1960]); and Waldemar Zacharasiewicz, *Images of Germany in American Literature* (Iowa City, 2007).

21 Napoleon III's meddling in Mexico still rankled, whereas German eagerness to help the Union cause by buying up US war bonds had left a legacy of goodwill. Only a few American newspapers declared the Germans' desire for unity in 1870–1 to be humbug: "If the war were for a German Republic or German unity in any sense save in a despotic one, American sympathies might tend in a widely different direction," wrote the *Boston Post* on 30 July 1870; cited in Schieber, *The Transformation*, 19; see also Junker, *The Manichaean Trap*, 11–12; Krüger, "Die Beurteilung," passim. Compare US views cited in ch. 2 of the present volume.

22 Wellenreuther, "Germans," notes (44) that early-nineteenth-century American travel reports did not stress regional Germany either; the usual stopping-off points were relatively few in number (the Rhine Valley, Heidelberg, Munich, Berlin, and Dresden), as John Adams noted early in the century. The British were prone to the same sin of omission: see my review of Richard Scully, *British Images of Germany: Admiration, Antagonism, and Ambivalence, 1860–1914* (Basingstoke, 2012), *German History* 31 (2013): 315–16.

23 See ch. 2 for the view of an American diplomat in Brussels, who wrote enthusiastically to US Secretary of State William Seward on 31 August 1866, linking the Prussian victory over Austria with the uncertain progress of democracy in Great Britain.

24 Thus Bancroft wrote to the US Secretary of State Hamilton Fish on 18 October 1870 that Germany was America's best ally in Europe, "because German institutions and ours most nearly resemble each other." Bancroft added that the Franco-German War "will leave Germany the most powerful state in Europe, and the most free." Cited in Schieber, *The Transformation*, 11.

25 "German Legislation," in *American Law Review* 10 (1875–6): 273, cited in Krüger, "Die Beurteilung," 280.

26 On 16 August 1866 an article in *The Nation* asked whether a "Prussianized" Germany would jeopardize the liberties of the people. "Will it not kill the little that is left of free and parliamentary institutions and, in the end, be a mere military despotism which knows only rulers and ruled? We believe not. There is no disaster in Germany's being Prussianized. On the contrary, if Prussia extends her influence over Germany, it will be a great blessing.

Prussia, with her good schools and freedom of commerce and industry, with her liberty of conscience and the self-government of the towns and villages, with an army established on a democratic basis [!], with her developed industrial resources, will confer the benefits of her own institutions upon the German people at large, and will soon make them feel one and the same." Cited in Krüger, "Die Beurteilung," 266.

27 George Bancroft (1800–1891) was US Minister at Berlin from 1867 to 1874. A trained historian, he had received his doctorate at the University of Göttingen in 1820.

28 Attempts to compare British diplomats' and travellers' accounts of German life have been sporadic, but see *inter alia* Günter Hollenberg, *Englisches Interesse am Kaiserreich* (Wiesbaden, 1874); Keith Robbins, *Present and Past: British Images of Germany in the First Half of the Twentieth Century and Their Historical Legacy* (Göttingen, 1999), esp. 19–29; M.E. Humble, "The Breakdown of a Consensus: British Writers and Anglo-German Relations 1900–1920," *Journal of European Studies* 7 (1977): 41–68; Paul M. Kennedy, "Idealists and Realists: British Views of Germany, 1864–1939," *Transactions of the Royal Historical Society*, Fifth Series, vol. 25 (London, 1975), 137–56; Kurt Weineck, *Deutschland und der Deutsche im Spiegel der englischen erzählenden Literatur seit 1830* (Halle, 1938); Schultz, *Der Deutsche in der englischen Literatur*; Günter Blaicher, *Das Deutschlandbild in der englishen Literatur* (Darmstadt, 1992), esp. chs. 2 and 6.

29 This was the description provided by the Positivist and political Radical Frederic Harrison; for similar comments from James Bryce, Henry Mayhew, and George Eliot, see Peter Pulzer, "Special Paths or Main Roads? Making Sense of German History," Elie Kedourie Memorial Lecture, *Proceedings of the British Academy* 21 (2003): 213–34 at 219. One of the most perceptive analyses of German society was provided by an American student in Berlin who personified more than one kind of hybridity: W.E.B. Du Bois, "The Present Condition of German Politics (1893)," reprinted with editorial comment by Kenneth Barkin in *Central European History* 31, no. 3 (1998): 171–88.

30 See, for example, Schieber, *The Transformation*, 27. Many American newspapers had "deplored the fact that France had stooped to the employment of African troops 'in this age of civilization to fight a civilized nation.'" But with the continuing bombardment, doubts quickly crept into US opinion on the legitimacy of Prussian tactics.

31 Walt Whitman and Julia Ward Howe, cited in Jarausch, "Huns," 148–9. See also Robbins, *Present and Past*, 19–20. The philosopher Frederick Harrison put it this way: "Let us embrace the savant, the artist, the poet of the

Fatherland. But let us keep our powder dry – and study the birth, the growth, and the future of Bismarckism." Frederick Harrison, *National and Social Problems* (London, 1908), cited in Kennedy, "Idealists and Realists," 140–1. See also Collier, *Germany*, 84–5. On France and Prussia, liberalism, and *Geist* and *Ungeist*, see Matthew Arnold, *Friendship's Garland: Being the Conversations, Letters, and Opinions of the late Arminius Baron von Thunder-ten-Tronckh* (London, 1903), 6–9.

32 Exceptions here include Lord Odo Russell's report of 7 September 1872, which has Hawthorne's ironic ring to it: "Berlin is in a blaze of Sunshine, Uniforms, and Imperial flags, tempered by clouds of Dust and horrid smells. – But everybody and his wife [*sic*] are overjoyed at the prospect of eternal Peace which the 3 Emperors are to decree to Europe." (The Russian tsar and the Austro-Hungarian emperor visited Berlin from 5 to 11 September 1872.) Cited in Paul Knaplund, ed., *Letters from the Berlin Embassy: Selections from the Private Correspondence of British Representatives at Berlin and Foreign Secretary Lord Granville, 1871–1874, 1880–1885*, 3 vols. (Washington, DC, 1942), 1: 65. Russell soured on Bismarck and the Germans later in the 1870s and early 1880s. In a letter to his friend and fellow German expert Robert Morier in 1882, Russell condemned the "shit-fear" (*Scheissangst*) of the Germans that made them kneel before the power of the Reich chancellor. Cited in Karina Urbach, *Bismarck's Favourite Englishman: Lord Odo Russell's Mission to Berlin* (London and New York, 1999), 86. Compare the humour in John Lothrop Motley's letter to his mother, written from Dresden, 3 February 1853: "His Majesty is a mild old gentleman, wadded and bolstered into very harmonious proportions. He has a single tooth worn carelessly on one side, which somewhat interferes with his eloquence … The Queen is very tall and very queenly … I am not at liberty to mention her conversation with myself. Indeed I did not understand a single word she said, and was entirely ignorant of what language she was speaking, but I have since ascertained that it was probably French … The ball was not particularly brilliant. The costumes of the gentlemen were slightly shabby. Those of the ladies were not remarkable … There were the statesmen of world-wide reputation, the sages and law-givers on whose accents the world hangs with enthusiasm, the generals … [who] must all be as eminent as Metternich or Talleyrand, Wellington or Blücher, Marshal Ney or King Murat, to judge from the trophies on their bosoms … I am quite satisfied that they are all destined for immortality … The etiquette is perhaps more formal since the reaction after '48. I suppose it is thought necessary to effect thorough repairs in the divinity which hedges kings, the said hedge having had so many gaps made in it by irreverent poachers in latter

days." *The Correspondence of John Lothrop Motley*, edited by George William Curtis, 2 vols. (New York, 1889), 1: 149–52.

33 See Heinz-Joachim Müllenbrock, "Trugbilder: Zum Dilemma imagologischer Forschung am Beispiel des englischen Deutschlandbildes 1870–1914," in *Anglia* 113, no. 3 (1995), 303–29 at 303 for the following passages. See also Keith Robbins, "National Identity and History: Past, Present and Future," in *History, Religion and Identity in Modern Britain* (London, 1993): 27–44; and Robbins, *Protestant Germany through British Eyes: A Complex Victorian Encounter*, 1992 Annual Lecture of the German Historical Institute, London (London, 1993).

34 For negative images of Germans in British literature that reflect both polarized and hybrid stereotypes after 1890, see Müllenbrock, "Trugbilder," 322–4, including the following lines from George Meredith, *One of Our Conquerers* (1891): "This German has the habit of pushing past politeness to carry his argumentative war into the enemy's country: and he presents on all sides a solid rampart of recent great deeds done, and mailed readiness for the doing of more, if we think of assailing him in that way. We are really like the poor beasts which have cast their shells or cases, helpless flesh to his beak. *So we are cousinly*" (324, emphasis added).

35 Having failed to find the word "imagology" in either my *Oxford English Dictionary* or my *Webster's Dictionary*, the following provided guidance: William W. Stowe, *Going Abroad: European Travel in Nineteenth-Century American Culture* (Princeton, 1994); Holger Klein, "Zerrspiegel? – Bilder von Preußen-Deutschland in englischer Prosa, 1890–1914," 71–101, and other essays in *Europa und das nationale Selbstverständnis. Imagologische Probleme in Literatur, Kunst und Kultur des 19. und 20. Jahrhunderts*, edited by Hugo Dyserinck and Karl Ulrich Syndram (Bonn, 1988); Hugo Dyserinck, "Zum Problem der 'images' und 'mirages' und ihrer Untersuchung im Rahmen der Vergleichenden Literaturwissenschaft," in *arcadia* 1 (1966): 107–20; Dyserinck, "Comparatistische Imagologie jenseits von 'Werkimmanenz' und 'Werktranszendenz,'" *Synthesis* 9 (1982): 27–40; M.S. Fischer, *Nationale Images als Gegenstand Vergleichender Literaturgeschichte* (Bonn, 1981); Peter Edgerly Firchow, *The Death of the German Cousin: Variations on a Literary Stereotype, 1890–1920* (Lewisburg, 1986); Gerd Dose, "'The Soul of Germany'. Bemerkungen zum angloamerikanischen Deutschlandbild vor und zu Beginn des Ersten Weltkrieges," in *Images of Germany*, edited by Hans-Jürgen Diller et al. (Heidelberg, 1986). See also Michael Werner and Bènédicte Zimmermann, "Beyond Comparison: *Histoire Croisée* and the Challenge of Reflexivity," *History and Theory* 45 (2006): 30–50.

36 I originally worked from a project outline titled "Imagology: A Handbook on the Literary Representation of National Characters," which is no longer on the internet; now see Manfred Beller and Joep Leerssen, eds., *Imagology: The Cultural Construction and Literary Representation of National Characters* (Amsterdam and New York, 2007), esp. sections on Germany (159–66) and "irony" (348–51), both with further references.

37 Colonel L. V. Swaine, letter of 28 March 1885 to Lord Granville's secretary, Sir Thomas H. (later Lord) Sanderson, cited in Knaplund, ed., *Letters from the Berlin Embassy*, 2: 393–4 (original emphasis).

38 From the former internet site noted above, "Imagology: A Handbook."

39 Robbins, *Present and Past*, 16.

40 Mayhew, *German Life*, 1: viii–ix and 2: 612. By the time British writers were skewering Germans during the First World War, George Bernard Shaw was outraged at his countrymen's inability to distinguish between *Sein* and *Schein* when they blamed Germans' wartime "barbarism" on Nietzscheanism: "O my brother journalists," he wrote, "if you must revile the Prussians, call them sheep led by snobs, call them beggars on horseback, call them sausage-eaters, depict them in the good English fashion in spectacles and comforter, seedy overcoat buttoned over paunchy figure, playing the contra-bass tuba in a street band; but do not flatter them with the heroic title of Superman, and hold up as magnificent villainies worthy of Milton's Lucifer these common crimes of violence and raid and lust that any drunken blackguard can commit when the police are away, and that no mere multiplication can dignify." Shaw, *What I Really Wrote about the War* (London, 1931), cited in Humble, "The Breakdown of a Consensus," 48.

41 The review appeared in *The Nation* 22, 30 March 1876, 355–8, rpt. in Henry James, *Literary Criticism*, vol. 1, *Essays on Literature: American Writers, English Writers*, edited by Leon Edel (New York, 1984), 300–2.

42 Consider Mayhew, writing from the home village of Luther's father, Möhra: "What may be the precise latitude and longitude of the '*Dörfchen*' (literally Thorpkin) bearing the name of Möhra, Heaven and Sir John Herschel only know. Suffice it to learn that it lies on the borders of Saxe-Meiningen, close to Saxe-Weimar, not above an hour or two from Saxe-Coburg-Gotha, and, indeed, in the immediate vicinity of Saxe-Everything" (*German Life and Manners*, 1: 4). Then compare Hawthorne: "We sallied forth this morning in quest of a representative Saxon village; but, save as regards situation, one is as representative as another ... Moreover, the names of fifteen out of twenty of these villages end in the same three mystic letters – 'itz.' What 'itz' signifies I know not; but I should fancy that whoever lives in a community whose name terminates differently would

feel like a kind of outlaw or alien. Loschwitz, Blasewitz, Pillnitz, Pulsnitz, Sedlitz, Gorbitz, – all are members of one family, and look, speak, and think in the family way. It is admirable the care they take to post up their names on a signboard at each entrance of the village, doubtless a safeguard against the serious danger of forgetting their own first syllables. Were some mischievous person, while the honest villagers slept, to interchange all their signboards, there would be no hope of their ever identifying themselves again. Perhaps, indeed, they might fail to perceive the alteration. Pillnitz or Pulsnitz – what odds?" (*SS*, 29–30).

43 For the following: M. Betham-Edwards's review in *The Academy* 9, 27 May 1876, 505–6; *Athenaeum* 2, 1 July 1876, 13–14, both cited in Knox, "Dissonance Abroad," 133; other reviews (134) appeared in the *New York Times*, 9 January 1876; the *New York Evening Post*, 27 December 1875; and *Appleton's Journal*, 8 January 1876. The *Athenaeum*'s reviewer found more truth in Hawthorne's observations, including his documentation of a growing spirit of philistinism in Germany. But this reviewer claimed that *Saxon Studies* was a misnomer: it should actually have been titled "*jeu d'esprit* on the human race as typified in Saxony."

44 Even Kaiser Wilhelm I was upset by his book, according to Hawthorne's claim in a literary column he wrote for the *Pasadena Star-News*, 22 October 1932, cited in Knox, "Dissonance Abroad," 141.

45 Julian Hawthorne appended the first of these reviews, as he later wrote, "to the fly-leaf of the essays." My edition of *Saxon Studies* does not include them, but Hawthorne's "accurate" translation of the first review, and George Knox's translation of the second, both appear in Knox, "Dissonance Abroad," 134–7, from which the following citations are taken. The reviews appeared in the *Dresdner Nachrichten* on 1 and 4 February 1876.

46 See ch. 2 of the present study for the British envoy's description of this newspaper's readership in the 1870s and 1880s.

47 Knox, "Dissonance Abroad," 136.

48 Nathaniel Hawthorne, *Passages from the English Note-Books of Nathaniel Hawthorne*, edited by Sophia Hawthorne, 2 vols. in 1 (Boston, 1871), 137 (2 November 1854); the *Dresdner Nachrichten*'s slightly divergent translation is cited in Knox, "Dissonance Abroad," 137.

49 Knox, "Dissonance Abroad," 137.

50 Richler, "Introduction," xlv.

51 Cited in Richler, "Introduction," xxxii.

52 For the following see Julian Hawthorne, *The Memoirs of Julian Hawthorne*, ed. Edith Garrigues Hawthorne (New York, 1938), esp. 179–87; Maurice Bassan, *Hawthorne's Son: The Life and Literary Career of Julian Hawthorne*

(Columbus, OH, 1970), esp. 46–53, 70–1, 89–91, 98–101. Scharnhorst's new biography, *Julian Hawthorne*, demonstrates that Hawthorne was an even worse hack, cheat, and eroticist than Bassan believed him to be – Hawthorne's constant penury was partly the result of supporting a mistress and two children – but it has little to say about *Saxon Studies* or the Germany of Hawthorne's day.

53 In a letter dated 7 September 1866, just prior to Julian's expulsion from Harvard, his mother Sophia had written to Lowell: "Silent as Julian is, he has a gift with his pen (inherited, no doubt –) which is remarkable."
54 Hawthorne, *The Memoirs*, 182.
55 Mark Twain, "The Awful German Language," Appendix D in *A Tramp Abroad* (New York, 2003), 315–31.
56 Hawthorne, *The Memoirs*, 187.
57 Cited in Scharnhorst, *Julian Hawthorne*, 49f.
58 Cited in Scharnhorst, *Julian Hawthorne*, 49.
59 In the 1860s it took about eighteen hours to get from Frankfurt am Main to Dresden: "the train went only as far as Leipzig, where the traveler arrived in the night and was obliged to take a ghostly vehicle – a night droschky – and drive from one station to the other; then recline on a bench in a pestilent smoking room reeking of stale tobacco, until, after a delay of several hours, a slow train, stopping at every station, took him on to Dresden." Whitman, *German Memories*, 19–20.
60 Cited in Scharnhorst, *Julian Hawthorne*, 49.
61 As Julian put it, while his sisters were otherwise busy, he studied "music, picture galleries, and beer." Scharnhorst, *Julian Hawthorne*, 49.
62 Hawthorne, *The Memoirs*, 180; see Scharnhorst, *Julian Hawthorne*, 49–50, for some of the following.
63 The opposite device is used in Bayard Taylor's description of his first glance at Raphael's *Madonna and Child* in Dresden; Taylor, *Views A-Foot*, 199–200.
64 These and other details from Sharnhorst, *Julian Hawthorne*, 51–74 at 51.
65 See lines from Hawthorne's notebook of 1871–2, cited in Bassan, *Hawthorne's Son*, 71.
66 Consider Julian's sister Rose's recollection of their father's reaction to her early efforts to enliven life in Concord by writing stories: "My father hung over me, dark as a prophetic flight of birds. 'Never let me hear of your writing stories!' he exclaimed, with as near an approach to anger as I had ever seen in him. 'I forbid you to write them!'" Cited in Bassan, *Hawthorne's Son*, 242.
67 Scharnhorst, *Julian Hawthorne*, 160–2, noting that Hawthorne added an "X" each time he had sex with his mistress Minna Desborough: for

example, "July 13 ... A heavenly day from first to last, & a [illegible] night. K[aihua Long Ding]" – a phallic-shaped Japanese tea-leaf – "down her throat. XXX." According to Scharnhorst, Hawthorne "defended his infidelity on the grounds that he was a free-born pagan unbound by convention."
68 *Appleton's Journal* 9, no. 189 (4 January 1873): 49, cited in Bassan, *Hawthorne's Son*, 70.
69 Bassan, *Hawthorne's Son*, 70–1.
70 Scharnhorst, *Julian Hawthorne*, 60f.
71 Scharnhorst, *Julian Hawthorne*, 63, describing *Bressant*, whose main character, like Hawthorne later, betrays two women.
72 As listed in the Dresden *Address Geschäfts-Handbuch* for 1873–4, cited in Knox, "Dissonance Abroad," 132; Scharnhorst, *Julian Hawthorne*, 61–2.
73 Julian Hawthorne, *Confessions and Criticisms* (Boston, 1887), 11f., cited in Bassan, *Hawthorne's Son*, 246.
74 Scharnhorst, *Julian Hawthorne*, 65, and for some of the following.
75 Bassan, *Hawthorne's Son*, 90.
76 Scharnhorst, *Julian Hawthorne*, 65.
77 *SS*, 211, with further charges against thievery and graft on 211–13.
78 Bassan, *Hawthorne's Son*, 91; Scharnhorst, *Julian Hawthorne*, 61, citing Will Morton.
79 Cited in Scharnhorst, *Julian Hawthorne*, 61.
80 Cited in Scharnhorst, *Julian Hawthorne*, 61.
81 See esp. Scharnhorst, *Julian Hawthorne*, 62–7.
82 Journal entry of 22 June 1873. In July 1873, Hawthorne wrote to his sister Una that they were "of course in extreme pecuniary distress"; his wife Minne was busy "painting silk fans like a maniac" to supplement their income. Hawthorne therefore had good reason to hope (if not to expect) that *Saxon Studies* "will be more popular than my unfortunate novels." Citations from Bassan, *Hawthorne's Son*, 89, 98.
83 Scharnhorst, *Julian Hawthorne*, 67–75, records how financially desperate Hawthorne was at the time. In September 1874, Hawthorne moved his family from Dresden to London, but their furniture remained in storage for many months because the bill could not be paid. When Hawthorne presented the incomplete manuscript for *Saxon Studies* to the English publisher Alexander Strahan, who wanted something for the *Contemporary Review*, Strahan looked at it for "inside of fifteen minutes," jumped up, clapped Hawthorne on the shoulder, and exclaimed "'Just the thing, my boy! ... Go on and finish it; give us as much as you like.'" Thereafter, though, Hawthorne frequently complained about late payments for his instalments of the book. Cited in Scharnhorst, *Julian Hawthorne*, 75.

84 Consider H.G. Wells's juxtaposition of discipline and organization on the one hand, and community and individualism on the other, in *Mr. Britling Sees It Through*: "To organize or discipline, or mould characters or press authority, is to assume that you have reached finality in your general philosophy. It implies an assured end ... Here [in Britain], we have none of these convictions. We know we haven't finality, and so we are open and apologetic and receptive, rather than wilful ... You see all organization, with its implication of finality, is death. We feel that. The Germans don't. What you organize you kill." Cited in Humble, "The Breakdown," 49. Compare Collier, *Germany*, 599: "Organization is only good as a means; it is stupefying as an end. Germany has organized herself into an organization, and is the most over-organized country in the world. What every democracy of free men wants is not as much, but as little, organization as possible ... You can think out a game of chess, but you cannot think out life ahead of the living of it without cramping it and finally killing it."

85 Compare D.H. Lawrence's comments in ch. 4 of *Fantasia of the Unconscious*, reflecting a moment when he was surrounded by the trees of the Black Forest: "The true German has something of the sap of trees in his veins even now: and a sort of pristine savageness, like trees, helpless, but most powerful, under all his mentality. He is a tree-soul, and his gods are not human ... The tree of life and death, the tree of good and evil, tree of abstraction and of immense, mindless life; tree of everything except the spirit, spirituality." Cited in Humble, "The Breakdown," 67–8. On this subject see Jeffrey K. Wilson, *The German Forest: Nature, Identity, and the Contestation of a National Symbol, 1871–1914* (Toronto, 2012); and Thomas M. Lekan, *Imagining the Nation in Nature: Landscape Preservation and German Identity, 1885–1945* (Cambridge, MA, 2004).

86 Heinrich von Treitschke, *Die Zukunft der norddeutschen Mittelstaaten*, 2nd ed. (Berlin, 1866), 17. See also ch. 5 in this volume.

87 Mrs Alfred Sidgwick, *Home Life in Germany* (New York, 1912), 2. "There are many Germanys, so that when you write of one corner you may easily write of ways and food and regulations that do not obtain in some other corner, and it is obviously impossible to remind the reader in every case that the part is not the whole ... You can only describe the side you know, and comment on the things you have seen. So you bring your mite to the store of knowledge which many have increased before you, and which many will add to again" (5–6).

88 After writing mainly novelettes and collections of stories while in London (September 1874 to October 1881), Hawthorne returned to America and again took up novels. He edited his father's posthumous work,

Dr. Grimshawe's Secret: A Romance (Boston, 1883) and completed the major work *Nathaniel Hawthorne and his Wife: A Biography*, 2nd ed., 2 vols. (Boston, 1884). Virtually every other relevant detail of his career – "chequered" hardly suffices to describe it – is found in Scharnhorst, *Julian Hawthorne*, chs. 4–8.

89 Hawthorne discussed his relationship with Samuel Clemens in "Mark Twain As I Knew Him," *Overland Monthly* n.s. 87 (April 1929): 111, 128, cited in Bassan, *Hawthorne's Son*, 253.

90 Arthur Miller, cited in Shelley Fisher Fishkin, "Foreword" to Mark Twain, *The Innocents Abroad*, xxii.

91 Bobbie Ann Mason, cited in Fishkin, "Foreword," xx.

92 Hawthorne, *Confessions and Criticisms*, cited in Bassan, *Hawthorne's Son*, 175.

93 Scharnhorst, *Julian Hawthorne*, chs. 5–7, amply illustrates Hawthorne's disdain for Naturalism.

94 These aspects of the book were not lost on Bassan: "The book, patched as it is from notebook jottings and from memory, has a mixed tone. Many of its observations of human nature are trite and sentimental, on a par with … passages of *Idolatry*; but the descriptions of Saxon life and customs are vivid and telling, and through these descriptions runs an irony (occasionally vindictive) that is itself uneven – sometimes heavy-handed, sometimes subtle." Bassan also notes that Henry James in his review "had obviously missed the point of Hawthorne's preface." Bassan, *Hawthorne's Son*, 99, 101. George Knox, "Dissonance Abroad," notes (138) that the "pastoral idyll" that constitutes Hawthorne's last substantive chapter – describing a trip into the mountains during his last days in Saxony – is "strongly ironic." In this chapter, Hawthorne's infatuation with a Saxon girl he meets is "coldly blasted" in the end when he discovers that she is only a vulgar shop girl he had previously known in Dresden. Hawthorne himself called this a "foolish, unsatisfactory little episode," but Knox concludes that "Julian meant this tacked-on anecdote to be typical of his entire Dresden experience, a parabolic interlude which should convey his disillusionment." Scharnhorst is less charitable, finding the book sarcastic, not ironic. For instance, he suggests that *Appleton's Journal* was unsuccessful in turning the author's "querulousness" to his advantage – the *Journal*'s reviewer wrote that Hawthorne's contempt was a kind of "genuine literary inspiration," but added that *Saxon Studies* "'will easily take the first place' among books of hate." Scharnhorst, *Julian Hawthorne*, 75–6, citing various reviews.

95 Cited in Scharnhorst, *Julian Hawthorne*, 76.

96 Hawthorne makes the implausible claim in his book's preface that the earlier, serialized version had prompted the founding of a "Native and Foreign Mutual Interest Protection Company" (Dresden) in June 1875, whose program was allegedly signed by a Baron von Stockhausen "as president" and that "aims to remedy some of those very abuses, for mentioning which the 'Studies' have been assailed."

97 These retrospective claims are found in Julian Hawthorne, "Our Experience Meetings: My Literary Autobiography," *Lippencott's Magazine* 37 (1886): 410, and "Recalling Heinrich Heine," a literary column written for the *Pasadena Star-News*, 22 October 1932, 24; both cited in Knox, "Dissonance Abroad," 131.

98 Julian Hawthorne, *Humors of the Fair* (Chicago, 1893), cited in Scharnhorst, *Julian Hawthorne*, 135.

99 This and other points draw on Beller and Leerssen, eds., *Imagology*.

100 Walt Whitman, *Leaves of Grass* (Oxford, 1998), 78 (orig. 1855). Consider also A.J.P. Taylor's pronouncement of 1946: "'German' has meant at one moment a being so sentimental, so trusting, so pious, as to be too good for this world; and at another a being so brutal, so unprincipled, so degraded, as to be not fit to live. Both descriptions are true: both types of Germans have existed not only at the same epoch, but in the same person. Only the normal person, not particularly good, not particularly bad, healthy, sane[,] moderate – he has never set his stamp on German history." Cited in Jarausch, "Huns," 145–6.

101 Jorge Luis Borges, *Tlön, Uqbar, Orbis Tertius* (1941), *Oxford Dictionary of Quotations*, ed. Knowles, 143.

102 W.H. Auden, "Shorts II" (1976), *Oxford Dictionary of Quotations*, ed. Knowles, 35.

103 See Knox, "Dissonance Abroad," 139.

104 Mordecai Richler, "Introduction," in Twain, *Innocents Abroad*, xxxi.

6 Bismarck and Engels:
The Role of Force in History

> War is not only a continuation of politics, it is the epitome of politics.
>
> V.I. Lenin, 5 December 1919[1]

Friedrich Engels's unfinished pamphlet *The Role of Force in History* was published (with alterations) by the revisionist Social Democrat Eduard Bernstein in *Die Neue Zeit* in 1896 – that is, during the twenty-fifth anniversary of Germany's Second Reich.[2] By the end of the 1890s, French, Russian, and Italian translations had appeared; an English edition was published belatedly in 1968.[3] In this pamphlet Engels planned to republish three chapters from his *Anti-Dühring*[4] (1878) and add a fourth chapter. That new chapter would explain the history of Germany from 1848 to 1888. Written between December 1887 and March 1888, *The Role of Force in History* charted the fate of the German bourgeoisie in a period when industrial capitalism, warfare, and struggles for national unification were all "modernized." Engels's aim was to demonstrate "why the policy of blood and iron was bound to be successful for a time and why it is bound to fail in the end."

In this chapter, after providing some background on why Engels had felt compelled to attack Eugen Dühring's "reinterpretation" of socialism in 1878, I focus on three aspects of the new chapter that Engels added to his *Anti-Dühring* in 1887–8. The first concerns the language he used to describe the heroes and anti-heroes of his narrative. The second concerns the sketch – only parts of which are included in the English edition – of how he planned to finish the fourth chapter. Third and last, I consider the German bourgeoisie's possible role in a violent confrontation between the state and Social Democracy in the 1890s.

Eugen Dühring was among the most radical and scurrilous antisemites in German public life during the late 1870s and early 1880s. He still awaits his modern biographer, but recent studies of antisemitism and Social Democracy's response to it illustrate why he was considered a threat by Karl Marx and Friedrich Engels.[5] Having studied philosophy, law, and political economy in Berlin, acquiring a doctorate and two Habilitation degrees, Dühring cultivated hatreds that were fuelled by the fact that, while never advancing beyond the rank of unsalaried university lecturer, he claimed competence as a "thinker, logician, mathematician, physicist, jurist, and political economist" – an expert in all "human interests." By the end of the 1870s, he had lost his licence to teach, not because he had gradually gone blind but because he had grown ever more radical in his attacks on universities and their faculties, whom he saw as "reptilian hangers-on" given to "monkish sneakishness." Dühring's list of enemies included Jews above all. For them he preached the most explicit forms of banishment and extermination any German antisemite dared utter at the time. His work titled *The Jewish Question as a Racial, Moral, and Cultural Question* (1881) and his call for "the elimination of Jewry by means of the modern *Volk*-spirit" (1883) are legitimately seen as anticipating the Final Solution. His teachings were incorporated into Theodor Fritsch's famous *Handbook on the Jewish Question*, with which Hitler was familiar.[6]

In the mid-1870s, Dühring entered the German political stage with his *Critical History of National Economy* and other works. Positive responses came from various members of Germany's Social Democratic Party (SPD), who made strange bedfellows even within their own ranks: the revisionist Eduard Bernstein, the later anarchist Johann Most, and even, for a short time, August Bebel. In 1875, Karl Marx and Wilhelm Liebknecht encouraged Friedrich Engels to tackle Dühring's blasphemous interpretation of dialectical materialism head-on. (Marx was busy with the next volume of *Das Kapital* at the time.) Two years later the result of Engels's effort was *Herr Eugen Dühring's Revolution in Science*.[7] It was serialized in the leading SPD newspaper, *Vorwärts*, between January 1877 and July 1878, causing a flurry of dissent at the SPD party congress of 1877. Part I and then Parts II and III were published separately as pamphlets – just in time to be banned under Bismarck's Anti-Socialist Law of October 1878. A third edition of this work, by then known as Engels's *Anti-Dühring*, was published in 1894, after the proscription against Social Democracy had expired (1890) and shortly before Engels's death. An English edition appeared in 1907.

Engels in 1878 was more eager to denounce his adversary than to state his own (and Marx's) case. His main objection to Dühring's supposed "conversion" to socialism was that the Berlin professor claimed to have discovered, with his "socialitary system," eternal truths and absolute theories in the realms of science, philosophy, and political economy. Yet in the process Engels produced a Marxist handbook that in its influence was similar to that of Bebel's *Woman under Socialism*, also published in 1878. Both books offered statements of Marxist theory that were "comprehensive, lucid, and convincing" for rank-and-file Social Democrats. Both books also brought young intellectuals such as Bernstein and Karl Kautsky firmly within the Marxist fold.[8]

By the time Engels returned to add a fourth chapter to the work, he no longer needed to defame the "Berlin apostle of revenge," as Friedrich Nietzsche once referred to Dühring. The "vehemence of his moralistic drivel" and his "offensive claptrap" (Nietzsche again) no longer deserved a rebuttal. Social Democracy was a power in its own right, and Engels's more urgent task was to "apply our theory to contemporary German history and its use of force." The progress of nationalism in the modern era, the "revolutionizing of Germany from above" under Bismarck, and the "political weakness of the German bourgeoisie" – these were the pressing issues of the day in 1887.

The Role of Force in History is thus very much a product of its time. It is forthright, even brutal, and it is filled with dismissive references to countless groups and individuals. It presents the reality of war and the discursive deployment of martial metaphors as two sides of a single coin. Consider what Engels has to say about Bismarck's insincere promise that Emperor Napoleon III would acquire the left bank of the Rhine for France if he remained neutral in the German Civil War of 1866.[9] "A diplomat, especially a Prussian diplomat, has his own ideas as to the limits within which one is justified, or even obliged, to do violence to the truth. Truth, after all, is like a woman, and according to a Junker's idea, she really quite likes it."[10]

Was Engels's allusion to female virtue unwise? Or did it correspond to the masculine coding of high politics, war, and diplomacy that Engels wanted to convey (albeit as secondary to economic circumstances)? Whatever the answer, here we see Engels's "take-no-prisoners" style, which runs throughout the work. In the same paragraph we find euphemisms and idioms that fit a moral universe predicated on domination, violence, and struggle, though they often appear in recognizably human guise. Thus we read of force, subjugation, and a "brisk, jolly war," but also of territorial and other advances, outwitted chauvinists, and alliances that pave the way for the "stab in the heart."[11]

Consider the lines Engels uses next to advance his thesis about the successes and failures of Bismarck's *Realpolitik*. "Philistines in many countries," he writes, "have been deeply affronted by this phrase ['stab in the heart']. Quite wrongly. *À la guerre comme à la guerre*. It simply proves that Bismarck understood the German Civil War of 1866 to be what it really was, namely, a *revolution*, and he was prepared to carry it through by revolutionary means." Engels hastens to applaud Bismarck for advancing history's dialectic in this fashion. He also provides a foretaste of his conclusion that the German Empire is doomed to fail. "Naturally," writes Engels, "we [socialists] are the last people to blame him for [using revolutionary means]. On the contrary, we blame him for not being revolutionary enough ... for beginning a whole revolution in a position in which he could only carry through half a revolution."[12]

Bismarck the Prussian diplomat can become the Prussian warmonger with only the slightest twist of *Realpolitik*. But once war is over, political "realism" shows its soft underbelly: Bismarck the peacemaker is unable to "carry it through." He reveals himself to be "satisfied" with "four paltry petty states" (*vier lumpigen Kleinstaaten*).[13] This moderation is Bismarck's fatal flaw. Yet it remains so only until Engels tells us that Bismarck's "first, colossal blunder" occurred in 1871, when he took the provinces of Alsace and Lorraine from the defeated French. Not for the last time Engels has reversed himself. That reversal, and others, reinforce V.G. Kiernan's supposition that Engels may have broken off *The Role of Force in History* in March 1888 not merely to attend to publication of the second and third volumes of *Das Kapital*: "Perhaps Engels lost confidence in his argument."[14]

There is something of the science fiction genre about Engels's book. The characters resemble cardboard cutouts: August Bebel as Luke Skywalker, Bismarck as Darth Vader. But the Junkers and the German bourgeoisie experience the same inversions that George Lucas later fashioned for Luke's Jedi knights and Darth Vader's myrmidons.[15] Engels's Junkers, cynical and ruthless, serve as reliable soldiers, but they are doomed as "die-hard, hopeless reactionaries, incapable of providing the basis for a great independent party."[16] If that is so, then the Prussian state is doomed too.[17] Darth Vader was once a knight and was turned to the dark side. Then he tried to turn others. But history's screenplay was not on his side.

Meanwhile, bourgeois Germans are cannily clad in white. The colour of their armour is unexpected and disconcerting, less so the unmistakable shape of their *Stahlhelme*. They are drones. They help others – the leaders of evil empires – secure the spoils of war (class wars, civil wars, and other, less interesting kinds of war, too). Bourgeois Germans are playing this role for posterity: "'Liberal' and 'national,'" Engels writes, "the dual nature from 1848, goes through even in Germany, 1870–1888." But actually their dominance is nothing more than a sham. "The revolution of 1848 had transformed the state into an outwardly constitutional form in which the bourgeoisie could establish and extend its political domination. Despite this, the bourgeoisie was still far from exercising real political power."[18] The bourgeoisie's fragile "domination" continues only until the next instalment is ready for prime time. It will feature the "inevitable conflict"[19] between the bourgeoisie and the proletariat.

Engels dates the beginning of this conflict to the time around 1871. It too is characterized by a reversal of roles: as opposed to 1848, "this time all the perplexity will be on the side of the bourgeoisie. The proletariat now knows what it wants."[20] Bebel and Liebknecht can say what they want "out the windows" of the Reichstag: No wars of conquest! No annexations![21] In a speech Bismarck cited years later as having convinced him that Social Democracy must be eradicated, Bebel outlined his party's position in a statement that produced the expected reaction from his listeners. "Gentlemen!," Bebel declared in the Reichstag on 25 May 1871, "the efforts of the [Paris] Commune may appear in your eyes to be reprehensible or … insane … Even though at this moment Paris is being suppressed, then remember that the struggle in Paris is only a preliminary skirmish, that the main issue in Europe still lies before us, and that before too many decades have passed the battle-cry of the Parisian proletariat – 'War on the palaces, Peace in the cottages, Death to misery and idleness!' – will become the battle cry of the entire European proletariat. (Amusement)."[22] Many months of imprisonment was the price Bebel and Liebknecht paid for their support of the Paris Commune.[23] Writing almost ten years after Bismarck rammed through the Anti-Socialist Law in 1878, Engels knew that while it helps to have the army on your side, he and his comrades had to reckon with other dark forces: judges and juries, gendarmes and jailers.

Bismarck and Engels 191

Figure 6.1 After being forced from office in 1890, Otto von Bismarck journeyed through Germany in June 1892 to attend his son Herbert's wedding in the Habsburg Empire. This displeased Kaiser Wilhelm II, not only because the former chancellor had been attacking his successor's (and his king's) policies for two years but also because Bismarck intentionally visited the "Greater German" (*großdeutsch*) territories of Austria, Bavaria, and Saxony on his trip. Dresden's Lord Mayor Paul Stübel can be seen, second from right, wearing the chain of office. To mark the occasion of Bismarck's visit, Saxony's King Albert allowed the mayor to wear the symbol of municipal authority for the first time. The "Bismarck cult," which swept up many bourgeois Saxons and other Germans in the 1890s, is already evident in this painting. *Fürst Bismarck in Dresden am 18. Juni 1892* (detail), by Ernst Max Pietschmann (1895). Städtische Galerie Dresden – Kunstsammlung, Museen der Stadt Dresden. Photograph: Franz Zadnicek.

In Engels's rough notes for the rest of the book's fourth chapter, historical materialism is conspicuous mainly by its absence. This is understandable given the nature of this sketch – it is only an outline. Still, if economic determinism was to be the bedrock of Engels's analysis as he carried the history of German unification through the 1880s, on that bedrock one hears the footsteps of the same heroes and villains found earlier in the manuscript: real people and lobby groups. Moreover, we discover that Engels's tone of disdain for those who can never hope to catch the coat-tails of history is likely to continue to the end of the book. Unfortunately, the English edition provides only an abbreviated, muted version of that outline.[24]

Engels broke off his manuscript while discussing the *Kulturkampf* – Bismarck's deployment of the Prussian authoritarian state against the Catholic Church. "The Catholic priest [is] no gendarme and police," he wrote, but the bourgeoisie was nonetheless "jubilant" about the cultural struggle of the 1870s. Other parts of Section II are rendered in the English edition simply as "Bismarck at the end of his tether" but in German as *"Bismarck am Ende – wird reaktionär, blödsinnig"* ("becomes reactionary, idiotic"). In that section Engels planned to discuss developments from the mid-1870s to the early 1880s. These included the economic recession and the allegedly dysfunctional liberal system of industrial capitalism; the "pettiness" and opposition to Bismarck's policy from Prussian Junkers, who are "just as dishonorable as the bourgeoisie"; protective tariffs and the colonial "swindle"; the Anti-Socialist Law and suppression of the Free Trade Unions (i.e., those unions associated with the SPD); and the beginning of Bismarck's social insurance program. Engels describes the latter as "à la Bonaparte" and characterizes it as that "social reform shit" (*Sozialreformscheiße*).

Section III was intended to discuss foreign policy in more detail, the problems of militarism and army expansion, and the annexation of Alsace and Lorraine in 1871. Referring to the war scares of 1874 and (most likely) 1886–7, Engels implies that the sands are beginning to run out for the chancellor (*die Zeit erfüllet*): he predicts that Bismarck will "revert to the years from before 1870, in order to hold the upper hand for a few more years." Engels makes this point to provide a segue to his fourth and last section of chapter 4. It appears under an unusual heading: "The Junker moves into the foreground, for lack of other ideas." But in his more detailed notes, Engels labels Section IV as the "consequence" of all that came before.

In Section IV, Part A, Engels expresses astonishment at Germany's domestic situation, "which breaks apart with the death of a couple of people: no Kaiserreich without a Kaiser!"[25] The pace of historical change then accelerates markedly. The proletariat is "pushed to revolution." Social Democracy expands "as never before" upon the expiry of the Anti-Socialist Law. And then comes – "chaos." One can guess that this chaos will afflict mainly the "perplexed" German bourgeoisie. Yet it may well be a chaos very similar to the "conflict" that was cited so often in the mid-1890s by Kaiser Wilhelm II and his chancellors. At that time, Germany's leaders contemplated a *coup d'état* against the Reichstag, a revision of the constitution, the abolition of universal manhood suffrage, and possibly dissolution of the federated empire.[26] This "battle plan" was formulated as the answer to the threat of Social Democracy.

One can only wish that Engels had expressed himself more explicitly on this point. Did he think Germany might have benefited if the Kaiser had unleashed a violent "conflict" – the endgame in his "war against subversion" – to keep German burghers and Reichstag parliamentarians in line? Whatever the case, from Engels's notes we know that in Section IV, Part B, the reader would have learned about "a peace [that is] worse than war ... – in the best case; or else a world war." Engels thus predicts a doubly apocalyptic outcome: domestic chaos, characterized by a "peace" better than anything else Germans could hope for; or "chaos" of the kind that Lenin would call the "epitome" of politics: war itself.

After Marx's death in 1883 it was up to Engels to forecast history wrongly.[27] Legions of citations can be mustered to illustrate how persistently he did so until his own death in 1895. Consider his reaction to the Social Democrats' electoral breakthrough in the Reichstag elections of 1890. "February 20, 1890, is the day marking the start of the German Revolution," wrote Engels to Marx's daughter. "It may be a few years before we'll experience the decisive crisis ... but the old stability is gone forever." As for Bismarck's right-wing *Kartell* of German Conservatives, Free Conservatives, and National Liberals, Engels disparaged the chancellor's hope that the anti-socialist coalition of 1887, which had produced a stunning setback for the SPD in the Reichstag elections of that year, could be revived: "all the King's horses and all the King's men cannot put Humpty Dumpty together again."[28] (The last line appeared in English in the original.)[29]

Figure 6.2 The text reads: "*Reviewing Officer Prince Bismarck*: My Heavens – How did that *civilian* get in here?!" The civilian in question is Prussian Minister of Justice Hermann von Schelling, who held office in Bismarck's state ministry from 1879 to 1889. The cartoonist meant to suggest not only that Bismarck demanded military-style obedience from his fellow cabinet members but also that non-military pedigrees and opinions among ministers of state were conspicuous mainly by their absence. "Unser Ministerium in Uniform (bis auf Einen)," by Friedrich Graetz, in *Lustige Blätter* (Berlin), vol. 4, no. 13 (28 March 1889). bpk, Berlin/Art Resource, NY.

Engels also falsely predicted Social Democracy's imminent penetration of the countryside and army ranks. As he wrote to Liebknecht after February 1890:

> Now, where we have the cities and the news of our victories penetrates into the most remote landed estates, we are able to ignite a very different blaze in rural areas than the grassfire of 12 years ago. In three years we will have the agricultural laborers and then we have the core regiments of the Prussian army. And to prevent that, only one means exists, whose ruthless deployment is the one point on which wee Wilhelm [*Wilhelmchen*] and Bismarck still agree: a brutal shooting spree with the obligatory, acute shock effect. They will use any pretext to do so.[30]

Engels had preceded these remarks with another derisory reference. This time his victims were the two conservative party leaders Otto von Helldorff and Wilhelm von Kardorff.[31] Characteristically, he punctuated his remarks by citing voting returns. After congratulating Liebknecht for winning 42,000 votes in Berlin, he added: "Now, if any Kar-, Hell-, or other sort of Junkerdorf should again interrupt you [in the Reichstag], you can tell him: draw yourself back into your foreskin, if you have one, for I represent as many voters as a dozen of your sort!"

Engels tended to be too optimistic. Yet shortly before his death he worried about Social Democracy's divergence from its theoretical orthodoxy based on the certainty of revolution. Engels chafed under the demand made by revisionist socialists that he moderate the views he expressed in his Preface to Marx's *Civil War in France*.[32] This was at a time when the SPD's leaders feared the worst from the Anti-Revolution Bill that had been introduced in the Reichstag in December 1894 in response to Wilhelm II's demand that "something" be done at last to defeat "the enemy within." What makes this parallelism significant is that Engels and German reactionaries conceived of the role of force in history in surprisingly similar ways.

True to revolutionary theory, Engels was not willing to wait for an eventual socialist majority in the Reichstag. The elements of stability that he could not fail to acknowledge in the final sections of *The Role of Force in History* compelled him to see the only hope for Social Democracy's triumph in the "chaos" he planned to elucidate there. "Our turn can only come," he had written to Bebel some years earlier, "when the bourgeois and petty-bourgeois parties have openly and in practice proved their inability to govern the country."[33]

This statement found its echo in the private views of Bismarck's two successors: General Leo von Caprivi (in office 1890–4) and Prince Chlodwig zu Hohenlohe-Schillingsfürst (1894–1900). In May 1893 the Reichstag was only a few hours from being dissolved over the government's Army Bill when Caprivi held a *tête-à-tête* with the government leader of the Kingdom of Saxony, Baron Georg von Metzsch.[34] Could Germany be ruled at all with the Reichstag "in its present composition," Caprivi asked his interlocutor? Caprivi answered his own question with a "no." One would then have to consider "upon which principles one might obtain a popular representation for the Reich ... that could be expected to approve all necessary funds to govern the Reich and endorse the other necessary legislative measures." Caprivi explained what suffrage revisions might yield the desired parliamentary representation: "a kind of representation by groups or interests, for example of the sort whereby business, trade, industry, [and] agriculture would find their own special representation in the Reichstag, though if possible by retaining the present general suffrage." Caprivi also floated the idea that Belgium's recently introduced system of plural balloting might be suitable. After this conversation, Metzsch noted without a hint of irony that "with such a transformation of popular representation on a more rational basis, the Reich chancellor hopes to facilitate a healthier alignment of parties in the Reichstag."

Like Caprivi, Chancellor Hohenlohe is credited with deflecting Kaiser Wilhelm II's most extreme plans to recast the role of force in history. At various times Wilhelm wanted to shoot socialists in the streets, to send the Reichstag packing, to muzzle the press, and to break the back of the Free Trade Unions. To be sure, Hohenlohe may have helped avert the worst during his term of office. Upon accepting his appointment in October 1894 he promptly demonstrated that he was no "conflict minister." In 1895, the year of Engels's death, he dissuaded Wilhelm II from demanding a law whose only virtue was its succinctness: "§1. All Social Democratic associations and assemblies are banned." This was the legislation Wilhelm wanted from his chancellor in August 1895: "This Reichstag can only be given thin gruel, like the budget, etc.," declared the Kaiser. "Something must be done in *Prussia* which the Empire can then copy. I have the feeling that a short and severe association law would best solve the problem."[35]

Upon closer scrutiny, Hohenlohe cannot bear the mantle of a reformist conservative that his biographers – even his recent ones – want to thrust upon him.³⁶ On the contrary: Hohenlohe wanted to see the Reichstag and universal suffrage abolished, and on this point he was remarkably consistent. Just days after the Anti-Revolution Bill was defeated, Hohenlohe made notes about the pros and cons of bringing about a showdown with parliament. Like the Kaiser's friend Philipp zu Eulenburg and others, Hohenlohe in May 1895 was worried about the ultimate outcome of dissolving the Reichstag and abolishing universal manhood suffrage with force of arms. But we need to ask: What was really different about his preferred alternative, "the path of waiting" and avoiding the worst? "The Reichstag," Hohenlohe wrote, "continues to lose its standing among the German people. If one lets it carry on as it has until now, in the end public opinion will push for its abolition ... Sooner or later there will come a moment when the general, direct suffrage produces a Reichstag that consists of the nation's worst elements and for which the German people will feel revulsion. Then it is time to step in, not with words but with armed force."³⁷

What can we conclude from these surprisingly similar reflections about the German bourgeoisie's readiness to endorse a bloodbath against Social Democracy? Two observations seem apt. First, Friedrich Engels lived up to his own subsidiary role in history when he appraised the course of German development by looking back in time. *The Role of Force in History* benefited from the fact that Engels did not devote himself to untangling the web of contingency that his allusion to future "chaos" might have added to his agenda. Second, historians would do well to follow both Engels and the reactionaries who concocted their *coup d'état* plans in the 1890s by paying more attention to the uncertain role German burghers might have played in a future showdown between the forces of revolution and those crusading, as they put it, "For Morality, Religion, and Order."³⁸

Since the early 1980s historians have increasingly stressed the many successes of the German bourgeoisie and their refusal to surrender their principles to the lures of profit or prestige – as Engels believed they had done long before 1888.³⁹ Nevertheless, German burghers were both more powerful and more "perplexed" than historians tend to believe. For that reason we have to follow them across the historical threshold of 1888–90, which divides the Bismarckian from the Wilhelmine era. Engels and others charted uncertain trajectories into the future for the German bourgeoisie. It could not reinvent itself in 1890 by throwing off the shackles forged by the Iron Chancellor. But neither did it continue an ineluctable slide into powerlessness. It remained "perplexed" even as it entered the new age Engels did not live to see.

NOTES

1 Report to the 7th All-Russian Congress of Soviets, cited in V.G. Kiernan, "War," in *A Dictionary of Marxist Thought*, edited by Tom Bottomore (Cambridge, MA, 1983), 522. On martial idioms common to socialist and anti-socialist rhetoric, see Roger Chickering, "Militarism and Radical Nationalism," in *Imperial Germany 1871–1918: The Short Oxford History of Germany*, edited by James Retallack (Oxford, 2008), 196–218, at 199–202.
2 *Die Rolle der Gewalt in der Geschichte*, in Karl Marx/Friedrich Engels, *Werke*, edited by the Institut für Marxismus-Leninismus beim ZK der SED (Berlin, 1962), 21: 405–61, 600–16; *Neue Zeit* 14 (1895–6), 1. Bd., 676–87, 708–18, 740–7, 772–81, 810–18, http://www.mlwerke.de/me/me21/me21_405.htm.
3 Friedrich Engels, *The Role of Force in History: A Study of Bismarck's Policy of Blood and Iron*, edited by Ernst Wangermann, translated by Jack Cohen (London, 1968). For the English text online: http://marxists.anu.edu.au/archive/marx/works/1887/role-force/index.htm.
4 See the next section of this chapter.
5 *NDB* 4 (1959): 157–8; Walter Bergmann, "Dühring," in *Handbuch des Antisemitismus*, 7 vols., edited by Wolfgang Benz (Berlin, 2009), 2/1: 188–91; Massimo Ferrari Zumbini, *Die Wurzeln des Bösen. Gründerjahre des Antisemitismus* (Frankfurt a.M., 2003), 174–82. On objections to Engels's attack on Dühring from the left wing of the party in 1877–8, see *inter alia* F.L. Carsten, *Eduard Bernstein 1850–1932* (Munich, 1993), 16; Rosemarie Leuschen-Scheppel, *Sozialdemokratie und Antisemitismus im Kaiserreich* (Bonn, 1978), 52.
6 Besides works cited above, see Birgitta Mogge-Stubbe's entry in *Antisemitism: An Encyclopedia of Prejudice and Persecution*, edited by Richard S. Levy, 2 vols. (Santa Barbara, CA, 2005), 1: 192–3. Dühring aggrandized many of his titles with each new edition, e.g. the 3rd edition of *Die Judenfrage* became *Die Judenfrage als Frage der Racenschädlichkeit für Existenz, Sitte und Cultur der Völker. Mit einer weltgeschichtlichen Antwort* (Karlsruhe and Leipzig, 1886).
7 Friedrich Engels, *Herrn Eugen Dühring's Umwälzung der Wissenschaft. Philosophie. Politische Oekonomie. Sozialismus* (Leipzig, 1878), rpt. Marx/Engels, *Werke*, 20: 1–303, http://www.mlwerke.de/me/me30/me20_001.htm;

Engels, *Landmarks of Scientific Socialism: "Anti-Dühring,"* translated by Austin Lewis (Chicago, 1907). English ed. (1947), https://www.marxists.org/archive/marx/works/1877/anti-duhring.
8   See Vernon Lidtke, *The Outlawed Party: Social Democracy in Germany, 1878–1890* (Princeton, 1966), 61.
9   Alternatively known as the Austro-Prussian War. See ch. 4 of the present volume.
10 Engels, *The Role of Force*, 64.
11 Engels, *The Role of Force*, 63–4.
12 Engels, *The Role of Force*, 65–6.
13 Here Engels refers to the territories, including the Kingdom of Hanover, that Prussia annexed outright in 1866.
14 Kiernan, "War," 520.
15 Engels's "misunderstandings" and "inversions" of Marxist teachings are discussed by Tristram Hunt in *Marx's General: The Revolutionary Life of Friedrich Engels* (New York, 2009), esp. 295. *The Role of Force in History* appears neither in Hunt's bibliography nor in his index.
16 Engels, *The Role of Force*, 106. Cf. Max Weber's inaugural lecture (May 1895) in Freiburg i.Br., "The Nation State and Economic Policy," in Weber, *Political Writings*, edited by Peter Lassman and Ronald Speirs (Cambridge, 1994), 1–28, esp. 9 on the "economic death throes of the old Prussian Junkerdom."
17 Engels, *The Role of Force*, 91.
18 Engels, *The Role of Force*, 92.
19 Engels, *The Role of Force*, 97.
20 Engels, *The Role of Force*, 97. In his *"Gliederung"* (outline), Engels notes that the workers "want only bourgeois fair play." Marx/Engels, *Werke*, 21: 464.
21 Engels understates the prerogatives of the Reichstag and overstates those of the Federal Council (*Bundesrat*); so does Ernst Wangermann in his Introduction; Engels, *The Role of Force*, 15, 99f.
22 *Stenographische Berichte über die Verhandlungen des Deutschen Reichstags* (Berlin, 1871), 2: 921; August Bebel, *Ausgewählte Reden und Schriften*, 10 vols. (Munich, 1995), 1: 150; Bismarck's retrospective remark was made in the Reichstag debate of 17 September 1878 on the Anti-Socialist Law. The Paris Commune instituted a revolutionary and socialist government in the French capital in the final phase of the Franco-German War of 1870–1. That government ruled Paris from 18 March to 28 May 1871 and was bloodily suppressed by French troops (including French prisoners of war released by Bismarck) loyal to the post-Napoleonic republican government of Adolphe Thiers. Debates about the bloodshed and historical

significance of the Commune inspired Marx to write *The Civil War in France*, published in London in June 1871.
23 See *Der Hochverrats-Prozeß wider Liebknecht, Bebel, Hepner vor dem Schwurgericht zu Leipzig vom 11. bis 26. März 1872*, 2nd ed. (Berlin, 1911).
24 Cf. Engels, *The Role of Force*, 9; Engels, *Rolle der Gewalt*, in Marx/Engels *Werke*, 21: 462–5.
25 In 1888, the "year of the three Kaisers," Kaiser Wilhelm I died on 9 March and Kaiser Friedrich III died on 15 June. Long before his reign of 99 days, Friedrich III was known to be terminally ill with throat cancer. Speculation had been rampant for months about what sort of regime, liberal or conservative, might be inaugurated in the time available to the dying emperor and, more importantly, with the ascension of his son Kaiser Wilhelm II. See the older J. Alden Nichols, *The Year of the Three Kaisers: Bismarck and the German Succession, 1887–88* (Chicago, 1987), and now Frank Lorenz Müller, *Our Fritz: Emperor Frederick III and the Political Culture of Imperial Germany* (Cambridge, MA, 2011).
26 See ch. 11 of the present volume.
27 See Manfred B. Steger and Terrell Carver, eds., *Engels after Marx* (University Park, PA, 1999).
28 Engels to Laura Lafargue, 26 February 1890, in James Retallack, ed., *Forging an Empire: Bismarckian Germany (1866–1890)*, vol. 4 of *German History in Documents and Images*, sec. 7, http://germanhistorydocs.ghi-dc.org/sub_document.cfm?document_id=692.
29 This prediction was false insofar as Chancellor Bernhard von Bülow (in office 1900–9) orchestrated a successful nationalist campaign for the Reichstag elections of January 1907. With considerable input from government forces, the nationalist parties, now including the left liberals, waged a chauvinistic campaign against the Social Democrats and Catholic Centre Party. The latter actually increased its number of Reichstag seats slightly, but the socialists were dealt a heavy blow, seeing their Reichstag caucus reduced from 81 to 43 members. See *inter alia* George Dunlap Crothers, *The German Elections of 1907* (New York, 1968).
30 Engels to Wilhelm Liebknecht, 9 March 1890; Wilhelm Liebknecht, *Briefwechsel mit Karl Marx und Friedrich Engels*, edited by Georg Eckert (The Hague, 1963), 366–7.
31 *NDB* 8 (1969): 474–5, and *NDB* 11 (1977): 150–1, respectively; Bernd Haunfelder, *Die konservativen Abgeordneten des Deutschen Reichstags 1871–1918. Ein biographisches Handbuch* (Münster, 2010), 125–7, 149–51; and the sketch of Helldorff in James Retallack, *The German Right, 1860–1920: Political Limits of the Authoritarian Imagination* (Toronto, 2006), 327–39.

32 Engels to Richard Fischer, 8 March 1895, cited by Wangermann in Engels, *The Role of Force*, 25.
33 Engels to Bebel, 28 October 1885, in *August Bebel. Briefwechsel mit Friedrich Engels* (The Hague, 1965), 242, cited by Wangermann in Engels, *The Role of Force*, 20.
34 Sächsisches Hauptstaatsarchiv Dresden, Ministerium des Auswärtigen Angelegenheiten, Nr. 1078a, Metzsch's Promemoria of 6 May 1893.
35 Wilhelm II to Hohenlohe (copy), 23 August 1895, in Chlodwig zu Hohenlohe-Schillingsfürst, *Denkwürdigkeiten der Reichskanzlerzeit*, edited by Karl Alexander von Müller (Osnabrück, 1967), 92.
36 Volker Stalmann, *Fürst Chlodwig zu Hohenlohe-Schillingsfürst. Ein deutscher Reichskanzler* (Stuttgart, 2009); Olav Zachau, *Die Kanzlerschaft des Fürsten Hohenlohe 1894–1900. Politik unter dem "Stempel der Beruhigung" im Zeitalter der Nervosität* (Hamburg, 2007).
37 See Hohenlohe's notes of 17 May 1895, Hohenlohe, *Denkwürdigkeiten der Reichskanzlerzeit*, 65–7.
38 The phrase was used in the Kaiser's speech in Königsberg on 6 September 1894 when he tried to rally loyal Germans against the alleged combination of socialist and anarchist threats. For more detail see ch. 11 in the present volume.
39 For guidance see Jonathan Sperber, "*Bürger, Bürgertum, Bürgerlichkeit, Bürgerliche Gesellschaft:* Studies of the German (Upper) Middle Class and Its Sociocultural World," *Journal of Modern History* 69 (1997): 271–97.

7 Heydebrand and Westarp: Leaving Behind the Second Reich

Introduction

To frame my analysis is to foreshadow my conclusion: the unpublished correspondence between Wilhelmine Germany's two leading Conservatives appears more lively if we bear in mind the words of the early biographer of Frederick the Great, Nancy Mitford, who contributed an essay on the English aristocracy to a volume titled *Noblesse Oblige*: "An aristocracy in a republic," Mitford wrote, "is like a chicken whose head has been cut off: it may run about in a lively way, but in fact it is dead."[1]

In this chapter I am less concerned with an aristocracy in a republic than with the fate of an anti-democratic political party, the German Conservative Party (Deutsch-Konservative Partei, or DKP), in two dramatically different political institutions. The first was Germany's semi-constitutional monarchy, which expired on 9 November 1918. The second was a parliamentary democracy, the Weimar Republic. The political cultures of Imperial and Weimar Germany are of course linked – historically, institutionally, and in the political thinking of leading statesmen of that time. Yet 9 November 1918 was a caesura as well as a transition. To say this is to say nothing new. But the unpublished correspondence discussed in this chapter allows us to view both continuities and discontinuities across 1918 in a new light. By painting a composite portrait of two political giants who drew very different lessons from the death throes of traditional German Conservatism, this chapter depicts multiple pathways out of the Wilhelmine era. It can thus be read against previous chapters on King Johann of Saxony and Friedrich Engels, which charted different paths into Bismarckian Germany.

Section I provides a brief introduction to Count Kuno von Westarp (1864–1945) and fuller biographical details on the less well-known party leader, Ernst von Heydebrand und der Lasa (1851–1924), who was Westarp's senior by thirteen years.[2] Section II discusses Heydebrand's political stature and historical significance in Imperial Germany. The third and fourth sections consider what insights into right-wing politics the Heydebrand–Westarp correspondence offers us.[3] Section III is devoted to the period up to 9 November 1918, Section IV to the period that followed. In the last two sections I offer more wide-ranging reflections about the Heydebrand–Westarp correspondence. Section V examines continuities in Conservative thinking on key issues across the threshold of 1918. Concluding remarks consider what the unpublished correspondence reveals – and what it hides.

I. "The Uncrowned King of Prussia"

Owner of a landed estate in the Prussian province of Silesia and a former county councillor (*Landrat*, 1883 to 1895), Ernst von Heydebrand und der Lasa served as de facto leader of the German Conservative Party from 1908 to 1918. As a member of the Prussian Landtag (1888–1918), he led the Conservative caucus in the House of Deputies – the lower chamber – after 1906. He was also elected to represent a rural Silesian constituency in the Reichstag (1903–18). A member of the Conservative Party's Committee of Five from 1902 onward, he was designated formal party chairman in 1913, a post he held until 1918.[4]

Count Kuno von Westarp was subordinate to Heydebrand in party ranks but has figured more prominently in the scholarly literature.[5] Westarp sprang from a family of aristocratic Prussian officers and civil servants in the eastern province of Posen, where he served as a county counsellor (*Landrat*) after 1893, as police director in Schöneberg after 1901, and as a jurist with the Prussian superior administrative court (*Oberverwaltungsgericht*) after 1903. Five years later he entered the Reichstag, where he rose quickly in prominence: by 1913 he was chairman of the Conservative Party's Reichstag caucus. But Westarp was destined for a second career after 1918 as a leading light in the German National People's Party (Deutschnationale Volkspartei, or DNVP), which was as much a "catch-all movement" (*Sammelbewegung*) as a party for the German Right.[6] He became the DNVP's caucus chairman in the Reichstag in 1925 and then its national chairman from 1925 to 1928.

Figure 7.1 Ernst von Heydebrand und der Lasa, the "uncrowned king of Prussia," was also known as "the little one" (*der Kleine*). From Kuno Graf von Westarp, *Konservative Politik im letzten Jahrzehnt des Kaiserreichs*, 2 vols. (Berlin: Deutsche Verlagsgesellschaft, 1935), vol. 1, facing 112.

Figure 7.2 Count Kuno von Westarp. From *Deutscher Aufstieg. Bilder aus der Vergangenheit und Gegenwart der rechtsstehenden Parteien*, edited by Hans von Arnim and Georg von Below (Berlin: F. Schneider, 1925), following 454.

As opposed to groups within the DNVP that were younger or more Pan-German in orientation, Westarp and his predecessor as party chairman, Oskar Hergt, belonged to an older and more moderate group. That group supported the new republic (though with great reluctance), and after 1924 it orchestrated the DNVP's participation in Weimar's ruling coalitions. With the rise of the Nazis and extra-parliamentary groups on the extreme Right, Westarp lost ground to Alfred Hugenberg, the powerful heavy industrialist and newspaper magnate who espoused a politics of uncompromising opposition to the Republic and who wrenched the DNVP chairmanship from Westarp in October 1928. From mid-1930 to mid-1932 Westarp attempted to rally the moderate Right in the form of a Conservative People's Party. But the Reichstag's dissolution in June 1932 led to the great Nazi breakthrough in elections the next month. Westarp's political star soon sank below the horizon.

Not so Westarp's place in German historical writing. To complement Westarp's own two-volume account of the Second Reich's last decade, in 2001 his account of the period from November 1918 to the summer of 1920 was published posthumously in a critical edition by his grandson, Baron Friedrich Hiller von Gaertringen. In May 2004 a conference was held in Gärtringen (not far from Stuttgart) to reconsider the life of "one of the most important Conservative politicians of the first third of the twentieth century." The resulting collection of essays reappraised Westarp's role in the evolution of the German Right, drawing upon two vast repositories of unpublished letters, manuscripts, and other writings, some of which lay behind the Iron Curtain until 1989 and some of which had been collected in Gärtringen, where they reside still. That essay collection's short title, "I am the last Prussian," was ironic in one sense because Heydebrand defended the old Prussia more steadfastly than did Westarp.

In both the German Reichstag and the Prussian Landtag, Heydebrand orchestrated his party's opposition to such government bills as the Finance Reform (1909), which effectively toppled Chancellor Bernhard von Bülow, and the Prussian Suffrage Reform (1910) – the first and perhaps most telling domestic defeat suffered by Bülow's successor, Chancellor Theobald von Bethmann Hollweg.[7] Heydebrand's resistance to domestic reform and democratization continued unabated during the war, even though Pan-German nationalists within the party challenged his authority after 1916.[8] A fanatical defender of Prussian – as opposed to German – interests, Heydebrand never established a personal relationship with his king and Kaiser, Wilhelm II. But it was no empty boast when Heydebrand once declared, "Prussian ministers must dance to my tune."[9]

In person, Heydebrand was blunt and haughty.[10] Always conscious of the historic power of his Junker class, he could be condescending and offensive. But he demanded and usually won unquestioning loyalty from members of the Conservative caucus. Remarkably small of stature, like Bismarck he possessed a weak speaking voice. Heydebrand was nonetheless a brilliant rhetorician and tactical leader in parliament – one of perhaps a half-dozen political superstars in Imperial Germany.[11] Because of his unbending will, even Bethmann Hollweg spoke of Heydebrand's dictatorial and demagogic strains.[12] His diminutive physical build stood in stark contrast to his Olympian political stature.

A common thread running through contemporary descriptions of Heydebrand is the focus and determination with which he worked to preserve the power of the Conservative Party and his native Prussia. Franz Sontag, the Pan-German enthusiast who once served on the editorial staffs of the Conservatives' *Neue Preußische Zeitung* (known as the *Kreuzzeitung*) and the Free Conservatives' *Post*, remarked in his unpublished memoirs that, for Heydebrand, the logic of the Reich ended at the frontier of Prussia.[13] Within his own party, added Sontag, Heyebrand's "Führer personality" allowed him to establish "an absolute regime." But Sontag was aware that Heydebrand's single-mindedness was a two-edged sword:

> Unfortunately, his [Heydebrand's] political strength was his weakness at the same time; for just as he had, before the war, interpreted the concept of conservatism all too narrowly in terms of conserving the status quo, he also regarded Prussia in particular not so much as the idea meant to shape Germany's destiny; instead, he viewed it as a concrete political reality that, in its historically evolved features, one had to maintain with the greatest tenacity. To be sure, this did not prevent him from affirming the notion of empire ... to whose existence one had been forced to resign oneself willy-nilly. However, to him the requirements of the Reich, having demanded enough sacrifices of people as it was, ended at the line marked with black-and-white boundary posts: This was where Prussia began, the most spotless [*sauberste*], best governed, most moral, and thus most perfect country in the world, whose divinely-ordained order needed no political imports from the western parts [of the empire] or from south of the Main River. Consequently, it was at these boundary posts that Herr von Heydebrand stood, of small stature but a knight without fear and without reproach,

wielding an unsheathed weapon at all times, always prepared to duel for this Prussia even against his king. When they buried him, they lowered into the Silesian soil of Klein Tschunkawe the last and most loyal guardian of old Prussia.

Eugen Schiffer, a leading National Liberal who periodically met secretly with Heydebrand, was also impressed by the directness of his manner and the sureness with which he pursued his goals. In his memoirs Schiffer recalled how Heydebrand expressed his innermost convictions in private conversation:[14] "As you see me before you here," Heydebrand told him once, "I do not show any consideration for my wife and family, my house and home, for things private; to me there exists only the one thing, [which is] the focus of my thoughts and my sentiments, of all my actions – the party." To defend his party while defending his Fatherland did not appear to Heydebrand as an irreconcilable challenge. "I intend at least to maintain its [the party's] size at the level at which I took it over and wish to pass it on to my successor. This is why I fight with all my strength against anything that threatens it – and there are plenty of threats, originating particularly from the government."

Theodor Wolff, chief editor of the left-liberal *Berliner Tageblatt*, referred to the Conservative leader as a huge talent.[15] The Conservative parliamentarian Alfred von Goßler, despite his differences with Heydebrand, described him as "the most important and most interesting personality, not only in the Conservative Party but overall in the political world of that time." According to Goßler, "a wholly uncommon consciousness of power, combined with a will that was unbending, hard as steel, made him a born leader."[16] Yet Goßler understood that Conservatives had to "let Heydebrand be Heydebrand," for better or worse:

> This consciousness of his power ... never degenerated into personal vanity, concentrating instead on his political goal, the advocacy of Conservative and Prussian ideas. Had he been vain, he could have earned an abundance of titles and decorations. But throughout, he remained a modest man concerning his own person, simple in his lifestyle almost to a fault – in the best and truest sense of the word a representative of the old Prussian ways. Considering the curtness and reservedness that characterized his political dealings, though, it was inevitable that ... he made enemies ... This phenomenon manifested itself particularly in his relations to others ... A little more personal willingness to cooperate, a little more pliability in small matters not only would have made his own position easier but

would also have been to his party's advantage ... Even at the zenith of his power, Heydebrand remained a lonely man, and only very few confidants ... knew his innermost political thoughts and objectives.

Many contemporary accounts echo Goßler's attempt to balance Heydebrand's political grandeur against his personal pettiness. But Heydebrand's tactical brilliance was inseparable from his willingness to go for the jugular – a combination that left no one unimpressed. Thus State Secretary of the Reich Treasury Office Reinhold von Sydow recalled in his memoirs that one question was repeatedly asked in the Prussian state ministry when a crucial issue of domestic policy was discussed: What does Heydebrand say about this?[17] When Heydebrand and Bethmann Hollweg clashed in 1911, Bethmann's secretary and confidant, Kurt Riezler, spoke of Heydebrand's ambition to topple the chancellor in titanic terms: he referred to the conflict as one not between two men but between Germany and Prussia.[18] But Eugen Schiffer's private account provides the most compelling portrait of Heydebrand:

> People really do call him the uncrowned King of Prussia with good reason. In parliament and among members of government he is dubbed the "little one," and again certainly not without good reason. He is conspicuously small of stature, which is why he never positions himself behind the lectern but rather next to it. Obviously, he does so on the right side, in order to stay close to his *garde du corps* and as far as possible away from the Left. There he stands, shaking his little head from time to time while formulating his sentences in a relatively soft voice. [They] sometimes resemble a throne speech rather than a parliamentary speech. From time to time, he turns to the government bench, reproaching those seated there, one moment condescendingly, the next moment even threateningly; or he hurls bolts of lightning against the Left, accompanied by the thundering applause of his myrmidons.

Like the most talented parliamentarians in the Second Reich, Heydebrand spoke freely on the floor of the house – according to Schiffer, "easily and effortlessly." However, Heydebrand once told Schiffer that "it costs him almost unbearable exertions to formulate his thoughts properly." Prior to a speech, Heydebrand would sometimes wander for hours in Berlin's *Tiergarten*; there he would try "to collect himself, to reflect, and to formulate his ideas." When he finally mounted the rostrum, he would "sometimes feel as though the veins on his temples [were] about to burst."[19]

II. Heydebrand and the Radical Nationalists

Transcriptions of the unpublished Heydebrand–Westarp correspondence were made available to me and countless other historians through the generosity of Baron Hiller von Gaertringen.[20] The correspondence begins in 1911, when Heydebrand appeared to move closer to the nationalist opposition to Chancellor Bethmann Hollweg. This political watershed is commonly associated with radical nationalist outrage over Bethmann's Moroccan policy. Can we discern here any real evidence that the Conservatives were prepared to endorse the kinds of foreign policy aims that animated Pan-Germans (both inside and outside the party) during the war? Or was the tension between moderate and radical Conservatism more complex, and its resolution less conclusive, than is generally believed?

The story of Bethmann's unsuccessful policy in the Second Moroccan Crisis of late 1911 is well-known.[21] On 9 November – a date that has acquired great resonance in German history – Bethmann defended his French settlement in the Reichstag.[22] It was on this occasion that Heydebrand, scheduled to speak after the chancellor, chose to prove that the Conservative Party was indeed a "people's party" with legitimate nationalist credentials. Heydebrand called the Morocco settlement a worthless agreement and declared that lasting peace could only be secured by the German sword. The import of Heydebrand's speech was not lost on anyone. For the first time, Heydebrand's bitter and aggressive words – towards England and towards Bethmann himself – were a match for what leaders of the Pan-German League had been saying for years. The crown prince underscored the importance of the occasion by applauding conspicuously from the royal box as Heydebrand's verbal attack on Bethmann reached its climax.

Contemporaries and historians have argued that Heydebrand's attack on the government was a clear indication that the Conservatives were willing to join the nationalist opposition. But Heydebrand was also attempting to redefine the Conservative Party's popular image and to reinvigorate a moribund anti-socialist campaign for the Reichstag elections fast approaching in January 1912. Germany's Social Democratic Party (SPD) had already built its election campaign around the accusation that the Conservatives formed a chauvinistic agrarian interest group. The Conservatives, claimed the SPD with some justification, were directly responsible for the new taxes of 1909 that had created economic hardship for consumers. Heydebrand wanted to counter SPD propaganda as forcefully as he could. His goal was to show voters that his party was a dynamic, committed, independent, and "national" party, worthy of the loyalty (and votes) not just of aristocrats but of all the little men of Germany who shared his shame over the defeat of Bethmann's Moroccan policy.[23]

The confrontation between Heydebrand and Bethmann on the floor of the Reichstag in November 1911 opened more questions about the viability of Bethmann Hollweg's government than Conservatives wanted to address at this juncture. Liberals immediately anticipated a new direction for government policy and a new alignment of pro-government parties.[24] Some liberals even dared to hope for a Grand Bloc of left-wing parties from the National Liberals to the socialists – from Ernst Bassermann on the middle-Right to August Bebel on the Left.[25] But more interesting is the response from members of the moderate conservative establishment.[26] Rudolf von Valentini, chief of the civil cabinet, wrote to Kaiser Wilhelm II's friend and shipping magnate, Albert Ballin, in mid-November about the recent speakers' duel in the Reichstag. Bethmann's political standing, Valentini wrote, had been considerably improved with the help of two people – Heydebrand and the crown prince.[27] Baroness Hildegard von Spitzemberg, wife of Württemberg's envoy in Berlin, agreed: the Kaiser must be firmly behind Bethmann if the chancellor was able to reply to Heydebrand's attack with such harsh words. Bethmann's rebuttal to Heydebrand, she noted, "threw the house into blank amazement and 'brought the retreat to a halt.'"[28] She added that "general outrage exists over the inappropriate behaviour of the crown prince." Upon exiting the Reichstag, the prince had remarked to the Bavarian envoy in Berlin, Count Hugo von Lerchenfeld-Köfering, that "Heydebrand's speech was certainly terrific!" To this Lerchenfeld replied, "Y[our] H[ighness], it was an election speech!'"

Acute conflict in the Reichstag was something to be avoided, at least for many Conservatives. A contributor to the *Allgemeine Konservative Monatsschrift* in December 1911 spoke for these moderates when he suggested that the current political situation was infected with the spirit of negativism. He called on the Conservative Party to preserve its political independence, not through opposition but rather through a kind of moderate governmentalism.[29] Similar efforts to define the limits of loyal opposition to the government afflicted Westarp and the German National People's Party in the 1920s. But at least in retrospect – that is, in his memoirs, published in 1935 – Westarp sided with those who saw the German Conservative Party confronted with a "crisis of authority" that had begun not long after the turn of the century. A sense of crisis became palpable with the Social Democrats' stunning Reichstag victories in June 1903 and January 1912; with the "loss of face" Germany experienced during the First and Second Moroccan crises; with the revision of parliamentary suffrages in almost all federal states except Prussia; and with the increasing power of the Reichstag to constrain the political course of the Reich chancellor or to censure him and his king.

Once Bethmann Hollweg replaced Bülow in July 1909 – after the Conservative and Catholic Centre parties had refused to grant the taxes Bülow requested – Westarp acknowledged that the Conservatives had become "an outspoken opposition party without a majority."[30] Yet Westarp also remembered occasional conversations in which he and Heydebrand could not decide whether Bethmann's "indecisiveness" or "lack of fighting spirit" was more fateful for their party and for Germany. Either way, "for reasons of state we took a strong stand against his [Bethmann Hollweg's] weakness in the face of Social Democracy and the democratic tendencies of the day and against the thirst for power of the parties in the Reichstag."[31]

III. To November 1918

The Heydebrand–Westarp correspondence up to November 1918 is best considered in tandem with Westarp's two-volume history, *Konservative Politik im letzten Jahrzehnt des Kaiserreichs*, as well as Westarp's other writings about the pre-revolutionary period.[32] Little of the Heydebrand–Westarp correspondence is devoted to the prewar years. Although it comprises 216 typewritten pages covering entries from 9 June 1911 to 11 November 1918, the transcription reaches 3 August 1914 on page 16. There is only one letter from 1911, and there are none at all from 1912 or 1913. The correspondence begins in earnest only at the end of March 1914.[33]

Even in those first fifteen pages we find glimmering nuggets. The correspondence reveals, for example, that Westarp recognized in mid-1911 that retention of public voting for Prussian Landtag elections actually held grave dangers for the Conservatives, who were known as the classic opponents of the secret ballot. In urban working-class districts, Westarp wrote to Heydebrand, public voting provided the Social Democrats with a "monstrous advantage." Hardly any shopkeepers or artisans dared to vote for non-socialist parties or stand as delegates in the two-stage voting procedure. However, Westarp doubted whether even the secret ballot for Prussian elections would help Conservatives in the cities.

Fears arose on the same issue when Heydebrand and Westarp corresponded about a possible suffrage reform initiative from the government in early 1914. Heydebrand counselled Westarp to sharpen his attacks against suffrage reform in the Conservative press. He suggested that Westarp should be more explicit in his warning to Bethmann Hollweg that the chancellor must not "drive a new wedge" between the non-socialist parties with a reform bill. On 7 April 1914, Heydebrand was still worried that Friedrich Wilhelm von Loebell, a former Conservative insider and about to become Bethmann's minister of the interior, might be asked to serve as a "suffrage reform minister."

Despite these details, this phase of the Heydebrand–Westarp correspondence mainly confirms what we already knew from other sources. Many challenges and few opportunities faced Conservative politicians seeking to break out of growing political isolation after the "red elections" of January 1912. Then as we move into the war years, we begin to uncover personal details – albeit more often from Heydebrand than from Westarp. On 3 August 1914, Heydebrand was effusive about the coming of war. "What a turn of events!" he wrote to Westarp from his estate in Silesia, only six miles from the Polish border. But Heydebrand also complained that the war had taken his estate's best workers and managers. Moreover, the army had requisitioned his desperately needed draught animals and his riding horses during the summer harvest. For these reasons, Heydebrand was unwilling to travel to Berlin. A Russian raid was expected at any moment, he announced. On 22 November, Heydebrand again complained to Westarp about the onerous requisitioning and billeting demands of the army, which required his constant presence on his estate.

These personal concerns did not prevent Heydebrand and Westarp from writing to each other about political matters of the highest priority. By 6 August 1914, Westarp was fully aware of the political profit Social Democrats would derive from the domestic truce (*Burgfrieden*) proclaimed by the Kaiser. With foresight, Westarp also conceived of an independent postwar Poland as "a difficult problem, which will cause us worries for decades even with a successful end to the war." Over the remaining war years, we catch glimpses of the shattering effect of political division and acrimony on Germany's political culture. The Heydebrand–Westarp correspondence offers intriguing details about intra-party factionalism, the peccadilloes of Conservative Party insiders, candidate selection, the divergent strategies pursued by Conservative press organs (from the *Kreuzzeitung* down to local news-sheets), and the difficult business of maintaining a party bureau in Berlin. On balance, it may be true that Westarp's published history of these years provides at least as much insight and detail as the unpublished correspondence, and sometimes more. For instance, the Conservatives' negotiations with Bethmann Hollweg, the Pan-German leader Heinrich Claß, and Alfred Hugenberg between September and December 1914 are better covered in the published volume.[34] Nevertheless, it is intriguing – and sometimes critically important – to read Heydebrand's remarks and marginalia verbatim: those remarks signalled the "go slow" policy over war aims that Heydebrand would pursue for the rest of the war.

Two examples suffice to illustrate the significance of the Conservatives' foot-dragging on this issue. On 26 September 1914, Westarp wrote to Heydebrand:

> Herr Hugenberg approached me for an informal meeting; it lasted two hours and covered next to all questions of foreign and domestic politics. His ideas concerning foreign policy resemble approximately those of the Pan-Germans; in terms of domestic politics, he has at hand a rather comprehensive program too ... [Hugenberg wanted] to discuss whether one could ... agree on common ground regarding the peace accord and the reconstruction of domestic politics and the economic system.
>
> I would like to propose that we reach out for such negotiations: even though many items he wishes to draw into the talks are rather premature, one might be able to work out something practical in time, and I do not, at any rate, wish to reject the extended hand ... Whether he intends to involve National Liberals as well, I could not determine clearly.

Beside the words "National Liberal," Heydebrand's marginal comment reads simply: "the main point."

The second example is from a letter Heydebrand wrote to Westarp on 30 December 1914. In it he noted that Heinrich Claß's Pan-German war aims were "far too extensive" and, for the most part, neither feasible nor even useful. Heydebrand had signalled "politely" to both Claß and Hugenberg that he was prepared to talk further about the issue, but confidentially to Westarp he wrote, "I cannot commit myself to the type of utopias and pure political twaddle of these gentlemen under any circumstances!"

The correspondence thus makes clear that the Conservatives were involved, at least initially, in their own two-front war: against Bethmann, and against the Pan-Germans. When Westarp wrote to Heydebrand on 18 November 1914, he offered clear evidence that the Conservative Party and the government were already drawing apart. Reporting on discussions between government representatives and the *Freie Kommission* that had been drawn from all parties of the Reichstag, Westarp wrote, "I emphasized that now one ought to concentrate on the war as the one mission and defer everything else." In short, Heydebrand was not the only one resisting Pan-German demands; Westarp offered his own critiques of unrealistic war aims and wanted to retain the Conservative Party's right to oppose them. As he wrote in one letter, "A meeting among an extended circle [of people] is scheduled for Monday, 30 Nov. at 1:30 p.m. [to discuss] the aims of domestic politics. I had been able to attend only the very end of the previous gathering with the Pan-Germans because a meeting at Delbrück's[35] office took place at the same time. I had arrived just in time to listen to the summaries of goals set for dividing up the world."[36]

IV. The Second Reich in the Rear-View Mirror

What insights can we draw from the Heydebrand–Westarp correspondence after November 1918? In this section it is *not* my intention to appraise the substance of Westarp's political philosophy, either as it was reflected in his correspondence with Heydebrand or as it is presented in his book, *Konservative Politik im Übergang*. In the latter we see that Westarp felt no reason to apologize for using terms and concepts that proved so poisonous in Weimar discourse. Even a cursory survey turns up such phrases as "liberation from enemy domination," "constitution without choice" (*Not-Verfassung*), "rule of the masses," "the methods and consequences of agitational bellowing for the favour of the voting masses," the "*Diktat* of Compiègne," and "the revolutionary treason of November [1918]."[37] Westarp did not try to disguise his wish for a monarchical restoration, his determination to preserve the pre-eminence of Prussia, or his support for Wolfgang Kapp's abortive Putsch in the spring of 1920.[38]

One of the most interesting aspects of the Heydebrand–Westarp correspondence in this period is these men's overwhelming focus on *Prussian* circumstances. This focus bordered on obsession. It appears in Heydebrand's very first letter to Westarp after his brief visit to Berlin on 12 November 1918. As Heydebrand wrote, "Undoubtedly Prussia will initially become a republic, like the rest of 'Germany.'"[39] Yet we learn little from either Westarp's published accounts or the unpublished portion of the Heydebrand–Westarp correspondence about Conservative Party affairs outside Prussia. For interest's sake I took the second volume of Westarp's history of pre-1918 Germany and counted references to its leading federal states in the subject index. I found there that Bavaria was mentioned on 4 pages; Saxony was mentioned on no pages at all (although the "uncrowned king of Saxony," Paul Mehnert, was mentioned twice); Baden was mentioned on 1 page, and Württemberg was mentioned on 3 pages. By contrast, the United States was mentioned on 41 pages, Belgium on 42 pages, Russia on 40 pages, and England more times than I could bear to count. When I consulted the index of place names in Westarp's *Konservative Politik im Übergang*, I discovered a similar pattern. Apart from localities lying within the various states, Bavaria was listed on 13 pages and Saxony on 8 pages. But there were 23 entries for the Prussian province of East Prussia alone and 21 entries for the province of Silesia (not counting a further 8 for Upper Silesia).

We catch glimpses of local affairs in the Heydebrand–Westarp correspondence, particularly when these leaders discuss the wrangling over local party candidacies.[40] But just as typical is Westarp's frustrated conclusion in a letter to Heydebrand, dated 6 January 1919, that the local and provincial Conservative Party organizations were largely responsible for his own inability to bring more "genuine" Conservative policy and personnel into the DNVP. This complaint is worth quoting because it reveals two things. It shows how much political distance remained between grassroots party activities and the caucus leaders. And it reminds us how little we still know about Conservative Party affairs in Germany's non-Prussian regions and localities:

> For the Conservative cause, the outcome [of preparations for the National Assembly elections] ... is very sad ... This flop is not connected with the central executive committee [of the DNVP], which saw the other three parties and [DNVP chairman Oskar] Hergt make every effort to live up to our requirements, but rather with the complete failure of the provincial and local associations. Considering the extremely poor links we had here with the provincial branches, it is very difficult for me to assess the degree to which, due to the transition toward the new form of party, the so-called "new" elements previously not Conservative or only Conservative on the surface have gained the upper hand as well, or whether our own people

failed. It seems to me that the latter was also the case to a great extent and that across the country the formerly Conservative folk join in the same chorus: "new men" – "no aristocrats," "no big landowners," "no names that have previously distinguished themselves," etc. Hergt claims that in this context the motive is not so much mistrust of our previous policies than the fear of voters running away. That may be. The result amounts to an exceedingly curious parliamentary group ... comprised of new but also minor people ... [and which] is supposed to draw up the constitution and make peace![41]

Both Heydebrand and Westarp strove to preserve as much as possible of the German Conservative Party's formal apparatus even after the founding of the German National People's Party. This strategy is well chronicled in Westarp's *Konservative Politik im Übergang*. Westarp observed that Heydebrand took a more dogmatic position than he did regarding the founding proclamation of the DNVP in November 1918. This difference of opinion between the two Conservative leaders is not unknown to historians. In 1978, Jens Flemming documented Heydebrand's conviction that the German Conservative Party could not be allowed simply to fade away.[42] But from the Heydebrand–Westarp correspondence we learn just how insistent Heydebrand could be on this point. In a letter of 4 January 1919, Heydebrand complained about "the composition of the new picture of the DNVP, [which] in appearance is essentially Free Conservative or middle-party." That party, Heydebrand continued, "will be difficult to provide with enough objective support ... for genuine conservative ideas." Westarp had conceded that any designation as a "people's party" signified "a dishonest bellowing for the favor of the masses." Even so, Heydebrand had proposed (in vain) that the new party be given the name Conservative People's Party or even German Conservative People's Party.[43] Clearly, he could not understand how tainted the word "Conservative" was, or why.

Regarding this divergence of opinion, Westarp was forthright in his published history. He acknowledged the different pressures, priorities, and proximity to information that necessarily distinguished his outlook from Heydebrand's. He also acknowledged Heydebrand's frustration, which is even more evident in the correspondence. This frustration arose from Heydebrand's sense that he was being shut out of daily decision-making. He also felt that he was being provided with too little information to judge the Conservative Party's available options, especially in the critical months of 1919. He observed more than once that he wanted to withdraw from political life entirely. Indeed, both men used this threat of resignation to bring their colleagues into line. However, such threats were taken less seriously by DNVP colleagues with each passing year. Thus Elard von Oldenburg-Januschau wrote to Hermann Kreth in 1920, shortly after Kreth had failed to win nomination as a DNVP candidate: "My dear Kreth, when it comes to dealing with your candidature, any malice can be ruled out. This confirms once again the insight that the old gods are soon forgotten once they leave the stage and must yield to those whose names appear in the newspapers."[44]

Westarp's experience of the "new politics" was very different from Heydebrand's. Westarp was quite literally front and centre on the DNVP's political stage. His columns in the *Kreuzzeitung* devoted to domestic politics were read avidly each week. By contrast, Heydebrand was hamstrung by his distance from Berlin and his reluctance to take part in meetings in the capital (or even in Breslau) unless absolutely necessary. All this was to a large extent dictated by the precarious situation of Heydebrand's estate. The complaints he had raised in August 1914 continued in a different form after 9 November 1918. Through 1919, Heydebrand was still obliged to quarter troops protecting the eastern border. His estate was used as an observation post for artillery battles on the border with Poland, and allegedly he was shot at a number of times while riding his fields.[45]

Tensions and misunderstandings between Westarp and Heydebrand arose from time to time. Those tensions often required one-on-one meetings to sort them out (which, Westarp claimed, was usually possible). But not all differences of opinion can be ascribed to the difficulties of long-range correspondence. Heydebrand's more direct manner comes through in his letters to Westarp. Consider his letter of 14 January 1919: "I do not know whether you would have managed, as you believe, to lead the Conservative Party toward the new structure; you hardly would have had me, for example, by your side in this endeavour."

One irreconcilable difference of opinion between the two men came to the fore in 1919–20. Westarp had gradually concluded that an independent German Conservative Party could not be sustained in parallel to the DNVP. By contrast, Heydebrand stubbornly refused to consider dissolving the DKP altogether. He adhered to a position he stated clearly for Westarp in a letter of 23 January 1919: "Now the *main* thing is that, amidst the turmoil and flood of things flowing and collapsing, we firmly and beyond doubt uphold *the banner of the party* [i.e., the German Conservative Party], around which a future might one day be built."

This divergence is richly documented in the correspondence, where we see how grand strategy and tactics fit together – or didn't. Each man pressed his campaign in his own way, which was not always in step with the other. It was far from obvious to Heydebrand and Westarp, for example, whether they should try to bring as many program points as possible from the German Conservative program into the DNVP platform, particularly given the apparent imminence of the DKP's final dissolution. Might a better strategy involve emphasizing those points that *divided* the parties, in an attempt to retain the DKP's political *raison d'être*? Heydebrand addressed this dilemma when he wrote to Westarp on 5 October 1919:

> The question concerning the program and the party convention that you touch upon is difficult. I suppose a certain degree of reservation lies in bringing the German National program in line with the Conservative counterpart to such an extent that one might deem the latter superfluous in the end?
>
> It would not hurt us Conservatives at all if unitary state [vs.] federal state – [if] preservation of Prussia – [if] constitutional Hohenzollern monarchy [vs.] parliamentarianism – were to remain key differences vis-à-vis the recently revised G[erman] N[ational] program. That, too, is a point on which some day opinions might differ between G[erman] N[ationals] and Conservatives (not to mention other issues).

Westarp was able to prevent Heydebrand from issuing a public statement calling for the preservation of the German Conservative Party. Westarp believed, correctly, that such a statement would have been received as a declaration of war against the DNVP. Silencing Heydebrand's public candidness in such matters was one of Westarp's most important accomplishments in these years. This achievement takes on added significance when one considers just how much effort was required to combat Oskar Hergt's demand for the outright and permanent dissolution of the Conservative Party and its Central Association.

A meeting between Heydebrand and Hergt in the autumn of 1919 was nothing less than disastrous. At that meeting, the two men discussed the question of Conservative candidacies on the DNVP's electoral list and early plans for what eventually became the Kapp Putsch in March 1920. Shortly after the meeting, on 8 November 1919, Heydebrand's hubris was blatant in his depiction of the conversation. He wrote to Westarp that Hergt had "sat on his high horse" and acted as though he was receiving a "verbal report" from an underling. Heydebrand felt that "it might not hurt to teach him" a thing or two, namely, that he was facing a man who could rightly claim "a certain measure of history for himself and his party." If Hergt was unwilling to act collegially, Heydebrand wrote, then he must not be allowed to adopt an air of superiority: that was "out of the question."

Three months later, Heydebrand expressed his dismissive attitude towards Hergt even more clearly. In response to a speech Hergt had recently delivered in Münster, Heydebrand wrote to Westarp on 20 February 1920. Again Heydebrand drew on what he (mistakenly) believed was the political clout to which his long career entitled him. Hergt's "manifesto" was so full of "inaccuracies, ignorance, and tactlessness" that any party should fear "the leadership of a man like this." Had Hergt perhaps been sleeping during the past fifteen years, Heydebrand asked rhetorically, while he had personally led the Conservative charge in the Prussian House of Deputies and when his speeches had helped defeat the Reich Finance Reform?

Heydebrand's personal animosity towards Hergt contributed to his feeling that Westarp was not sufficiently critical of the DNVP leader or his policies. In December 1919, after Hergt had taken a public stand against the DKP, Heydebrand insinuated to Westarp that his inability to criticize Hergt sufficiently or defend the Conservative Party's prerogatives derived from Westarp's hope to be nominated as a DNVP candidate. On another occasion, in the margins of a letter from Westarp describing his decision to take on the role of chief editor with the *Kreuzzeitung*, Heydebrand scribbled a particularly ungenerous comment: "With editorial posts Westarp is continually feathering his own nest."[46] In his published history, Westarp did his best to ascribe these hurtful accusations to Heydebrand's suspicious nature. But he did not conceal the depth of their disagreement or the fact that Heydebrand was so obviously disappointed in his actions. He wrote that "even my reports about the extent to which I had managed to incorporate Conservative demands into the German National party program did not meet with his [Heydebrand's] approval."[47]

Westarp was willing to concede that he had erred in accepting Hergt's request that he address the first party congress of the DNVP in July 1919. That address significantly raised Westarp's profile in the DNVP. And for that reason it aroused Heydebrand's ire. Even before the DNVP congress, in a letter of 9 July, Heydebrand had written to Westarp: "Your dual position entails quite a bit of awkwardness both for you and for us, e.g., the circumstance [has] now arisen that these fine German

National gentlemen have the nerve to want to drag you, as it were, before their court to account for measures you took in the Conservative Party." After the congress, Heydebrand again refused to gaze admiringly at Westarp's rising star. On 19 August he wrote, "I frankly admit that your exceedingly brilliant speech would have met with my wholehearted approval at a *Conservative* party convention."[48] But in Heydebrand's eyes, Westarp's speech "failed to improve the awkward situation of our party" – indeed, it had worsened it. Westarp defended himself against Heydebrand's accusation by observing that his address to the party congress had had one positive outcome: "Hergt was afforded the opportunity to keep antisemitic debates on the back burner, continuing to have the antisemitic question treated in a dilatory way."[49]

Tensions between Heydebrand and Westarp reached their high point in the winter of 1919–20. With growing insistence, Heydebrand demanded that the DKP's Committee of Fifty be convened. He expected that it would agree on a resolution calling on the DKP to maintain its independence. Westarp was aware that such a resolution would likely lead to a showdown with the DNVP's leaders and perhaps even a disavowal of his and Heydebrand's leadership within the rump Conservative Party. So he did everything in his power to postpone such a meeting. Westarp's efforts here were aided by the difficult transportation situation in Germany over that winter, and then by the Kapp Putsch in the spring of 1920.

Eventually the Conservative Party's Committee of Fifty did meet, on 11 May 1920. At that meeting it declared that it supported "adherence to the continued existence of the Conservative Party as an unconditional political necessity." The victory was pyrrhic. By the end of the summer of 1920, Westarp realized that the fate of the old party had been sealed. It was no longer politically possible for a separate right-wing party to exist alongside the DNVP. The need for right-wing unity, the immediate challenges still facing the anti-Republican Right, the DNVP's demonstrated self-sufficiency – all these factors now demanded unity above all else.

Westarp's decision to part with the DKP was one of the most difficult he ever made. Yet his account of the "crisis of conscience" he went through in the summer of 1920 is noteworthy for its lack of sentimentality:

> The negotiations with v. Heydebrand about relations between the Conservative Party and the DNVP were particularly painful to me, and the

decisions I had to take and advocate in this context ranked among the most difficult ones in my political life ... Our factual difference of opinion, the first and only one of any significance separating us during a decade and a half of working together, was profound ...

As to the substance of the matter, the tragic destiny that was the demise of the Conservative Party took its ultimate course only now. [Herr] v. Heydebrand experienced the dismantling of the Conservative party edifice in the role of a casual bystander with the grim sentiment of being shut out, not being heard, and not being able to change anything. I incurred the duty of participating personally in the final demolition of our life's work ... The time when parliamentary decisions had to wait upon the presence of the "uncrowned king" had passed ... Indeed, my election [to the Reichstag] on 6 June 1920 ended any possibility of bringing the Conservative Party back to active life.[50]

V. Continuities

If we compare the challenges Westarp faced between 1918 and 1920 and those that the Conservative Party faced earlier in its history, intriguing continuities come to light. First, Westarp never warmed to the idea of trying to increase the party's appeal among women and youth.[51] In early 1914 he had written to Heydebrand that one had to put the best face possible on efforts to form a Young Conservative faction within the DKP. After 1918, when the DNVP was forced to inaugurate new appeals to this clientele, Westarp's view was essentially unchanged. Second, it did not become easier for Westarp and Heydebrand to reconcile their defence of Prussian interests with a warm embrace of national goals. They continued to equate anything that was good or bearable in Weimar Germany – their list was not long – with Prussia's historic role. Third, Westarp's speeches rarely failed to cite the need to distinguish between the working classes and Social Democracy. This perpetuated a familiar trope from Conservative propaganda on the social question dating from the Imperial period. It is impossible to overlook the continuity between Westarp's abiding suspicion of the Christian Social Party (CSP) and its affiliated Protestant Workers' Associations – "relations between the German National workers' organization and me were not free of intrinsic scruples"[52] – and similar doubts within the German Conservative Party during and after the alliance with Court Preacher Adolf Stöcker's CSP in the 1880s and 1890s. For these reasons it remains an open question just how and why Westarp was able to make his peace with a new party, the DNVP, whose program revolved around the "triad of the national, Christian, social idea."[53]

The German Revolution of 1918 did not make it any easier than it had been during the Second Reich to distinguish between conservatives who were also antisemitic and antisemites who were also conservative.[54] In both Westarp's published work and his letters to Heydebrand, one finds little of the radical antisemitism that jumps off the page in Conservative propaganda from the Imperial and Weimar eras. In Westarp's *Konservative Politik im Übergang*, antisemitism only occasionally rears its head. For example, in decrying the willingness of socialist and communist agitators to whip up public outrage against the bourgeoisie, Westarp wrote, "They were provided with the material toward that end less by the undeniable mistakes of a sated, materialistic, democratic-Jewish bourgeoisie than by the rancorous envy of the 'unpropertied classes' against any type of possession and any type of educated refinement, resentments that they fuelled artificially."[55]

Nevertheless, the list of conservative newspapers that Westarp read avidly (besides the *Kreuzzeitung*) contained a disproportionate number of antisemitic organs.[56] Westarp was not averse to echoing familiar conservative calls for the protection of an independent *Mittelstand* in the face of "international, mainly Jewish big capital."[57] And he blamed the Jews themselves, in particular Jewish immigrants from eastern Europe, for the dramatic rise of extreme antisemitism in the final years of the war and the immediate postwar years.[58]

Such instances of antisemitic opinion are not the main story here. As Stephan Malinowski's research on the German Society of Nobles has demonstrated, we would be surprised if antisemitic tropes did *not* crop up in an aristocratic Conservative leader's public record in this era.[59] The more striking continuity is the difficulty Westarp experienced in setting the limits to what he felt was a demagogic, dangerous, "unworthy" kind of agitation against the Jews. Why is *that* continuity so important?

On the one hand, Westarp's position seems relatively clear, even laudable. One of his goals was "to set certain limits [within the DNVP] to the fight against Jewry, the violation of which only a few antisemitic outsiders failed to view as an impossible exaggeration." Westarp's weekly review published in the *Kreuzzeitung* on 30 November 1919 was written in response to renewed attempts by Albrecht von Graefe-Goldebee and other prominent antisemites within the party to push the DNVP in a more radical direction. In that review Westarp was programmatic: "It is obvious that any politician who deserves to be taken seriously rejects acts of violence against Jews."⁶⁰ Westarp also endorsed the DNVP leadership when it refused to accept a motion that Jews be barred from membership in the party and when it opposed the plans of its younger, *völkisch* members to establish a German-Racist Working Group within the party.

On the other hand, it is equally clear that Westarp, like many Conservative Party leaders from the 1880s and 1890s, felt that an extreme, demagogic form of antisemitism undermined the more lofty, "legitimate" struggle against Jewish dominance in Germany. After claiming that he had distanced himself from Weimar antisemites in order to preserve peace within the DNVP, he added:

> In doing so, I not only wished to serve the unity of the DNVP. From the pre-war period, I remembered quite clearly how the overly radical antisemitism after about 1890 had contributed to fragmenting and paralyzing the defense against aggressive Jewry. A repeat of that was to be avoided; instead, the aim was to pave the way for a struggle against the Jewish threat with goals and methods that were supported by strict German views but could still be regarded as just and feasible.⁶¹

In that same overview of 30 November 1919, Westarp conceded that the Conservative Party's infamous Tivoli program of December 1892, which contained an explicit attack against the "pervasive" and "corrosive" Jewish influence in German life,⁶² had been overtaken. But it had been overtaken, he wrote, *only* insofar as it had conceived of "the struggle against the destructive influence of Jewry" as a religious question. By contrast, Westarp stated, the Conservative Party's own political practice had transformed the "Jewish Question" into a matter of race. And properly understood as a matter of race rather than religion, the "Jewish Question" deserved its place among the most compelling issues currently facing the German people. This was true, Westarp wrote retrospectively, because the Weimar Coalition, which included Social Democracy, had opened the floodgates of Jewish immigration from eastern Europe:

> Anyone who did not witness those days can hardly conceive today the significance that public opinion rightly attached at the time to the immigration of East European Jews. The government opened all doors to them, one had to watch at every turn how these immigrants, inferior and of

foreign nationality, proliferated and, favored by the powers that be, ensconced themselves with mounting influence in private and public, economic, cultural, and political life.[63]

Earlier, in November 1919, Westarp had written that the war had made Germans conscious of something they already felt instinctively: "Jews are a foreign race." There could be no question of expelling the German Jews who had already assimilated. But, Westarp added tellingly, "All the more urgent and unavoidable is the need to protect oneself against the further growth of this foreign body."[64]

Westarp also felt that the Conservative Party's 1892 Tivoli Program – in particular its anti-Jewish clause – remained relevant insofar as it demanded a spiritual and moral struggle to preserve the German race (*Volkstum*). Westarp wrote that "Jewish influence is becoming a special danger to Germandom [*Deutschtum*] in two respects." This double threat consisted in the pairing of Jews as a racial "other" with their influence over German socialism. "The German worker must be enlightened to the fact," Westarp wrote in the *Kreuzzeitung*, "that he risks placing himself under the influence of an alien people when entrusting his guidance to a Cohn and a Hirsch, a Haase and a Wurm, and to all the countless Jews in Social Democracy."[65] For this reason, he believed that the spiritual and moral struggle against "Jewish domination" had to become a political struggle as well: against Jews sitting in parliament, against the "dictatorial rule by terror" (*Diktatur der Schreckenherrschaft*), and in favour of those parties that, like the DNVP, committed themselves to explicit political antisemitism.

Against this backdrop, it is hardly astounding to discover that the Pan-German publicist Franz Sontag – after keeping in close touch with Heydebrand and Westarp in 1920 as relations between the DKP and the DNVP became acute – counselled Westarp to travel to Munich in 1921 to meet the "interesting people" who, Sontag felt, could be useful to "our camp."[66] Sontag singled out one such person for special mention:

Yesterday, a Herr Hitler from Munich, the leader of the local National Social workers' movement, called on me. The fellow is inspired by a fervent nationalism, a worker, an intelligent mind, apparently of stirring eloquence, a clever tactician, and harmless [!] in terms of his social program. Today I introduced him to Dr. [Karl] Steiniger, who held that one ought to try at all cost to utilize this force in northern Germany for agitational purposes. Herr Dr. Steiniger now believes that you, highly esteemed Count, ought to have a look at this man in Munich (incidentally, [Erich] Ludendorff also recommends him warmly), because according to Steiniger, the remaining gentlemen of the local party executive have neither the appreciation nor the initiative for such means. Hitler lives in Munich: Am Tal 54.

There is no evidence that Westarp took up Sontag's suggestion to drop in on Hitler. He did, however, follow the logic of his own conviction that the moral and economic struggle against the Jews had to become an explicitly political one.

Once he had thus committed himself, Westarp's political agitation in the unfamiliar world of genuinely mass meetings proved more effective than he ever expected. In his published recollections Westarp used words and phrases that provide a chilling echo of Hitler's lines in *Mein Kampf* – lines that instruct the reader how to rouse his listeners to frenzied excitement and command even a room filled with political heretics:

> When addressing individual grievances [wrote Westarp], it was not difficult to highlight again and again – to hammer home through agitation – the Jewification of the ruling system and of the revolutionary forces. Just the names of the persons involved served as a reminder, whether it be a ministers' list of the Independents [Social Democrats], the hostage murder in Munich, the undignified events in the committee of inquiry, the wasting of military goods ... Besides, I was often able to observe that a meeting that had turned drowsy came to life, and the building resounded with applause, as soon as I started speaking about the Jews.[67]

Westarp spoke frequently to crowds of two thousand listeners or more. Again recalling Hitler's own learning processes, Westarp documented how he gradually learned to master tumultuous meetings and the "concerts of Pfuis" (*Pfeifkonzerte*) from the audience: "In principle, I welcomed heckling by opponents, and I did not particularly appreciate overzealous chairmen – e.g., older officers who set great store in discipline – who wished to ban it altogether. Although such instances cost time, they infused life into the audience and afforded an opportunity for polemics that sometimes involved rudeness or indignation, other times supercilious irony, to good effect. In this respect it was easy to earn the glory of quick repartee."[68]

Conclusion

How, then, do we appraise the value of the Heydebrand–Westarp correspondence in relation to other primary sources at our disposal for a history of German Conservatism in these years? We could do worse than to take Westarp at his word when he cites Goethe in the Foreword to his published memoir: "Try to do your duty, and you will know immediately what you must do. But what is your duty? The demands of the day." Westarp's ability to confront the "demands of the day" is chronicled in his own memoirs and in his correspondence with Ernst von Heydebrand. The same is true of his day-to-day leadership of the Conservative Reichstag caucus and the editorials he wrote for the *Kreuzzeitung*. When we add to the mix Westarp's other publications,[69] the Heydebrand–Westarp correspondence enriches the historical record in significant ways. It will enlighten students of the German Right for years to come.

NOTES

1 Nancy Mitford, "The English Aristocracy," in *Noblesse Oblige: An Enquiry into the Identifiable Characteristics of the English Aristocracy*, edited by Alan S.C. Ross et al. (London, 1956), 39.
2 For consistency I will use the spelling of Heydebrand's name, ending in "Lasa," not "Lase," that he adopted in 1920. This is also the spelling found most often in scholarly literature.
3 This chapter was written before publication of an important new collection of essays: Larry Eugene Jones, ed., *The German Right in the Weimar Republic: Studies in the History of German Conservatism, Nationalism, and Antisemitism* (New York and Oxford, 2014). The chapters by Rainer Hering, Björn Hofmeister, Barry A. Jackisch, and Brian E. Crim go well beyond my own reflections on relations between the Conservative Party, the DNVP, and the radical nationalist Right. Chapters by Larry Jones and Ulrike Ehret examine Conservatives and antisemites. The most pertinent contribution complements rather than supersedes my own analysis, in part because it focuses not on Westarp's relationship with Heydebrand but on his dealings with the Central Association of German Conservatives and the *völkisch* politician Albrecht von Graefe-Goldebee: Daniela Gasteiger, "From Friends to Foes: Count Kuno von Westarp and the Transformation

of the German Right," 48–78. The book's comprehensive bibliography adds to histories of German conservatism listed in Larry Eugene Jones and James Retallack, eds., *Between Reform, Reaction, and Resistance: Studies in the History of German Conservatism from 1789 to 1945* (Providence, RI, and Oxford, 1993), 503–23, and in the notes to James Retallack, *The German Right, 1860–1920: Political Limits of the Authoritarian Imagination* (Toronto, 2006).

4 Kuno von Westarp, "Heydebrand," in *Deutscher Aufstieg. Bilder aus der Vergangenheit und Gegenwart der rechtsstehenden Parteien*, edited by Hans von Arnim and Georg von Below (Berlin, 1925), 337–55 (hereafter cited as *Deutscher Aufstieg*); *NDB* 9 (1972): 66–7; Rudolf Martin, "Von Heydebrand," in *Deutsche Machthaber*, edited by Martin, 3rd ed. (Berlin and Leipzig, 1910), 401–21; Bernd Haunfelder, *Die konservativen Abgeordneten des Deutschen Reichstags 1871–1918. Ein biographisches Handbuch* (Münster, 2010), 129–31.

5 Friedrich Everling, "Westarp," *Deutscher Aufstieg*, 453–8; Haunfelder, *Die konservativen Abgeordneten*, 286–7; Kuno von Westarp, *Konservative Politik im letzten Jahrzehnt des Kaiserreiches*, 2 vols. (Berlin, 1935); Westarp, *Konservative Politik im Übergang vom Kaiserreich zur Weimarer Republik*, edited by Friedrich Hiller von Gaertringen, Reinhold Weber, and Karl J. Mayer (Düsseldorf, 2001) (these three vols. are hereafter cited as Westarp I, II, and III). See the overviews of Westarp's career and the history of his unpublished private papers in Westarp III, 13–23. See also Larry Eugene Jones and Wolfram Pyta, eds., *"'Ich bin der letzte Preuße.' Der politische Lebensweg des konservativen Politikers Kuno Graf von Westarp (1864–1945)* (Cologne, Weimar, Vienna, 2006) (hereafter cited as Jones/Pyta, *Preuße*).

6 Gasteiger, "From Friends to Foes," 48.

7 See "Die konservative Partei und die Reichsfinanzreform. Rede des Abgeordneten Dr. von Heydebrand und der Lasa" [1909]; "Die Aufgaben der konservativen Partei. Rede des Reichstags- und Landtagsabgeordneten Dr. v. Heyebrand auf dem Konservativen Parteitag der Provinz Hannover in Hildesheim am 3. Februar 1910": both in Bundesarchiv Koblenz (now Berlin) (hereafter BAK), Zeitgeschichtliche Sammlung 1 (hereafter ZSg. 1) 70/1 (7) und (10). Westarp's obituary for Heydebrand (16 November 1924) in ZSg. 1, 70/1 (19).

8 The somewhat idiosyncratic analysis by Abraham J. Peck, *Radicals and Reactionaries: The Crisis of Conservatism in Wilhelmine Germany* (Washington, DC, 1978), has been superseded by Joachim Bohlmann, "Die Deutschkonservative Partei am Ende des Kaiserreichs: Stillstand und Wandel einer untergehenden Organisation" (D.Phil. diss., University of Greifswald, 2011), which I first discovered after drafting this chapter; see ch. 6 on the election

of January 1912; chs. 7–8 on 1912–14; ch. 9 on 1914–18; and ch. 10 on the early Weimar Republic.

9 BA-Militärarchiv, Freiburg i.Br., Nachlaß (hereafter NL) Alfred von Goßler, NL 98/1, "Erinnerungen" (MS), 43. For permission to use this NL I am grateful to Frau Toni von Goßler.

10 For example, toward the National Liberal leader Eugen Schiffer; undated diary entry in BAK, NL Eugen Schiffer, Nr. 1, "Memorien" (MS), Heft 1, 43.

11 In the quality of its parliamentary rhetoric, the Wilhelmine era was arguably poorer than the Bismarckian, though not as poor as in the 1920s. Cf. Hans-Peter Goldberg, Bismarck und seine Gegner. Die politische Rhetorik im kaiserlichen Reichstag (Düsseldorf, 1998); Thomas Mergel, Parlamentarische Kultur in der Weimarer Republik. Politische Kommunikation, symbolische Politik und Öffentlichkeit im Reichstag (Düsseldorf, 2002).

12 Bethmann Hollweg to Carl von Eisendecher, 27 December 1910, 16 November 1911, 22 February 1912: Politisches Archiv des Auswärtigen Amts, Bonn (now Berlin) (hereafter PAAAB), NL Eisendecher, Nrn. 1–2. Eugen Schiffer once observed that relations between the DKP and the National Liberal Party were unlikely to improve as long as Heydebrand's "permanent dictatorship" (Dauerdiktatur) persisted. Schiffer could not fathom why Bethmann avoided a showdown with the "uncrowned king": "You lay Heydebrand out in the sand," he told Bethmann, "but then you help him up, shake the dust off his coat, and ask him if he has been hurt." BAK, NL Schiffer, Nr. 1, Heft 2. For context to this section, see James Retallack, "The Road to Philippi: The Conservative Party and Bethmann Hollweg's 'Politics of the Diagonal,' 1909–14," in Between Reform, Reaction, and Resistance, edited by Jones and Retallack, 261–98, esp. 290.

13 BAK, NL Junius Alter [pseudonym for Franz Sontag], Nr. 6, "Kampfjahre der Vorkriegszeit" (MS), 27–8, for this and the following remarks. Sontag continued in the next paragraph: "A considerable distance behind him [Heydebrand] followed Count Westarp, an upright, noble man with the best of intentions, who unfortunately lacked the firmness [Härte] that a time of political struggle demanded. His greatest years were those when he stood in the shadow of Heydebrand, whose own energies shone upon him." Nr. 13 of this NL contains eight letters between Heydebrand and Sontag from 1920 to 1922.

14 BAK, NL Eugen Schiffer, Nr. 1, Heft 1 (MS), 44.

15 Theodor Wolff, Tagebücher 1914–1919. Der Erste Weltkrieg und die Entstehung der Weimarer Republik in Tagebüchern, edited by Bernd Sösemann, 2 pts (Boppard a.R., 1984), 1: 160, 350.

16 BA-Militärarchiv, Freiburg i.Br., NL Goßler, NL 98/1, "Erinnerungen" (MS), 43–4.
17 Cited in David Schoenbaum, *Zabern 1913: Consensus Politics in Imperial Germany* (London, 1982), 34.
18 Kurt Riezler, *Tagebücher, Aufsätze, Dokumente*, edited by Karl Dietrich Erdmann (Göttingen, 1972), 168, 172.
19 BAK, NL Schiffer, Nr. 1, Heft 1 (MS), 46.
20 During my doctoral research, I drove from Koblenz to Freiburg where Friedrich Freiherr Hiller von Gaertringen kindly put into my hands a typed transcription of the correspondence for the period up to November 1918 – some 216 pages. In 2004, Karl J. Mayer generously provided me with a typescript of the correspondence covering 1919 to 1924 (174 typed pages). In this chapter I have chosen, due to limits of space, to focus on the years up to 1920. For the later period see the essays by Jones, Jackisch, Pyta, and Mayer, besides others cited below, in Jones/Pyta, *Preuße*, as well as Gasteiger, "From Friends to Foes." Instead of citing page numbers from the typescripts in Gärtringen, which would not be helpful to most historians, wherever possible I have cited the date of specific letters instead (except when they are taken from Westarp I–III).
21 Cf. Fritz Fischer, *War of Illusions: German Policies from 1911 to 1914* (London, 1975), 71–94; and the briefer account in Roger Chickering, *We Men Who Feel Most German: A Cultural Study of the Pan-German League, 1886–1914* (Boston, 1984), 262–7.
22 *Stenographische Berichte über die Verhandlungen des Reichstags*, 268: 7721ff. (9 November 1911), und 7756ff. (10 November 1911).
23 See Stephan Malinowski, "Kuno Graf von Westarp – ein *missing link* im preußischen Adel. Anmerkungen zur Einordnung eines untypischen Grafen," in Jones/Pyta, *Preuße*, 9–32. At a provincial party congress in 1910 Heydebrand was already trying to heal the wounds of 1909 and depict the DKP as a people's party (*Volkspartei*): "We as Conservatives can be happy and satisfied that complete unity within our ranks has once again been attained ... We Conservatives are confident in ourselves that we are called to be the *party of the future* ... [and] that we have the right and the duty to be a *true people's party*." *Parteitag des Konservativen Provinzialvereins für Pommern am Mittwoch, den 30. November 1910 (Stenographischer Bericht)* (n.p., n.d.), 87; BAK, ZSg. 1, 70/1 (15).
24 See, for example, Albert Ballin to Bethmann, 17 November 1911, in Zentrales Staatsarchiv (hereafter ZStA) II, Merseburg (now Geheimes Staatsarchiv Preußischer Kulturbesitz, Berlin), 2.2.1, Nr. 667; and Arthur

von Huhn (of the National Liberals' *Kölnische Zeitung*) to former Chancellor Bernhard von Bülow, 20 November 1911, BAK, NL Bernhard von Bülow, Nr. 108.

25 See Beverly Heckart, *From Bassermann to Bebel: The Grand Bloc's Quest for Reform in the Kaiserreich, 1900–1914* (New Haven, 1974). Cf. Alastair P. Thompson, *Left Liberals, the State, and Popular Politics in Wilhelmine Germany* (Oxford, 2000).

26 See BAK, Reichskanzlei, Nr. 1391/5, Bl. 204, discussing the election campaign; and reports from Prussian envoys in Stuttgart, Munich, and Dresden, in PAAAB, I.A.A.b. Deutschland Nr. 125, Nr. 3, Bd. 25, and I.A.A.m. Sachsen (Königreich) Nr. 48, Bd. 20. Still indispensable: Jürgen Bertram, *Die Wahlen zum Deutschen Reichstag vom Jahre 1912* (Düsseldorf, 1964).

27 [Valentini] to Ballin, 15 Nov. 1911, ZStA II, Merseburg, 2.2.1, Nr. 667.

28 *Das Tagebuch der Baronin Spitzemberg geb. Freiin v. Varnbüler. Aufzeichnungen aus der Hofgesellschaft des Hohenzollernreiches*, edited by Rudolf Vierhaus, 5th ed. (Göttingen, 1989), 537–8, for this and the following.

29 "Die Regierung und die konservative Partei. Ein Exkurs in die deutsche Verfassung," *Konservative Monatsschrift* 69, Heft 3 (December 1911): 233.

30 Westarp to Rudolf Beyendorff, 13 March 1920, cited in Gasteiger, "From Friends to Foes," 52.

31 Westarp I, 379. Greater detail and further references in Retallack, "The Road to Philippi," 261–98 at 297. An overview of the party's radicalization and collapse (1909–18) is found in Retallack, *Notables of the Right: The Conservative Party and Political Mobilization in Germany, 1876–1918* (London and Boston, 1988), 208–26.

32 The same logic inclined me to seek alternatives to Dr von Heydebrand, "Beiträge zu einer Geschichte der konservativen Partei in den letzten 30 Jahren (1888 bis 1919)," *Konservative Monatsschrift* 77 (1920): 497–504, 539–45, 569–75, 605–11, 638–44.

33 See ZStA I (Potsdam) (now BA Berlin), NL Kuno Graf von Westarp (90 We 4, now Bestand N 2329), Nr. 1, for the period to June 1920; the NL covering 1920 to 1945 is found in Gärtringen.

34 Westarp II.

35 Reich State Secretary of the Interior Clemens von Delbrück.

36 See also *Rede des Reichstagsabgeordneten Graf von Westarp im Reichstage am 10. Oktober 1917 über auswärtige Politik* (Konservative Flugschriften, Nr. 1) (Berlin, n.d. [1917]). More generally, see Raffael Scheck, "Kuno Graf von Westarp's Kriegsziele und Gedanken zur Kriegführung im Ersten Weltkrieg," in Jones/Pyta, *Preuße*, 61–76, also with further references.

37 Westarp III, 4–6.
38 Westarp was involved in planning the Putsch but escaped direct association with it for a number of reasons.
39 Heydebrand to Westarp, 14 November 1918, cited in Westarp III, 15. Cf. *Für Preußen! Reden der Abgeordneten Dr. von Heydebrand und der Lase, von der Osten-Warnitz und Graef bei der 1. Lesung der Wahlrechtsvorlagen im Hause der Abgeordneten im Dezember 1917* (Konservative Flugschriften, Nr. 6) (Berlin, n.d. [1918]); Kuno Graf von Westarp, *Preußens Verwaltung und Verfassung als Grundlage seiner Führerstellung im Reich*. In *Preußen. Deutschlands Vergangenheit und Deutschlands Zukunft. Vier Vorträge*, 2nd ed. (Berlin, 1916); Westarp, *Zwei Gedenktage in schwerer Zeit* (Berlin, 1916).
40 The reports of the Hauptverein der Deutsch-Konservativen to Heydebrand covered much of the same ground; excerpts in ZStA I (Potsdam), NL Westarp, for example, Nr. 98. On the Hauptverein's later dealings with the DNVP and Westarp, see Gasteiger, "From Friends to Foes," 59–71.
41 Westarp to Heydebrand, 6 January 1919, excerpt in Westarp, *Konservative Politik im Übergang*, 33.
42 Jens Flemming, "Konservatismus als 'nationalrevolutionäre Bewegung.' Konservative Kritik an der Deutschnationalen Volkspartei 1918–1933," in *Deutscher Konservatismus im 19. und 20. Jahrhundert*, edited by Dirk Stegmann, Bernd-Jürgen Wendt, and Peter-Christian Witt (Bonn, 1983), 306. See also Dirk Stegmann, "Vom Neokonservatismus zum Proto-Faschismus: Konservative Partei, Vereine und Verbände 1893–1920," in the same collection (199–230).
43 Westarp III, 20, replying to Heydebrand's proposal in a letter of 25 November 1918.
44 Westarp III, 56.
45 Westarp III, 34.
46 Westarp III, 77.
47 Westarp III, 62.
48 Emphasis added.
49 Westarp's note for Heydebrand, 30 August 1919; Westarp III, 48.
50 Westarp III, 62f. Gasteiger, "From Friends to Foes," argues correctly that the matter hung in doubt longer than Westarp suggests here.
51 On Conservative women, see Kirsten Heinsohn, *Konservative Parteien in Deutschland 1912 bis 1933. Demokratisierung und Partizipation in geschlechterhistorischer Perspektive* (Düsseldorf, 2010); Heinsohn, "Das konservative Dilemma und die Frauen. Anmerkungen zum Scheitern eines republikanischen Konservatismus in Deutschland 1912 bis 1930," in Jones/Pyta,

Preuße, 77–108. The literature on women in the late Wilhelmine and Weimar periods has grown too large to cite here. For a taste of arguments that appeared in their larger monographs, see the contributions by Andrea Hänger, Ute Planert, Raffael Scheck, Julia Sneeringer, and the co-editors in *Ihrem Volk verantwortlich. Frauen der politischen Rechten (1890–1933)*, edited by Eva Schöck-Quinteros and Christiane Streubel (Berlin, 2007).
52 Westarp III, 119.
53 Westarp III, 113.
54 See also Retallack, *The German Right*, 273–324, and ch. 8 in the present volume.
55 Westarp III, 118.
56 Westarp III, 150.
57 Westarp III, 132.
58 Westarp III, 139ff.
59 Stephan Malinowski, *Vom König zum Führer. Sozialer Niedergang und politische Radikalisierung im deutschen Adel zwischen Kaiserreich und NS-Staat* (Berlin, 2003); Malinowski, "Westarp"; and chapters on the DNVP and antisemitism cited earlier from Jones, ed., *The German Right*. An important study on antisemitism on the Weimar moderate Right has appeared recently: Maik Ohnezeit, *Zwischen "schärfster Opposition" und den "Willen zur Macht." Die Deutschnationale Volkspartei (DNVP) in der Weimarer Republik 1918–1928* (Düsseldorf, 2012).
60 *Kreuzzeitung*, Nr. 581, 30 November 1919, "Innere Politik der Woche," cited in Westarp III, 141.
61 Westarp III, 144.
62 The text of the Tivoli program is found in Roger Chickering and Steven Chase Gummer with Seth Rotramel, eds, *Wilhelmine Germany and the First World War (1890–1918)*, vol. 5 of *German History in Documents and Images*, ch. 5. The relevant lines read: "1. We desire the preservation and strengthening of the Christian life-view in the nation and the state and regard its practical activation in legislation as the indispensable foundation of every healthy development ... We fight against the often obtrusive and corrosive Jewish influence on our national life. We demand Christian authorities for the Christian people and Christian teachers for Christian students." http://germanhistorydocs.ghi-dc.org/sub_document.cfm?document_id=758. Gasteiger seems to take at face value Westarp's pronouncement that the Tivoli program was formulated only on the basis of religious, not racial, antisemitism.
63 Westarp III, 145.
64 *Kreuzzeitung*, Nr. 581, 30 November 1919, cited in Westarp III, 145.

65 Westarp III, 145f.
66 Sontag to Westarp, 10 June 1921, in BAK, NL Alter, Nr. 14 (MS), 146. Sontag's earlier correspondence with Westarp (and others) about Heydebrand's activities and the possible dissolution of the Conservative Party in 1920 is found in the same Nr. 14. Sontag's description of his meeting with Hitler is followed in his NL by undated notes listing the "Sins of the Conservatives." That list identifies the Conservatives' traditional lack of attention to workers' and urban issues, their one-sided orientation toward domestic rather than foreign policy, their neglect "of the political, cultural, and social tasks of the party in favor of purely agrarian interests," their "neglect for the organization of a effective and popular right-wing press [in favor of] beggarly, boring, and therefore aimless journalism," their "acceptance of the Jewification of the nation instead of the rational organization of its defensive instincts," and their "willingness to abide the moral and physical Jewification of the nobility especially." In early 1921, Sontag was involved with plans to fuse the *Konservative Monatsschrift* with his own journal, *Die Tradition* – which itself had been conceived under the name *Der Junker* in 1919; see correspondence from February to March 1919 in BAK, NL Alter, Nr. 13.
67 Westarp III, 147, 149. Compare Baron Heinrich von Friesen-Rötha's assessment of this kind of agitation in the 1890s, cited in chapter 8 of this book.
68 Westarp III, 171. Yet see Gasteiger, "From Friends to Foes," 54, citing a letter from Graefe-Goldebee to Westarp, 8 January 1922. Graefe was responding to Westarp's request (6 January) for "a fiery irredenta speech." Graefe replied that such a speech would be useless – "the very idea makes me shiver with disgust" – until the DNVP "in its innermost core" had grasped "the *völkisch* principle." Graefe was unwilling to use his "sharp tongue" (*Schnauze*) for agitation in a way that seemed "stupid" to him.
69 See also Westarp, *Die Regierung des Prinzen Max von Baden und die Konservative Partei 1918. Material zu den Verhandlungen des Parlamentarischen Untersuchungsausschusses für die Kriegsschuldfragen* (Berlin, 1928); Westarp, *Das Ende der Monarchie am 9. November 1918. Abschließender Bericht nach den Aussagen der Beteiligten*, edited by Werner Conze (Stollhamm and Berlin, 1952); and Westarp, *Am Grab der Parteiherrschaft. Bilanz des deutschen Parlamentarismus von 1918–1932* (Berlin, 1932). On the transition of October–November 1918 that figured so centrally in Westarp's writing, see the important new biography by Lothar Machtan, *Prinz Max von Baden. Der letzte Kanzler des Kaisers* (Berlin, 2013).

TWIST

8 Get Out the Vote! Electioneering without Democracy

You can certainly tell small children that a ringing bell means the ice-cream truck is out of ice cream. But that's about it, I think.

Jeffrey Goldberg, advice columnist [1]

George Eliot's novel *Felix Holt* was published in 1866 – when Prussia's victory in the German Civil War excluded Austria from the future Germany.[2] Eighteen-sixty-six was also the year when Bismarck decided to use the "revolutionary" idea of universal manhood suffrage for a new, national parliament. He deployed it as a weapon against Austria and against Prussian liberals.[3] German liberals saw universal suffrage in exactly these terms. As one of their newspapers put it in 1867, "Even the vote is a rifle, and ballots are also bullets."[4] (Abraham Lincoln made a similar remark a decade earlier.)[5] George Eliot viewed the act of voting more cynically. In *Felix Holt* she wrote, "An election is coming. Universal peace is declared, and the foxes have a sincere interest in prolonging the lives of the poultry."[6]

Eliot's *bon mot* prompts reflection on three open questions that characterize past scholarship on German elections. First: If barnyards and the familiar rhythms of country life had begun to disappear by the last third of the nineteenth century under the impact of modern industrial capitalism, how do we calibrate the speed and direction of socioeconomic change, on the one hand, against the speed and direction of political change, on the other? Did social dislocation transform the German electorate more than any single event or decision?[7] Assuming for a moment that it did, how best do we gauge the political manifestations of divisions, cleavages, conflicts, and exclusionary practices in rapidly changing societies? And how do the X-factors of locality and region complicate things?

More than three decades ago, when the history of everyday life (*Alltagsgeschichte*) was just beginning to be taken seriously, the political scientist Peter Steinbach offered a convincing argument about why students of German elections and democratic institutions need to address these questions head-on:

> Whereas previously, histories of parties, associations, and elections would jump all too quickly from the social structure of a district to the articulation of politics, research on the history of everyday life offers the opportunity to ... describe more precisely the social structures that are considered primarily as statistical categories ... Even though the much-cited "linkage problem" between social structure and political articulation can be resolved at the empirical level only in the rarest cases, this does not eliminate the [historian's] duty to recognize that it is a new task of historical-sociological regional history to find a solution.[8]

Second: If the great questions of modern German history revolve around the so-called Third Reich, Hitler, and the Holocaust, when voting was inconsequential to politics and democracy was on the mat, why should we care about "elections without democracy" in an earlier period? One fragile consensus holds that there are three institutional attributes of democracy: universal manhood suffrage,[9] an autonomous legislature, and civil liberties. Did these attributes actually characterize the Second Reich? Even if they did, such a view ignores important elements of Imperial Germany's political culture, for example, the role played by the state and political leaders in defining the choices voters faced. Historians have done a good job of charting the increasing levels of competition among German political parties during what has been called Europe's "participation revolution" of the nineteenth century. But they have tended to overemphasize the role of "populist" outsiders – rascals and others who wanted to get inside the party-political tent – in determining who profited from changes to the system. Therefore we need to know more about how anti-democratic leaders and representatives of the authoritarian state worked together at all three tiers of government (national, state, and municipal) to change the rules of the electoral game to their own advantage. Was the "motor of change" in Germany's electoral culture driven mainly by mendacious élites operating from above? Or was the "terror of the street" more important – for example, when tens of thousands of German citizens called for suffrage reform in mass demonstrations?[10] The easy answer is that both kinds of pressure combined to favour change. In fact the easy answer is wrong.

Third: Did the "red spectre" or the "Jewish threat" determine how Germany's electoral culture was transformed by the processes of democratization? Interrogating the fate of socialists and Jews together forces us to consider the *longue durée* stretching from the mid-nineteenth to the mid-twentieth century. Germany's Social Democratic Party (SPD) won more votes in Reichstag elections than any other party from 1890 onwards. By 1912 the SPD fielded the largest caucus in the Reichstag: 110 of 397 seats. Clearly, it had expanded its following beyond Germany's working classes alone. Even though the party became more reformist and less revolutionary over this period, the SPD was poised to push Germany over the threshold to democracy on the eve of the First World War. Or was it?

Socialists were not the only ones in Imperial Germany who suffered persecution, defamation, and political isolation. Other alleged "enemies of the Reich" (*Reichsfeinde*) did not fit into the national community defined by Bismarck, Hitler, and middle-class opponents of democracy. Why consider socialists, Jews, and their enemies together when talking about democracy and efforts to mobilize a changing electorate? Because democracy and voting laws are fundamentally about inclusion and exclusion. In the late 1920s, Hitler became the impresario of attacks on Marxists and the Jews – attacks that ascribed pariah status, and much worse, to both groups.

I am not suggesting here that Imperial Germany was Nazi Germany in embryonic form.[11] Even though the Kaiser chose his own government ministers and had exclusive power to declare war and peace, the Second Reich was not a fascist state or a dictatorship ruled by terror. It was not a state where you could line your enemies up against a wall and mow them down. It was a semi-parliamentary constitutional monarchy, where the rule of law still prevailed (with notable interruptions and exceptions). The Reichstag had the power of the purse and grew more important over time as a sounding board of public opinion. It became a forum for airing demands for participation and grievances against the authoritarian state – something that chancellors and the Kaiser ignored at their peril.

That said, Hitler was conspicuously unoriginal in targeting Marxists and Jews and profiting at the polls by doing so. The dystopia of a future Germany overrun by "Sozis" and "Semites" – as conservatives put it in the 1880s and as depicted in Max Bewer's semi-pornographic *Politische Bilderbogen* in the 1890s[12] – was a spectre made frighteningly real not despite universal manhood suffrage but because of it. That spectre was not born in 1933 or 1919. It had already become a German nightmare by 1900. This continuity from the nineteenth century to the twentieth is not unique to German history, and the concept of Germany's "special path" to modernity – its *Sonderweg* – cannot explain it. Democrats everywhere pay a terrible price when their enemies become responsive to the masses without wishing to be responsible to the people. Nevertheless, historians have yet to explain the interconnectedness of three dimensions of German electoral culture before 1918: exclusionary strategies targeting socialists and Jews, efforts to hold back the tide of democracy, and mendacious campaign tactics that succeeded in turning the weapon of universal manhood suffrage against revolutionaries and reformers. We do not need to invoke the *Sonderweg* to sense that Imperial German elections hold important clues to what went so terribly wrong in the 1920s and 1930s.

What partial answers have scholars lately provided to these open questions of social change, democratic institutions, and continuity? Good history is like a Swiss Army knife: it offers different tools for different situations rather than only the sharp edge of a blade. Students of German elections have learned a great deal from political scientists and political sociologists in particular: one thinks of Stein Rokkan, M. Rainer Lepsius, Ralf Dahrendorf, and Karl Rohe. Rokkan wrote about the cleavages dividing societies on the cusp of modernity. These included conflicts between centre and periphery, between agriculture and industry, between state and church, and between employers and employees.[13] Lepsius asked why the main social/moral milieux that formed in Germany in the 1860s – at the moment that universal manhood suffrage (but not democracy) was introduced – persisted more or less in the same form until the Nazis broke the mould after 1928.[14] Dahrendorf's "German Question" is almost too familiar to bear repeating: "Why," he asked, "is it that so few in Germany embraced the principle of liberal democracy?"[15] And Rohe developed the idea of political camps (*Lager*), taking over Lepsius's thesis about a socialist camp and a Catholic camp but lumping the other milieux into a "nationalist" camp.[16]

I cite Rohe's camps as a "partial answer" because the nationalist camp is actually very difficult to find in the historical record. Nonetheless, political historians have always tried to incorporate factors such as socio-economic dislocation and cultural anxiety into their analyses. For example, the émigré historian Hans Rosenberg argued in the 1940s that the "Great Depression" from 1873 to 1896 drove up the anxiety level of the German lower-middle class (petit bourgeoisie or *Mittelstand*).[17] Rosenberg's thesis was not dissimilar to Richard Hofstadter's thesis dating from the mid-1960s, about the *Paranoid Style in American Politics*.[18] This lower-middle-class grouping *was* fractured, in flux, cut loose from its traditional political moorings and susceptible to the siren call of antisemitism. After 1928 its members flocked to the Nazis, who appealed to their real and imagined fears. Even though recent research has cut away at the thesis that this group provided the overwhelming mass of Nazi supporters, the idea of *Panik im Mittelstand* remains important if we are to explore Rohe's nationalist camp further or understand the first wave of racial antisemitism.

A second partial answer highlights the importance of democratization as a social *process* but remains ambivalent about democracy as a political *institution*.[19] German and non-German scholars have focused mainly on the latter, as Daniel Ziblatt made clear when he asked, "How did Europe Democratize?"[20] A notable ambivalence about these twin aspects of democratization is evident in the best work on Imperial German elections: *The Kaiser's Voters* by Jonathan Sperber; *Democracy in the Undemocratic State* by Brett Fairbairn; and *Practicing Democracy* by Margaret Lavinia Anderson.[21] Sperber is not speaking of citizen-voters, but subject-voters. Fairbairn's paradoxical title acknowledges the power of social democratization but also the persistence of undemocratic state institutions. And Anderson argues that Germans, by practising democracy with such fervour and dedication before 1918, were actually more ready to make the Weimar Republic a political success than we previously believed.[22] Each of these works provides a piece of the interpretive puzzle of Germany's democratization. Yet that puzzle, even when it is assembled, remains slightly out of focus – rather like a 3-D movie viewed without the right glasses.

These studies have built on a mountain of previous research that tells us how unusual Imperial Germany was in having universal manhood suffrage without a liberal democracy based on the parliamentary system. The broad suffrage provided German Social Democrats with the opportunity to develop a modern, mass-based party apparatus at a time when the Reichstag's prerogatives and ambitions were still uncertain. And the gradual transition from a "politics of notables" (*Honoratiorenpolitik*) to a "political mass market"[23] frightened those who wanted to protect (as they put it) the established social and political order. Germany in 1914 still did not possess a legislature that determined the make-up of the government or could rein in a powerful military and bureaucracy.

To be sure, *one* kind of democratization, the "fundamental politicization" (*Fundamentalpolitisierung*)[24] of German society, was far advanced. Civil liberties also protected a free vote – usually. But Germany was not a democracy just because the ballot was exercised and the secret ballot was defended. As Tom Stoppard once wrote, "It's not the voting that's democracy; it's the counting."[25] I don't mean that corruption precluded a "fair count" in the narrow sense. Rather I mean that the Reichstag, if it was an autonomous legislature, was *too* autonomous: it didn't "count" for as much as many historians of the Empire like to think.

Including herself among those who stress the importance of inclusiveness and habituation in making the free vote a reality, Margaret Lavinia Anderson has argued that in 1866, when Bismarck tossed universal manhood suffrage into his "national omelet" – the one he didn't want liberals or foreign powers poking their fingers into – only two other countries in Europe had a broader suffrage: Greece after 1844, France after 1852. Almost all other countries had to wait until after 1900 for an equitable franchise. The United States was encumbered by any number of racial and other barriers to fairness, based on states' rights. And Britain could not boast of democracy after the First, Second, or Third Reform Acts of 1832, 1867, or 1884; it arrived only with the "Fourth" Reform Act of 1918.[26] These assertions are not contentious. I'm less sure, however, that we should sign on to Anderson's more provocative claim. Implicitly alluding to Wilhelm Liebknecht's famous pronouncement that the Reichstag was merely the "fig-leaf of absolutism,"[27] Anderson writes that Germany in 1914 was not just "a monarchy with democratic adornments"; rather, it was a "'democratic' monarchy" – full stop.[28] The inverted commas around "democratic" preserve the modesty of her claim, though only just.

Anderson is the world's leading scholar on Imperial German elections. She has studied the myriad rules, regulations, and election protests that protected the secret ballot. In the process she has exploded the myth that German voters were frog-marched to the polls by their agrarian landlords, urban employers, and Catholic priests. Anderson's broader thesis is that those rules and regulations prepared Germans well for democracy after 1918. They ensured that Imperial Germany's oppositional parties could mobilize their voters and get them to the polls, with little chicanery to prevent them from doing so. Those rules also ensured that every word spoken in the Reichstag could be published in any party's newspaper the next day: hence even opposition deputies could declare their disdain for the monarchy – even their "*hatred* for the person of the Kaiser," as the SPD leader August Bebel did in January 1903.[29] During election campaigns, which typically lasted eight weeks or so, there were (still according to Anderson) no restrictions on the media of modern elections: pamphlets, flyers, posters, placards, even the distribution of printed ballots before voting day. All parties had access to new technologies in their campaigning, from the rotary printing press to the slide show to mechanized transportation for party *Schlepper* who brought supporters to the polls. And German civil servants, the police, and the parties' own scrutinizers ensured that graft, bribery, and other forms of what the English call "treating" had no meaningful impact on German elections.

With this evidence Anderson concludes that strict adherence to elaborate rules of electoral procedure provided "the early handholds, the rough crevices in the smooth system of authority, which allowed some groups of voters as early as the 1870s to gain a purchase on the wall of authority."[30] Both the metaphor and Anderson's analysis are illuminating. What they each fail to convey is that the enemies of democracy did their utmost to fill in those handholds, smooth those crevices, and loosen the grasp of democrats trying to conquer the bastions of authority. They were aided in this task by the harsh political climate of authoritarianism. The many successes scored by democracy's enemies cast doubt on Anderson's central conclusion, namely, that advocates of democracy had successfully turned the weapons of the old order upon itself before 1918. Substantial intimidation and other barriers to a free vote persisted, for Social Democrats above all.

What about other successes scored by the enemies of democracy? Limits of space allow me to cite only one example: the rolling back of "democratic" voting laws in countless municipal and regional parliaments after 1890. In municipal councils and state *Landtage* across Germany, either unequal suffrage laws were retained or new ones were introduced in order to privilege income, property, education, military service, and age (this list is not exhaustive).[31] Retrenchment and experimentation with new suffrages were advertised – and accepted by German burghers – as means to keep socialists out of these parliaments.[32] Like a storm lashing our climber from all sides, such anti-democratic practices and strategies increased the slipperiness of the face of the authoritarian state. They weakened the resolve of all but the most resilient adventurers to continue the upward struggle. That this ascent continued at all is of profound historical significance. Without question it deserves our attention. But for precisely that reason, historians should not diminish the durability of obstacles that remained in the path of those for whom we – as small-"D" democrats ourselves – would like to reserve our most enthusiastic cheers.

In this section I offer a case study based on the Reichstag elections of June 1893, to bolster the preceding argument and to make three further points. First, democracy's enemies in Germany hated the *style* of democratic politics at least as much as they hated its content. Yet they could not entirely resist new pressures to get "up close and personal" with voters. Second, for all their distrust of "rabble-rousing" campaign tactics, many conservative insiders were just as willing to play the "Jewish card" in 1893 as were their more radical opponents, the independent antisemitic parties. Third, I hope to provide a hint of the look and feel of a contemporary election campaign.

By 1893, three years after Bismarck's dismissal, the German party system was in upheaval. The right-wing parties that Bismarck had been manipulating for two decades were in disarray, and "enemies of the Reich" were on the cusp of their remarkable period of growth in the 1890s. The successes of Social Democrats and radical antisemites indicated that the older, informal style of politics was in its death throes; it seemed that a new, more "in your face" style of mass politics had arrived. Election campaigns that exhibited various features of political *Hetzerei* – rabble-rousing attacks, mischievousness, maliciousness – demonstrated how badly Bismarck had miscalculated in 1866–7 when he gambled that the German masses, peasants *and* workers, were pliable monarchists and thus likely to defer to their betters. By the 1893 election, the Conservative Party leader Otto von Helldorff was expressing his disdain for the vulgar, racist antisemitism that was penetrating even his own party. Helldorff referred to "the frightful brutalization of public opinion" that was the hallmark of modern campaigning.[33]

Conservative prejudice against unsavoury mass politics and against the Jews was neither new nor exclusively German. Conservatives had long preferred to run in "Riviera constituencies," where one might issue a short statement in the first week of the campaign and spend the rest of the contest relaxing on the south coast of France. Moreover, curmudgeons elsewhere have expressed disdain for the "unwashed" or "uneducated" masses who clamoured for attention. One thinks here of the crusty American journalist H.L. Mencken, who liked to refer to the American middle classes as the "booboisie." Mencken once observed that "democracy is the theory that the common people know what they want, and deserve to get it good and hard."[34]

To look ahead for a moment to the outcome of the 1893 Reichstag elections, it seemed to be a case of grand larceny. At least that is how it was seen by Conservative Junkers in the rural, backwoods provinces of Prussia. When the independent antisemites made off with a record high of sixteen Reichstag seats in that election (won with over 250,000 votes or 3.4 per cent of the national total), the Junkers cried "Foul!" These interlopers had stolen their safe seats. When the Junkers claimed that the independent antisemites promised everything to everybody, the independent antisemites also cried "Foul!" But Prussian Junkers were not the only losers in 1893: radical antisemites also stole seats from solidly bourgeois Saxon Conservatives.

A primer on *How to Win an Election* – in the form of a letter from Quintus Tullius Cicero to his famous brother Marcus, written in the summer of 64 BC when the latter was vying to become a Roman consul – tells us that the rules of the game had not changed much in two millennia. Quintus gave Marcus the following nuggets of advice: don't leave town; call in all favours; build a wide base of support; "promise everything to everybody"; know the weaknesses of your opponents – and exploit them; give people hope; and "flatter voters shamelessly."[35] In 1893, radical antisemites found a lot of traction with voters by using the same methods. They also won a hearing for themselves when they claimed that the "little man" in Germany was the victim of Jews and Junkers alike. Conversely, Junkers and other conservatives charged that the scatter-shot attacks of the antisemites were doing the dirty work of Social Democrats. "The frightful brutalization of public opinion," they argued, was "plowing the furrows" in which socialists planted the seeds of revolution.

Helmut von Gerlach, who had a foot in both the antisemitic and Conservative camps, described the rural campaigning that proved successful around this time for one of the loosest cannons in the antisemitic camp. Hermann Ahlwardt offered prospective voters in backwoods Pomerania electoral bait in the form of lies, flattery, and innuendo: "Along with his secretary, [Ahlwardt] systematically called on farms, asking each farmer how many acres of land and how much livestock he owned. Then he turned to the secretary, who flashed a gigantic notebook, and dictated to him: 'Take this down! [Farmer] Gussow owns 30 acres, 5 cows, 4 pigs; he *ought* to own: 60 acres, 12 cows, and 10 pigs.'"[36]

With their close ties to the state, the civil service, and the army, mainstream Conservatives objected to such dishonesty on the hustings. Even more fiercely they hated the tenor – the noise and rough language – of antisemitic rallies. Consider what one high-born Conservative, Baron Heinrich von Friesen-Rötha, defined as "rowdyism" shortly after he and other Conservatives lost their seats to the independent antisemitic parties in 1893. In Friesen's pamphlet titled *Honour the Truth!* – which could also be translated as *Call a Spade a Spade!* – it was virtually impossible to distinguish between the "rabble-rousing" tactics used by Social Democrats and those used by radical antisemites. Even the beer-bench politics of Pan-Germans, student corps, and veterans' associations loomed in his dystopia, which reflected all his class pretensions and political prejudices:

> "Rowdyism" [*der "Radau"*] is a singular sport of the uneducated masses ... One shouts, one stamps one's feet, and in this way one achieves a certain gymnastic exercise ... Rowdyism in meetings sets the mob into [a] kind of drunkenness ...
>
> Whether one has announced that the meeting will exhibit a calf with six feet or the inevitable "Jew" is completely irrelevant ...
>
> It is mandatory to greet the speaker with rowdy applause, and even here there is an opportunity to set lungs, hands, feet, and the lids of beer steins into the desired state of motion. A hired group of applauders has to make sure that this movement does not cease. The ... alcoholic atmosphere increase[s] the need to call out and rave. If the word "Jew" is mentioned, then the jubilation has no end ...
>
> Rowdyism is infectious. Soon one demands these kinds of rabble-rousing meetings in every village ... Always new meetings ... The leaders [of the antisemitic movement] soon feel themselves to be the people's representatives, from whom the governments, in sheer amazement, declare themselves obligated to seek counsel.
>
> One could proclaim this "rowdyism," in and of itself, to be benign. However, it is *a big lie*, it relies on deception and breeds deception, and therein resides a danger that cannot be underestimated.[37]

I have cited these attempts to define what Hitler (after Friesen) called the "big lie" in order to bring Conservatives and antisemites into the same picture. As David Blackbourn explained long ago, their competition for votes was not merely a challenge-and-response development.[38] Rather, it was part of a spiral of escalating radicalism that continued from the 1890s right up to Hitler's seizure of power in 1933. I cannot chart the longer path that transformed the "traditional" Right into the "radical" Right and then the fascist Right in Germany. But I hope I can illuminate the timing and the trajectory of that path with a few final reflections. With one more example of "demagogic" politics I want to argue that antisemites, in 1893, did not steal the Conservative vote at all. Instead that election proved there is no honour among thieves.

In February 1880 – that is, more than a decade before the Reichstag election I have been describing – another Conservative bigwig, Dr Paul Mehnert, who later became known as the "uncrowned king of Saxony," delivered a programmatic speech to the Dresden Conservative Association.[39] This address was delivered at the height of the first wave of antisemitic excitement in Germany, after the nationalist historian Heinrich von Treitschke had famously proclaimed, "The Jews are our misfortune."[40] Mehnert levelled the following charges against the Jews: The French Revolution had helped German Jews begin their rise to influence and power. Sweden and Norway severely limited the rights of Jews, whereas Germany had allowed "Semitism" to become a "moneyed power" in its own right. It was wrong to speak of Jew-baiting any more, he declared: "One could better speak of Christian-baiting."

Next Mehnert drew his audience's attention to an American group called the "Society for the Eradication of the Jews." After claiming that this "society" sought to relocate all American Jews to Jerusalem, Mehnert cited a resolution it had supposedly passed demanding "the complete extermination of the Jews." Some gentle jabs at a local antisemitic club in Dresden followed, but Mehnert claimed that its policies merely repeated what the Conservatives had been demanding for years: a stock exchange tax (meant to hit Jews hard), the demand for cash payments from Jews in business dealings, and other measures to address the "dysfunctional economy" that Bismarck and his liberal supporters – also identified as Jews – had put in place during the 1870s.

During the Reichstag election campaign of 1893, Conservatives in the Kingdom of Saxony offered only variations on this speech Mehnert had delivered thirteen years earlier.[41] They acknowledged the "good kernel" in German antisemitism; they reworked age-old myths to sharpen

Figure 8.1 This antisemitic postcard from 1897, garishly coloured in the original, sends greetings from the *Kölner Hof* in Frankfurt am Main, located at Scharnhorststrasse 37–9. It advertises itself as the "only Jew-free hotel in the city," also as "New Jerusalem on the frankisch Jordan." Lest the artist's nationalist credentials be in doubt, the immense monument to Kaiser Wilhelm I on the *Deutsches Eck* in Koblenz is inserted in the lower left corner. bpk, Berlin/Art Resource, NY.

the Conservative message; they coquetted with the spectre of physical violence; they excoriated the Jews for their "dominance" of the press and public opinion; and they reaffirmed the Conservative Party's claim to have defended the "rights of Christians" longer and more diligently than any other party, old or new. Conservatives never conceded that their own party was insincere – mendacious. They never conceded that they were insufficiently engaged – unable to mobilize their troops – in the struggle against the Jews. The "big lie" was still working. To be sure, fresh recruits were needed in the Conservative army: "genuine" antisemites were welcome. But "whole new regiments" – that is, independent antisemitic parties – definitely were not. So: Grand larceny? Stealing the vote? Not quite. From the beginning, the fix was in.

In later elections, German Conservatives drew to their side antisemites who had grown disaffected with the rancour and confusion in the independent antisemitic parties. All the while, Conservatives did not moderate their views on the "Jewish question" or scale back their rhetoric on the hustings. Quite the reverse: as Yeats would say, their innocence had been drowned: "The best lack all conviction, while the worst are full of passionate intensity."[42] In the Reichstag election campaign of 1893, the independent antisemites won 93,364 votes in Saxony (15.8 per cent) compared to just 4,788 votes in 1890. Six antisemites were elected in Saxony, compared to none in 1890. Over the same two elections the Saxon Conservatives saw their own Reichstag contingent decline from twelve to six. The exact congruency between these gains and losses was more apparent than real. Yet only slight differences of strategy separated the two groups. For "radical" antisemites, the "Jewish question" was beguilingly simple. For them, there was no harm in fighting elections as single-issue parties. For "moderate" Conservatives, the "Jewish question" was fraught with dangerous complexities. But there was no harm in playing the "Jewish card" either.[43]

This example suggests that Conservatives preferred defiance over decorum when targeting German Jews at election time. Their rhetoric was belligerent and clangorous – certainly not aloof and measured, as Baron von Friesen-Rötha would have preferred. It does not much matter when and where Conservatives learned this language. Recent scholarship suggests it was earlier than historians have believed, namely, in the years 1855 to 1873.[44] At that time another Conservative antisemite, Hermann Wagener, taught his party comrades to "get out the vote" – also to recruit new members and to sell newspapers – by making scapegoats of Jews, even though German liberalism was on the rise. Regional particularities determined the success of such strategies at the subnational level; but the more important point is that both groups, "radical" antisemites and "moderate" Conservatives, identified feckless liberalism and dysfunctional "democracy" as their chief enemies in the 1890s as in the 1860s. Jew-baiting provided the bridge that brought these two groups together – so closely together that they became virtually indistinguishable.

What is the benefit of posing open questions, reviewing tentative answers, and applying the case-study approach to elections in Imperial

Germany? I have tried to suggest that as a trans-Atlantic and a global phenomenon, democracy was not a single river that kept adding new tributaries through history as it flowed to some blue sea we call "modernity." At the dawn of the twentieth century, democracy's tributaries were still distinct. Some of them trickled into nothing or went over a cliff. They were all attacked or defended by statesmen, party leaders, and ordinary voters who had their own opinions about the ultimate purpose of voting (and counting votes). Nevertheless, by the end of the first decade of the twentieth century most European countries had accomplished a significant expansion of their national electorate. That expansion was based on the premise that elections served a worthwhile transmissive function, funnelling pressures upwards from society and downwards from the state. Those pressures were always ultimately about power, and as in military conflicts, power usually rested with those who had the biggest armies. "Ballots are also bullets," and regiments of conservatives could not resist democracy on a world-historical scale.

I have also argued that the secret ballot and a free vote did not necessarily mean a *fair* or *equal* vote. The principle of "one man, one vote" had a beguiling simplicity to contemporaries, as it has to historians. But that principle was always fraught with complexities, many of which favoured democracy's enemies. Contemporaries were aware of this. In 1900 the left-liberal politician Friedrich Naumann referred to the Conservatives as "authoritarian types with democratic gloves."[45] Conservatives and other opponents of democracy were not *always* imbued with a meanness of spirit or a willingness to pander to the lowest common denominator. However, often they were – particularly when they declared that socialists and Jews presented a clear and present danger to the homogenous, Christian, national community (*Volksgemeinschaft*) that was their ideal.

Lastly: in Germany, as elsewhere, bumpy and potentially reversible transitions to democracy unfolded in the context of local, regional, national, and transnational conversations about inclusion, exclusion, and political fairness. Who belonged to the political nation? Which "cautionary measures" were compatible with what Thomas Jefferson called "the decent opinion of mankind"? What bulwarks against democracy could ensure that "enemies of the Reich" would not overturn the political status quo or overthrow the authoritarian state? (Tellingly, contemporaries used the term *Umsturz* to describe a revolution that would topple the existing order.) If the rules of the game could be changed, what oversight could be exerted to make sure that neither side could game the system with unpredictable ramifications and irreversible consequences?[46]

Get Out the Vote! Electioneering without Democracy 251

Figure 8.2 A Reichstag voter is dismayed by the range of parties for which he might cast his ballot. His choice is made more difficult by the quantity of printed materials outlining the parties' platforms and the vehemence with which their functionaries attempt to win his support just before he enters the polling station. They attempt to push a printed ballot in favour of their candidate into this "philistine's" hands while a policeman (far left) looks on benignly. *Ein Wahlphilister*, original woodcut by Ferdinand Lindner, *Die Gartenlaube* 19, no. 44 (November 1881): 737.

In this context – where voters and politicians were abandoning ingrained traditions but accommodating new conflicts fitfully or reluctantly – Elmer Eric Schattschneider's observations about a "semi-sovereign people" are germane. "Political conflict," he wrote in 1960, "is not like a football game, played on a measured field by a fixed number of players in the presence of an audience scrupulously excluded from the playing field. Politics is much more like the original primitive game of football in which everybody was free to join, a game in which the whole population of one town play the entire population of another town moving freely back and forth across the countryside."⁴⁷ Politics is rough business, especially when players and the crowd come into such close proximity. The analogy is not watertight, but Schattschneider's idea of opposing teams (and their supporters) roaming freely back and forth across the political landscape calls to mind groups of people studied by historians of another, darker era in German history. Electoral politics, too, has its victims, bystanders, and perpetrators. In the high-stakes contests that unfolded with mounting ferocity after 1890, mobilizing electoral support at whatever cost meant that fewer and fewer unsavoury tactics were declared out of bounds.

In the decades before 1914, neither the advocates of reform nor the advocates of retrenchment were willing to cede the field to the other, but they were not equally matched. We cannot say what Germany's future would have been if the First World War had not intervened: a liberal democracy was only one of many possible outcomes. Germans before 1914 had many opportunities to undertake significant constitutional reform. In most cases they sidestepped them.⁴⁸ In 1908 they refused to censor the impetuous Kaiser in any meaningful way, even after he called the British "mad, mad as March hares." In 1910 they refused to abolish the notorious three-class suffrage in Prussia. And they never significantly reformed most upper houses of parliament, even after the British showed the way by clipping the tail feathers of the House of Lords.⁴⁹

Nevertheless, it is unlikely that conservative enemies of democracy could have inaugurated anything resembling the Third Reich absent the horror of the First World War. More plausibly, they would have embraced a kind of pragmatic, reformist conservatism – because no other option was available. G.K. Chesterton suggested as much in his work *Orthodoxy* (1908). His words underscore the ambiguities inherent in German transitions to democracy. They also suggest why the traditional Right's prospects at the polls were growing dimmer in a democratizing age. In a chapter titled "The Eternal Revolution," Chesterton wrote: "All conservatism is based upon the idea that if you leave things alone you leave them as they are. But you do not. If you leave a thing alone you leave it to a torrent of change."⁵⁰

NOTES

1 *The Atlantic* 310, no. 1 (July–August 2012): 148.
2 The German Civil War is also known as the Austro-Prussian War.

3 See Christian Müller, "Das Wahlrecht als Waffe. Die Wahlrechtsdiskussionen in Deutschland zwischen Revolution und Reichsgründungszeit (1848–1881)" (PhD diss., University of Heidelberg, 2005), esp. ch. 4; Andreas Biefang, "Modernität wider Willen. Bemerkungen zur Entstehung des demokratischen Wahlrechts des Kaiserreichs," in *Gestaltungskraft des Politischen. Festschrift für Eberhard Kolb*, edited by Wolfram Pyta and Ludwig Richter (Berlin, 1998), 239–59; Biefang, "La mobilization politique dans l'Empire autoritaire. Le spectacle des élections au Reichstag (1871–1912)," *Revue d'histoire du XIXe siècle* 46, no. 1 (2013): 95–117; cf. Walter Gagel, *Die Wahlrechtsfrage in der Geschichte der deutschen liberalen Parteien 1848–1918* (Düsseldorf, 1958), esp. 38–63.
4 *Volks-Zeitung* (Berlin), 30 August 1867.
5 "The ballot is stronger than the bullet." Abraham Lincoln, speech of 19 May 1856.
6 George Eliot, *Felix Holt: The Radical*, 3 vols. (Edinburgh and London, 1866; online edition Cambridge: Chadwyck-Healey Ltd., 1999–2000), vol. 1, ch. 5, 127.
7 Cf. recent overviews in Brett Fairbairn, "Economic and Social Developments," in *Imperial Germany 1871–1918: The Short Oxford History of Germany*, edited by James Retallack (Oxford, New York, 2008), 61–82; Cornelius Torp, "The Great Transformation: German Economy and Society, 1850–1914," in *The Oxford Handbook of Modern German History*, edited by Helmut Walser Smith (Oxford, New York, 2011), 336–58.
8 Peter Steinbach, "Alltagsleben und Landesgeschichte. Zur Kritik an einem neuen Forschungsinteresse," *Hessisches Jahrbuch für Landesgeschichte* 29 (1979): 225–305 at 304.
9 Daniel Ziblatt, "How Did Europe Democratize?" *World Politics* 58 (2006): 311–38 at 325. Of course a suffrage is not universal if it is *manhood* suffrage, but the context of this chapter is Germany and Europe before 1918. Even today, many other criteria besides gender – e.g., age – prevent certain members of a population from voting.
10 The complexity and importance of these issues is suggested in Simone Lässig, "Der 'Terror der Straße' als Motor des Fortschritts? Zum Wandel der politischen Kultur im 'Musterland der Reaktion,'" in *Sachsen im Kaiserreich. Politik, Wirtschaft und Gesellschaft im Umbruch*, edited by Lässig and Karl Heinrich Pohl (Weimar, 1997), 191–239; Lässig, "Wahlrechtskämpfe im Kaiserreich. Lernprozesse, Reformimpulse, Modernisierungsfaktoren: das Beispiel Sachsen, " *Neues Archiv für sächsische Geschichte* 65 (1994): 137–68. Cf. Bernd Jürgen Warneken et al., *Als die Deutschen demonstrieren lernten. Das Kulturmuster "friedliche Straßendemonstration" im preußischen Wahlrechtskampf 1908–1910* (Tübingen, 1986).

11 For an appraisal of recent work on this theme see Lars Fischer, "Continuity and Discontinuity in Nineteenth- and Twentieth-Century German History," *Canadian Journal of History* 45 (2010): 565–88.
12 See Thomas Gräfe, *Antisemitismus in Gesellschaft und Karikatur des Kaiserreichs. Glöß' Politische Bilderbogen 1892–1901* (Norderstedt, 2005); Gräfe, "Zwischen katholischem und völkischem Antisemitismus. Die Bücher, Broschüren und Bilderbogen des Schriftstellers Max Bewer (1861–1921)," *Internationales Archiv für Sozialgeschichte der deutschen Literatur* 34, no. 2 (2009): 121–56.
13 Stein Rokkan, *State Formation, Nation-Building, and Mass Politics in Europe*, edited by Peter Flora, Stein Kuhnle, and Derek W. Urwin (Oxford and New York, 1999).
14 M. Rainer Lepsius, *Demokratie in Deutschland. Soziologisch-historische Konstellationsanalysen* (Göttingen, 1993).
15 Ralf Dahrendorf, *Society and Democracy in Germany*, orig. 1965 (Garden City, NY, 1967); see further reflections in ch. 10 of this book.
16 Karl Rohe, *Wahlen und Wählertraditionen in Deutschland* (Frankfurt a.M., 1992).
17 Hans Rosenberg, "Political and Social Consequences of the Great Depression of 1873–1896 in Central Europe," *Economic History Review* 13 (1943): 58–73, rpt. in *Imperial Germany*, edited by James J. Sheehan (New York, 1976), 39–60.
18 Richard Hofstadter, *The Paranoid Style in American Politics, and Other Essays* (New York, 1965).
19 See also chapter 10 of this book.
20 Ziblatt, "How Did Europe Democratize?" Cf. other comparative studies including Markus Mattmüller, "Die Durchsetzung des allgemeinen Wahlrechts als gesamteuropäischer Vorgang," in *Geschichte und politische Wissenschaft. Festschrift für Erich Gruner zum 60. Geburtstag*, edited by Beat Junker, Peter Gilg, and Richard Reich (Bern, 1975), 213–36; Alan S. Kahan, *Liberalism in Nineteenth-Century Europe: The Political Culture of Limited Suffrage* (Basingstoke, 2003); Elfi Bendikat, *Wahlkämpfe in Europa 1884 bis 1889. Parteiensysteme und Politikstile in Deutschland, Frankreich und Großbritannien* (Wiesbaden, 1988).
21 Jonathan Sperber, *The Kaiser's Voters: Electors and Elections in Imperial Germany* (Cambridge, New York, 1997); Brett Fairbairn, *Democracy in the Undemocratic State: The German Reichstag Elections of 1898 and 1903* (Toronto, 1997); Margaret Lavinia Anderson, *Practicing Democracy: Elections and Political Culture in Imperial Germany* (Princeton, 2000).
22 See also Stanley Suval, *Electoral Politics in Wilhelmine Germany* (Chapel Hill, NC, 1985).

23 The term originated with Hans Rosenberg. See chapter 8 of this book.
24 Karl Mannheim, *Man and Society in an Age of Reconstruction* (orig. German ed. 1935), translated by Edward Shils (New York, 1967), 44.
25 Tom Stoppard, *Jumpers* (London, 1972), act 1.
26 Forcefully argued in H.C.G. Matthew, Ross I. McKibbin, and J.A. Kay, "The Franchise Factor in the Rise of the Labour Party," *English Historical Review* 91 (1976): 723–52.
27 *Stenographische Berichte über die Verhandlungen des Reichstags des Norddeutschen Bund* (17 October 1867), 452. All Reichstag speeches from 1867 to 1942 can easily be located online by date and page number: www.reichstagsprotokolle.de.
28 Margaret Lavinia Anderson, "Demokratie auf schwierigem Pflaster. Wie das deutsche Kaiserreich demokratisch wurde," in *Logos im Dialogos. Auf der Such nach der Orthodoxie*, edited by Anna Briskina-Müller, Armenuhi Drost-Abgarjan, and Axel Meißner (Münster, 2011), 245–62 at 246.
29 *Stenographische Berichte über die Verhandlungen des Deutschen Reichstags* (22 January 1903), 7484.
30 Margaret Lavinia Anderson, "Voter, Junker, *Landrat*, Priest: The Old Authorities and the New Franchise in Imperial Germany," *American Historical Review* 98 (1993): 1448–74 at 1460.
31 Besides chapter 11 in the present book and works cited in the following note, see my forthcoming monograph with Oxford University Press: *Red Saxony: Election Battles and the Spectre of Democracy in Germany, 1860–1918*.
32 My preliminary statements of this thesis include James Retallack, "Anti-Socialism and Electoral Politics in Regional Perspective: The Kingdom of Saxony," in *Elections, Mass Politics, and Social Change in Modern Germany*, edited by Larry Eugene Jones and Retallack (Cambridge, New York, 1992), 49–91; Retallack, "'What is to Be Done?' The Red Spectre, Franchise Questions, and the Crisis of Conservative Hegemony in Saxony, 1896–1909," *Central European History* 23 (December 1990): 271–312 [appeared 1992]; Retallack and Thomas Adam, "*Philanthropy* und politische Macht in deutschen Kommunen," in *Zwischen Markt und Staat. Stifter und Stiftungen im transatlantischen Vergleich*, special double issue edited by Adam and Retallack, *Comparativ* 11, Hefte 5–6 (2001): 106–38. The latter essay was published in English and with different emphases as ch. 6 in James Retallack, *The German Right 1860–1920: Political Limits of the Authoritarian Imagination* (Toronto, 2006), 192–222.
33 Helldorff to Philipp Eulenburg, 11 December 1892, and other correspondence in *Philipp Eulenburgs Politische Korrespondenz*, edited by John C.G. Röhl, 3 vols. (Boppard am Rhein, 1976–83), 2: 988–98.
34 H.L. Mencken, *A Little Book in C Major* (New York, 1916), 19.

35 Quintus Tullius Cicero, *How to Win an Election: An Ancient Guide for Modern Politicians*, translated by Philip Freeman (Princeton, 2012). Cf. Peter Stothard's lively review, "The Ancient Art of Fooling Voters," in the *Wall Street Journal*, 8 March 2012, http://www.wsj.com/articles/SB10001424052970203458604577263291359761910.
36 Helmut von Gerlach, *Von rechts nach links* (Zurich, 1937), 113–14 (emphasis added).
37 Anon. [Heinrich Freiherr von Friesen-Rötha], *Der Wahrheit die Ehre!* (Leipzig, n.d. [1893]), 17–19 (emphasis added), Sächsisches Staatsarchiv, Leipzig, Rittergut Rötha mit Trachenau, Nr. 1576, Mappe: Aufzeichnungen und Notizen.
38 David Blackbourn, "Peasants and Politics in Germany, 1871–1914," and "The Politics of Demagoguery in Imperial Germany," in *Populists and Patricians: Essays in Modern German History* (London, 1987), 114–39, 217–45.
39 For the following, *Sächsischer Volksfreund*, 21 February 1880. On Mehnert see also ch. 11 in this book.
40 See Heinrich von Treitschke, "Unsere Aussichten," *Preußische Jahrbücher* 44, Heft 5 (Nov. 1879): 572–6.
41 Here I draw on campaign flyers and other publicity materials in the Sächsische Landesbibliothek. Staats- und Universitätsbibliothek, Dresden, H. Sax. C 500, and the Geheimes Staatsarchiv Preußischer Kulturbesitz, Berlin, XII. Haupt-Abteilung, Abt. IV, Nr. 200.
42 William Butler Yeats, "The Second Coming" (1919), www.online-literature.com/yeats/780.
43 Further reflections on the interpenetration of German conservatism and antisemitism are found in Retallack, *The German Right*, esp. chs. 2, 8, and 9. The entire first stanza of Yeats's "Second Coming" seems apposite:

> Turning and turning in the widening gyre
> The falcon cannot hear the falconer;
> Things fall apart; the centre cannot hold;
> Mere anarchy is loosed upon the world,
> The blood-dimmed tide is loosed, and everywhere
> The ceremony of innocence is drowned;
> The best lack all conviction, while the worst
> Are full of passionate intensity.

44 See Henning Albrecht, *Antiliberalismus und Antisemitismus. Hermann Wagener und die preussischen Sozialkonservativen, 1855–1873* (Paderborn, 2010); also Massimo Ferrari Zumbini, *Die Wurzeln des Bösen. Gründerjahre des Antisemitismus: Von der Bismarckzeit zu Hitler* (Frankfurt a.M., 2003).

45 Friedrich Naumann, *Demokratie und Kaisertum* (Berlin, 1900), 92–3.
46 From a modern perspective see Andre Blais, Louis Massicotte, and Antoine Yoshinaka, *Establishing the Rules of the Game: Election Laws in Democracies* (Toronto, 2003).
47 Elmer Eric Schattschneider, *The Semisovereign People: A Realist's View of Democracy in America* (New York, 1960), 18. He also draws a distinction between "the idea that the people are involved in politics by the contagion of conflict" and the "classical definition of democracy as 'government by the people'" (129).
48 Cf. Thomas Kühne, "Demokratisierung und Parlamentarisierung: Neue Forschungen zur politischen Entwicklungsfähigkeit Deutschlands vor dem Ersten Weltkrieg," *Geschichte und Gesellschaft* 31 (2005): 293–316; Kühne, "Die Jahrhundertwende, die 'lange' Bismarckzeit und die Demokratisierung der politischen Kultur, " in *Otto von Bismarck und Wilhelm II.*, edited by Lothar Gall (Paderborn, 2000), 85–118; Hartwin Spenkuch, "Vergleichsweise besonders? Politisches System und Strukturen Preußens als Kern des 'deutschen Sonderwegs,'" *Geschichte und Gesellschaft* 29 (2003): 262–93; Mark Hewitson, "The *Kaiserreich* in Question: Constitutional Crisis in Germany before the First World War," *Journal of Modern History* 73 (2001): 725–80; Hewitson, "The Wilhelmine Regime and the Problem of Reform: German Debates about Modern Nation-States," and James Retallack, "Ideas into Politics: Meanings of 'Stasis' in Wilhelmine Germany," both in *Wilhelminism and Its Legacies: German Modernities, Imperialism, and the Meanings of Reform, 1890–1930*, edited by Geoff Eley and Retallack (New York and Oxford, 2003), 73–90, 235–52. The latter essay, with slight amendments and updated references, appeared as "Meanings of Stasis" (ch. 3) in Retallack, *The German Right 1860–1920*, 108–34.
49 Thomas Kühne, *Dreiklassenwahlrecht und Wahlkultur in Preußen 1867–1914* (Düsseldorf, 1994); Hartwin Spenkuch, *Das Preußische Herrenhaus. Adel und Bürgertum in der Ersten Kammer des Landtages 1854–1918* (Düsseldorf, 1998).
50 G.K. Chesterton, *Orthodoxy* (London, 1908, eBook 1994), ch. 7.

9 The Authoritarian State and the Political Mass Market

In this chapter I consider how research on the German authoritarian state and its "political mass market" has evolved since the 1980s. In the process I try to identify some open questions for future research. Some initial observations are required to place my twin subjects in the context of other works dealing with the First World War, culture, and transnationalism. Those observations also begin the task of explaining why the two bodies of scholarly writing on the authoritarian state and on the political mass market have relied so heavily on each other in the past – and should continue to do so.[1]

Don't Fence Me In

Did the First World War decide the fate of the German authoritarian state or deflect the evolution of mass politics? Yes and no. Many elements of the thesis about Germany's *Sonderweg* (special path) to modernity hinge on what happened at the beginning and end of the war. Whether the German Revolution of 1918–19 represented a likely or even plausible outcome to the processes of democratization and constitutional reform is a question that has been tackled less often in recent years than we might suppose.[2] Nevertheless, the prospects of democracy in the transition from empire to republic have drawn the attention of such scholars as Stanley Suval, Brett Fairbairn, and Margaret Lavinia Anderson. They have argued that an undemocratic political culture inherited from the prewar era was *not* one of the burdens afflicting the Weimar Republic.[3] Instead they have stressed the importance of "affirming voting," legal guarantees underpinning the secret ballot, and the concept of electoral "fairness." Germans learned about "democracy in the undemocratic state" – this is Fairbairn's provocative term – by practising it *avant la lettre*.

What of the war's beginning and middle? With reference to the "polarized" and "stalemated" condition of Imperial Germany's political parties, Volker Berghahn has argued that the most important question about the Second Reich remains, "Why did Germany go to war in 1914?"[4] I disagree not with the question but with the priority assigned to it. There are more interesting questions about Germany's political modernization than can fit under the harsh spotlight of July 1914. We are immeasurably better informed than we were just twenty years ago about the authoritarian state's loss of legitimacy in the middle years of the war – as seen, for example, from the trenches and from the cities, towns, and villages of southern Germany.[5] When we speak of burdens that exhausted the resources and undermined the legitimacy of the authoritarian state, it is there that we are finding new clues about why the dysfunctional German state of 1914–18 was essentially the same state that Bismarck had put in the saddle in 1871. Why, then, should we give the authoritarian state credit for flexibility, generosity, and commitment to serving the interests of a pluralistic society in *either* the war years or the decades that preceded them?

A second point is that historians of German political culture are by definition interested in culture. This interest has grown more intense with each passing decade since the 1970s. Symptomatic here is the evolution of approaches to confessional conflict, class conflict, gender relations, and the antagonism among political camps (*Lager*). We can appreciate how far we have travelled when we contrast, say, Ronald Ross's study of Bismarck's *Kulturkampf*, which was already more sceptical of the power of the authoritarian state than anything written in the 1970s, with more recent books by David Blackbourn, Michael Gross, and Róisín Healy.[6] Each of these authors considers confessional conflict from the vantage point of perceptions, meanings, and experiences. Not incidentally, each has also questioned the operation of gender norms.

Third, transnational history focuses attention on relationships, constellations, and "flows" rather than on events. Transnational history helps us move beyond a fixation on the German nation-state as the self-evident, paradigmatic unit of analysis.[7] But these strengths are no less constitutive of political culture research in which the authoritarian state and political modernization figure centrally. Two examples are provided by Thomas Kühne's study of electoral culture in Prussia and Thomas Mergel's study of parliamentary culture in the Weimar Republic.[8]

Notwithstanding contemporary complaints about the hateful Americanization of German electioneering, the old adage that "all politics is local" reminds us that comparisons among different tiers of governance can help us assess just where and when and how the "mass" in mass politics operated. Margaret Lavinia Anderson showed us what mass politics looked like at the local level; but she also reassessed German political culture in European and global contexts. Contemporaries judged the norms and practices of their political culture not just as seen from the village church steeple but in light of cultural transfers across national borders.

Border crossers enjoy other advantages. Consider the colonizing efforts of Germany's political parties to win new territory in the political mass market. One can emphasize manipulation from above, self-mobilization from below, or – better still – the sparks that flew between them when different ways of fishing for popularity collided.[9] One might also consider the willingness of Conservatives and others on the Right to recruit female auxiliaries before 1918. My point is that crossing borders helps reveal how asymmetrical relations of power and alterities emerged as smaller political cultures became enmeshed in larger ones. As they often did in transnational settings, they might alleviate marginality and misery; but they could also cause loss and humiliation.

"Playing with scales" (*jeu d'échelles*) helps us discover how winners and losers transgressed or transcended established political boundaries, for example, when they left small-town politics and "arrived" in Dresden, Munich, or Berlin. As Michael Geyer has written, "even the most parochial and inward-turned worlds are imbricated in other worlds of action and imagination that range beyond parish and nation."[10] Yet that imbrication was not quite as "natural" as we sometimes think. To say that politics at a given time and place was "parochial" still seems to imply that what happened in local and regional settings was necessarily more small-minded than what took place on a larger stage.[11] This implication echoes an early – and untenable – variant of modernization theory. My point is that it also reflects the disdain we tend to feel for the authoritarian state and the politics of notables (*Honoratiorenpolitik*), as well as for the "anachronistic" élites who defended them. We look right through those élites or hope they will hurry off the stage because they are too arrogant to belong there any longer. Yet if we avoid historical hubris and redirect our gaze, we can profit from Geyer's advice about how to study border crossers: "you notice them only when the transnational 'pie' is no longer in the sky, but manifestly in your face."

The Authoritarian State

Konrad Jarausch and Michael Geyer contended in their book *Shattered Past* that to speak of the "authoritarian" Second Reich is to invoke an "empty cliché."[12] Because their book appeared in English, it is unclear whether they would have used the German term *autoritär* or *obrigkeitsstaatlich*. But that distinction is hardly the central issue, because in neither case are we invoking an empty cliché. Let me suggest five reasons why it may still be helpful – and not only heuristically – to describe Imperial Germany as an authoritarian state.

The first way to determine whether a concept has become a cliché is to examine its linguistic usage and to parse its changing inflections over time. Authority (*Obrigkeit*) and the authoritarian state (*Obrigkeitsstaat*) do not appear in the *Geschichtliche Grundbegriffe* – a historical lexicon of social and political language in Germany.[13] But this absence should not distract us from the way "authoritarian" was used as a polemical term before, during, and after the First World War. Otto von Gierke and his pupil Hugo Preuß lent the authoritarian state currency when they asserted its opposition to a people's state or one where the rule of law prevailed. By 1915, Preuß's use of the term had become even more barbed. It conjured up a host of hateful associations, each of which identified realms in which the state helped preserve "anomalous" spheres of power – the police and the military, for example – and made them immune from the constitutional and political influence of a bourgeois society.[14] From Max Weber's perspective in 1917, the authoritarian state was bankrupt: it had failed to produce the charismatic leaders and talented parliamentarians who might have educated Germans politically.[15] Then in 1930, Gustav Radbruch famously attacked the idea "that the government stood above the parties": this, he wrote, "was precisely the legend, the life-giving lie [*Lebenslüge*], of the authoritarian state."[16] Arguably, the concept of the authoritarian state is with us still – as a polemical superweapon and as part of historiographical memory. Before 1918, socialists and left liberals used the term as a catch-all for everything they disliked about Imperial Germany. Have liberal historians avoided this pitfall?

Second, we should acknowledge that the concept of the authoritarian state has frequently been deployed in ways that make it functionally equivalent to a lightning rod. A symptom of this usage is historians' uncertainty about whether the term "Prussia–Germany" is to be understood as Greater Prussia or Lesser Germany (*Kleindeutschland*). Hartwin

Spenkuch has argued convincingly that Prussian particularities have often been ignored by critics of the *Sonderweg* idea.[17] When historians use terms like *Junkerstaat, Militärstaat, Machtstaat* (power state), and *Beamtenstaat* (civil servant state), they may be striving for both precision and nuance. Often they deliver neither. Such ersatz terms allow historians to avoid thorny questions about how the authoritarian state actually functioned – or didn't.

A third strategy is to break down the false polarity between society-centred and state-centred analyses. An exaggerated distinction between state and society veils interesting questions about how a modern society can accommodate an authoritarian state, and vice versa. Of course to speak of "the state" in the singular is to start on the wrong foot. Different authorities existed in Prussia, Bavaria, Saxony, Württemberg, Baden, and the other federal states. Yet only recently have historians of modern Germany begun in earnest to follow the example of Abigail Green, whose book *Fatherlands* was pioneering.[18] Green demonstrated for the pre-1870 period that the middle-sized German states used schoolbooks, press policies, and various symbols of nationhood to enhance the authority of German princes and their administrations. Green's findings chart a different path to the same conclusion reached by Celia Applegate, who illustrated that attachment to one's homeland (*Heimat*) was perfectly compatible with a modern sense of nationalism.[19] Still, more work is required before we will understand how "a nation of provincials," understood sociologically, evolved in tandem with authoritarian states at the subnational level when they faced new challenges.[20]

Fourth, it is worth asking whether state and society "tolerated" each other only in the sense that that each sought to guarantee its own hegemony. David Blackbourn has remarked that the German state was never particularly successful at wringing "wide-eyed obedience" from politically emancipated citizens. But where did the "mystique of the state" begin and where did it end? Was the authoritarian state the "provider" or the "scourge" of bourgeois hegemony? Or did it function mainly as a "sternly benevolent umpire" among competing social, economic, and political interests?[21] And what other forms of authority filled this role when the deficiencies of the central German state were plain to see? Mark Hewitson, Christoph Schönberger, and Thomas Kühne, building on earlier work by Dieter Langewiesche and others, have helped clarify why the "silent parliamentarization" thesis is a dead letter: they have correctly distinguished between the political, institutional processes of parliamentarization, on the one hand, and the social and emotional significance of democratization, on the other.[22] This distinction helps

The Authoritarian State and the Political Mass Market 263

Figure 9.1 This painting shows Prussian Crown Prince Friedrich Wilhelm (1831–1888) in robust health, conversing with dignitaries at a court ball some ten years before his death. As German Kaiser Friedrich III he ruled for just 99 days in the spring of 1888 before he died of throat cancer. The figure in the doorway at the right is the painter Adolph Menzel, who stood less than 4½ feet tall. Anton von Werner captured the imperial pomp of Germany's Second Reich, as did Menzel; but the latter better understood that a dynamic Germany, with its fine social layerings, needed a new style. Many of his sketches and paintings sympathetically depict the hardships faced by ordinary workers. *Kronprinz Friedrich Wilhelm auf dem Hofball 1878*, by Anton von Werner, 1895. bpk, Berlin/Nationalgalerie, Staatliche Museen, Berlin/ Photograph: Klaus Göken/Art Resource, NY.

explain why suffrage reform movements generated far more resonance – in speeches, printed propaganda, street demonstrations, and riots – than, say, efforts to reform or abolish the upper chambers in Prussia and other federal states.[23] This distinction also suggests why parliamentarization and democratization are best understood as learning processes: both required practice and habituation. Unfortunately, sometimes, the longer view still gets lost.[24] I am tempted to agree with the British political scientist Peter Stirk, who has posed this question: When did the authoritarian state die? Not yet!, some might say. Or it died in November 1918. "A more interesting possibility," Stirk suggests, "is that it was in a sense dead even before then. It was a façade of strength lacking true substance. The 'life-giving lie' gave life to a walking corpse."[25]

Fifth and lastly, the authoritarian state is invoked *less* frequently than we might imagine in descriptions of Imperial Germany's constitutional structure. In his *Deutsche Gesellschaftsgeschichte*, Hans-Ulrich Wehler conceded that the couplet "constitutional monarchy" is not precise enough to get at the real nature of Germany's Second Reich.[26] He preferred to explore the contours of charismatic rule. Thomas Nipperdey took a different tack to describe his *Machtstaat vor der Demokratie*. The authoritarian state was conspicuously absent: "The Empire of 1871 was many things rolled into one: federal state, constitutional state, imperial state, Prussian hegemonic state, power state and military state, above all it was a national state."[27] Winfried Becker hitched up the same wagons and sent them off on the *Sonderweg* at the outset of his slim book titled *Das Bismarck-Reich – eine Obrigkeitsstaat?* Yet in his conclusion he conceded that his principal question can only be answered if we continue to explore what Karl Mannheim in the 1930s referred to as the fundamental politicization of German society.[28] In suggesting that a new socio-political dynamic in Imperial Germany conditioned the principle and *Praxis* of authority, Becker put it this way:

> The politicization of wide circles of the population, which already began in the Bismarckian era, was by no means only the reflex of authoritarian state action that deliberately awakened and conflated the interests of the dominated in order to guarantee its own hold on power. Rather, precisely the many conflicts at the regional and national levels led members of various classes of the population toward political life via increased participation. The disputes leading up to elections created and reflected a growing multiplicity of highly diverse motivations, which included not only burgeoning class, confessional, and milieu loyalties, which tended to stiffen quickly, but also everyday problems as well as questions about

political culture and about the common welfare viewed either as a particularist or a nationalist matter.[29]

Coming at the same problem from a different direction, Thomas Kühne has asked: Was the "authoritarian essence" of Imperial Germany fundamentally transformed by the processes of democratization?[30] Did the beginnings of political pluralization overcome the socio-cultural fragmentation of the party system? To each question Kühne answers no. It is not easy to reconcile Becker's and Kühne's conclusions; but what is centrally important here, and will remain so in the future, is that the idea of the authoritarian state is not a cliché. On the contrary, further study will underscore just how unpredictably representatives of the German authoritarian state reacted to social, economic, and political transformations they could not control.

The Political Mass Market

What elements of a political system or a political culture have the strongest transmissive function between state and society? Elections play such a role, as has long been recognized. But so do electoral cultures, regional political cultures, and the public sphere (the latter includes the press, associational life, and civil liberties). In studying each of these areas, scholars writing in the past fifteen years have made tremendous strides. They have linked political and cultural ways of invoking authority. They have demonstrated the reciprocal relationship between parliamentarization and democratization, whereby the latter actually inhibited progress of the former. And they have helped us learn to balance (though not necessarily reconcile) the views of statesmen, ordinary voters, and other citizens who entertained one of two very different visions of Germany's future. On the one hand we find those who viewed the Second Reich as dysfunctional: it was hamstrung by irreconcilable religious, ideological, ethnic, and other conflicts, and it appeared to be teetering on the brink of revolution or collapse. On the other hand we find those who viewed the Reich as amazingly liberal and as likely to become more so every day: its pluralistic, modern face was Germany's most recognizable feature.

Scholars' efforts to "emphasize the positive" in the German Empire have achieved mixed results. Some have elicited groans of impatience or howls of protest. Such studies include the volume that purported to find *Another Germany*. A more extreme example of muddled thinking was provided recently by social scientists who tried to link movements of the Berlin stock market to the rise and fall of prospects for Saxon suffrage reform in order to deduce "the economic effects of democracy."[31] Done well, a refusal to see only Imperial Germany's dark side has its merits, as do efforts to link political developments in one federal state with their economic or other ramifications elsewhere. Edward Ross Dickinson, Kevin Repp, and Andrew Lees have demonstrated the breadth and cohesion of a reformist movement in Wilhelmine Germany, principally in Germany's municipal arenas, though not only there.[32] Two handbooks on Germany's reform and *völkisch* movements have also demonstrated the priority Germans placed on overcoming perceived deficiencies in their country's cultural and political heritage.[33]

Unfortunately, the existence of a modern, pluralist, steadfastly reformist empire is often asserted but not demonstrated by scholars whose research agendas have become narrow and self-referential and who rely on theories that spiral inward on themselves.[34] How many valences of modernity do we really need? Such arguments are particularly unconvincing when they present a caricature of Imperial Germany as sclerotic, backward-looking, and ruled by pre-modern élites. This caricature is then used to prop up two other unsupportable claims: that if the Second Reich was modern, it cannot also have been authoritarian; and that Bismarckian and Wilhelmine styles of politics were so fundamentally different that they are best studied separately.

Scholars thus hold divergent opinions about Hans Rosenberg's concept of a "political mass market." Does the term satisfactorily describe a polity that had been transformed by the introduction of universal manhood suffrage in 1866–7 but continued to evolve?[35] Critics of Rosenberg's thesis object that the notion of a political mass market connotes a passivity among voters that is belied by the evidence. Such critics say we cannot regard the German voter as a "consumer" of politics because he did not choose his party or candidate the way a supermarket shopper chooses one brand over another.[36] (Stanley Suval's thesis about the "affirming" habits of Reichstag voters runs in the same groove.) Others contend that voters expressed their political preferences in groups and not, like a consumer, by individual choice.[37] These criticisms miss the mark, for reasons I will outline in the balance of this chapter.

When speaking of consumers in a political mass market, it would seem helpful to consider the cut-throat competition among the *purveyors* of political wares – the parties. With the de facto deregulation of the electoral arena, the government gradually became unable to control either the medium or the message of politics. Both aspects were denigrated when contemporaries complained about the unseemly business of cattle-trading in the political marketplace. But one can argue that the chief commodity being bought and sold was influence. Influence was bartered on a new scale, in new venues, and with new middlemen wanting a piece of the action. Such middlemen included party functionaries, newspaper editors, and municipal counsellors, to list only a few. But each of these intermediary types focused their attention on parliamentary candidates who, if elected, could serve the interests of local constituents and wire-pullers.[38] Thus, when a voter entered a polling booth, he could legitimately ask: If I cast my vote for this candidate over that one, what is it going to cost me and how might I profit? Thinking in these terms helps us understand why Anderson, Fairbairn, and Suval are correct to stress the agency of voters, who were once considered "voting fodder" by local notables and historians alike. But it is just as important to recognize that each voter's cost–benefit analysis had its own short-, medium-, and long-term ramifications. Collectively these voters determined whether a candidate was given the opportunity to represent them in the next legislative period of a municipal, state, or national parliament. However, the daily business of politicking had implications that stretched far beyond the next legislative session.

Even the most future-oriented politicians, among whom we can count the Social Democratic leader August Bebel, sometimes had to be reminded not to let their entrepreneurial spirit sag. Consider the words that Friedrich Engels, "Marx's general," directed to Bebel in May 1883. Bebel had recently expressed some satisfaction that he was now sitting as a member of the Saxon Landtag, not in Berlin's Reichstag. (In 1881, Bebel had lost the Reichstag constituency of Dresden-Altstadt to the "parties of order.") Forced to live away from his family in the village of Borsdorf because the Minor State of Siege had been imposed on Leipzig and its environs by the Saxon government in June 1881,[39] Bebel was trying to recover his health and recharge his political batteries. Engels was worried that competing interpretations of Marxist "orthodoxy" were taking market share in the movement during Bebel's absence.[40] Hence he urged Bebel to invest in the future, roll up his sleeves, and get back to work:

> My dear Bebel! That you would rather *not* sit in the Reichstag I can well believe. But you see what your absence has made possible ... Certainly agitational and parliamentary work become very boring in the long run. It is the same as with advertising, launching promotions, and traveling around on business: success comes only slowly and, for many, not at all. But there's no alternative, and once you're in it, the thing must be carried through to the end or else all the previous effort is lost.[41]

Figure 9.2 This working-class tavern is the setting for a political discussion during the Reichstag election campaign of 1877. The solid-looking socialist functionary holds a copy of a socialist newspaper, the *Volksfreund* (*The People's Friend*). This apparently provides him with prompts as he informs the others about the main points of the Social Democratic platform. The painting underscores the importance of taverns as places where Social Democrats could get the message out to audiences that often consisted, as shown here, of a mix of rural and urban, lower-class and middle-class elements – and even those who were not entitled to cast a ballot (i.e., women and children). *Wirtshausszene*, by Ernst Henseler, 1877. bpk, Berlin/Hessisches Landesmuseum, Darmstadt/ Photograph: Lutz Braun/Art Resource, NY.

Were the Social Democratic Party and the Catholic Centre Party the Best Buys and Walmarts of Imperial Germany? At the very least, these parties' activities in the first years of the German Empire helped create a marketplace of ideas, niches of opportunity where none had existed before. Who can doubt that they sought to mobilize a particular kind of acquisitiveness – the hunger to be heard – among society's "little men"? Conversely, had not the defenders of throne and altar, the leaders of veterans' associations, and other agents of the authoritarian state been market-testing their own brand of subliminal advertising for years before Bismarck fell from power? Insofar as they learned the art of successful political mobilization, they could calculate their profit and assess the benefits of possible mergers and acquisitions by counting the number of votes and Reichstag seats they won. Consensus-building and coercion, too, went hand in hand, as they do in any good marketing strategy or public relations campaign.

Neither the authoritarian state nor its enemies could ever hope to achieve anything like a competitive monopoly – but they kept trying. Anti-democrats, whose flavour of the month never changed, referred to their parties of choice as the "state-supporting parties" (*staatserhaltende Parteien*), the "parties of order" (*Ordnungsparteien*), or simply the "bourgeois parties" (*bürgerliche Parteien*). Left liberals came and went from these political coalitions, but the Social Democrats were always excluded. Long before a decisive majority of Reichstag deputies willingly voted for Bismarck's Anti-Socialist Law (1878–90), it was axiomatic that the *bürgerlich* parties included *all* parties besides the SPD. Although they experimented endlessly with new forms of political mobilization, these parties tended to put more effort into perfecting the arts of repression and exclusion that made such mobilization either easier or unnecessary. Meanwhile the Social Democrats and other parties who joined them in opposition from time to time learned new ways to pitch their own ideals of liberty and democracy to mass recruits. And those recruits, year after year, proved more receptive to their appeals than to the state's. In the process, new political practices were tested and retested under constantly changing marketplace conditions.

These processes, even after 1909, did not lead to political stalemate or gridlock, as standard works on German history still claim when describing the prewar phase of Theobald von Bethmann Hollweg's chancellorship (1909–17). Germany was not paralysed by equally matched opponents, it was not at the end of its tether in domestic politics, and it did not opt for war in July 1914 simply because it could not bear further wrangles between the forces of order and revolution. These notions, insofar as they constituted an erroneous consensus, no longer hold sway. Rather, it was collisions between competing strategies for political mobilization that were decisive. Those collisions transformed political styles in the Second Reich and gave rise to new ones. In the process they opened up an uncertain future for all those who chose to engage in election battles (and who could avoid them?). For all these reasons, it is wrong-headed to look for the agents of change in only one camp or the other, that is, among the revolutionary "masses" – who were not so revolutionary after all – or among the self-proclaimed defenders of "the established social and political order," who by 1909 were flocking to the radical nationalist opposition. Although it will never become a paradigmatic superweapon, Rosenberg's idea of a "political mass market" asks of us nothing more than that we widen our conception of mass politics. It suggests that we must study the unpredictable combination of pressures that determined the rise and fall, success or failure, of political stratagems to win voters to "the good cause." And it suggests that we should do so the same way experts today try to analyse unpredictable consumer preferences to steer world markets in a "favourable" direction.[42]

Rosenberg's term also helps focus attention on the early date at which "modern" mass politics came to characterize national politics in Germany. Under universal manhood suffrage, introduced for elections to the North German Confederation in 1867 and then for the German Reich in 1871, no one could accurately predict which strategies would work in competitive environments still largely shaped by local, personal relationships. One is tempted to say that no one could *initially* predict election outcomes because the broad suffrage was so new and unfamiliar. But predictability did not lie around the corner, even though corporate magnates, cartels, and other actors in a competitive society or economy cherish exactly that quality. William Sheridan Allen, in his pioneering study of Nazism's rise in the town of Northeim, stressed the self-correcting, "capitalist" principle that forced rank-and-file Nazis to learn (on the job) what attracted voters and what alienated them.[43] Who can say that the same principle did not operate in the political culture of Bismarckian Germany? The liberal Gustav Freytag certainly thought it did. Even in the midst of the first Reichstag election campaign in the winter of 1866–7, Freytag was exhausted by the demands of his voter-clientele. "Fie, Bismarck, that was no master stroke," Freytag wrote, referring to the principle of one man, one vote. "Worst of all ... no one knows whether he'll be elected or not."[44] Members of the "state supporting" parties were voicing the same complaint on the eve of the First World War.

It is not difficult to discover why the advent of "mass politics" has so often been ascribed to the 1890s. According to this line of argument, the mobilization of previously passive social constituencies was accompanied by the appearance of new economic interest groups and nationalist pressure groups, and also by the development of new technologies (for instance, slide shows and naval displays) that made it easier to "spread the word." Moreover, Carl Schorske's term "politics in a new key" *was* meant to describe innovations that occurred after 1890.[45] Rosenberg himself endorsed Friedrich Naumann's withering critique of agrarian self-interest as exemplified by the Agrarian League after its founding in 1893.[46] An "agitating aristocracy" and "authoritarian types with democratic gloves" – what a thought!, exclaimed Naumann. These descriptions were cited by Rosenberg, and then subsequently by Wehler and others, as evidence that pre-modern élites learned to play the modern game of politics with unheard-of skill and cunning. Offering an "outward accommodation with democratization," those élites accepted the need to participate in a political competition with its inevitable "levelling" tendencies.[47]

It is ironic that many of the same historians who have stressed the "modern," dynamic nature of German politics after 1890 have themselves provided arguments that highlight the historically more significant period of political innovation and mobilization between 1867 and 1881. David Blackbourn convincingly demonstrated the newness of political institutions set in place by Bismarck at the founding of the empire. These included constitutional, administrative, parliamentary, and electoral institutions that would remain largely unchanged over the next half-century. Geoff Eley has drawn attention to the relatively early date – not later than the mid-1870s – by which time both bourgeois and (national) liberal Germans exerted economic, social, and cultural dominance but irrepressible political influence as well. Margaret Lavinia Anderson and Helmut Walser Smith, among others, have illustrated that although openness and dynamism characterized the 1870s due to conflicts pitting the authoritarian state against the Catholic Church and Social Democracy, those battle lines had already hardened by the early 1880s into political polarities that remained largely static until the end of the empire.[48]

According to one view of Germany's political modernization, the decade of the 1890s witnessed the "reconstitution of the political nation," "a major moment of flux," a "vital moment of transition," a time of political "fission," a "populist moment," a "major enlargement of the public sphere," a "reordering of the public domain," and "a fundamental change in the scale and intensity of public life."[49] But a growing number of historians, including Alastair Thompson and Axel Grießmer, have shown that it is misleading to single out the 1890s so categorically.[50] To be sure, we are hampered by a paucity of good studies of domestic politics in the 1870s and 1880s, especially ones that take the performative aspects of Germany's electoral and parliamentary cultures seriously.

Hans-Peter Goldberg's study of "Bismarck and his opponents" and Andreas Biefang's consideration of "Reichstag elections as democratic ritual" are notable exceptions.[51] As these two studies suggest, when we consider the decades in which truly innovative strategies were not just formulated but actually implemented by the political parties, economic lobby groups, and nationalist associations, the 1890s recede as a decade of fundamental change.

Exaggerating only slightly, one could say that mass politics arrived in the guise of a *Weihnachtsmarkt* (Christmas market) when, to Freytag's dismay, that first Reichstag election campaign heated up in December 1866. There was no turning back. The participation rate for Reichstag elections rose from 1867 through 1887, when it reached 77.5 per cent; that figure was not exceeded until 1907. The Catholic and Social Democratic milieux were mobilized in the 1870s and 1880s, respectively. Antisemites, whether in the Conservative Party or outside it, were mainly unoriginal in their take on the "Jewish question" in the 1890s.[52] SPD membership climbed steeply after 1903. And the nationalist camp, if it ever existed, could have been consolidated only once the agrarian movement, mass imperialist agitation, and popular anti-socialism were fully functional, that is, *after* 1900. Women, too, found opportunities in the new century to become active in voluntary associations, suffrage movements and, eventually, the political parties themselves. When Eve Rosenhaft proposed an expanded definition of "mass" politics at a University of Toronto conference twenty-five years ago, she feared that scholars had no choice but to accept the conscious, regretful practice of excluding women from historical accounts that chart the formal structures and informal pathways of politics.[53] Happily, other scholars have shown that Rosenhaft was too pessimistic. The proliferation of works on the political activities of right-wing women alone, spanning the divide of 1918–19, suggests the vibrancy of this field.[54]

All new? New and improved? These make good marketing slogans. But they do a poor job of describing Germany's political culture at the dawn of the twentieth century.

Conclusion

Obrigkeitsstaat is still regularly used by historians as a shorthand description of Imperial Germany *tout court*, even though the term itself is so obviously state-oriented. The closest approximation to an "authoritarian society" one finds in the literature is reference to a society of subjects or a spirit of servility (*Untertanengeist*). The general trend of recent research has been in the opposite direction. It depicts a bourgeois society where subjects have been replaced by citizens; where civil liberties, individual rights, and the rule of law are scrupulously protected; where professional, entrepreneurial, and intellectual merit are rewarded in ways typical of modern societies; and where Germans enjoyed many opportunities to adapt their society to new circumstances, indeed to "transform" it fundamentally – as the authoritarian state and its institutions could not be transformed. However, as this chapter has tried to suggest, there is no longer any need to ask students of Imperial Germany to choose between such stark alternatives. The Second Reich was modern and it was authoritarian. No single decade, no single party, and no single political "idiom" can be privileged in the way they once were. Future scholars will probe more deeply into the cross-cutting pressures that contributed to both the "unchaining" (*Entfesselung*) and the "taming" (*Zähmung*) of the political mass market.[55] In doing so they will surely reveal new facets of authoritarianism as well.

NOTES

1 The best historiographical primers include Matthew Jefferies, ed., *The Ashgate Research Companion to Imperial Germany* (Farnham, Surrey, 2015); Jefferies, *Contesting the German Empire, 1871–1918* (Oxford, 2007); Ewald Frie, *Das Deutsche Kaiserreich* (Darmstadt, 2004, 2nd ed. 2013); and Hans-Peter Ullmann, *Politik im Deutschen Kaiserreich 1871–1918* (Munich, 1999). See also James Retallack, *Germany in the Age of Kaiser Wilhelm II* (Basingstoke and New York, 1996), and Retallack, ed., *Imperial Germany 1871–1918: The Short Oxford History of Germany* (Oxford and New York, 2008).
2 See, however, Marcus Llanque, *Demokratisches Denken im Krieg. Die deutsche Debatte im Ersten Weltkrieg* (Berlin, 2000), and further references there.
3 Cf. Stanley Suval, *Electoral Politics in Wilhelmine Germany* (Chapel Hill, NC, 1985); Brett Fairbairn, *Democracy in the Undemocratic State: The Reichstag Elections of 1897 and 1903* (Toronto, 1987); Margaret Lavinia Anderson, *Practicing Democracy: Elections and Political Culture in Imperial Germany* (Princeton, 2000).
4 Volker Berghahn, "The German Empire, 1871–1914: Reflections on the Direction of Recent Research," *Central European History* 35 (2002): 75–82.
5 See *inter alia* Benjamin Ziemann, *War Experiences in Rural Germany, 1914– 1923* (orig. German ed. 1997) (Oxford, 2007); Roger Chickering, *The Great War and Urban Life in Germany: Freiburg, 1914–1918* (Cambridge, 2007).

6 Ronald J. Ross, *The Failure of Bismarck's Kulturkampf: Catholicism and State Power in Imperial Germany, 1871–1887* (Washington, DC, 1998); David Blackbourn, *Marpingen: Apparitions of the Virgin Mary in Bismarckian Germany* (Oxford, 1993); Michael Gross, *The War against Catholicism: Liberalism and the Anti-Catholic Imagination in Nineteenth-Century Germany* (Ann Arbor, 2004); Róisín Healy, *The Jesuit Specter in Imperial Germany* (Boston, 2003).
7 Start with Sebastian Conrad and Jürgen Osterhammel, eds., *Das Kaiserreich transnational. Deutschland in der Welt 1871–1914*, 2nd ed. (Göttingen, 2006). The literature is now too large to cite here. See the essays in pt 4 of Sven Oliver Müller and Cornelius Torp, eds., *Imperial Germany Revisited: Continuing Debates and New Perspectives* (New York and Oxford, 2011).
8 Thomas Kühne, *Dreiklassenwahlrecht und Wahlkultur in Preussen 1867–1914. Landtagswahlen zwischen korporativer Tradition und politischem Massenmarkt* (Düsseldorf, 1994); Thomas Mergel, *Parlamentarische Kultur in der Weimarer Republik. Politische Kommunikation, symbolische Politik und Öffentlichkeit im Reichstag* (Düsseldorf, 2002).
9 I have previously grappled with the usefulness of "populism" and "demagogy" as terms describing politicians' efforts to win mass appeal; see ch. 2, "'Fishing for Popularity,'" in James Retallack, *The German Right: Political Limits of the Authoritarian Imagination* (Toronto, 2006), 76–107, and further references there.
10 Michael Geyer, "Forum: "Reviewsymposium 'Transnationale Geschichte': The New Consensus," http://hsozkult.geschichte.hu-berlin.de/rezensionen/id=812&type=revsymp, and for the following citation.
11 See David Blackbourn and James Retallack, eds, *Localism, Landscape, and the Ambiguities of Place: German-Speaking Central Europe, 1860–1930* (Toronto, 2007), "Introduction," 3–35.
12 Konrad H. Jarausch and Michael Geyer, *Shattered Past: Reconstructing German Histories* (Princeton, 2003), 19.
13 Otto Brunner et al., eds., *Geschichtliche Grundbegriffe. Historisches Lexikon zur politisch-sozialen Sprache in Deutschland*, 8 vols. (Stuttgart, 1972–97); see Horst Rabe, "Autorität," 1: 382–406; Horst Günther et al., "Herrschaft," 3: 1–102; Hans Boldt et al., "Staat," 6: 1–154.
14 Hugo Preuß, *Staat, Recht und Freiheit* (Tübingen, 1926), pts I and III and 365–8; Preuß, *Das deutsche Volk und die Politik*, orig. 1915 (Jena, 1919), esp. 170–99. Cf. Julius Hatschek, *Das Parlamentsrecht des Deutschen Reiches* (Berlin, 1915); Detlef Lehnert, *Verfassungsdemokratie als Bürgergenossenschaft. Politisches Denken, Öffentliches Recht und Geschichtsdeutungen bei Hugo Preuß* (Baden-Baden, 1998), esp. ch. 8.
15 Max Weber, "Parlament und Regierung im neugeordneten Deutschland. Zur politischen Kritik des Beamtentums und Parteiwesens" [1917], in Max

Weber, *Gesamtausgabe*, vol. 15, *Zur Politik im Weltkrieg. Schriften und Reden 1914–1918*, edited by Wolfgang J. Mommsen (Tübingen, 1984), 432–596. See also Klaus von Beyme, *Die parlamentarische Demokratie. Entstehung und Funktionsweise 1789–1999*, 3rd ed. (Opladen, 1999).

16 Gustav Radbruch, "Die politischen Parteien im System des deutschen Verfassungsrechts," in *Handbuch des deutschen Staatsrechts*, edited by Gerhard Anschütz and Richard Thoma, 2 vols. (Tübingen, 1930), 1: 289.

17 Hartwin Spenkuch, "Vergleichsweise besonders? Politisches System und Strukturen Preußens als Kern des 'deutschen Sonderwegs,'" *Geschichte und Gesellschaft* 29 (2003): 262–93. See also Christopher Clark, *Iron Kingdom: The Rise and Downfall of Prussia, 1600–1947* (Cambridge, 2006).

18 Abigail Green, *Fatherlands: State-Building and Nationhood in Nineteenth-Century Germany* (Cambridge, 2001).

19 Celia Applegate, *A Nation of Provincials: The German Idea of Heimat* (Berkeley, 1990).

20 See, for example, Siegfried Weichlein, *Region und Nation. Integrationsprozesse im Bismarckreich* (Düsseldorf, 2004).

21 David Blackbourn, *Populists and Patricians: Essays in Modern German History* (London, 1987), 18–19.

22 Christoph Schönberger, "Die überholte Parlamentarisierung. Einflußgewinn und fehlende Herrschaftsfähigkeit des Reichstags im sich demokratisierenden Kaiserreich," *Historische Zeitschrift* 272 (2001): 623–66; Mark Hewitson, "The Wilhelmine Regime and the Problem of Reform: German Debates about Modern Nation-States," in *Wilhelminism and Its Legacies: German Modernities, Imperialism, and the Meanings of Reform*, edited by Geoff Eley and James Retallack (New York, 2003), 73–90; Thomas Kühne, "Demokratisierung und Parlamentarisierung: Neue Forschungen zur politischen Entwicklungsfähigkeit Deutschlands vor dem Ersten Weltkrieg," *Geschichte und Gesellschaft* 31 (2005): 293–316. See Manfred Rauh, *Die Parlamentarisierung des Deutschen Reiches* (Düsseldorf, 1977) and the withering critique by Dieter Langewiesche, "Das Deutsche Kaiserreich: Bemerkungen zur Diskussion über Parlamentarisierung und Demokratisierung Deutschlands," *Archiv für Sozialgeschichte* 19 (1979): 628–42. See also ch. 10 in the present volume.

23 See e.g., Simone Lässig, "Wahlrechtsreformen in den deutschen Einzelstaaten. Indikatoren für Modernisierungstendenzen und Reformfähigkeit im Kaiserreich?", in *Modernisierung und Region im wilhelminischen Deutschland. Wahlen, Wahlrecht und Politische Kultur*, edited by Lässig, Karl Heinrich Pohl, and James Retallack, 2nd ed. (Bielefeld, 1998), 127–69.

24 See Anderson, *Practicing Democracy*, and the critical appreciations in Gerhard A. Ritter, "Die Reichstagswahlen und die Wurzeln der deutschen

Demokratie im Kaiserreich," *Historische Zeitschrift* 275 (2002): 385–403; Kühne, "Demokratisierung"; and ch. 8 of this book. More sceptical: Robert Arsenschek, *Der Kampf um die Wahlfreiheit im Kaiserreich. Zur parlamentarischen Wahlprüfung und politischen Realität der Reichstagswahlen 1871–1914* (Düsseldorf, 2003).

25 Peter Stirk, "The Obrigkeitsstaat: when was it born and when did it die?," unpublished paper delivered at the Annual Meeting of the Political Studies Association, April 2004 (MS.), 12; cf. Stirk, "Hugo Preuss, German Political Thought and the Weimar Constitution," *History of Political Thought* 23 (2002): 497–516; Stirk, *Twentieth-Century German Political Thought* (Edinburgh, 2006), chs. 2–3.

26 Hans-Ulrich Wehler, *Deutsche Gesellschaftsgeschichte*, vol. 3, *Von der "Deutschen Doppelrevolution" bis zum Beginn des Ersten Weltkrieges 1849–1914* (Munich, 1995), 361–2.

27 Thomas Nipperdey, *Deutsche Geschichte 1866–1918*, 2 vols., vol. 2, *Machtstaat vor der Demokratie* (Munich, 1992), 80.

28 Karl Mannheim, *Man and Society in an Age of Reconstruction* (orig. German ed. 1935), translated by Edward Shils (New York, 1967), 44.

29 Winfried Becker, *Das Bismarck-Reich – ein Obrigkeitsstaat? Die Entwicklung des Parlamentarismus und der Parteien 1871–1890* (Friedrichsruh, 2000), 34. Becker takes issue with the idea (in Ullmann, *Politik*, 31–3) that political mobilization began around 1900 and worked principally through the ideologies of nationalism and antisemitism.

30 Kühne's term was "obrigkeitsstaatliche Verfaßtheit." Thomas Kühne, "Die Jahrhundertwende, die 'lange' Bismarckzeit und die Demokratisierung der politischen Kultur," in *Otto von Bismarck und Wilhelm II. Repräsentanten eines Epochenwechsels?*, edited by Lothar Gall (Paderborn, 2000), 85–118.

31 Jack R. Dukes and Joachim Remak, eds., *Another Germany: A Reconsideration of the Imperial Era* (Boulder, CO, 1988); Sibylle Lehmann-Hasemeyera, Philipp Haubera, and Alexander Opitza, "The Political Stock Market in the German Kaiserreich – Do Markets Punish the Extension of the Suffrage to the Benefit of the Working Class? Evidence from Saxony," *Journal of Economic History* 74, no. 4 (December 2014): 1140–67.

32 Edward Ross Dickinson, "The Bourgeoisie and Reform," in *Imperial Germany*, ed. Retallack, 151–73; Dickinson, *Sex, Freedom, and Power in Imperial Germany, 1880–1914* (Cambridge and New York, 2014); Kevin Repp, *Reformers, Critics, and the Paths of German Modernity: Anti-politics and the Search for Alternatives, 1890–1914* (Cambridge, MA, 2000); Andrew Lees, *Cities, Sin, and Social Reform in Imperial Germany* (Ann Arbor, 2002).

33 Diethart Kerbs and Jürgen Reulecke, *Handbuch der Deutschen Reformbewegungen 1880–1933* (Wuppertal, 1998); Uwe Puschner, Walter Schmitz, and

Justus H. Ulbricht, eds, *Handbuch zur "Völkischen Bewegung" 1871–1918* (Munich, 1996).

34 See the unfortunate trans-Atlantic polemic over Geoff Eley, ed., *Society, Culture, and the State in Germany, 1870–1930* (Ann Arbor, 1996): Hans-Ulrich Wehler, "A Guide to Future Research on the Kaiserreich?" *Central European History* 29 (1996): 541–72; and Eley, "Theory and the Kaiserreich: Problems with Culture: German History after the Linguistic Turn," *Central European History* 31 (1998): 197–227.

35 Hans Rosenberg, *Große Depression und Bismarckzeit. Wirtschaftsablauf, Gesellschaft und Politik in Mitteleuropa* (Berlin, 1967), esp. ch. 4.

36 See *inter alia* Blackbourn, *Populists and Patricians*, 222.

37 For example, Anderson, *Practicing Democracy*; cf. Suval, *Electoral Politics*; Fairbairn, *Democracy*; Karl Rohe, *Wahlen und Wählertraditionen in Deutschland. Kulturelle Grundlagen deutscher Parteien und Parteiensysteme im 19. und 20. Jahrhundert* (Frankfurt a.M., 1992).

38 See Thomas Kühne, "From Electoral Campaigning to the Politics of Togetherness: Localism and Democracy," in *Localism, Landscape, and the Ambiguities of Place*, ed. Blackbourn and Retallack, 101–23.

39 The imposition of §28 of the Anti-Socialist Law on Leipzig is discussed in ch. 2 of the present volume.

40 Engels was alluding to the increasing influence of Johann Most and other Social Democrats who were drawn to anarchism. See the important new study by Elun T. Gabriel, *Assassins and Conspirators: Anarchism, Socialism, and Political Culture in Imperial Germany* (DeKalb, IL, 2014), especially ch. 3.

41 Friedrich Engels to August Bebel, 10[-11] May 1883, in Bebel, *Aus meinem Leben*, 3rd. ed. (Berlin-GDR, 1961), 822–3.

42 For promising work in this direction see Dieter Langewiesche, *Politikstile im Kaiserreich. Zum Wandel von Politik und Öffentlichkeit im Zeitalter des "politischen Massenmarktes"* (Friedrichsruh, 2002); Dieter Dowe et al., eds., *Parteien im Wandel. Vom Kaiserreich zur Weimarer Republik* (Munich, 1999); Gerhard A. Ritter, ed., *Wahlen und Wahlkämpfe in Deutschland. Von den Anfängen im 19. Jahrhundert bis zur Bundesrepublik* (Düsseldorf, 1997).

43 William Sheridan Allen, *The Nazi Seizure of Power: The Experience of a Single German Town, 1922–1945*, 2nd rev. ed. (New York, 1984). Cf. Roger Chickering, "Political Mobilization and Associational Life: Some Thoughts on the National Socialist German Workers' Club (e.V.)," in *Elections, Mass Politics, and Social Change in Modern Germany*, edited by Larry Eugene Jones and James Retallack (Cambridge, 1992), 307–28.

44 Gustav Freytag to Duke Ernst von Coburg, 21/30 January 1867, in *Gustav Freytag und Herzog Ernst von Coburg im Briefwechsel 1853 bis 1893*, edited by Eduard Tempeltey (Leipzig, 1904), 212–17.

45 Albeit with reference to Karl Lueger and Christian Socialism in Austria: Carl Schorske, "Politics in a New Key: An Austrian Trio," *Journal of Modern History* 39 (1967): 343–86.
46 Friedrich Naumann, *Demokratie und Kaisertum* (Berlin, 1900), 92–3; Hans Rosenberg, "Die Pseudodemokratisierung der Rittergutsbesitzerklasse" [1958], in Rosenberg, *Probleme der deutschen Sozialgeschichte* (Frankfurt a.M., 1969), 11–12.
47 See *inter alia* Wehler, *Deutsche Gesellschaftsgeschichte*, 3: 825.
48 David Blackbourn, "New Legislatures: Germany, 1871–1914," *Historical Research* 65 (1992): 201–14; Geoff Eley, "Society and Politics in Bismarckian Germany," *German History* 15 (1997): 101–32, esp. 111, 121, 128; Margaret Lavinia Anderson, "Voter, Junker, *Landrat*, Priest: The Old Authorities and the New Franchise in Imperial Germany," *American Historical Review* 98 (1993): 1448–74; Helmut Walser Smith, *German Nationalism and Religious Conflict* (Princeton, 1995), esp. 113.
49 Geoff Eley, "Anti-Semitism, Agrarian Mobilization, and the Conservative Party: Radicalism and Containment in the Founding of the Agrarian League, 1890–93," in *Between Reform, Reaction, and Resistance: Studies in the History of German Conservatism from 1789 to 1945*, edited by Larry Eugene Jones and James Retallack (Providence, RI, and Oxford, 1993), 194; Eley, "Notable Politics, the Crisis of German Liberalism, and the Electoral Transition of the 1890s," in *In Search of a Liberal Germany*, edited by Konrad H. Jarausch and Larry Eugene Jones (New York, Oxford, Munich, 1990), 192, 210–11; Eley, *Reshaping the German Right: Radical Nationalism and Political Change after Bismarck* (New Haven, 1980), 184–205.
50 Alastair P. Thompson, *Left Liberals, the State, and Popular Politics in Wilhelmine Germany* (Oxford, 2000), 21; Axel Grießmer, *Massenverbände und Massenparteien im wilhelminischen Reich. Zum Wandel der Wahlkultur 1903–1912* (Düsseldorf, 2000), 49f.; Cf. Helmut Walser Smith's contribution to "Forum. The Long Nineteenth Century," *German History* 26 (2008): 79–80.
51 Hans-Peter Goldberg, *Bismarck und seine Gegner. Die politische Rhetorik im kaiserlichen Reichstag* (Düsseldorf, 1998). In an important new series devoted to *Parlament und Öffentlichkeit*, sponsored by the Kommission für Geschichte des Parlamentarismus und der politischen Parteien, see the pioneering essays and excellent illustrations in *Das politische Zeremoniell im Deutschen Kaiserreich 1871–1918*, edited by Andreas Biefang, Michael Epkenhans, and Klaus Tenfelde, 2nd ed. (Düsseldorf, 2009), including Biefang, "Die Reichstagswahlen als demokratisches Zeremoniell," 233–70.
52 Consider the example of Paul Mehnert's speech to Dresden Conservatives in 1880, cited in ch. 8 of this volume. Exceptions include Max Bewer's

Politische Bilderbogen in the 1890s; see Thomas Gräfe, *Antisemitismus in Gesellschaft und Karikatur des Kaiserreichs. Glöß' Politische Bilderbogen 1892–1901* (Norderstedt, 2005).

53 Eve Rosenhaft, "Women, Gender, and the Limits of Political History in the Age of 'Mass' Politics," in *Elections, Mass Politics, and Social Change*, ed. Jones and Retallack, 149–73.

54 See *inter alia* Andrea Süchting-Hänger, *Das "Gewissen der Nation." Nationales Engagement und politisches Handeln konservativer Frauenorganisationen 1900 bis 1937* (Düsseldorf, 2002); Eva Schöck-Quinteros and Christiane Streubel, eds., *"Ihrem Volk verantwortlich." Frauen der politischen Rechten (1890–1933)* (Bremen, 2007); Kirsten Heinsohn, *Konservative Parteien in Deutschland 1912 bis 1933. Demokratisierung und Partizipation in geschlechterhistorischer Perspektive* (Düsseldorf, 2009); Julia Sneeringer, *Winning Women's Votes: Propaganda and Politics in Weimar Germany* (Chapel Hill, NC, 2002); Raffael Scheck, *Mothers of the Nation: Right-Wing Women in Weimar Germany* (Oxford and New York, 2004). Cf. Ute Planert, *Antifeminismus im Kaiserreich. Diskurs, soziale Formation und politische Mentalität* (Göttingen, 1998); Matthew Stibbe, "Anti-Feminism, Nationalism, and the German Right, 1914–1920: A Reappraisal," *German History* 20, no. 2 (2002): 185–210.

55 These terms allude to Peter Steinbach, *Die Zähmung des politischen Massenmarktes. Wahlen und Wahlkämpfe im Bismarckreich*, 3 vols. (Passau, 1990).

10 Society and Democracy in Germany: Why Dahrendorf Still Matters

Ralf Dahrendorf's *Society and Democracy in Germany* was published in German in 1965; two years later an English edition appeared.[1] As a provocation and a synthesis, Dahrendorf's book was soon recognized as seminal. Is it still seen this way? The book continues to be read, as far as I can determine, principally because it was wrong or overstated on so many points. One thinks here of its similarity to pioneering but flawed books by Hans-Ulrich Wehler, Hannah Arendt, and Jürgen Habermas.[2] Today, *Society and Democracy in Germany* must be read against the grain and in contexts very different from those prevailing in the 1960s. Yet in this chapter I want to suggest that Dahrendorf's work should not be dismissed by young scholars, no matter whether they want to challenge, defend, or (most likely) move beyond the thesis of Germany's "special path" (*Sonderweg*) to modernity.[3] I also want to reassess the book's importance in the context of scholarly debates about German democratization between 1848 and 1933.

Specifically, I ask whether Dahrendorf was sufficiently attuned to the differences and the reciprocal interactions among four distinct but interrelated historical processes. The first of these is the democratization of German *society*, referred to by Karl Mannheim as its "fundamental politicization."[4] The second process is the democratization of German *politics*, sometimes referred to as the advent of "mass politics," of a "political mass market" (Hans Rosenberg), or of "politics in a new key" (Carl Schorske).[5] I want, third, to consider the democratization of German *governance* (or its lack) between 1890 and 1918, and fourth, also for the Wilhelmine period, to take up the issue of German *parliamentarization* (or lack thereof).[6] Read generously, *Society and Democracy in Germany* can still offer useful counsel on each of these issues.

At this point I need to make a personal declaration of faith and ascribe one to Dahrendorf. He and I are agnostic on the question of whether a special path can be discerned in German history leading from the "failed bourgeois revolutions" of 1848–9 to the horrors of Nazism and the Holocaust. But agnosticism by definition encourages an openness to other points of view. For us, the operative terminus or *Fluchtpunkt* for historical analysis is 1933, not 1941. I use this word *Fluchtpunkt* as part of an ongoing conversation with Helmut Walser Smith, and others, about continuities from the nineteenth to the twentieth century and about the best way to study them. In his essay on "vanishing points" and his book *The Continuities of German History*, Smith has suggested that the story of history – not just German history – is often written according to "who has the Gatling gun," who has genocidal instincts, who has gas chambers, and – not least – who has genuine authority.[7] Smith (and others) have made a compelling case for seeing 1941 as the most appropriate *Fluchtpunkt* to help us consider the longer sweep of German history. For them, the horrific acts of violence that 1941 represents – above all, the construction of the first extermination camps within months of the German invasion of the Soviet Union – provide historians with a useful and compelling shorthand.[8] However, it is not difficult to find dates and arguments that redirect our attention towards developments in German history that have nothing to do with genocide or war. The *Fluchtpunkt* of 1941 leaves open many questions about why German liberalism and German democracy could not withstand the onslaught of Nazism. Those questions can be addressed better by focusing instead on 30 January 1933, when Reich President Paul von Hindenburg formally appointed Adolf Hitler as chancellor.

By valorizing arguments closely connected with Hitler's rise to power, I find myself in the company of historians who have thought deeply about the connections between voting, mass appeal, and the institutions of state governance. Building on the insights of such scholars, my own work has tended to focus on Germans who not only harboured antisemitic, anti-socialist, anti-liberal, and anti-democratic instincts but also used elections and parliaments to put them into practice.[9] Not *murderous* practice, perhaps; but just as 1941 saw a fateful convergence of views among the Jews' most determined enemies, January 1933 represented the triumph of our perpetrators – those who killed liberalism and democracy in Germany, at least for a time.

The differences of outlook among scholars who are warm or cool towards Dahrendorf and his book should not be overplayed. All such scholars are interested in the fragility of boundaries, of ideals, of moral certitudes. They share an interest in how institutions and habits of mind interact to sustain or break down established patterns of authority. Thomas Kühne's writing on comradeship (*Kamaradschaft*) reveals his interest in questions of "sentiment" and "sunderings."[10] These are not unlike the questions that Helmut Smith has examined through the lens of German–Jewish relations. It could easily have been Kühne, not Smith, who posed a question that suggests why Dahrendorf remains relevant: How did *humanity* come to think of itself as divided with some parts less human than others?[11] Answering his own question, Smith observed that 1933 was not a "civilizational break." I agree. In the same breath, though – and this is my thesis – I would argue that 1933 was a necessary precondition for the Nazis' later implementation of a racialized world view. The failures of liberalism and democracy were part of that "collapse of fellow feeling" that makes German history unique.

I remember the moment I was struck with the idea of initiating a new conversation about Ralf Dahrendorf. I was frustrated that yet another overarching model of German politics had been posited by a political scientist, not only to explain the dynamic of domestic politics in Imperial Germany but also to categorize the scholars who studied it into one camp or another. Was the Second Reich a "good" or an "evil" empire? Are historians of Imperial Germany "optimists" or "pessimists?"[12] To explore my own dissatisfaction with the premises underlying such questions, I thought: Why not take the work of one of Germany's most respected political scientists from the 1960s and consider its relevance today? You can imagine my chagrin when I pulled down my tattered copy of Dahrendorf from the 1970s – with the Trent University Bookstore price sticker ($3.25) safely preserved inside the back cover – and remembered that the fellow was a *sociologist*. I read the book from beginning to end and then, a few months later, I read it again. Both times Dahrendorf repaid my effort and dispelled my hubris.

More ably than in my undergraduate days I was able to take in stride Dahrendorf's obvious indebtedness to modernization theory, which still marks the book as a product of the 1960s. But now I could also better appreciate the preparatory homework he had done across many disciplines. In his early chapter devoted to "posing the question," I was cheered that Dahrendorf travelled back to 1866, citing Constantin Frantz's assertion that "the German question is the most obscure, most involved and most comprehensive problem in the whole of modern history."[13] Frantz helped Dahrendorf dismiss previous statements of "the" German question in short order, although the modern scholar was characteristically generous in crediting those who had gone before.[14] Hans Kohn's study *The Mind of Germany* is only one of many approaches Dahrendorf considered, and superseded, on the way to posing his own "German Question." That question is *almost* (but not quite) too familiar to bear repeating: "Why," Dahrendorf asked, "is it that so few in Germany embraced the principle of liberal democracy?"[15]

We have now reached the half-century mark since Dahrendorf wrote his book – five decades of sophisticated, sobering research on the question of how Germans arrived at 30 January 1933. That research has revealed at least four difficulties inherent in the way Dahrendorf posed his question (leaving his answer entirely aside for the moment). First, the negative syntax and premise of Dahrendorf's "German Problem" – "Why so few …" – gave impetus to two unconvincing premises of the *Sonderweg* thesis: that the German bourgeoisie was somehow deficient, and that German history diverged from a "normal" Western path. Second, and no less important, fifty years of research has shown how unwise it is to precede the word "democracy" with the modifier "liberal" in such a foundational statement of intent. This was no unconsidered coupling in Dahrendorf's book; it was programmatic. As he wrote, "Democracy means many things to many men … In this study the term democracy is used … always in the sense of 'softened by liberal admixtures.'" To which he added: "There is no shortage of discussion about the aroma of these admixtures." But he was firm in defining liberal democracy as "a basic attitude, political in intention and effect, that is characterized by the search for institutional means to control the powerful in order to keep the political system open for ever new solutions." Thus the principle of liberal democracy remained, for Dahrendorf, "the safeguarding of liberty by effective protection from the dogmatic establishment of one-sided positions."[16]

That it is unwise to conflate bourgeois, liberal, and democratic attitudes in Germany – third – was already apparent to historians before 1984. Such worries were given pointed expression in that year when David Blackbourn and Geoff Eley's *Peculiarities of German History* appeared in English.[17] One of their key arguments was that the German bourgeoisie may have exerted hegemony in the economic, social, and cultural spheres before 1914 but nevertheless accepted a form of government that fell far short of the "liberal democratic ideal." Fourth, I would argue that a sociologist's inquiry into the "principle of democracy" is insufficient for historians, perhaps even unattractive to them, because they believe it is more important to study the *processes* of democratization. At the same time, good history does not examine *only* processes (such as democratization); nor does it ignore ideals (such as democracy).[18]

On these four counts, then, the very terms in which Dahrendorf formulated "his" German Question provoked many of the objections subsequently raised against his book.

What did Dahrendorf have to say about democratization in the 1. social, 2. political, 3. governmental, and 4. parliamentary realms?

1. Any German history textbook worth its salt tells us that German society was modernized quickly and thoroughly from the mid-nineteenth century onward. Germans were on the move; industrial capitalism transformed a society of estates (*Stände*) into a class society; the middle classes grew more powerful and their vision of the ideal state more influential; the world and its culture and its commodities penetrated everyday life. Many readers of Dahrendorf remember his argument that Germans sought consensus and community as a reaction to unprecedented upheaval in their social world. Hence Germans never properly learned the mechanics of democracy, which is based on the limited battle of contending positions. As Dahrendorf reminded us, though – for example, when he took the sociologist Ferdinand Tönnies to task – Germans were not as naive as we might think in swallowing the notion that society had to be a community, let alone a people's community (*Volksgemeinschaft*), to function well. Nor were Dahrendorf's Germans as allergic to discord as he claimed (after Kant) in certain other parts of his book. On the contrary: "The confrontation of a sweet community of minds in the past with the heartless contractual society of the present is historically misleading." He continued: "Community is indeed an unsociety … The success of the German ideology of social classlessness and national community consisted less in the power of conviction it carried than in its advocates' ability to distract people's interest from the immediate, real, and acutely threatening and turn it to the more distant and obscure."[19]

My point in citing Dahrendorf's ambivalence on the issue of society's democratization is twofold. I would suggest that, as a sociologist, he was well placed to consider the historical ramifications of a situation

Figure 10.1 © Estate of Thomas Theodor Heine/SODRAC (2015). "Fortschritt im Schulwesen," by Thomas Theodor Heine, *Simplicissimus* 15, no. 50 (13 March 1911): 846. In this critique of Prussian militarism, a Prussian police officer, seated at a classroom lectern, gives his obedient pupils a lesson with the aid of his sword. The text reads: "Progress in the Education System: Civics is to be introduced as a new subject of study in Prussian schools. It goes without saying that instruction will be given by policemen." Note the ruler readily available for the corporal punishment of pupils and the programmatic pictures of a lion and a sheep on the wall – two further aspects of a "modern" curriculum for German children.

– one that prevailed in Germany at least by the 1890s – where, as he put it, "everybody counts, everybody can participate and has the right to secure the range of his existence against the claims of others."[20] Furthermore, it is helpful (albeit not sufficient) to cite as evidence of the fundamental democratization of German society the introduction of universal manhood suffrage in 1866–7, the subsequent rise in turnout rates for Reichstag elections, the triumph of the mass press, and the rapid growth of voluntary associations (especially economic lobbies and radical nationalist pressure groups). Dahrendorf seemed to understand this instinctively, even though he did not or could not draw upon supporting arguments from such political scientists as Stein Rokkan, M. Rainer Lepsius, Karl Rohe, and Peter Steinbach.[21] A prickly passage from Dahrendorf makes the point: "I am not concerned with an electoral participation of 99.9 per cent, or with people who spend their entire leisure time reading newspapers and carrying on political debates. Apart from the borderline situations of massive protest, politics will always remain a domain of active minorities."[22]

2. Dahrendorf is remembered for claiming that Germans have long cherished private over public virtues, that they are obsessed with chasing universal truth, and that political discussion in Germany has perennially been "dominated by the search for the specialist of the general."[23] Dahrendorf concluded (using the passive voice) that conflict is "solved" and that Germany is "governed." Nevertheless, he devoted considerable attention to those aspects of Germany's political culture that have been taken up in books whose titles reflect his own scepticism regarding the de facto liberty of (male) Germans entitled to vote.[24] Dahrendorf's warning was clear: "The belief that the establishment of the rule of law must bring about democracy more or less automatically is in itself a German misunderstanding."

As recent historians have done with increasing frequency and insight, Dahrendorf – following T.H. Marshall's discussion of the development of citizenship in England – divided citizenship into the civil, the social, and the political.[25] By the political element he meant "the right to participate in the exercise of political power, as a member of a body invested with political authority or as an elector of the members of such a body." Dahrendorf cited many elements of unfairness in the "universality" and "equality" of the Reichstag suffrage, although he did not tip his hand as to whether the Reichstag actually constituted a "body invested with political authority."[26] No matter. Doubts on this score continue to be raised by historians who consider, for example, the power of the Prussian Landtag, the temerity of the Reichstag's Election

Ostelbischer Wahlzauber.

Eine reizende Neuerung

zur Erzielung „guter" Wahlen.

Figure 10.2 The text reads: "Voting-Magic, East of the Elbe [River] – A charming innovation to achieve 'good' elections." The Prussian district administrator (*Landrat*) looms over the peasant voter at every turn. "Ostelbischer Wahlzauber," *Ulk*, no. 37 (12 September 1913). bpk, Berlin/Art Resource, NY.

Oversight Committee, or the influence of the Kaiser and his court as permanent impediments to the fulfilment of the social, civil, and political rights of citizenship before 1918.[27]

This brings me to "blockages" in German history to 3. democratic governance and 4. parliamentarism. On both topics Dahrendorf wrote passionately. What we tend to remember are those phrases that found a home in the *Sonderweg* thesis, for instance, about the "cartel of anxiety" and the "rallying together" (*Sammlung*) of "pre-industrial élites" to block constitutional reform (at least before October 1918). From such arguments Dahrendorf rushed to a conclusion that took him to the Third Reich and even the Federal Republic after 1949. In a chapter titled "The Path to Dictatorship," he wrote that in 1918, "one of the most skillful elites of modern history ... lost its political basis. The state ... began to float. No counter-elite emerged to fasten it."[28] We all know what happened fifteen years later.

Yes, we do; but the trajectories stretching from 1867 to 1933 remain contentious, and we ought to give Dahrendorf some of the credit for keeping them so.[29] Not long ago Volker Berghahn cited such authorities as Gerhard A. Ritter, Christoph Schönberger, and Mark Hewitson to explain the hardening of ideological positions among party caucuses in the Reichstag and between the Reichstag, the government, and the mass of enfranchised voters. Lack of ministerial responsibility – which is really just the tip of the iceberg in any discussion of parliamentarism – was one of the most important reasons why reform *appeared* to be hamstrung by political, institutional, and attitudinal stasis. By 1914, Berghahn concluded, "constitutional reform ... would have been tantamount to a constitutional revolution, and neither the crown nor the non-socialist parties were prepared even to consider it. Instead they stubbornly asserted that all was well."[30] If Berghahn's assessment of the situation on the eve of the First World War deserves further debate, so does Dahrendorf's book, which provided much of its premise.

We cannot and we should not ignore Dahrendorf's blind spots about the processes of social and political democratization or their relationship to German governance and parliamentarism. To these we can add his disinclination to deal with the period of the Weimar Republic systematically and his neglect of grassroots electoral politics. What did he accomplish instead? By ranging broadly across History's sister disciplines, by delving deeply into the social, economic, and intellectual history of the Second Reich, and by asking forthright questions about comparability and continuity, Dahrendorf worked with the evidence and the interpretive models available to him in the early 1960s. He stretched the *longue durée* of modern German history more vigorously than most historians were doing at the time, until it became taut. In these ways he pushed his readers to move beyond talking about only abstract notions of "full democracy." He provoked them to embrace thornier debates about the complex processes of political modernization and the contingent ways authoritarian governments attempt to deal with them. Such debates will not likely be settled any time soon.

NOTES

1 Ralf Dahrendorf, *Gesellschaft und Demokratie in Deutschland* (Munich, 1965); *Society and Democracy in Germany* (Garden City, NY, 1967); my Anchor Books edition of 1969 was used for citations in this chapter.
2 Hans-Ulrich Wehler, *Das Deutsche Kaiserreich 1871–1918* (Göttingen, 1973, 7th ed. 1994), *The German Empire, 1871–1918*, trans. Kim Traynor (Leamington Spa and Dover, NH, 1985, Oxford and New York, 1997); Hannah Arendt, *Eichmann in Jerusalem: A Report on the Banality of Evil* (New York, 1963, rev. eds. 1994, 2006); Jürgen Habermas, *Strukturwandel der Öffentlichkeit: Untersuchungen zu einer Kategorie der bürgerlichen Gesellschaft*, orig. 1962, 5th ed. (Neuwied, 1971), *The Structural Transformation of the Public Sphere: An Inquiry into a Category of Bourgeois Society*, trans. Thomas Burger with Frederick Lawrence (Cambridge, MA, 1989).
3 On the *Sonderweg* thesis, see also the preface and other chapters in this book.
4 Karl Mannheim, *Man and Society in an Age of Reconstruction* (orig. German ed. 1935), translated by Edward Shils (New York, 1967), 44.
5 Hans Rosenberg, *Große Depression und Bismarckzeit. Wirtschaftsablauf, Gesellschaft und Politik in Mitteleuropa* (Berlin, 1967), ch. 4; Carl Schorske, "Politics in a New Key: An Austrian Trio," *Journal of Modern History* 39 (1967): 343–86. See also ch. 9 above.
6 Manfred Rauh, *Die Parlamentarisierung des Deutschen Reiches* (Düsseldorf, 1977), appropriately criticized in Dieter Langewiesche, "Das Deutsche Kaiserreich: Bemerkungen zur Diskussion über Parlamentarisierung und Demokratisierung Deutschlands," *Archiv für Sozialgeschichte* 19 (1979): 628–42.
7 Helmut Walser Smith, "The Vanishing Point in German History: An Essay on Perspective," *History and Memory* 17 (2005): 269–95; Smith, *The Continuities of German History: Nation, Religion, and Race across the Long Nineteenth Century* (Cambridge and New York, 2008), esp. ch. 1; Smith "When the *Sonderweg* Debate Left Us," in *Imperial Germany Revisited: Continuing*

Debates and New Perspectives, edited by Sven Oliver Müller and Cornelius Torp (New York and Oxford, 2011), 21–36.

8 Explained from somewhat different points of view in Smith, *The Continuities of German History*, 30–6 and 211–14, citing the arguments of Detlev Peukert, Ulrich Herbert, Omer Bartov, and Saul Friedländer, among others.

9 Margaret Lavinia Anderson, *Practicing Democracy: Elections and Political Culture in Imperial Germany* (Princeton, 2000); Brett Fairbairn, *Democracy in the Undemocratic State: The German Reichstag Elections of 1898 and 1903* (Toronto, 1997); Fairbairn, "Interpreting Wilhelmine Elections: National Issues, Fairness Issues, and Electoral Mobilization," in *Elections, Mass Politics, and Social Change in Modern Germany*, edited by Larry Eugene Jones and James Retallack (Cambridge and New York, 1992), 17–48. Thomas Kühne provided the concept of "electoral culture" (*Wahlkultur*): Kühne, *Dreiklassenwahlrecht und Wahlkultur in Preussen 1867–1914. Landtagswahlen zwischen korporativer Tradition und politischem Massenmarkt* (Düsseldorf, 1994); see also Kühne's early *tour d'horizon*, "Wahlrecht – Wahlverhalten – Wahlkultur. Tradition und Innovation in der historischen Wahlforschung," *Archiv für Sozialgeschichte* 33 (1993): 481–547.

10 Thomas Kühne, *Kameradschaft. Die Soldaten des nationalsozialistischen Krieges und das 20. Jahrhundert* (Göttingen, 2006); Kühne, *Belonging and Genocide: Hitler's Community, 1918–1945* (New Haven, 2010).

11 Smith, *The Continuities of German History*, 37, emphasis added; and 37–8 for the following phrases.

12 See *inter alia* Chris Lorenz, "Beyond Good and Evil? The German Empire of 1871 and Modern German Historiography," *Journal of Contemporary History* 30 (1995): 729–65; Marcus Kreuzer, "Parliamentarization and the Question of German Exceptionalism, 1867–1918," *Central European History* 36 (2003): 327–57.

13 Cited in Dahrendorf, *Society and Democracy*, 4. It has taken too long, but historians have lately come to appreciate the significance of antisemitic "images of history" (*Geschichtsbilder*) proselytised by Constantin Frantz, Heinrich von Treitschke, Theodor Fritsch, and Heinrich Claß (among others). See essays on these thinkers, as well as Andrea Hopp's and Michaela Haibl's analyses of picture postcards, satirical cartoons, memorabilia, and other media that brought their message to the masses, in Werner Bergmann and Ulrich Sieg, eds., *Antisemitische Geschichtsbilder* (Essen, 2009).

14 A partial, alphabetical list includes Otto von Bismarck, Karl Dietrich Bracher, Ernest K. Bramsted, Fritz Fischer, Ernst Fraenkel, Hans Kohn, Leonard Krieger, three Manns (Thomas, Heinrich, Golo), Karl Mannheim, Wolfgang J. Mommsen, Franz Neumann, Helmuth Plessner, Gerhard

Ritter, Guenther Roth, Fritz Stern, A.J.P. Taylor, Alexis de Tocqueville, and Thorstein Veblen.
15 Dahrendorf, *Society and Democracy*, 14.
16 Dahrendorf, *Society and Democracy*, 12–13.
17 Geoff Eley and David Blackbourn, *Mythen deutscher Geschichtsschreibung. Die gescheiterte bürgerliche Revolution von 1848* (Frankfurt a.M., 1980), published in a revised and expanded edition as Blackbourn and Eley, *The Peculiarities of German History: Bourgeois Society and Politics in Nineteenth-Century Germany* (Oxford and New York, 1984).
18 See the useful entries in the online *International Encyclopedia of the Social and Behavioral Sciences* (2001): "Democracy" by Robert A. Dahl (3405–8); "Democracy, History of" by James J. Sheehan (3408–13); and "Liberalism: Historical Aspects" by Dieter Langewiesche (8792–7). Sheehan refers to the democratic vision and the democratic tradition but also to democratic pressures and markers of democracy's progress. http://www.science direct.com/science/referenceworks/9780080430768.
19 Dahrendorf, *Society and Democracy*, 121–4.
20 Dahrendorf, *Society and Democracy*, 65.
21 Stein Rokkan, *Citizens, Elections, Parties: Approaches to the Comparative Study of the Processes of Development* (Oslo, 1970); Rokkan, *State Formation, Nation-Building, and Mass Politics in Europe*, edited by Peter Flora et al. (Oxford and New York, 1999); M. Rainer Lepsius, *Demokratie in Deutschland. Soziologisch-historische Konstellationsanalysen* (Göttingen, 1993); Karl Rohe, "Wahlanalyse im historischen Kontext: Zur Kontinuität und Wandel von Wählerverhalten," *Historische Zeitschrift* 234 (1982): 337–57; Rohe, "German Elections and Party Systems in Historical and Regional Perspective: An Introduction," in *Elections, Parties and Political Traditions: Social Foundations of German Parties and Party Systems, 1867–1987*, edited by Rohe (New York, Oxford, Munich, 1990), 1–15; Rohe, *Wahlen und Wählertraditionen in Deutschland. Kulturelle Grundlagen deutscher Parteien und Parteiensysteme im 19. und 20. Jahrhundert* (Frankfurt a.M., 1992); Peter Steinbach, "Deutungsmuster der historischen Modernisierungstheorie für die Analyse westeuropäischer Wahlen," in *Vergleichende europäische Wahlforschung*, edited by Otto Büsch and Steinbach (Berlin, 1982), 158–246; Steinbach, "Nationalisierung, soziale Differenzierung und Urbanisierung als Bedingungsfaktoren des Wahlverhaltens im Kaiserreich," *Historical Social Research* 15 (1990): 63–82; Steinbach, "Einleitung. Probleme politischer Partizipation im Modernisierungsprozeß" in *Probleme politischer Partizipation im Modernisierungsprozeß*, edited by Steinbach (Stuttgart, 1982), 7–19.
22 Dahrendorf, *Society and Democracy*, 65.

23 Dahrendorf, *Society and Democracy*, 153.
24 Fairbairn, *Democracy in the Undemocratic State*; Jonathan Sperber, *The Kaiser's Voters: Electors and Elections in Imperial Germany* (Cambridge and New York, 1997); Anderson, *Practicing Democracy*.
25 For further references see Geoff Eley and Jan Palmowski, eds, *Citizenship and National Identity in Twentieth-Century Germany* (Stanford, 2008).
26 For the preceding, Dahrendorf, *Society and Democracy*, 66–7.
27 Kühne, *Dreiklassenwahlrecht*; Robert Arsenschek, *Der Kampf um die Wahlfreiheit im Kaiserreich. Zur parlamentarischen Wahlprüfung und politischen Realität der Reichstagswahlen 1871–1914* (Düsseldorf, 2003); John C.G. Röhl, *Wilhelm II*, vol. 3, *Into the Abyss of War and Exile, 1900–1941* (Cambridge and New York, 2014).
28 Dahrendorf, *Society and Democracy*, 377.
29 Contrast, for example, Smith, *The Continuities of German History*, with Geoff Eley, *Nazism as Fascism: Violence, Ideology, and the Ground of Consent in Germany 1930–1945* (London, 1913).
30 Volker Berghahn, "Industrial Capitalism and Universal Suffrage: German, American, and British Paths into the Twentieth Century," in *Rechtsstaat statt Revolution, Verrechtlichung statt Demokratie?*, edited by Detlev Schulze et al. (Münster, 2010), pt 1, 361–80; also Berghahn, "The German Empire, 1871–1914: Reflections on the Direction of Recent Research," *Central European History* 35 (2002): 75–82; cf. Christoph Schönberger, *Das Parlament im Anstaltsstaat. Zur Theorie parlamentarischer Repräsentation in der Staatsrechtslehre des Kaiserreichs (1871–1918)* (Frankfurt a.M., 1997); Schönberger, "Die überholte Parlamentarisierung. Einflußgewinn und fehlende Herrschaftsfähigkeit des Reichstags im sich demokratisierenden Kaiserreich," *Historische Zeitschrift* 272 (2001): 623–66; Gerhard A. Ritter, "Entwicklungsprobleme des deutschen Parlamentarismus," in *Gesellschaft, Parlament und Regierung. Zur Geschichte des Parlamentarismus in Deutschland*, edited by G.A. Ritter (Düsseldorf, 1974), 11–54; Ritter, "Die Reichstagswahlen und die Wurzeln der deutschen Demokratie im Kaiserreich," *Historische Zeitschrift* 275 (2002): 385–403; Mark Hewitson, "The *Kaiserreich* in Question: Constitutional Crisis in Germany before the First World War," *Journal of Modern History* 73 (2001): 725–80; and Hewitson, "The Wilhelmine Regime and the Problem of Reform: German Debates about Modern Nation-States," in *Wilhelminism and Its Legacies: German Modernities, Imperialism, and the Meanings of Reform, 1890–1930*, edited by Geoff Eley and James Retallack (Oxford and New York, 2003), 73–90.

11 Democracy in Disappearing Ink: Suffrage Robbery as *Coup d'État*

All these men [the liberals] regard as revolutionary the abolition of anciently established institutions and evils, whereas by counter-revolution they understand the restoration of these or of other abuses. Their adversaries, on the other hand, understand by revolution the aggregate of all the follies and crimes that have ever been committed, whereas by counter-revolution they mean the re-establishment of order, of authority, of religion, and so on.

Friedrich von Raumer,
Briefe aus Paris und Frankreich im Jahre 1830[1]

Introduction

"The Kaiser is like a balloon," Bismarck famously remarked. "You have to hold tight to the string or you never know where he'll be off to next." Kaiser Wilhelm II, who came to the throne at the age of twenty-nine in 1888 and dismissed Bismarck a scant two years later, fully deserves the bad press he has received. It was said at the time that Wilhelm approached every issue with an open mouth. Even before 1900, many people in high political circles were sure that Wilhelm was mad. John Röhl's three-volume biography of Wilhelm, the final volume of which just appeared in English, hammers home the point.[2]

In this chapter I address a problem that merits more consideration than the Kaiser's mental state or his personal peccadilloes: the progress of the democratic idea in Germany on the cusp of the twentieth century. I want to pull together and reconsider three aspects of this issue – without, however, leaving aside what Röhl called the "kingship mechanism" and its role in the governance of the Second Reich.[3]

Older scholarship suggests that Bismarck's departure from office in 1890 introduced a period characterized both by "polycratic chaos" and by "the permanent threat of a *coup d'état*" against the democratically elected Reichstag.[4] I want, first, to suggest that these two interpretations of how politics functioned in the 1890s are compatible in some ways but incompatible in others. More recent scholarship, second, has suggested that Germans were successfully "practising democracy" during the Wilhelmine era. By this reading, after the introduction of universal manhood suffrage for Reichstag elections in 1867, right up until the outbreak of war in 1914, German political culture was not characterized by a deficit of democratic values. On the contrary: ordinary Germans were remarkably successful in learning and implementing the lessons of democracy. They protected the principle of "one man, one vote," they increased the power and prestige of the Reichstag, and they ensured that electoral chicanery played little or no part in German political culture. This conclusion, too, merits re-examination.

Third, Germany's erratic policy has been ascribed to an increasingly isolated emperor whose manic-depressive episodes and whose rants against the Reichstag were dismissed by contemporaries as nonsense. In oblique reference to his chancellors' continuing problems cobbling together party majorities in parliament, Wilhelm himself once claimed that he did not care which monkeys jumped around in the monkey cage he called the Reichstag. Actually, people in influential positions knew he cared very much. Nevertheless, according to standard accounts, almost no one supported Wilhelm's extreme efforts to domesticate the unruly beast, *demos*. A coup against the Reichstag, even when its members voted down government legislation, was too dangerous a course even to contemplate seriously, let alone carry out.

My hypothesis is that these claims begin to wobble when we widen our focus to include political sentiments and initiatives beyond the confines of the Kaiser's court and the halls of the Reich chancellory. A new perspective that takes into account reactionary plans hatched in Germany's federal states – including Prussia, but more interestingly in the next largest states of Bavaria, Saxony, Baden, and Württemberg – demonstrates that Germany was not embarked on an "odyssey toward democracy" – a journey of epic proportions from which there could be no turning back. That very term "odyssey" commits historians who use it to see the processes of democratization through a teleological lens. Exaggerating only slightly, the argument that the Kaiser never carried through with his threats to revise universal manhood suffrage or abolish the Reichstag suggests that the Weimar Republic and its parliamentary democracy were, in large measure, the natural outcome of what *didn't* happen in the Second Reich. Germany's missing *coup d'état* has become German historiography's dog that didn't bark in the night.

The following analysis asks what "polycratic chaos" and an attack on the prerogatives of the Reichstag really looked like to statesmen, politicians, and other observers outside Berlin. It asks, next, whether a liberal, reformist consensus, which has been emphasized in much of the recent literature on Imperial Germany, really existed among the powerful bourgeois class of that age. If such a consensus did exist, what are we to make of the schemes and dreams of anti-democrats who argued that the Reichstag, because it was already dysfunctional in a democratizing age, was the *last* place from which attacks on socialism and democracy should be launched? Lastly, I ask whether Germany in the mid-1890s might have been closer to the brink of a civil war than standard accounts of the period suggest.

Was the Kaiser really all that isolated or out of touch with reality? No. Was Wilhelm's aggressiveness – towards the exercise of civil liberties, towards the Social Democratic movement, towards the national parliament – really what determined the outcome of legislative crises in the 1890s? For a time, yes, but in the long run, no. It was his *timidness*, his hesitancy, his unwillingness to take the final plunge into all-out war against "subversion," that proved decisive. As I argue, that hesitancy emboldened others who were willing to initiate draconian measures against the "inner enemies of the Reich" (*innere Reichsfeinde*). I will not draw explicit parallels between the 1890s and Germany's role in precipitating the First World War. But scholarly work spawned by the one-hundredth anniversary of the outbreak of hostilities in the summer of 1914 has made us more aware than ever that the Kaiser was under intense pressure during the July Crisis not to appear weak and not to choose the path of compromise. This chapter suggests that constitutional brinkmanship in the mid-1890s was not entirely dissimilar from the diplomatic brinkmanship of mid-summer 1914, even though the stakes and outcomes were very different.

The Kaiser's *Coup d'État* Plans

Between 1894 and 1900, Wilhelm II floated many trial balloons that were allowed to drift in troubling directions. They drifted towards street battles with Social Democrats, possibly leading to bloodshed or civil war;

towards serial dissolutions of the Reichstag and new elections, possibly leading to the dismantling of universal manhood suffrage; and towards stricter provisions for the Criminal Code and laws of association and assembly, possibly leading to much stronger influence for the Church, censors, and the police. The fate of these trial balloons depended on where and how they were moored in German political culture (in Prussia, in the courts, in local administration, in the public sphere). Some of the lines tethering them were strong and taut. Others were weak and elastic. Still others were strong *because* they were elastic.

Early in the decade, conservatives lined up in support of the Lex Heinze – a term that subsumed an initial scandal, a series of legislative bills, and a public debate that dragged on from February 1892 to June 1900. The murder trial of a Berlin pimp (named Heinze) had prompted Bismarck's successor as chancellor, General Leo von Caprivi, to introduce a bill imposing stiff penalties on a range of "morally offensive" practices, most of them sexual in nature. The bill was opposed by liberal academics, writers, artists, and journalists, who wanted to protect artistic and scholarly freedom. They ensured that only a rump bill passed in 1900.[5]

Dreams that Wilhelm II would inaugurate a "social monarchy" were already dashed by 1894, when the so-called Stumm era began. Named after the Saar industrialist Baron Karl Ferdinand von Stumm-Halberg, it was characterized by harsh workplace policies designed to limit the growth of the Social Democratic trade union movement and preserve the *Herr-im-Haus* model of industrial relations. As one representative of heavy industry in the Rhine–Ruhr district put it, "the workshop and the army are very much alike in that strict discipline must prevail for all classes."[6] One Conservative denounced the whole idea of social reform as "fanatical humanitarianism."[7] At the end of the decade, echoes of the Stumm era were still heard in the Hard Labour Bill (*Zuchthausvorlage*), introduced into the Reichstag in May 1899. This bill would have punished all those who attempted to resist or break up strikes and other forms of industrial action with hard labour in a workhouse. It was reluctantly supported by Chancellor Chlodwig zu Hohenlohe-Schillingsfürst, who served from 1894 to 1900. Again socialists and liberals defeated the bill.[8]

Why, then, can the mid-1890s be characterized as a turning point in Germany's democratization? In May and June 1894, law-abiding citizens in European capitals were shocked by a wave of anarchist attacks.[9] These included the attempted assassination of the Italian premier

Figure 11.1 Under the revealing title, *A German Socialist Propounding His Bloodthirsty Ideas*, this painting was exhibited in 1885 at the National Academy of Design in New York. The aggressive posture and evident vehemence of this Social Democratic orator are highlighted by the red tablecloth at the bottom of the painting and the handkerchief of the same colour tucked into the speaker's vest pocket. Yet the painting's real title is simply *The Socialist*. Indicative of the international reach of the Social Democratic and anarchist movements, the scene depicted here by the artist – who emigrated as a child from Germany to Milwaukee – might plausibly have taken place in either Germany or America. In both the Bismarckian and Wilhelmine eras, prominent leftists traveled across the Atlantic and addressed large crowds in New York, Boston, Philadelphia, and Chicago. Robert Koehler, *Der Sozialist*, 1885. bpk, Berlin/Deutsches Historisches Museum/Photograph: Jürgen Liepe/Art Resource, NY.

Francesco Crispi and the stabbing death of French President Sadi Carnot by an Italian revolutionary on 24 June 1894. Bombs were set off in London and Paris and Prague. Barcelona's governor was shot, Chicago's mayor murdered in his home. As anarchists became the target of legislation in Europe, Britain, and the United States, characteristically the Kaiser wanted Germany to take the lead.[10] Wilhelm telegraphed Chancellor Caprivi that an anti-anarchist bill should be prepared for the Reichstag with the utmost haste.[11] Wilhelm warned Caprivi that the Social Democrats would try to distance themselves from the anarchists, but the two groups had to be "thrown into one pot." In October, however, the Prussian state ministry backed Caprivi's more moderate plans, which steered clear of a new Anti-Socialist Law. Meanwhile the battle against revolution had become hopelessly enmeshed with court and ministerial intrigues, which led to the appointment of the seventy-five-year-old Hohenlohe as chancellor in October 1894. Part of the Kaiser's frustration was that it was taking so long for his ministers to formulate concrete plans against Social Democracy. As one insider reported from Berlin, the more Wilhelm saw signs of a vigorous response to the threat of revolutionary violence, "the more he likes it."[12]

With obvious lack of enthusiasm, Hohenlohe reverted to part of the Kaiser's original plan and introduced an Anti-Revolution Bill into the Reichstag in December 1894.[13] Again, leftist critics helped defeat the bill, on 11 May 1895. The Kaiser's anger was palpable. In a telegram he shot off to Hohenlohe upon hearing the news, he wrote, "Now we are left with fire hoses for ordinary situations and grapeshot as a last resort."[14] Taking stock of the liberals' many successes in defeating reactionary legislation between 1894 and 1900, the historian Robert Lougee has concluded that although public attention was aroused, there was no consensus – even among the right-wing parties, let alone more broadly – that the state should hit out hard against the "inner enemy." According to Lougee, such attention produced the opposite effect: it became "abundantly clear" that "fear of revolution was not an overriding anxiety of the German people or one which would induce them to accept repression or manipulation."[15] Does Lougee's assertion hold water?

To answer this question we need to take a short journey from Berlin to Dresden, the capital of the Kingdom of Saxony. In this federal state – Imperial Germany's third largest, with almost 5 million inhabitants – urban industrial and rural agrarian interests were represented mainly by bourgeois politicians. The Conservative and National Liberal parties dominated state politics, with Conservatives clearly holding the upper hand. Saxon burghers, many of whom appeared to have solidly liberal credentials, were among the most determined enemies of socialism. Saxon history thus allows us to reframe the *Sonderweg* debate about Germany's "special path" to modernity. It adds flesh to the bones of a counter-*Sonderweg* thesis proposed more than thirty years ago by David Blackbourn and Geoff Eley. In their view, an ascendant bourgeoisie may exercise hegemony in the social, economic, and cultural realms even while rejecting the ideals of liberalism and democracy.[16] But the Saxon example does more than that.

Throughout the imperial period, Saxony provided models of successful repression, but never more so than during the 1890s, when its politicians led the rhetorical charge against subversion. With uncommon candour, Saxony's King Albert (ruled 1873–1902) and his ministers assured other monarchs and government leaders that they were ready for a *coup d'état* against the Reichstag and revision of universal manhood suffrage. With uncommon unanimity, Saxon civil servants, police commissioners, and civic leaders defended the "Saxon Jewel" – Saxony's harsh Association Law, dating from 1850, which was envied by Prussian reactionaries. With uncommon alacrity, Saxon parliamentarians revised suffrage laws to disadvantage Social Democrats seeking election to state and municipal parliaments. And with uncommon success, Saxon statesmen demonstrated that bourgeois public opinion, properly channelled, could overcome legislative roadblocks that frustrated reactionaries in Prussia and the Reich.

Right away we can dispense with the notion that a murderous anarchist in June 1894 triggered the Kaiser's call three months later for a crusade for "religion, morality, and order." Similarly, we can abandon the carefully prepared fiction that a provocative socialist motion in November 1895 to broaden the Saxon Landtag suffrage prompted what followed: the replacement of a relatively liberal suffrage with one closely modelled on the plutocratic three-class suffrage that had prevailed in Prussia since 1850. When we juxtapose these two battles against the "forces of subversion," we discover how Saxons thought the war could be won. Victory was impossible without a coordinated effort between the authoritarian state and the burgher class. Even with bayonets and grapeshot, no coup against parliament, no round-up of subversives, no abolition of universal suffrage would be possible unless a broader offensive was unleashed against the "enemy within." That offensive could only hope to succeed if it captured the imagination of the bourgeoisie and mobilized its ranks to united action.

In January 1894, even before that wave of assassinations, the heads of forty-two local councils on the outskirts of Dresden sent a petition to the Saxon Landtag asking for protection from Social Democratic "revolutionaries" and demanding a larger police force. The petition offered a carefully crafted narrative whereby evidence of *local* subversion was shaped to evoke a mood of *national* emergency:

> At nightfall, young men, often in sizable groups, roam the towns, attempting to "insult probable opponents of revolution" – decent people – and they respond to words of criticism offered in defense with abusive and threatening tirades and sometimes with actual assaults. Women walking alone even short distances through parts of town incur the risk that their honour will be severely violated. On Sundays and holidays, groups frequently numbering several hundred persons wander from town to town ... singing revolutionary songs and blocking the streets, thus forcing anyone coming from the opposite direction to give way ... They demand that proprietors of dancehalls and their musical bands play revolutionary songs. If they refuse, the patrons then stop consuming any food or drink "as if on command." ... "As a rule, this manoeuvre is carried out on the same Sunday in different dance halls. It is almost impossible to express one's monarchical conviction or love of country on the birthdays of His Majesty the Emperor or the [Saxon] King, just as it is impossible for many people – particularly business-people – to attend mass."[17]

When this petition was debated in the upper chamber of the Saxon Landtag, one Conservative spokesman hoped that increased vigilance might prevent the "blind masses" from falling prey to the "banal slogans" of Social Democratic leaders. He seconded the petition's call for "the energetic deployment of the power of the state" and the "urgent wish that not only our Saxony will proceed on the charted path but that those [in Berlin] who occupy the positions where power is concentrated will use this power to the benefit of our great Fatherland." This was an obvious plea to politicians and statesmen in the Reich capital to recognize the emergency and respond accordingly.

In the lower house, the Conservatives' spokesman was Paul Mehnert, a non-noble wirepuller who had close ties to agricultural, industrial,

Democracy in Disappearing Ink 301

Figure 11.2 Dr Paul Mehnert, Jr (1852–1922). Sächsisches Hauptstaatsarchiv Dresden, X 742, Die Abgeordneten der Ständeversammlung, Nachlaß Philipp, Nr. 28, Fotografien von Abgeordneten.

and commercial interests. Known as "the uncrowned king of Saxony," Mehnert exemplified the bourgeois German politician whose anti-socialist, anti-democratic, and antisemitic ideas sometimes trumped his statist ideals. As Mehnert cited examples of Social Democratic "terrorism," he elicited cries of horror on the Right and laughter on the Left. His speech, too, was carefully constructed to achieve maximum effect, in at least three ways.

First, in what was undoubtedly a prearranged incident, Mehnert interrupted his speech at one point to say that he had just been handed a slip of paper citing another example of Social Democratic outrage. "Mayor Förster of Hohnstein," he read aloud, "while attending a Social Democratic meeting that was dissolved [by police], received four knife wounds." Mehnert wanted, second, to demonstrate the SPD's brutality towards women. In his telling, a certain "widow Kosche" was approached by a socialist functionary and instructed that she should allow no clergy at her husband's funeral: if she refused she would receive nothing from the Social Democratic fund to support widows. She eventually agreed to the SPD's demand, whereupon she was given ten Marks and "not a penny more." Mehnert provided his third example only after he had shared more stories of betrayal, broken teeth, and the socialists' alleged endorsement of wife-swapping ("*Oh je! Oh je!* from the Social Democrats"). Mehnert wanted his audience to know that SPD boycotts were implemented "in the most despicable ways" imaginable. In October 1892, a fishmonger named Andreas Schulz in Pieschen was visited by two SPD members who insisted he join their party. After refusing, Schulz awoke the next morning to see placards calling for a boycott of his wares. Schulz's store railings were "blasted apart," reported Mehnert, and "his shop window was smeared with human excrement."[18] Mehnert ended his *cri du cœur* by demanding that Saxony's state ministry provide the "parties of order" (*Ordnungsparteien*) with "a wake-up call." "Gentlemen!" he declared: *"To live means to struggle, and if ever in life it appeared that a struggle appears necessary, so it is in today's struggle for political existence!"*[19]

Another sign that Saxons had no patience for half-hearted measures against "murderous ruffians" was identified by the British envoy stationed in Dresden, George Strachey. In February 1894 he reported that Dresden's semi-official gazette had singled out Great Britain as "the friendly host" and "rallying point" for the "scum of all nations." The Dresden organ excoriated the British cabinet for tolerating "so-called 'advanced' Socialists" and providing them "freedom and asylum."

London had become a "den of international criminals" and "thus a danger to the whole world." This gazette claimed to have discovered the reason behind the British government's "tolerance of ... crimes of violence against society and individuals": it had a "wretched majority" of only 40 seats at Westminster.[20] Strachey accurately caught the public mood in Dresden. In July 1894, barely a week after the French president was assassinated, Dresden Conservatives drew up their own petition. In it they claimed that socialists – "for years and with incomprehensible leniency" – had been allowed "to pursue the extermination of Christian and patriotic sensibility and the vilification and subversion of everything the German people [feel] to be holy and precious!"[21]

Historians have generally considered Saxon King Albert's support for the Kaiser's crusade "for religion, morality, and order" as evidence that these two monarchs were out of touch with public opinion in the autumn of 1894 – as the failure of the Anti-Revolution Bill the next spring supposedly demonstrated. In fact Albert's views reflected sentiments found at many levels of Saxon political society: in local councils, in Conservative clubs, in the upper house of the Landtag, and among Conservative, National Liberal, and Saxon Progressive deputies in the lower house. Nor was King Albert out of touch with the views of other monarchs in Germany's federal states. Kaiser Wilhelm later described their conversation about the previous summer's revolutionary violence at a meeting in early September 1894:[22]

> The matter must at all costs be regulated nationally [said the Saxon king] ... Existing regulations must be strengthened by introducing sharper paragraphs [in the Reich Criminal Code] ... [The Saxon king] is aware that this might involve a dissolution of the Reichstag, perhaps even two. However, he stated determinedly that if the Reichstag repeatedly refused to pass measures to protect civil society, it had outlived its usefulness. Then the moment would arrive when the bombs have to go off and the Federal Council (that is, the German princes) would have to propose, or promulgate, a new [Reichstag] election law. In other words, the *ultima ratio*, a *coup d'état*.

When Wilhelm asked what Prince Regent Luitpold of Bavaria thought about this drastic course, King Albert replied, "certainly Bavaria too; he would take care of that personally: things cannot go on like this any longer ... The King of Württemberg is of the same mind: as he put it, none of us has sworn loyalty to the Reich constitution, so it can be revised." Up to this point the royal conversation would appear to support the standard historical interpretation that any notion of a *coup d'état* came exclusively "from above." But we must not dismiss as bombast Albert's promise that Saxon burghers would prove as reliable as German monarchs when the final showdown arrived. "The law-and-order loving segment of the population," Albert told Wilhelm, "would welcome such a solution," because their "fear of revolution increases daily."

At the other end of the political spectrum, we find someone who confirmed Albert's assessment that the German bourgeoisie was not dedicated to the free vote or civil liberties. Shortly after the Social Democratic breakthrough in the Reichstag elections of 1890, Marx's collaborator and friend Friedrich Engels wrote to Wilhelm Liebknecht, one of Germany's most prominent Social Democrats:

> In three years we will have the agricultural labourers and then we have the core regiments of the Prussian army. And to prevent that, only one means exists ...: a brutal shooting spree with the obligatory, acute shock effect. They will use any pretext to do so, and once [the Prussian minister of the interior's] "cannon" have discharged their shrapnel in a few large cities, then a state of siege will be imposed on all Germany; the [bourgeois] philistines will once again be in the right mood, they will blindly vote as they are told, and we will be paralyzed for years.[23]

Between the introduction of Caprivi's Anti-Revolution Bill and its ultimate defeat in May 1895, some Berlin insiders were convinced that Wilhelm was ready to undertake a *coup d'état*. One of them believed that Wilhelm had decided on major action against the socialists, even if it meant parting with Chancellor Caprivi. The dangers appeared not to worry Wilhelm "because he *seems* to want a *decision* ... His Majesty wants to 'sort things out.'"[24]

When the Kaiser met with Caprivi on 5 October 1894, not long before he was dismissed, Wilhelm declared that parliament "must be taken completely *by surprise*" by his new crusade, "and the dissolution of the Reichstag must follow at once." To Caprivi's doubts Wilhelm replied with "a long and enthusiastic exposition of the entire *coup d'état* program which he had agreed with the King of Saxony."[25] The Bavarian envoy to Prussia noted around this time that differences of opinion among state ministers in Berlin and between them and the Kaiser had raised the standing of "an array of people here who have adopted the standpoint that one cannot rule any longer with universal suffrage and who would rather bring about a conflict sooner rather than later – a conflict that would lead to the elimination of [the Reichstag]."[26]

Through 1895, as the Kaiser attempted to overcome opposition to his more extreme plans by sharpening Prussia's own Association Law and raiding Social Democratic headquarters in Berlin, he more frequently cited Saxony as the example Prussia must follow. As a case in point, when he received a clutch of newspaper clippings about the Saxon government's harsh application of its own Association Law against Social Democrats, he wrote in the margin: "Why isn't that possible here [in Prussia]?"[27] On another occasion Wilhelm wanted a bill to be submitted to the Prussian Landtag, "consisting if possible of only one paragraph – ... which bans all Social Democratic assemblies (such as Saxony has). Nothing more than that."[28]

As Caprivi's successor from October 1894 onward, Chancellor Hohenlohe had the unenviable task of dissuading the Kaiser from following his most violent instincts. But Hohenlohe's reputation as a liberal who "avoided the worst" has been overdrawn. Like Saxony's King Albert and like Friedrich Engels, Hohenlohe saw the best hope of defeating Social Democracy in fundamental changes to the make-up and constitutional prerogatives of the Reichstag, which would be both cause and effect of a turn towards conservative ideals among German voters. Just days after the Anti-Revolution Bill was defeated in 1895, Hohenlohe conceded in private that he would happily see the Reichstag abolished, though only under the right circumstances. "The Reichstag," he wrote, "is the result of a unhealthy mood in German public opinion ... If one lets it carry on as it has until now, in the end public opinion will push for its abolition ... Then one will be able to count on general agreement. When the moment will have come that the Reichstag has sunk so low that one can sweep it away like so much rubbish, that is the time to show courage. And I'll be right there too, if I am still alive."[29]

In September 1895, when revisions to Prussia's Association Law were being debated, Hohenlohe showed no more respect for the national parliament:

> We must find a way so that the German people elect another Reichstag. But right now the thing that keeps people from voting conservative is nothing other than the fear that conservative or bourgeois elections will precipitate the Reaction ... The fear of Social Democracy must be larger and carry more weight than the fear of a *coup d'état*. If we then have a reasonable

Reichstag, we can complete the reorientation by legal means: yes, we could even attain a reform of the [universal] suffrage (perhaps by partly supplementing the Reichstag from the individual [state] chambers?).

Sharpening Prussia's Association Law would be counterproductive, Hohenlohe concluded, despite the hue and cry since June 1894 that "something" must be done. "If one objects that the excitement of this summer must be exploited, then one should remember that one cannot make policy with festive cheers; for these last only as long as the festival itself, as long as the flags wave and the beer flows. The monarchical ideal and love of order that prevail among the German people – these will remain and can be turned to account later."[30] In short: It may be true that Hohenlohe, believing that "patience is needed," avoided a *coup d'état* against the Reichstag and violent street battles. There would be no bloodbath on his watch.[31] It is far from clear, however, whether the threat of a *coup d'état* in the mid-1890s was "without realistic content," as one of Hohenlohe's recent biographers has claimed.[32]

Why did King Albert, Saxon Conservatives, and other advocates of a showdown with the "inner enemy" draw back from a *coup d'état* against the Reichstag? The short answer is that political infighting in Berlin and the erratic policies emanating from it in the years 1894 to 1897 made them lose faith that the Kaiser would pursue a reactionary course steadfastly enough to strike a major blow at Social Democracy. "What a way to behave," commented former Chief of the Prussian General Staff, General Alfred von Waldersee, one of the most extreme advocates of a coup: "and what vacillation!"[33] But the short answer is insufficient.

John Röhl and Peter Winzen are among a small group of historians who fully understand the complex, duplicitous machinations through which a half-dozen high-ranking individuals in Berlin fought for power – either their own or Wilhelm's – in the second half of the 1890s.[34] The period 1894 to 1897 was decisive in putting in place what Röhl has called the Kaiser's personal regime (*persönliches Regiment*), which for the next ten years provided Wilhelm with unprecedented – and disastrous – influence over Germany's domestic and foreign policy. For our purposes it is sufficient to note that three of these men supported the Kaiser when he demanded forceful or violent measures. They did so when he proposed to abolish the Reichstag and universal manhood suffrage, to revise other features of the 1871 constitution, to eradicate Social Democracy, and to renegotiate the premise of German unity as a "federation of princes." These men were Prussian Minister President

Botho zu Eulenburg (in office 1892–4), Prussian Minister of the Interior Ernst von Köller (1894–7), and Waldersee. Two other men steadfastly opposed the Kaiser's on-again, off-again readiness to unleash what was described in coded language as some variation of "an inner conflict" or "a larger campaign in domestic policy."[35] These were Friedrich von Holstein, the *éminence grise* of the Foreign Office, and Reich Secretary of State for Foreign Affairs Adolf Marschall von Bieberstein (1890–7), who in previous decades had been a leader of the tiny Conservative movement in his native Baden and then its envoy to Prussia. Lastly, two other figures, perhaps the most duplicitous of all, found themselves arguing both sides of the question before they concluded that a full-scale *coup* was too dangerous to consider. These were Bernhard von Bülow, who succeeded Marschall as State Secretary for Foreign Affairs (1897–1900) before he was appointed chancellor (1900–9), and Philipp zu Eulenburg, the Kaiser's closest friend until he was brought down by a series of homosexual scandals and trials after the turn of the century.

A maximal policy of repression, which would attempt to achieve all the Kaiser's reactionary goals at the same time, was opposed loudly and often by Holstein and Marschall. They argued that the non-Prussian kingdoms (Bavaria, Saxony, and Württemberg) would refuse to support such a plan; that such refusal, in combination with violent conflict with Social Democrats, would plunge the Reich into a civil war; and that as the empire broke up, France and Russia, and perhaps even Austria-Hungary, would use the situation as an opportunity to intervene. In short, a *coup d'état* would unravel German unification as it had been achieved in 1866–71.[36] If the Second Reich flew apart due to the centrifugal forces that Bismarck had overcome decades earlier, it would be reconstituted, if at all, on a basis that undermined Prussia's dominant position. Worst-case scenarios depicted Germany disappearing beneath the tide of socialism or anarchy.

In two letters to Philipp Eulenburg, sent in February and September 1895, Bülow summarized the scenario outlined above. The first was sent when the whole country was pondering the fate of Köller's Association Bill in the Prussian Landtag:

> In my opinion [Bülow wrote], there can be no doubt that Germany cannot be governed from the exclusionary standpoint of a single party, or one political, economic, or confessional tendency [*Richtung*]. Ultimately it would not be smart, naturally, to have the reds [SPD] and the blacks [Catholic Centre Party] against us at the same time. A larger campaign domestically, if it is to succeed in the long run, demands – besides the unconditional

collaboration of the middle states – two further prerequisites: 1. That the Catholics do not fear a new *Kulturkampf* unleashed ... by a monarchy freed of parliamentary constraints. 2. Also that the liberal middle classes do not worry that an absolutist (or more absolutist) regime will endanger "enlightenment," "education," and "freedom of conscience." In a word: the extremes must be avoided in domestic policy and all state-supporting elements must be drawn in as far as possible.[37]

In the second letter, when national tensions were even higher, Bülow again concluded that a full-scale coup was unwise, and now he offered even more reasons (which he wanted Eulenburg to pass on to Hohenlohe). A serious war on subversion was "hardly conceivable without the cooperation of Prince Bismarck." This was another *idée fixe* among the anti-coup clique: not only foreign powers, but the Bismarck family, too, would exploit a chancellor crisis for its own advancement. Moreover, "the struggle against Social Democracy" required actual assassination attempts against the Kaiser and his family as well as "the actual penetration of the army by the revolutionary movement." Unless both these conditions were met, wrote Bülow, it would "be advisable not to cut off the abscess before it is mature." Besides reiterating his points about having Catholics on board and keeping foreign powers at bay, Bülow also believed that the "large domestic campaign" – the *coup d'état* – would succeed in the long term "only if the bourgeoisie is even more intimidated by the communist danger than it is today."

If all these conditions were not in place, it would be politically disastrous to replace Hohenlohe with a chancellor – such as Köller or Waldersee – who would mount coordinated attacks on Social Democracy and the German constitution. Nevertheless, when Bülow tried to put into Philipp Eulenburg's mouth the exact words he should convey to Hohenlohe, they typified the subtle hedging for which Bülow became famous as chancellor (his nickname was "the eel"). They also registered the ambivalence that intruded when Wilhelm and other reactionaries talked about the need for "serious action" at home. According to Bülow, Eulenburg should spell it out for Hohenlohe as an either/or decision: "'Either a truly drastic [Anti-]Socialist Law must be drawn up, and one feels strong enough to accept the consequences, or one must leave alone a question that endlessly stirs up dust.'"

Even before Bülow had conveyed this advice to his superiors, Saxony's King Albert understood that Holstein's and Marschall's opposition to a *coup d'état* had carried the day. In fact he too had given up hope that

Kaiser Wilhelm would "get to the root of things." That is why he advised against dissolving the Reichstag over the Anti-Revolution Bill in early 1895. Such a dissolution would force the government to try to "achieve conservative elections" on the basis of "an agrarian program" – a dubious prospect, as Albert put it, because "farmers [are] radical."[38] Albert's scepticism grew as Wilhelm continued to take advice from friends and advisers who did not hold office. Among the latter, of course, was Philipp Eulenburg himself. Yet months later, in the spring of 1897, it was Eulenburg who had to tell the Kaiser what he should have known already: King Albert was not on board.[39] The Saxon king had met with Chancellor Hohenlohe in Berlin and told him that "there can arise moments when one must dissolve the Reichstag, but now, with the current mood in the country, it would be a *grave* mistake. And as for the *coup d'état*," – Albert continued – "the German princes can *not* follow the Kaiser *in that respect*. They would thereby be risking a great deal."

Existing accounts of the "permanent crisis" in Wilhelmine Germany may be misleading insofar as they fail to recognize that the Kaiser, his fellow monarchs, and most of his influential advisers had disavowed a major revision of the constitution and abolition of the Reichstag. However, the notion of permanent crisis is still useful if we consider smaller versions of the *Kladderadatsch* – the disaster, the chaos, the "bust-up" – that pessimists always believed lay on the horizon. That word was used by contemporaries to describe both the situation that might precipitate a *coup d'état* in the first place and the situation that would prevail if an attempted coup failed. In both cases, opponents of the Reichstag's prerogatives and enemies of Social Democracy continued to suggest that disaster might befall Germany even without constitutional upheaval. For this reason they hinted that an alternative strategy was viable – we can call it *coup d'état* on the instalment plan. They argued that Germany could sidestep disaster in stages: by making adjustments to universal manhood suffrage when the proper moment arrived, by devising new means to combat Social Democracy on a legal basis, or, best of all, by pursuing both strategies in tandem. Hohenlohe was right: patience was needed. But patience was not Field Marshall von Waldersee's long suit. He continued through the spring of 1897 to press the Kaiser at every turn to undertake a coup, preferably with himself as chancellor. He made it abundantly clear that he was willing to have Social Democratic blood on his hands – it would not weigh heavily on his conscience. But Waldersee also despaired, rightly, that Wilhelm would never have the courage to take this step.[40]

So what are we to make of the "dog that didn't bark"? John Röhl has written that "it is by no means easy to unravel the tangle of conflicting sources" that might reveal what paths lay open in these critical years.⁴¹ Röhl is correct. But if we refuse to worry about tying up every loose end, a general picture comes into view. In the spring of 1897, the Kaiser almost certainly sounded out members of the right-wing parties, Hohenlohe, the Grand Duke of Baden, and others about the feasibility of a coup. When these discussions were reported back to Wilhelm, he wrote "Absolute lies!" in the margin. What is more important than determining the truth of these claims is that they set a pattern – a pattern whereby the Kaiser's "lively temper" and "aggressive tone" kept others guessing whether a *Kladderadatsch* might be in the cards after all. When the Kaiser met Philipp Eulenburg in Vienna on 21 April 1897, he denied Hohenlohe's claim that he had mentioned the word *Staatsstreich* to him. Wilhelm used the chancellor's decrepitude to deflect blame from himself. However, with his own overheated rhetoric he let slip that he had used precisely those phrases that kept his fellow monarchs, his responsible ministers, and his irresponsible advisers uncertain what course he would chart in the future:

> If old Hohenlohe imagines that I am planning a *coup d'état*, he is playing a dishonest game too. He *knows* that I have no such intention ... I perhaps spoke to him once in confidence about the possibility or impossibility of changing the electoral law – but I am sure you have done that too, we have *all* done that! To deduce a policy of violence [*Gewaltpolitik*] from that – that is bad faith! ... How did the King of Saxony come to speak in this way? ... I have never said anything ambiguous about the matter to the king ... I have only once spoken lately to the Grand Duke of Baden about the electoral law *in an academic sense*, without any ulterior motive, purely by chance.⁴²

Saxony's Suffrage Robbery

Let us turn back the clock eighteen months. As the Kaiser faced mounting opposition to his reactionary plans in the autumn of 1895, the "parties of order" (*Ordnungsparteien*) in Saxony had already set a new course.⁴³ Their shift of strategy was more fitful and more calculated than they claimed at the time. But it was dramatic enough. Most representatives of the Saxon state would have agreed with Waldersee: "When the Kaiser called for a struggle for religion, morality, and order, he had to lead it with all possible energy, or else he should have kept his fingers off it."[44] Hence a new answer had to be found to that lingering question, "What is to be done?"

Not long after the defeat of the Anti-Revolution Bill in Berlin, the prospect of socialist victories in the Saxon Landtag elections of autumn 1895 began to loom. The Austrian envoy in Dresden noted that "under such circumstances it is understandable that in Saxony, perhaps more than in other federal states, one hears calls for resort to repressive measures against the Social Democratic movement ... The Conservative press in Saxony ... has spoken tirelessly of exceptional laws against the party [the SPD] and its increasingly audacious methods of agitation."[45] It would be wrong, however, to imagine that only Conservative newspapers expressed extreme dissatisfaction with parliament or that they had begun to do so only in the summer of 1894 under the impact of foreign violence.

Although his reports to Britain's Foreign Office had been disparaging the Germans' understanding of politics since he was appointed British envoy to Saxony in 1873, George Strachey wrote more scathingly in the 1890s than ever before about Saxons' willingness to embrace an assault on democratic prerogatives. Strachey reported in early 1893 that Saxon government leader Georg von Metzsch and his state ministry would support the Kaiser's wish for more recruits, and the means to get them, if Caprivi's Army Bill of 1892–3 was not passed by the Reichstag. "Saxony would support an arbitrary solution of difficulties, even to the extent of a breach of the constitution," Strachey wrote. "In this kingdom, resistance to an invasion of popular rights, whether by material or moral force, is utterly unthinkable. If Germany is not now in the hands of 'Major-Generals,' the credit is due to the rulers of the 26 states of the Empire, and not to their subjects, who, at present, are incapable of firing a shot in defence of their liberties and laws."[46] A few months later, when a Reichstag dissolution and new elections were on the horizon, Strachey again chronicled the positive echo Wilhelm's bluster would elicit in Saxony:

> Such warnings were understood to foreshadow the eventuality of a coup d'état, a form of settlement to which ... the Emperor and his advisers would, if other methods failed, probably resort. In numerous confidential discussions of the subject, I found it to be universally admitted as an axiom, that a violation of the constitution of the Empire would meet with no obstacles on the part of the confederated Governments, or with any resistance, however faint, even in the way of protest, from the German public.

That Saxony and Dresden are actually in the condition of political impotence thus implied, is unquestionable.

Strachey's conclusion was emphatic: in Saxony, as in Prussia to the north, "authority would command implicit obedience by a few strokes of the pen."

Returning to the year 1895, Social Democrats did not disavow the connection between the Kaiser's threats and the outcome of *regional* elections either. They replied in kind after Wilhelm famously declared on 2 September 1895 (Sedan Day) that they were "scoundrels not worthy to bear the name German" (*eine Rotte von Menschen, nicht werth, den Namen Deutscher zu tragen*).[47] One of the SPD's Saxon election manifestos declared that "this year's Landtag elections have a special significance, not only for Saxony's workers but for all of Germany's. *The outcome of the Saxon Landtag elections will give the appropriate answer to the question: 'Can the Social Democratic workers' movement be suppressed by force or not?'*" After noting how ruthlessly Saxony's Association Law had been used to dissolve socialist meetings and clubs over the past two years, prompting "orgies of celebration by reactionaries," the SPD's national newspaper, *Vorwärts*, observed that "Saxony is, in effect, the test case for everything that happens to workers. If the Saxon government's system of repression should prove itself viable, the governments of the other federal states will not waste a moment in introducing this system for all of Germany. They would be assured the support of all the non-socialist parties."[48]

After the Saxon Landtag election was over, at the ceremonial opening of the new session in mid-November 1895, storm signals were flying.[49] When the president of the lower house called for the usual oath of loyalty to the Saxon king, the fourteen Social Democrats quickly exited the chamber. Metzsch felt the SPD deputies had made themselves "laughable" with this fruitless gesture, but he also foresaw a difficult session ahead. That Leipzig's police director had recently been the target of an (unsuccessful) assassination attempt only added to the tension.[50]

Within two days of parliament's opening the SPD caucus introduced a motion calling for universal manhood suffrage for Landtag elections (and municipal assemblies). They had done so at the opening of each Landtag session almost as long as anyone could remember, but the "parties of order" had silently moved on to other business each time.

This time those parties went on the offensive. The Conservatives' Paul Mehnert led the attack with a counter-motion. It had just been signed by all members of the Conservative, National Liberal, and Saxon Progressive caucuses. In a polemical speech lasting one-and-a-half hours, Mehnert announced that these *Kartell* parties had finally accepted their responsibility to respond to an emergency situation.[51]

In Mehnert's telling, the "parties of order" had had an epiphany. The SPD's continual attempts to transplant the Reichstag suffrage to the Landtag had to be stopped. "On the basis of universal suffrage," declared Mehnert, "the [candidate] who has the greatest success ... is the one who ... is the most ruthless in his choice of methods, who piles it on most crudely, and who best flatters ... the instincts of the people."[52] The "parties of order" had also had a terrible fright: like Dickens's Scrooge, they had glimpsed the future. Social Democratic victories in the Landtag elections of October 1895 and their party's "wild agitation" during that campaign underscored the need for urgent action. If a decisive response were not taken, the Social Democrats stood poised to win a Landtag majority after the next election. They would then be in a position to introduce the socialist state of the future (*Zukunftsstaat*), destroying the existing social and political order in the process. One did not have to read between the lines to understand that the Saxon "parties of order" had finally lost patience waiting for statesmen in Berlin or Dresden to take the initiative. So they had drawn up a set of general principles on which a new Saxon suffrage should be based.

Mehnert's tale was plausible. It convinced most Saxon burghers at the time and many historians since. But it was artfully constructed fiction. If the Saxon suffrage of 1868 was about to be "assassinated," as the socialists claimed, this was going to happen with malice aforethought. Sources in the Saxon State Archive in Dresden show how assiduously anti-socialist politicians in Saxony had prepared for this moment: not for days or weeks but for months and years. Mehnert chose the first full day of debate in the Landtag session to throw down the gauntlet. He sought maximum dramatic effect, for instance by conjuring up spine-chilling defamations Germans could expect to hear from Social Democrats when the twenty-fifth anniversary of the founding of the Reich was celebrated a few months hence (January 1896). He also intended his Landtag speech to be a provocation. It served its purpose. The Social Democrats were caught off-guard, and they were genuinely outraged.

Some of the preparations for this dramatic announcement had unfolded in public view. Since the Reichstag elections of June 1893 the "parties of order" had done their utmost to emphasize what united them. Two other developments leading to Saxony's 1896 suffrage reform occurred with less fanfare. The first was a reform of Leipzig's municipal suffrage. That reform sought to block if not completely bar the door to socialist candidates. Its success sowed the seeds of reform in other municipalities and at the state level. The second was a series of secret memoranda and meetings among leaders of the *Kartell* parties – meetings also attended by civil servants and statesmen in both Berlin and Dresden.[53] The Kaiser's failure to diminish the power of the Reichstag convinced Saxon conspirators that their only recourse lay in killing off the relatively liberal Landtag suffrage of 1868 as quickly as possible. Thus, in the winter of 1895–6, the enemies of socialism in Saxony once again bolstered their reputation as pioneers. They carefully stage-managed a coup against the existing suffrage, replacing it with a three-class voting system that would remain in place until 1909.

This patently unfair suffrage differed only slightly from Prussia's more notorious law.[54] It lumped the richest 5 per cent of taxpayers into a first voting class. The next wealthiest taxpayers, roughly 15 per cent, constituted the second voting class. The third class included the other 80 per cent of male adults. In this system, each class voted for its own delegates, who then met to elect the actual parliamentary deputy. In almost every case the first two classes combined to ensure that no socialist would actually be elected to the Saxon Landtag. Immediately dubbed "Mehnert's Law," the new suffrage achieved its goal. In the three partial renewals of the Saxon Landtag in 1897, 1899, and 1901 – each time one-third of the seats were contested – those fourteen sitting Social Democrats failed to win re-election, so that at the dawn of the twentieth century not a single one was left in Saxony's parliament. The Conservative Party held a two-thirds majority, ensuring that no constitutional amendment could be passed against its wishes.

To be sure, the new suffrage remained "universal" in the technical sense that no Saxon voter was disenfranchised. This made it easier for Conservatives and National Liberals to claim, on the one hand, that Social Democratic "revolutionaries" had themselves corrupted the principle of democracy and, on the other, that the defenders of state and society had provided the only possible response. That claim was a palpable lie, and the left-wing press lost no time in declaring it one. The

Progressives' *Dresdner Zeitung* sounded a note of shame: "Among all cultured nations, Saxony seeks to take a step backward. Our narrower Fatherland has no reason to be proud of that." When the law was passed in March 1896, the *Arbeiterzeitung* issued a more stirring battle cry: "Woe to the 'victors'! The people, those who work, those who are disenfranchised, recognize their enemy! The struggle begins! All of Saxony [is] an armed camp!" Later the same month the *Arbeiterzeitung* drew the obvious comparisons with Saxony's neighbour to the north. Prussia's three-class suffrage was the "most vile" (*elendste*) thing imaginable; but the Saxon suffrage "will be the most ignoble" (*gemein*). The socialist jeremiad continued: "The Prussian [suffrage] is brutal, yet honest. The Saxon [suffrage], when it becomes law, is no less brutal, no less an offence against the people's rights, but therefore hypocritical, duplicitous, perfidious." To Saxon Social Democrats, "Mehnert's Law" was "suffrage robbery" (*Wahlrechtsraub*). Justice itself had been "murdered."[55]

These protests counted for little – in the short run. The Conservatives' two leading newspapers in Saxony offered hyperbolic assessments of the authoritarian state's victory over sedition. *Das Vaterland* hoped that the rest of Germany would appreciate "that a little parliament had the courage to take up the decisive battle against Social Democracy." A new age was dawning, and no one could be left in doubt that the showdown "between order and revolution" had begun – in Saxony.[56] The *Dresdner Nachrichten* advised against compromise and "half-measures." As the father of Saxony's three-class suffrage,[57] Mehnert could soon boast that his initiative had received the blessing of other German observers. In April 1896 the Bavarian government was allegedly "gazing toward Dresden, full of envy." Its minister president, Baron Friedrich Krafft von Crailsheim, had doubted that Saxony's suffrage reform would be approved, but when it passed it became a "great victory," which he characterized as "an advance backwards" (*ein Fortschritt nach rückwärts*).[58] Regressive suffrage reforms were also enacted around this time in Anhalt, Hamburg, and Braunschweig.

King Albert was initially worried about the repercussions of introducing a three-class suffrage.[59] As late as February 1896, Metzsch too was taking "every possible opportunity" to stress that responsibility for suffrage reform would have to rest with the majority parties in the Landtag and the voters who had elected them, not with the Saxon government. The king and his first minister also experienced "bitter disappointment that the opposition [to the bill] by no means originated only with the small but noisy Social Democratic caucus."⁶⁰ "Learned but grizzled" professors at the University of Leipzig had been "doctrinaire" and "tactless" in defending the old 1868 suffrage. Metzsch was "in low spirits" about these "turnip scholars" – he felt they were completely out of touch with the public mood in Saxony. When it became clear that the bill would pass, King Albert was more favourably disposed to recognize its long-term benefits. The bill "did credit to the sound sense of the [Saxon] population." It would provide "a very useful barrier against Social Democracy," whose "semi-educated mediocrities sitting here in the *Landhaus*" were intent on "seizing the upper hand."⁶¹

Yet opinions differed about exactly what had been accomplished. Some prominent Conservatives asserted that the Saxon SPD had "received a blow from which it will not recover."⁶² By contrast, Metzsch believed that the very first test of the new suffrage – more so than later ones – might be a "flop" for the government.⁶³ One of Saxony's state ministers observed privately that he would be satisfied if the new suffrage merely prevented the Social Democrats from increasing the size of their present caucus in future elections.⁶⁴ He had no expectation that they would be eliminated from the Landtag.

There was more joy in Berlin. Even before the suffrage bill was ready, the Kaiser had expressed "the highest praise for the sound political sense of the Saxon people." He added "appreciatively" that "this time Saxony is leading the way in Germany." The Kaiser also "showed himself very well informed about the details of the corresponding action by the Saxon parties of order."⁶⁵ The same was true when he asked Metzsch to call on him during a visit to Berlin in late January 1896.⁶⁶ In March the Kaiser told the Saxon envoy in Berlin "that He hopes the Reich will follow the Saxon example some day. But He will probably 'turn old and grey' first."⁶⁷ Wilhelm was equally pleased when Mehnert used the occasion of King Albert's birthday (23 April 1896) to announce that the *Kartell* binding together the "parties of order" in Saxony had been renewed the previous day.⁶⁸ To this agreement, which also renewed their pledge of unity against Social Democracy, 108 deputies from the upper and lower houses of the Saxon Landtag had attached their signature. The Kaiser could hardly contain his enthusiasm when he reflected on the counter-revolutionary possibilities such a constellation of parties opened up. "Bravo! Saxonia!" he wrote. "What about us?! ... That must be tried here! ... Who could best take the matter in hand?"⁶⁹

Conclusion

To ask whether the "reactionary '90s" were really so reactionary after all is to pose the wrong question. The 1890s were *differently* reactionary than historians have believed. With a new perspective it becomes impossible to proclaim winners and losers. The liberals' success in defending popular rights deserves our attention. It is much less clear whether "legislative stalemate" properly describes the outcome of these battles. That term may apply reasonably well to the national scene. The notion of stalemate is far less convincing at the sub-national level. In Saxony, the tide of democratization was stemmed and reversed. That reversal held ramifications for the entire Reich.

After 1896, the prospects for meeting the "red threat" with grapeshot and fire hoses or by dismantling the "monkey-house" in Berlin slipped further from view, even in the Kaiser's imagination. But more hard-headed politicians across Germany achieved similar goals with different means, and Saxons really did lead the way. They knew that unleashing genuine violence against Social Democrats might cost them dearly, so they sidestepped that option and found others. As Social Democracy's own leaders began to opt for the path of reformism over revolution, anti-democrats devised new voting laws for Saxony's largest cities that moved further away from the principle of "one man, one vote." Leipzig's municipal suffrage reform of 1894 led the way. It was a coup to prevent a Social Democratic flood, and soon the instalment plan came to Chemnitz (1898) and Dresden (1905).[70]

In 1909, in his last political act of national importance, Paul Mehnert led the charge that introduced another "suffrage of the future": a plural ballot system for Saxon Landtag elections that grotesquely disadvantaged working-class voters. Saxon statisticians played a nasty trick on themselves and on legislators who relied on their forecasts: they didn't anticipate how many working-class voters would qualify for a second or even a third ballot. The first test of the new suffrage came in October 1909, and the SPD did far better than expected. Suddenly the sky was falling again. But the plural suffrage ensured that Saxon workers were not represented fairly: one of every two voters supported the "party of revolution," yet the SPD received only 38 per cent of the ballots cast and twenty-five of ninety-one seats in the Landtag. Those new "reds" in Dresden's parliament were a shock to the system, as were the 110 Social Democrats who sat in the Reichstag after January 1912. What was to be done? The next general elections in Saxony were scheduled for the autumn of 1915: a six-year wait between elections was deemed prudent to prevent election skirmishes from becoming all-out war. But those elections were never held. War came anyway.

The spectre of democracy never disappeared during the Second Reich, because the fundamental politicization of German society continued from the time of Bismarck up to and through the First World War. But the enemies of Social Democracy helped ensure that the Reichstag and the Saxon Landtag, though they served as sounding boards of public opinion, did not become legitimate contenders for power. That so many bourgeois Germans applauded this outcome, exactly as Saxony's crowned and uncrowned kings had anticipated in the 1890s, suggests that practising democracy was not uppermost in their minds.

NOTES

1 Cited in Robert Michels, *Political Parties: A Sociological Study of the Oligarchical Tendencies of Modern Democracy*, translated by Eden and Cedar Paul (New York, 1968), 45 (orig. German ed. 1925).
2 See vols. 2 and 3 of John C.G. Röhl's immense study: *Wilhelm II: The Kaiser's Personal Monarchy, 1888–1900* (Cambridge, 2004), and *Wilhelm II: Into the Abyss of War and Exile, 1900–1941* (Cambridge, 2014).
3 Developed most fully in John C.G. Röhl, *The Kaiser and His Court: Wilhelm II and the Government of Germany* (Cambridge and New York, 1994), 107–30; see also Röhl, ed., *Der Ort Kaiser Wilhelms II. in der deutschen Geschichte* (Munich, 1991).
4 As representative of many other works see Hans-Ulrich Wehler, *The German Empire, 1871–1918* (Leamington Spa, 1985), 62–5 (orig. German ed. 1973); Michael Stürmer, "Staatsstreichgedanken im Bismarckreich," *Historische Zeitschrift* 209 (1969): 566–615.
5 In this chapter all dates are cited in dd.mm.yy format. I have kept references to a minimum because general background on the 1890s is easily gleaned either from two standard works – J. Alden Nichols, *Germany after Bismarck: The Caprivi Era, 1890–1894* (Cambridge, MA, 1958), and John C.G. Röhl, *Germany without Bismarck: The Crisis of Government in the Second Reich, 1890–1900* (London, 1967) – or from works cited in other chapters of this book. See also Röhl, *Wilhelm II*, vols. 2 and 3, and *Philipp Eulenburgs Politische Korrespondenz*, edited by Röhl, 3 vols. (Boppard a.R., 1976–83),

vol. 2, *Im Brennpunkt der Regierungskrise 1892–1895*, and vol. 3, *Krisen, Krieg und Katastrophen 1895–1921*.

6 Wilhelm Beumer, general secretary of the Langnamverein, 12.4.90, cited in Dirk Stegmann, "Between Economic Interests and Radical Nationalism: Attempts to Found a New Right-Wing Party in Imperial Germany, 1887–94," in *Between Reform, Reaction, and Resistance: Studies in the History of German Conservatism from 1789 to 1945*, edited by Larry Eugene Jones and James Retallack (Providence, RI, and Oxford, 1993), 157–85 at 163.

7 Baron Wilhelm von Minnigerode-Rositten, January 1893, cited in Nichols, *Germany after Bismarck*, 258.

8 See Eleanor L. Turk, "The Political Press and the People's Rights: The Role of the Political Press in the Debates Over the Association Right in Germany, 1894–1899" (PhD diss., University of Wisconsin – Madison, 1975); Turk, "Holding the Line: The National Liberals and the Prussian Association Law of 1897," *German Studies Review* 2 (1979): 297–316; Turk, "The Berlin Socialist Trials of 1896: An Examination of Civil Liberty in Wilhelmian Germany," *Central European History* 19 (1986): 323–42; Turk, "German Liberals and the Genesis of the Association Law of 1908," in *In Search of a Liberal Germany: Studies in the History of German Liberalism From 1789 to the Present*, edited by Konrad H. Jarausch and Larry Eugene Jones (New York, 1990), 237–60; Turk, "Thwarting the Imperial Will: A Perspective on the Labor Regulation Bill and the Press of Wilhelmian Germany," in *Another Germany: A Reconsideration of the Imperial Era*, edited by Jack R. Dukes and Joachim Remak (Boulder, CO, and London, 1988), 115–38. A more recent contribution is Gary Stark, *Banned in Berlin: Literary Censorship in Imperial Germany, 1871–1918* (New York, 2009), drawing on his many earlier treatments of the subject.

9 See Elun T. Gabriel, *Assassins and Conspirators: Anarchism, Socialism, and Political Culture in Imperial Germany* (Dekalb, IL, 2014), esp. chs. 5–6.

10 More than a year later he was still convinced that a new Anti-Socialist Law would enhance his own personal security and that of his family; those who were trying to rein in Wilhelm believed the exact opposite. See, for example, Friedrich von Holstein to Philipp Eulenburg, 27.9.95, *Philipp Eulenburgs Politische Korrespondenz*, 3: 1547.

11 The relevant documents are in Bundesarchiv, Abteilungen Potsdam (now Berlin) (hereafter BAP), Reichskanzlei (hereafter Rkz), Nr. 755/1, including Alfred von Kiderlen-Wächter's telegrams from the German Foreign Office to Caprivi, 15/16/17.7.94.

12 Wilhelm von Hohenthal und Bergen, Saxony's envoy to Prussia, to Saxon government leader (and foreign minister) Georg von Metzsch, Dresden,

14.9.94, 29.10.94; Sächsisches Hauptstaatsarchiv, Dresden (hereafter SHStAD), Ministerium des Auswärtigen Angelegenheiten (hereafter MdAA), Nr. 3305; Egmont Zechlin, *Staatsstreichpläne Bismarcks und Wilhelms II. 1890–1894* (Stuttgart, 1929), 223–5.

13 First reading 17.12.94, 8.–12.1.95.

14 Wilhelm II to Hohenlohe, telegram, 11.5.95, in Fürst Chlodwig zu Hohenlohe-Schillingsfürst, *Denkwürdigkeiten der Reichskanzlerzeit*, edited by Karl Alexander von Müller (Osnabrück, 1967), 63 (orig. 1931). Cf. Hohenlohe, *Denkwürdigkeiten des Fürsten Chlodwig zu Hohenlohe-Schillingsfürst*, edited by Alexander von Hohenlohe-Schillingsfürst, 2 vols. (Stuttgart and Leipzig, 1907), 2: 516ff.

15 Robert W. Lougee, "The Anti-Revolution Bill of 1894 in Wilhelmine Germany," *Central European History* 15 (1982): 224–40 at 240; cf. Marven H. Krug, "Civil Liberties in Imperial Germany" (PhD diss., University of Toronto, 1995), 354–5.

16 David Blackbourn and Geoff Eley, *The Peculiarities of German History: Bourgeois Society and Politics in Nineteenth-Century Germany* (Oxford and New York, 1984).

17 *Leipziger Zeitung*, 16.1.94, Beilage: internal quotations are from the petition. Cf. the Austrian envoy to Saxony, Count Bohuslav Chotek, Dresden, to the Austrian Foreign Office (hereafter FO), Vienna, 17.1.[94], Österreichisches Staatsarchiv, Haus-, Hof- und Staatsarchiv, Vienna (hereafter HHStAV), Politisches Archiv (hereafter PA), V/48. The petition was debated in the Saxon upper house (Erste Kammer, hereafter I.K.) and lower house (Zweite Kammer, hereafter II.K.) during the Landtag session of 1893/4: I.K. (18.1.94) and II.K. (27.2.94): *Mitteilungen aus der Verhandlungen des Landtags des Königreichs Sachsens* (hereafter *LTMitt*), I.K. 1893/4, 104–18; II.K. 1893/4, 767–800; petition and committee report (10.1.94) in *Verhandlungen des ordentlichen Landtags im Königreich Sachsen, Landtagsakten*, I.K. 1893/4, Drucksachen, Nrn. 34 and 255; these and other materials are also found in the SHStAD, Ministerium des Innern (hereafter MdI), Nr. 10989. Although they do not include *Drucksachen, Ständische Schriften*, and other printed matter gathered under the rubric Landtags-Akten, the *LTMitt* for both the I.K. and the II.K. are available online for the entire period 1833–1933: http://landtagsprotokolle.sachsendigital.de/startseite.

18 Saxon *LTMitt*, II.K., 1895/6, 791–3.

19 Saxon *LTMitt*, II.K., 1895/6, 795 (original emphasis).

20 George Strachey, Dresden, to British FO, 22.3.94, The National Archives, Kew (formerly the Public Record Office, or PRO, hereafter cited as TNA), FO 68/179.

21 "Petition betr. Abwehr-Maßregeln gegen die Socialdemokratie, Aenderung des Preßgesetzes und der Gewerbeordnung," Dresden, 3.7.94, HHStAV, PAV/48. Cf. Prussian envoy to Saxony, Carl von Dönhoff, Dresden, to Prussian FO, 8.7.94, Politisches Archiv des Auswärtigen Amts, Bonn (now Berlin) (PAAAB), Europa Generalia, No. 82 Nr. 1 Nr. 1 (Geheim), Bd. 4.
22 Telegram from Botho Eulenburg to Caprivi, 8.9.94, in Zechlin, *Staatsstreichpläne*, 189–92; telegram, Wilhelm II to Caprivi, 9.9.94, BAP, Rkz 755/1; B. Eulenburg's telegram reports that he also spoke directly with King Albert. See also Turk, "Political Press," 80; Nichols, *Germany after Bismarck*, 340.
23 Engels to Liebknecht, 9.3.90, in Liebknecht, *Briefwechsel mit Karl Marx und Friedrich Engels*, edited by Georg Eckert (The Hague, 1963), 366–7. See also ch. 6 in the present volume.
24 Adolf Marschall von Bieberstein to Philipp Eulenburg, 6.10.94, *Philipp Eulenburgs Politische Korrespondenz*, 2: 1366–7.
25 *Philipp Eulenburgs Politische Korrespondenz*, 2: 1366–7.
26 Count Hugo von Lerchenfeld-Köfering, Berlin, to Bavarian FO (draft), 16.10.94, in Peter Rassow and Karl Erich Born, eds, *Akten zur staatlichen Sozialpolitik in Deutschland 1890–1914* (Wiesbaden, 1959), 50.
27 Reported in Hohenthal, Berlin, to Metzsch, Dresden, 18.3.94, SHStAD, MdAA, Nr. 3305.
28 P. Eulenburg to Hohenlohe, 12.9.95; see confirmation of the Kaiser's determination to follow King Albert's advice in Eulenburg's follow-up letter of 21.9.95; both in Hohenlohe, *Denkwürdigkeiten der Reichskanzlerzeit*, 97, 100.
29 Hohenlohe's notes of 17.5.95, Hohenlohe, *Denkwürdigkeiten*, 65–7.
30 Hohenlohe, *Denkwürdigkeiten*, 99 (notes of 19.9.95). Hohenlohe felt the Bismarckian press was using the excitement of the twenty-fifth anniversary of the Battle of Sedan to demand action against the SPD. But so was the Kaiser, who was appalled by socialist insults against him and his grandfather on 1/2.9.95 and who feared that his wife and children might be assassinated by "this horde." P. Eulenburg to Hohenlohe ("Geheim!"), 21.9.95, *Denkwürdigkeiten*, 99–101; cf. *Norddeutsche Allgemeine Zeitung*, 4.9.95; Saxon Legations-Sekretär von Stieglitz, Berlin, to Metzsch, Dresden, 15.10.95, SHStAD, MdAA, Nr. 3305.
31 Volker Stalmann, *Fürst Chlodwig zu Hohenlohe-Schillingsfürst 1819–1901. Ein deutscher Reichskanzler* (Paderborn, 2009). Cf. Thomas Nipperdey, *Deutsche Geschichte 1866–1918*, vol. 2, *Machtstaat vor der Demokratie* (Munich, 1992), 713.
32 Stalmann, *Fürst Chlodwig zu Hohenlohe*, 239.
33 Alfred Graf von Waldersee, *Denkwürdigkeiten des General-Feldmarschalls Alfred Grafen von Waldersee*, 3 vols., ed. Heinrich Otto Meisner (Stuttgart

and Berlin, 1922), 2: 327–9, and Röhl, *Wilhelm II*, 2: 616–7. Cf. Zechlin, *Staatsstreichpläne*, 129–30.

34 Besides Röhl's work cited above, see Peter Winzen, *Im Schatten Wilhelms II. Bülows und Eulenburgs Poker um die Macht im Kaiserreich* (Cologne, 2011). The literature on the Eulenburg scandals is extensive; one can profitably begin with Winzen, *Das Ende der Kaiserherrlichkeit. Die Skandalprozesse um die homosexuellen Berater Wilhelms II. 1907–1909* (Cologne, 2010).

35 See *inter alia* Bernhard von Bülow to P. Eulenburg, 23.2.95, *Philipp Eulenburgs Politische Korrespondenz*, 3: 1482: "*Eine größere Aktion im Innern...*"

36 As noted in correspondence from John Röhl dated 22.11.2011, for which I am grateful. As Röhl suggested in that communication, the Berlin dimension, especially the fear that the south Germans would in the end not follow the Kaiser's lead, points up the relevance of the controversy in Saxony all the more sharply.

37 Bülow to P. Eulenburg, 23.2.95, 28.9.95, *Philipp Eulenburgs Politische Korrespondenz*, 3: 1482, 1552, respectively. Here I cite the first letter.

38 Journal entry [Jan. 1895], Hohenlohe, *Denkwürdigkeiten der Reichskanzlerzeit*, 31–2.

39 P. Eulenburg to Wilhelm II, 8.4.97, Anlage I, in *Philipp Eulenburgs Politische Korrespondenz*, 3: 1813. See ibid., 1815, for Holstein to Eulenburg, 18.4.97, predicting bad Reichstag elections in 1898 but also emphasizing that the German princes would abandon the Kaiser if he embarked on a coup, no matter whether he made ministerial changes before or after that setback: they would hold him responsible in either case. As Holstein put it: "Then He [Kaiser Wilhelm] will sit there. What does he want to do? Do you [Eulenburg] know? Does He know? There is nothing he can do then but give in."

40 Detailed in Röhl, *Wilhelm II*, 2: 852–60.

41 Röhl, *Wilhelm II*, 2: 859, and for some of the following.

42 P. Eulenburg to Bülow, 24.4.97, *Philipp Eulenburgs Politische Korrespondenz*, 3: 1818–22 (original emphasis); cited in part in Röhl, *Wilhelm II*, 2: 859.

43 See the reports of Hohenthal, Berlin, to Metzsch, Dresden, 3/5/9/11.12.95, SHStAD, MdAA, Nr. 3305.

44 Waldersee added: "Eulenburg's bill would have been workable; but Caprivi's, to which [the government] retreated, was a monstrosity." Waldersee, *Denkwürdigkeiten*, 2: 348 (11.5.95).

45 Austrian envoy Count Bohuslav Chotek, Dresden, to Austrian FO, 4.10.95, HHStAV, PAV/49.

46 For this and the following see Strachey, Dresden, to British FO, 14.1.93, 11.5.93, TNA, FO 68/178. I am grateful to Markus Mößlang for providing

me transcripts of these reports, which I had seen only as drafts in FO 215/40.
47 *Vorwärts*, 4.9.95; cf. reactions from Hohenthal's deputy in Berlin, Legations-Sekretär von Stieglitz, to Metzsch's deputy in the Saxon FO, Geheimer Legationsrat von Friesen, 4.9.95, SHStAD, MdAA, Nr. 3305; also Strachey, Dresden, to British FO, 16.9.95, 9.12.95, TNA, FO 68/180.
48 *Sächsische Arbeiter-Zeitung*, 7.9.95; *Vorwärts*, 20.10.95.
49 The following is based on paraphrased speeches and reflections in Dönhoff, Dresden, to Prussian FO, 13/14.11.95 and 4/5/12/15/19.12.95, PAAAB, Sachsen 60, Bd. 3; Dönhoff, Dresden, to Prussian FO, 21.11.95, PAAAB, Sachsen 48, Bd. 18; Dönhoff's report of 4.12.95 referred explicitly to the "anti-Social-Democratic deputies" in the Saxon II.K.
50 Dönhoff, Dresden, to Prussian FO, 24.10.95, PAAAB, Sachsen 48, Bd. 18.
51 Mehnert's speech in Saxon *LTMitt* II.K. 1895/6, 1: 163–75 (10.12.95). The dramatic debate is reported in Dönhoff, Dresden, to Prussian FO, 12.12.95, PAAAB, Sachsen 60, Bd. 3.
52 Saxon *LTMitt* II.K., 1895/6, 1: 166 (10.12.95).
53 Mehnert to Metzsch, 25.11.95, and other memoranda and correspondence, in SHStAD, MdI, Nr. 5414.
54 The two best sources at present are Simone Lässig, *Wahlrechtskampf und Wahlreform in Sachsen, 1895–1909* (Weimar, 1996) and Thomas Kühne, *Dreiklassenwahlrecht und Wahlkultur in Preussen 1867–1914* (Düsseldorf, 1994).
55 "Justizmord" was the term used. *Sächsische Arbeiter-Zeitung*, 12.12.95, 7/10/29.3.96, and *Dresdner Zeitung*, 13.12.95, cited in Gerhard Schmidt, "Der sächsische Landtag 1833–1918. Sein Wahlrecht und seine soziale Zusammensetzung," in *Beiträge zur Archivwissenschaft und Geschichtsforschung*, edited by Reiner Groß and Manfred Kobuch (Weimar, 1977), 445–65 at 460–1.
56 *Das Vaterland*, 13.12.95; cf. Dönhoff, Dresden, to Prussian FO, 15.12.95, cited above.
57 Dönhoff, Dresden, to Prussian FO, 24.4.96, PAAAB, Sachsen 60, Bd. 4.
58 A conversation reported by Saxony's envoy to Bavaria, 10.4.96, cited in Marga Beyer, "Der Kampf der deutschen Sozialdemokratie um ein demokratisches Wahlrecht in den Jahren 1895–1897 anhand der sächsischen Wahlrechtskämpfe 1896 und der Diskussion um die Beteiligung an den preußischen Landtagswahlen" (PhD diss., Institut für Gesellschaftswissenschaften beim ZK der SED – Lehrstuhl Geschichte der Arbeiterbewegung, Berlin-GDR, 1970), 212.
59 Count Heinrich Lützow, Dresden, to Austrian FO, 1.2.96, HHStAV, PAV/49, and for the following.

60 Lützow, Dresden, to Austrian FO, 29.2.96, HHStAV, PAV/49.
61 Lützow, Dresden, to Austrian FO, 15.2.96, HHStAV, PAV/49, and for the following.
62 Strachey, Dresden, to British FO, 30.5.96, TNA, FO 68/181.
63 Dönhoff, Dresden, to Prussian FO, 22.9.97, PAAAB, Sachsen 60, Bd. 5.
64 Strachey, Dresden, to British FO, 30.5.96, cited above.
65 Chotek, Dresden, to Austrian FO, 29.12.95, HHStAV, PAV/49.
66 Lützow, Dresden, to Austrian FO, 1.2.96.
67 Hohenthal, Berlin, to Metzsch, Dresden, 9.3.96, SHStAD, MdAA, Nr. 3308.
68 *Dresdner Journal*, 22.4.96; *Das Vaterland*, 1.5.96.
69 Dönhoff, Dresden, to Prussian FO, 24.4.96, PAAAB, Sachsen 60, Bd. 4.
70 See "Citadels of Democracy," originally co-authored with Thomas Adam, as ch. 6 in James Retallack, *The German Right, 1860–1920: Political Limits of the Authoritarian Imagination* (Toronto, 2006), 192–222. One of the best primary sources on these developments is Verein für Socialpolik, ed., *Verfassung und Verwaltungsorganisation der Städte*, vol. 4, no. 1, *Königreich Sachsen* (Leipzig, 1905).

Acknowledgments

Most of the people and institutions who were acknowledged in my earlier collection of essays with the University of Toronto Press, *The German Right* (2006), deserve to be thanked again. To all of them I express my sincere gratitude, even as I cite the new debts I have incurred in the past decade and indicate the provenance of each of the foregoing chapters.

My research and writing since 2006 have been greatly assisted by a Standard Research Grant from the Social Sciences and Humanities Research Council of Canada; by a two-year Research Fellowship from the Gerda Henkel Foundation; by a three-month renewal of the Friedrich-Wilhelm-Bessel Research Prize from the Alexander von Humboldt Foundation, which I first held in 2002–3 and took up again at the University of Wuppertal in the last three months of 2014; and by six-month Research Fellowships from the Connaught Committee and the Jackman Humanities Institute, both at the University of Toronto. I am grateful to my Henkel and Humboldt hosts in Berlin and Wuppertal, Jürgen Kocka and Ute Planert, respectively, and to successive chairs of my department who allowed me to accept these opportunities: Lorna Jane Abray, Kenneth Mills, Adrienne Hood, and Nicholas Terpstra. I have also found support through my affiliation with the Joint Initiative in German and European Studies (JIGES) and the Centre for European, Russian, and Eurasian Studies (CERES), both of which provide a congenial home under the able stewardship of Randall Hansen at the Munk School of Global Affairs, University of Toronto.

My undergraduate research assistants provided me essential support with hundreds of trips to and from our university's outstanding Robarts Library, with photocopying and proofreading, and with much else.

They include Robin Buller, Diana Chen, Candice Cheung, Madeline Klimek, Angela Petersen, Yunjie Shi, Allison Spiegel, and Jordan Stone. Different kinds of input and support have been provided by all my PhD supervisees not listed in my last book: Anthony Cantor, Evan Dokos, Marc-André Dufour, Geoff Hamm, and Gavin Wiens, as well as Rebecca Carter-Chand. Again my former supervisee, Dr Erwin Fink (Freiburg i.Br.), deserves special thanks: he helped me with numerous translations. Drs Daniel Fischer and Swen Steinberg helped me acquire or check documents from the Saxon Central State Archive in Dresden. Many colleagues and friends in Toronto continue to let me seek their advice, above all Doris Bergen, Deborah Neill (York University), Andrea Geddes Poole, and Lynne Viola. My trips overseas have invariably drawn on the logistical support and encouragement of dear friends from the 1970s and 1980s, especially Johannes Hahn, Hans Horn, Gurli Jacobsen, Jef McAllister, Ann Olivarius, and the Schilfert family. I profited in more ways than I can count from the year (2012–13) that Ute Planert spent in Toronto as the DAAD Hannah Arendt Visiting Chair for German and European Studies at the Munk School.

To the editors and publishers of journals and books in which some of these chapters first appeared, I am grateful for permission to publish them in revised form here. I also wish to thank the libraries, archives, and other institutions from which I have drawn the illustrations for this book. The provenance of each image is indicated where it appears. I welcome any communication from holders of copyright whom I have not been able to reach directly.

CHAPTER 1, FORGING AN EMPIRE: ECONOMY, SOCIETY, CULTURE, AND POLITICS, 1866–1890, owes a great deal to the support of Roger Chickering and other editors of the *German History in Documents and Images* project, to the generous sponsors of that project, to the director of the German Historical Institute (GHI), Washington, DC, at the time of its inception, Christof Mauch, and especially to Project Director Dr Kelly McCullough, who helped hone earlier versions of this text. For this chapter I have revised the online "Introduction" to *Forging an Empire: Bismarckian Germany (1866–1890)*, edited by James Retallack, vol. 4 of *German History in Documents and Images* (10 vols.), on the website of the GHI, Washington, DC: http://germanhistorydocs.ghi-dc.org/section.cfm?section_id=10&language=english. I hope readers will consult that online edition for hyperlinks to the texts and images to which I allude in this chapter. In the summer of 2014 I significantly updated the "Suggestions for Further Reading" found at the end of this chapter.

CHAPTER 2, BRITISH VIEWS OF GERMANY, 1815–1914, took shape initially as a review essay devoted to the *British Envoys to Germany* project, among whose editors Markus Mößlang and Torsten Riotte provided me crucial advice, support, and images from the Public Record Office, Kew (now The National Archives or TNA). They did so at the cost of considerable time and effort that might have been spent pushing their own project to completion. I am grateful to Moritz Föllmer, former editor of *German History*, for giving me the green light to write an extended review of this edited collection, allowing me to present some of my own research in the process. This chapter is drawn from James Retallack, "Reform or Revolution? British Envoys to Germany and the Culture of Diplomacy, 1816–1905," *German History* 31, no. 4 (2013): 550–78. It benefited from critical readings by Moritz Föllmer, Dr Geoff Hamm (who also provided documents from TNA), and Eckart Conze (University of Marburg).

CHAPTER 3, DIGITAL HISTORY ANTHOLOGIES ON THE WEB, was originally co-authored with Kelly McCullough. I am deeply grateful for her permission to let me include it in this volume. My revisions to our joint text have been minimal – mainly adding an opening few paragraphs, deleting some technical details about the project, and inserting URLs near the end of the chapter. Of course Kelly bears no responsibility for any errors of fact or judgment that may now infect the text. This chapter's pre-history is unusual in another way. It originated as a series of panels I organized at the annual meetings of the German Studies Association and the American Historical Association, held in Washington, DC, in October 2009 and San Diego in January 2010, respectively. As at those sessions, the essay and this chapter drew on insights not only from other panelists but from the entire group of editors who produced the ten volumes of *German History in Documents and Images:* they made time to reflect upon the questions we posed to them and provided stimulating answers. The project itself was made possible by the generous support of the Max Kade Foundation and the ZEIT-Stiftung Ebelin und Gerd Bucerius, and was undertaken in cooperation with the Friends of the GHI. Both Christoph Mauch and his successor as GHI Director, Hartmut Berghoff, supported the project generously. Kenneth Ledford's enthusiasm was indispensable in encouraging us to work up a report from those panels for *Central European History*, which he edited at that time. Thus I was able to help make the project known to more colleagues in the field. The chapter originally appeared as Kelly McCullough and James Retallack, "Digital History Anthologies on the Web: *German History in Documents and Images,*" *Central European History* 46, no. 2 (2013): 346–61.

CHAPTER 4, KING JOHANN OF SAXONY AND THE GERMAN CIVIL WAR OF 1866, draws upon some of the same sources I have used for other studies of the Prussian occupation of Saxony in 1866, but it includes new material from my last extended archival visit to Berlin and Dresden: there I found the reports that Prussian Civil Commissar Lothar von Wurmb sent to Bismarck during the occupation. For scans of the diary kept by the de facto secretary of Saxony's provisional government during the occupation, Carl von Weber, now in Saxony's Central State Archive, I am grateful to Gavin Wiens. I am also indebted to audiences who have heard oral presentation of this material in Toronto and elsewhere. Most of all I wish to thank the organizers and sponsors of the conference on monarchy and exile held at the GHI London in December 2007, whose director, Andreas Gestrich, was a gracious host on that occasion, as he and his staff have been each time I visit their institute. I am grateful to the editors and publishers of the volume in which a different version of this text first appeared: James Retallack, "'To My Loyal Saxons!' King Johann in Exile, 1866," in *Monarchy and Exile: The Politics of Legitimacy from Marie de Médici to Wilhelm II*, edited by Philip Mansel and Torsten Riotte (London and New York: Palgrave, 2011), 279–304.

CHAPTER 5, JULIAN HAWTHORNE'S *SAXON STUDIES*, was first drafted in 2004–5 and then reduced in length for presentation at a conference I co-organized with David Blackbourn (Vanderbilt University) in May 2005 as part of the academic program of the Joint Initiative in German and European Studies. The short title of the conference paper – "When Localism Goes Bad" – reflected the playfulness I hope the present chapter retains. Although I have drawn upon a longer draft here, I have not neglected the useful critiques I received early on from Andrea Geddes Poole and John Zilcosky and later from Alon Confino and David Blackbourn. Other conference participants, including Celia Applegate, also helped improve the piece. The appearance of Gary Scharnhorst's new biography of Hawthorne in 2014 necessitated more than a few revisions. The shorter version appeared in print as James Retallack, "'Native Son': Julian Hawthorne's *Saxon Studies*," in *Localism, Landscape, and the Ambiguities of Place: German-Speaking Central Europe,*

1860–1930, edited by David Blackbourn and James Retallack (Toronto: University of Toronto Press, 2007), 76–98. For his assistance in bringing that volume to press and supporting a paperback edition in 2014, David and I are grateful to our editor at the University of Toronto Press, Len Husband.

CHAPTER 6, BISMARCK AND ENGELS: *THE ROLE OF FORCE IN HISTORY*, was drafted in response to an invitation to contribute to a *Festschrift* for Bernd Weisbrod (Berlin), my host and mentor at the University of Göttingen in 2002–3. Bernd has been a friend, supporter, and gentle critic of my work for many years, and it was a pleasure to have the opportunity to join so many esteemed colleagues in honouring him upon his retirement. The concept of the *Festschrift* was that every contributor should offer his or her thoughts on a historical "classic." So many chapters were squeezed between the covers of Weisbrod's *Festschrift* that each one had to be short; I have therefore added necessary background material to an early draft of the chapter and tried to clarify some points. It first appeared as James Retallack, "Bismarck, Engels, and The Role of Force in History. Friedrich Engels: *Die Rolle der Gewalt in der Geschichte* (1896)," in *Gewalt und Gesellschaft. Klassiker modernen Denkens neu gelesen*, edited by Uffa Jensen, Habbo Knoch, Daniel Morat, and Miriam Rürup (Göttingen: Wallstein Verlag, 2011), 47–56.

CHAPTER 7, HEYDEBRAND AND WESTARP: LEAVING BEHIND THE SECOND REICH, also has its genesis in an overseas conference. A shorter version was presented at the conference "'Ich bin der letzte Preusse': Kuno Graf von Westarp und die deutsche Politik," held in Villa Schwalbenhof, Gärtringen, Germany, in May 2004. The larger rationale behind the conference, the paper, and the sources they were based on is explained in the chapter itself. I am grateful to Larry Eugene Jones above all for inviting me to this gathering; to Karl J. Mayer's kind hospitality during my trip; to the late Hans Freiherr von Gaertringen and his family for graciously opening their doors to so many guests; and to the other volume authors, many of whom I count as close friends. Because parts of this chapter were drafted in English and translated into German, whereas the original German passages had to be translated into English here, I owe another debt of gratitude to my translator Erwin Fink and to the careful scrutiny of Wolfram Pyta. This chapter has previously appeared only in German, but very recently new research has been published on Weimar Conservatism, which I felt compelled to integrate into the present version. Otherwise the text was first published as James Retallack, "Zwei Vertreter des preußischen

Konservatismus im Spiegel ihres Briefwechsels: Die Heydebrand-Westarp Korrespondenz," in *"Ich bin der letzte Preuße." Der politische Lebensweg des konservativen Politikers Kuno Graf von Westarp*, edited by Larry Eugene Jones and Wolfram Pyta (Cologne, Weimar, Vienna: Böhlau Verlag, 2006), 33–60.

CHAPTER 8, GET OUT THE VOTE! ELECTIONEERING WITHOUT DEMOCRACY, originated as an invited lecture delivered at the German Historical Institute, Washington, DC, on 12 April 2012. That lecture was part of a series of talks titled "Get Out the Vote! Mobilization, Media, and Money." For the invitation I am indebted to the series organizers David Lazar and Jan Logemann. Again I tried to preserve the tone of the original oral presentation both when it was first published and when I revised it for this book. As before, I dedicate this chapter to my dear friend and not-always-so-gentle critic Margaret Lavinia Anderson, whose work continues to inspire my own. A somewhat shorter version of the text was published both in print and online as James Retallack, "'Get Out the Vote!' Elections without Democracy in Imperial Germany," *Bulletin of the German Historical Institute, Washington DC*, no. 51 (Fall 2012): 23–38.

CHAPTER 9, THE AUTHORITARIAN STATE AND THE POLITICAL MASS MARKET, was drafted as a contribution to a Berlin conference honouring Hans-Ulrich Wehler after his retirement. I am grateful for input I received from other conference participants and for the chance to re-establish many personal friendships during an extraordinary meeting. The organizers of the conference proved to be wonderful hosts and editors as well, although revising this chapter in July 2014 was emotionally painful due to the untimely death of my friend and mentor, Uli Wehler. This chapter was drafted in English but published first in German, so the translation help of Erwin Fink and the editors is gratefully acknowledged. For this volume I have added to and updated some of the references in the notes and filled out the argument in one section. First published as James Retallack, "Obrigkeitsstaat und politischer Massenmarkt," in *Das Deutsche Kaiserreich in der Kontroverse*, edited by Sven Oliver Müller and Cornelius Torp (Göttingen: Vandenhoeck & Ruprecht, 2009), 121–35, only minor revisions were made when it appeared as James Retallack, "The Authoritarian State and the Political Mass Market," in *Imperial Germany Revisited: Continuing Debates and New Perspectives*, edited by Sven Oliver Müller and Cornelius Torp (Oxford and New York: Berghahn Books, 2011), 83–96.

CHAPTER 10, SOCIETY AND DEMOCRACY IN GERMANY: WHY DAHRENDORF STILL MATTERS, has not previously appeared in print. It was written for a conference panel I organized with Helmut Walser Smith (Vanderbilt University) and Thomas Kühne (Clark University). Originally titled "Democratization and German Society: Why the *Fluchtpunkt* of 1933 Still Matters," it was presented at the Annual Meeting of the German Studies Association in Louisville, Kentucky, in September 2011. I am grateful to Helmut, Thomas, and our commentator, Volker Berghahn (Columbia University), for their critical reflections and suggestions for improvement. I have added citations to the original presentation, expanded the argument in places, and revised it to avoid repetition with other chapters.

CHAPTER 11, DEMOCRACY IN DISAPPEARING INK: SUFFRAGE ROBBERY AS *COUP D'ÉTAT*, is an expanded version of a colloquium paper I presented at the Max Kade Center for German and European Studies, Vanderbilt University, Nashville, in April 2011. I am grateful to Helmut Walser Smith for the invitation (and for the honky-tonk evening afterward), to his wife Meike Werner for her hospitality, to his graduate students for intellectual stimulation and logistical help, and to all those who participated in the colloquium. In April 2011, I had already drafted separate sections of my monograph, *Red Saxony*, that dealt with the *coup d'état* and suffrage "crises" of 1894–6, but it was tremendously helpful to test the idea of juxtaposing these events in a new way. For the present volume I have added substantially to the sections depicting reactions to the Kaiser's *coup d'état* plans. I was able to do so partly because John Röhl (University of Sussex, Emeritus) kindly provided critical reflections on the corresponding draft chapter of my book. John was a mentor even before he served as external examiner for my D.Phil. in 1983: he kindly shared with me proofs from his edition of the *Eulenburg Korrespondenz* because he knew they would enrich my dissertation. I am grateful not only to have all three English volumes of his remarkable biography of Wilhelm II on my shelf – besides his many other works – but to count him as a friend.

During the past half-decade I have become more mindful than ever of the importance of health and family. For their unflinching efforts since 2011 I am grateful to the staff of West Park Rehab Plus, above all my therapists Daniel, Emily, and Lauren, and to Dr Rajka Soric at West Park Healthcare Centre in Toronto. For his encouragement from the moment he first heard about this book, for his stewardship of the UTP series on *German and European Studies*, and for years of support and advice, I am indebted to my editor at the University of Toronto Press, Richard Ratzlaff (as I am to the two anonymous referees he recruited). I also owe a debt of thanks to Matthew Kudelka, who copy edited the manuscript with a light touch, to Gavin Wiens, who helped me check page proofs, and to Rebecca Carter-Chand, who compiled the index.

For their continuing forbearance as one writing project follows quickly on the heels of the last, I dedicate this book to my son Stuart and my daughter Hanna: they do a better job than I do of shrinking the time and distance that keep us apart. Above all I am grateful for the love and support of Helen E. Graham, who deserves to have a bigger book than this one dedicated to her – and soon.

Index

The following terms were not indexed: Germany; international relations; Kaiserreich; Second Reich; state

1848–9, revolutions of, 108, 190, 281
1918–19, revolution of, 223, 258

absolutism, 93
Academy, The, 152
Africa, 149
Agrarian League, agrarian movement, 271, 272, 309
agriculture, 8, 10, 61, 62, 245, 304. *See also* economy: agricultural economy; rural communities, rural life
Ahlwardt, Hermann, 245
Albert (King of Saxony), xii, 127–8, 191, 299, 300, 303–4, 305–6, 308–9, 310, 312, 315, 316; as crown prince, 55, 113, 127
alcohol, drinking customs, 142–4, 148, 155, 160, 165–6
Allen, William Sheridan, 270
Allgemeine Konservative Monatsschrift, 211
Alsace and Lorraine, 22, 26, 56, 189, 192

Amelung, May Albertina (Minne), 157
Americanization, 92, 260
anarchist movement, 296–8, 299, 307
Anderson, Margaret Lavinia, 241–2, 258, 260, 267, 271; *Practicing Democracy*, 241
Anglophobia, 51
Anhalt, 315
animals, 10, 151, 152, 160, 162, 213
anti-anarchist bill, 298
Anti-Revolution Bill (1894), 195, 197, 298, 303, 304, 305, 311
Anti-Socialist Law (1878–90), 26, 28, 51, 62, 65, 68, 69, 187, 190, 192, 193, 269, 298, 308; Minor State of Siege (§28), 68, 69, 70–1, 267. *See also* Social Democratic Party of Germany (SPD), Social Democrats; socialism, socialists
antisemitism, antisemites, xiv, 18, 29, 62, 100–1, 152, 187, 221, 223, 224–6, 239, 241, 244, 245, 247, 248, 249, 272, 281, 302; "Berlin Antisemitic Dispute" (1879–81), 18, 100;

Tivoli program (1892), 224–5. *See also* conservatism, conservatives; "Jewish question"; Jews
Anton (King of Saxony), 108
Applegate, Celia, 262
Arendt, Hannah, 280
army. *See* military, militarism; Prussia: officer corps
Army Bill (1893), 196, 311
Arnim, Hans von, 205
Arnould, George Ludwig Wilhelm, 99
art, artistic movements, 1, 4, 6, 11, 13, 15, 16, 17, 94, 99, 100, 108, 119, 143, 145, 151, 155, 160, 168, 170, 194, 248, 251, 263, 268, 287, 296, 297
Association of German Students, 19
associational life, 265
Auden, W.H., 170
Auer, Ignaz, 70
August the Strong (August II, King of Saxony), 108
Augusta (Queen of Prussia), 123
Austria, 22, 51, 61, 68, 110–11, 112, 113, 115, 116, 117, 118, 120–1, 123, 124, 237; diplomacy, diplomats, 66, 71, 191, 311
Austro-Hungarian Empire, 22, 23, 307
Austro-Prussian War (1866). *See* German Civil War
authoritarianism, authoritarian state, 3, 4, 5, 30, 50–1, 65, 144, 192, 238, 243, 250, 258–73, 289

Baden, 10, 68, 216, 262, 294, 307, 310
Ballin, Albert, 211
Bancroft, George, 64, 146
Barmen Rhine Missionary Society, 24
Bassan, Maurice, 159

Bassermann, Ernst, 211
Bastei, Die, 163
Battle of Nations (1813), 108
Bavaria, 26, 46, 51, 63, 68, 111, 115, 191, 216, 262, 294, 303, 307, 315; diplomacy, diplomats, 66, 68, 71, 211, 304
Bayreuth, 16
Bebel, August, 14, 25, 28, 62, 70, 71, 187–90, 195, 211, 243, 267; *Woman under Socialism*, 188
Becker, Winfried, 264, 265
Beethoven, Ludwig van, 144
Behrenberg, Carl von, 112–13; *Einmarsch preußischer Truppen am 18. Juni 1866*, 112–13
Belgium, 196, 216
Below, Georg von, 205
Berghahn, Volker, 92, 94, 97, 259, 288
Berlin, 7, 15, 30, 46, 50, 51, 52, 53, 55, 61, 65, 68, 69, 70, 100, 112, 114, 127, 187, 214, 218, 260, 266, 296, 298, 304, 306, 309, 311, 313, 314, 316, 317; Berlin Wall, 46, 91; *Tiergarten*, 209
Berlin Conference (1884–5), 63
Berliner Tageblatt, 208
Bernstein, Eduard, 186–8
Bethmann Hollweg, Theobald von, 206, 207, 209, 212, 214, 269; Moroccan policy, 210–11
Beust, Friedrich Ferdinand von, 109–10, 112, 115, 120, 122
Bewer, Max, 240; *Politische Bilderbogen*, 240
Biedermann, Karl, 116
Biefang, Andreas, 272
Bismarck, Herbert von, 191
Bismarck, Otto von, xi, xii, xiii, 3, 4, 5, 17, 19, 20–3, 25, 26–8, 30, 44, 48,

49, 50, 54, 62, 63–4, 67, 68, 69, 70, 71, 86, 109, 110, 111, 115, 116–17, 118, 120, 122, 123, 128, 144, 165, 186–98, 237, 239, 244, 247, 259, 269, 270, 271, 272, 293–4, 307, 308, 318
Blackbourn, David, 50, 247, 259, 262, 271, 299; *The Peculiarities of German History* (co-author), 383
Bleichröder, Gerson von, 116
Blount, Roy, Jr, 140
Böcklin, Arnold, 16
Bohemia, 109, 110, 113, 114, 115
Borges, Jorge Luis, 169–70
Boston, 161–2, 297
bourgeoisie. *See* middle classes
Brady, Thomas, 94
Brahms, Johannes: *Ein Deutsches Requiem*, 16
Brandt, Willy, 96
Brauneis, Rudolf, 160
Braunschweig, 315
Breitman, Richard, 92, 95
Bremen, 155
Breslau, 218
Breuilly, John, xiii
Britain, 25, 47, 65, 202, 210, 216, 242, 252, 286, 298, 302–3; Anglo–German relations, 48–9, 63, 71; British views of Germany, xii, 44–72, 145; diplomacy, diplomats, 44–72, 110, 111, 112, 124, 127, 147, 302, 311; Foreign Office, foreign policy, 45, 46, 47, 50–2, 54, 56, 58, 61, 62, 64, 118, 311; National Archives, 47, 53. *See also* diplomacy, diplomats
Brussels, 65
Bülow, Bernhard von, 63, 206, 212, 307–8
Bürgertum. *See* middle classes
Bull, John (national figure), 148

Burbach Smelting Works, 99
Burgk–Roßthal, Carl von, 62
Burnley, J. Hume, 61, 62

Cameroon, 25
capitalism, 12, 20, 94
Caprivi, Leo von, 196, 296, 298, 304, 305, 311
Carlsbad Decrees, 54, 57, 58
Carnot, Sadi, 298
Cartwright, William, 61
Catholicism, Catholics, 17–18, 26–7, 27–32, 50, 54, 70, 108, 117, 192, 240, 242, 308. *See also Kulturkampf*; religion
Central Europe, 46, 47
Centre Party, German, 27, 28, 212, 268, 307–8
Cham (Amédée Charles de Noé), 119
Charivari, Le, 119
Chartism, 54
Chemnitz, 70, 317
Chesterton, G.K., 252; *Orthodoxy*, 252
Chicago, 169, 297, 298
Chickering, Roger, 88–9, 93, 97, 98; *The Great War and Urban Life in Germany: Freiburg 1914–1918*, 93
China, 107
Christian Social Party, 222
Cicero, Marcus, 245
Cicero, Quintus Tullius, 245; *How to Win an Election*, 245
civil liberties, 26, 238, 265, 273, 295, 304
Clarendon, Lord (George William Frederick Villiers), 52
class, class conflict, 11, 12, 19, 31, 190, 259, 284
Claß, Heinrich, 214
Clinton, Hillary, 45

Cohen, Daniel J., 87
Cold War, 94
Coleridge, Samuel Taylor, 168
Cologne Cathedral, 63
colonialism, colonies, 24–5. See also Cameroon; German East Africa; South-West Africa; Togo
communism, 308
Congress of Berlin, 23
Congress of Vienna, 57, 118
Conservative People's Party, 206
conservatism, conservatives, 50, 120, 126, 152, 195, 202, 207, 210–15, 216–18, 245–7, 248, 249, 252, 260, 272, 296, 300, 303, 306, 307, 311, 313–16. See also Conservative People's Party; Free Conservative Party; German Conservative Party; Junkers
constitutional monarchy, xiv, 21, 55, 202, 219, 239, 242, 264, 308
constitutionalism, 54, 56, 146, 258, 288, 304
Contemporary Review, The, 138
Crailsheim, Friedrich Krafft von, 315
Criminal Code, 62, 296, 303
Crispi, Francesco, 298
Crowe, Joseph Archer, 52, 55, 56, 60
culture, 6, 16, 17, 25, 27, 30, 68, 139, 147, 241

Dahrendorf, Ralf, xiii, 240, 280–9; *Society and Democracy in Germany*, 280–9
Daimler, Gottlieb, 31
Dante, 108; *Divine Comedy*, 108
Davis, John R., 48
democracy, democratization, xiii, xiv, xv, 4, 31, 57, 60, 92, 202, 238–52, 258–9, 263–5, 269, 271, 280–9, 295, 296, 299, 317–18; opponents of, 239–40, 243–4, 249, 269, 281, 295, 302. *See also* parliament, parliamentarism; reform; suffrage
Derby, Lord (Edward Henry Stanley), 53
Dickinson, Edward Ross, 266
digital anthologies, 47–8, 86–101. See also *German History in Documents and Images*
diplomacy, diplomats, 45, 46, 48, 59, 66, 71, 115, 125, 145. *See also under* Austria; Bavaria; Britain; Germany; Saxony; United States
Disraeli, Benjamin, 22, 49
Dönhoff, Carl von, 70
Dohm, Hedwig, 14
Don Quixote (national figure), 148
Dresden, 11, 15–16, 46, 51, 53, 55, 57–8, 61–2, 64–5, 68, 70, 108, 109–10, 112–15, 122, 124–7, 139, 140, 141, 142, 145, 150, 152–4, 155–7, 158–9, 163, 166–7, 169, 170, 191, 260, 267, 298, 300, 302–3, 311–12, 313, 314, 315, 317; American Club in, 161; Dresden Conservative Association, 247; Dresden Uprising (1849), 108
Dresdner Nachrichten, 152–3, 168, 315
Dresdner Zeitung, 315
Du Bois, W.E.B., 64
Dühring, Eugen, 186–7; *The Jewish Question as a Racial, Moral, and Cultural Question*, 187

East Germany. *See* German Democratic Republic (GDR)
economy, 7–8
Eden, Charles, 124, 125, 126–7
education, 18–19, 285; opportunities for women, 14, 18, 19

elections, 25, 27, 28, 29, 116, 125, 164, 193, 213, 237–52, 258, 265, 266–7, 270, 272, 281, 286, 294, 296, 304, 311, 312, 318. *See also* suffrage; Reichstag
Eley, Geoff, 50, 271, 299; *The Peculiarities of German History* (co-author), 383
Eliot, George, 237; *Felix Holt*, 237
Emerson, Ralph Waldo, 151, 168; *English Traits*, 151
Ems Dispatch, 20
Engels, Friedrich, xii, 186–98, 202, 267, 304, 305; "*Anti–Dühring,*" 186, 187; *Herr Eugen Dühring's Revolution in Science*, 187; *The Role of Force in History*, 186–95, 197–8
England. *See* Britain
enemies of the Reich, 244, 250, 295, 298, 306. *See also* Catholicism, Catholics; Jews; liberalism, liberals; socialism, socialists
Erzgebirge (Ore Mountains), 113
Essen, 98–9
estates, social (*Stände*), 11, 284
Eulenberg, Botho zu, 307
Eulenburg, Philipp zu, 197, 307, 308–10
Evarts, William M., 65
Everett, H. Sidney, 65

Fahrmeir, Andreas, 48
Fairbairn, Brett, 241, 258–9, 267; *Democracy in the Undemocratic State*, 241
Falk, Adalbert, 26
families, 11–12, 14
farmers. *See* agriculture
Fechter, Peter, 91
Federal Act (1815), 57

federal princes, 20
Federal Republic of Germany (West Germany), 46, 95, 139, 288
federalism, federal states, 15, 22, 54, 71, 124, 146, 264, 294, 303, 312. *See also* regionalism
Feldman, Gerald, 89
Finance Reform (1909), 206
First Reform Act (Britain), 54
First World War, 60, 61, 93, 252, 258, 259, 261, 270, 288, 295, 318; July Crisis (1914), 295
Flemming, Jens, 217
Fontane, Theodor, 11, 16, 22; *Der Stechlin*, 16
France, 22, 49, 51, 53–4, 57, 58, 108, 117, 120, 123, 124, 146–7, 154, 242, 303, 307
Franco-German War (1870–1), 49, 127, 158
Frankfurt am Main, 49, 51, 57, 58, 248
Frantz, Constantin, 282–3
Frederick the Great (Friedrich II, King of Prussia), 111, 202
Free Conservative Party, 25, 193, 207, 217
free speech, 68
Free Trade Unions, 196
Freie Kommission, 215
French Revolution, 46, 49, 56, 72
Freud, Sigmund, 140
Freytag, Gustav, 120, 270, 272
Friedrich III (King of Prussia, Kaiser of Germany) (Crown Prince Friedrich Wilhelm), 22, 25, 30, 63, 117, 121, 123, 263
Friedrich August I (King of Saxony), 108
Friedrich August II (King of Saxony), 108

Friedrichsruh, 30
Friesen, Richard von, 114, 115, 116
Friesen-Rötha, Heinrich von, 246, 249
Fritsch, Theodor, 187; *Handbook on the Jewish Question*, 187

Gartenlaube, Die, 251
gender relations, 14, 259. *See also* women
Gerlach, Helmut von, 245
German Centre Party. *See* Centre Party
German Civil War (1866), 47, 64, 107–28, 188–9, 237; military convention, Prussian–Saxon (1867), 117; peace treaty, Prussian–Saxon (1866), 122, 124, 126; Provisional Government, Saxon, 114, 116, 120. *See also* Nikolsburg armistice negotiations
German Confederation, 45, 46, 51, 57, 58, 65, 109
German Conservative Party, 193, 202–27, 244, 272, 299
German Democratic Republic (GDR), 16, 46, 47, 95, 139
German East Africa, 25
German Historical Institute London, 45, 47
German Historical Institute, Washington, DC, 48, 87–8
German History in Documents and Images (GHDI), 48, 87–101
German National People's Party, 202–27
German Question, 47, 125, 283–4. See also *Großdeutschland*; *Kleindeutschland*
German Society of Nobles, 223

Germany: reunification (1989–90), 16, 44; unification (1871), 3, 16, 44, 46, 49, 50, 146, 192, 307
Gestrich, Andreas, 45
Geyer, Michael, 260–1; *Shattered Past* (co-author), 261
Gierke, Otto von, 261
Glebe, Ellen Yutzy, 94
Goethe, Johann Wolfgang von, 47, 151, 227; *Faust*, 155, 156
Goldberg, Hans-Peter, 272
Goldberg, Jeffrey, 237
Gorbachev, Mikhail, 16
Goßler, Alfred von, 208
Gotha Program, 29
Göttingen, 146
Graefe-Goldebee, Albrecht von, 223
Graetz, Friedrich, 194
"Great Deflation," 7
Great Depression (1873–96), 7, 241
Greece, 242
Green, Abigail, 262
Green movement, 99
Grenzboten, Die, 120
Grießmer, Axel, 271
Gross, Michael, 259
Großdeutschland (Greater Germany), 109–10, 191
Günther, Otto, 143; *Am Tagelöhnertisch*, 143

Habermas, Jürgen, 280
Habsburg Empire. *See* Austria; Austro-Hungarian Empire
Hagen, William W., 91–2, 93–4; *Ordinary Prussians: Brandenburg Junkers and Villagers, 1500–1840*, 94
Hall of Mirrors (Palace of Versailles), 20, 23
Halsall, Paul, 88

Hamburg, 30, 63, 68, 70, 315
Hanover, 51, 58, 110, 118, 123
Hard Labour Bill, 296
Harte, Bret, 160
Harvard University, 154–5, 160
Hauptmann, Gerhart, 15
Hawthorne, Julian, xii, 109, 138–70; "A Golden Wedding in the Best Society," 159; *Bressant*, 158, 161; *Humours of the Fair*, 169; *Idolatry*, 158, 159–61; "The Real Romance," 159; *Saxon Studies*, 138–70
Hawthorne, Nathaniel, 109, 138, 149, 153, 154, 155, 158, 159, 161; *English Notebooks*, 153
Hawthorne, Rose, 156
Hawthorne, Una, 156
Healy, Róisín, 259
Heidelberg, 146
Heimat, 262
Heine, Heinrich, 100, 169
Heine, Thomas Theodor, 67, 285
Heinze, Lex, 296
Helldorff, Otto von, 195, 244
Henseler, Ernst, *Wirtshausszene*, 268
Hergt, Oskar, 206, 216, 219–21
Hertling, Georg von, 46
Hesse-Cassel, 110
Hessen, 58
Hewitson, Mark, 262, 288
Heydebrand und der Lasa, Ernst von, xii, 202–27
Hiller von Gaertringen, Friedrich, 206, 210, 230
Hindenburg, Paul von, 281
historical genre, historical methodology, 46–7, 68, 86, 88, 91–4, 100, 192, 258–60; history of everyday life (*Alltagsgeschichte*), 238; images as sources, 88–9, 92; transnationalism, 250, 258–60. *See also* postcolonial studies
historiography, xiv, xv, 6, 18, 31, 44, 46, 47–8, 49, 50, 63, 68, 69, 94, 240–4, 249–51, 259, 260, 261–2, 265–6, 280, 295, 303. *See also* digital anthologies
Hitler, Adolf, xi, xiii, xiv, 187, 225–6, 238–9, 246–7, 281; *Mein Kampf*, 226
Hoffmann von Fallersleben, August Heinrich, 16
Hofstadter, Richard, 241; *The Paranoid Style in American Politics*, 241
Hohenlohe-Schillingsfürst, Chlodwig zu, 196–7, 296, 298, 305–6, 308–9, 310
Hohenthal, Karl Adolf von, 120
Hohenthal und Bergen, Wilhelm von, 46
Hohenzollern dynasty, 115, 117
Hollenberg, Günter, 48
Holocaust, xiii, 238, 281
Holstein, Friedrich von, 307
Holy Roman Empire, xi, 65
Honecker, Erich, 16
Hugenberg, Alfred, 206, 214
"Hungarian Legion," 116
hybridity, hybrid identities, 148, 162, 168, 169

Illustrirte Zeitung, 115, 125
imagology, 147–8
Imperial navy, 23, 63
Industrial Revolution, 46, 72
industrialization, industrial capitalism, 8, 10, 12, 61, 63, 68, 93, 99, 108, 186, 192, 237
Ireland, 54

340   Index

Italy, 46, 55, 154, 296, 298

James, Henry, 139, 149–51, 154, 155, 161, 166, 168
Japan, 46, 54, 107
Jarausch, Konrad H., 88–9, 91, 92, 95, 97, 99, 261; *Shattered Past* (co-author), 261
Jefferson, Thomas, 250
"Jewish question," 224, 249, 272. *See also* antisemitism, antisemites
Jews, 18, 20, 68, 94, 116, 223, 239–40, 247, 249, 250, 282. *See also* antisemitism, antisemites
Johann (King of Saxony), xii, 62, 107–13, 115–16, 118, 120–1, 123, 124, 125, 126, 127, 159, 202
Jones, Raymond, 45, 46, 51
Junkers, 10, 50, 188–9, 192, 195, 207, 245

Kant, Immanuel, 47, 284
Kapp, Friedrich, 25
Kapp, Wolfgang, 215
Kapp Putsch, 219, 221
Kardorff, Wilhelm von, 195
Kartell parties, 69, 193, 313, 314, 316
Kautsky, Karl, 188
Kennedy, Paul, 48
Kiernan, V.G., 189
Kladderadatsch, 145
Kleindeutschland (Lesser Germany), 56, 261
Koblenz, 248
Kohn, Hans, 283; *The Mind of Germany*, 283
Köller, Ernst von, 307, 308
Koehler, Robert, 297; *Der Sozialist*, 297
Kölner Hof, 248

Königgrätz, Battle of (1866), 47, 55, 110, 117, 119, 123, 124, 125, 127, 155
Königstein fortress, 116
Kotzebue, August von, 57
Kreth, Hermann, 218
Kreuzzeitung (Neue Preußische Zeitung), 207, 214, 218, 220, 223, 225, 227
Krupp, Alfred, 9, 11, 98
Krupp, Friedrich, 9
Krupp factory, 98–9
Kühne, Thomas, 259, 262, 265, 282
Kulturkampf, 17, 26, 27, 28, 62–3, 192, 259, 308

"La Marseillaise," 70
Lamb, Frederick, 58
Landrat (county councillor), 203, 287
landscape, 140, 141, 163
Landtag (Prussian), 26, 55, 58, 203, 206, 212, 286, 305, 307
Landtag (Saxon), 28, 50, 61, 62, 66, 109, 110, 115, 116, 267, 299, 300, 303, 311–12, 313, 314–18
Langewiesche, Dieter, 50, 262
Lawrence Scientific School, 155
Leacock, Stephen, 154
Lees, Andrew, 266
Lehmann, Emil, 18
Leibl, Wilhelm, 16
Leipzig, 48, 56, 68, 70–1, 108, 116, 118, 120, 123, 146, 152, 153, 155, 267, 314, 317
Leipzig, University of, 316
Lenin, Vladimir Ilyich, 186
Lepsius, M. Rainer, 28, 240, 286
Lerchenfeld-Köfering, Hugo von, 46, 211
liberal era (1870s), 22
liberalism, liberals, 21, 26–7, 49–50, 54–5, 56, 58, 237, 271, 281–2, 293,

295, 296, 298–9, 317; left liberals, 21, 26, 29, 261, 269; opponents of, 249, 281. *See also* National Liberal Party; Protestants: Protestant liberals
Liebermann, Max, 15
Liebknecht, Wilhelm, 28, 62, 187, 190, 195, 242, 304
Lincoln, Abraham, 237
literature, 15, 16, 151. *See also* reading, reading habits
local politics, 243, 260, 296
localism, local communities, 24, 29, 60, 145, 146, 148, 167, 250, 260, 296. *See also* regionalism, regional diversity
Lodge, David, 147; *Nice Work*, 147
Loebell, Friedrich Wilhelm von, 213
Loftus, Augustus, 52, 53, 110–11, 112, 118, 123
London, 298, 303
Lougee, Robert, 298
Lowell, James Russell, 155
Ludendorff, Erich, 226
Lübeck, 10
Luitpold, Prince Regent (of Bavaria), 303
Lusatia (*Die Lausitz*), 118, 120
Lustige Blätter, 194

Madai, Guido von, 69
Magdeburg, 155
Mainz, 123
Major, Patrick, 48
Malinowski, Stephan, 223
Mann, Heinrich, 11
Mannheim, 57
Mannheim, Karl, 264, 280
Mansfield, Katherine, 147; *In a German Pension*, 147

Marées, Hans, 16
Marschall von Bieberstein, Adolf, 307, 308
Marshall, T.H., 286
Marx, Karl, 19, 28, 187–8, 193, 304; *The Civil War in France*, 195; *Das Kapital*, 187, 189
Mason, Bobbie Ann, 168
mass politics, xiv, 29, 244, 260, 270, 272, 280. *See also* democratization; political modernization, political mobilization
Mauch, Christof, 88
May Laws (1873), 27. See also *Kulturkampf*
Maybach, Wilhelm, 31
Mayhew, Henry, 64; *German Life and Manners as Seen in Saxony*, 149, 151
McClellan, George B., 158
McDermott, John, 48
Mecklenburg, 50
Mehnert, Paul, Jr, xii, 203, 204, 209, 216, 222, 247, 300–2, 313, 315–16, 317
Mencken, H.L., 245
Menzel, Adolph, 15, 263; *Iron Rolling Mill*, 17
Mergel, Thomas, 259
Metternich, Clemens von, 44, 57, 60
Metzsch, Georg von, 196, 311, 312, 315–16
Michel (national figure), 148
middle classes (bourgeoisie, *Bürgertum*), xiv, 11–12, 14, 15, 24, 25, 27, 50, 51, 145, 147, 186, 188, 190, 192, 193, 197, 223, 245, 269, 271, 273, 283–4, 299, 300, 302, 304, 308; burghers, 11, 94, 193, 197, 243, 299, 304, 313; *Mittelstand* (lower-middle classes), 12, 68, 223, 241

migration, 7, 10, 24, 153, 165–6, 224–5, 297
milieu, milieu theory, 28
military, militarism, 22–5, 58, 98, 99, 112, 145, 146, 148, 192, 194, 261, 285. *See also* Imperial navy; Prussia: army; Prussia: officer corps
Miller, Arthur, 168
Mitford, Nancy, 202
"mixed race" children, 92
modernity, modernization, 3, 6, 30, 47, 51, 72, 141, 186, 259, 260, 266, 273, 282, 284. See also *Sonderweg*
Moltke, Helmuth von, 20, 111
monarchy. *See* constitutional monarchy
Montreal, 170
Morier, David Richard, 60
Morier, Robert, 47, 48, 52, 55, 56, 57, 58, 60
Moroccan Crises (first and second), 59, 210, 212
Most, Johann, 187
Motley, John Lothrop, 64
Müller, Frank Lorenz, 48, 52
Munich, 15, 16, 61, 116, 260
municipalities, 15, 164, 266. *See also* urbanization
Murray, Charles, 124
Murray, Scott R., 48, 55
music, 16, 144
Muthesius, Hermann, 14

Napoleon I (Emperor of France), Napoleonic era, 50, 56, 93, 108
Napoleon III (Emperor of France), 56, 117, 123, 188
nation, nation-state, 18, 27
Nation, The, 146, 161
National Association, 49

"national character," 148
National Gallery (Berlin), 17
National Liberal Party, National Liberals, 21, 25, 26, 49, 58, 116, 118, 120, 126, 193, 208, 211, 214, 299, 303, 313–14
nationalism, nationalists, 23, 25, 44, 49–51, 54, 142, 148, 165, 188, 225, 240, 241, 286
Naumann, Friedrich, 250, 271
navy. *See* Imperial navy
Nazi Germany, xi, 47, 238, 239, 252, 288
Nazism, Nazi Party, xiii, 14, 92, 93, 94, 100–1, 206, 225, 241, 270, 281
Neue Zeit, Die, 186
Neumann, Ilse, 48
New York City, 152–3, 168, 297
newspapers. *See* reading, reading habits; press
Nietzsche, Friedrich, 15, 54, 56, 143, 188; *Untimely Meditations*, 143
Nikolsburg armistice negotiations (1866), 110–11, 117, 118, 120
Nipperdey, Thomas, 264
North German Confederation, xiii, 28, 64, 110, 121, 125, 270
Northeim, 270
Nostitz-Wallwitz, Hermann von, 62–3, 69, 70–1

Oldenburg, 120
Oldenburg-Januschau, Elard von, 218
Osterhammel, Jürgen, 107

Palmerston, Lord (Henry John Temple), 49, 54
Pan-Germanism, Pan-German League, 23, 206, 207, 210, 214–15, 225, 246

Paris, 56, 146, 190, 298
Paris Commune (1871), 190
parliament, parliamentarianism, 50, 51, 58, 116, 146, 193, 196, 202, 207, 209, 219, 238, 243, 261, 264, 265, 267, 280, 281, 288, 295, 311. See also democracy, democratization; suffrage
"parties of order" (Ordnungsparteien), 69, 70, 267, 269, 302, 310, 312–14, 316
Paulmann, Johannes, 45
peasantry, 15, 140, 141, 142, 152
Peterloo, 54
Peters, Carl, 24, 25
Pfau, Ludwig, 21
Philadelphia, 297
Pieschen, 302
Pietschmann, Ernst Max, 191; *Fürst Bismarck in Dresden am 18. Juni 1892*, 191
Pillnitz, 125, 126
Pius IX (Pope), 27
Poiger, Ute, 92, 94, 97
Poland, 108, 213, 218
police, 27, 68, 69, 70, 114, 145, 151, 261, 295, 299, 300, 302
"political mass market," 241, 258–73, 280
political modernization, political mobilization, 25, 242, 252, 269. See also democracy, democratization; mass politics
political parties, 26–9, 266, 269
politics of notables (Honoratiorenpolitik), 29, 241, 260
Pomerania, 245
Pope, Alexander, 123
populism, populists, 238
Posen, 203

Post, Die, 207
postcolonial studies, 147–8
Prague, 120, 124, 298
press, 57, 58, 68, 151, 196, 213, 223, 248, 265, 286, 311; mass, 11, 29, 45, 286; Reich Press Law (1874), 62
Preuß, Hugo, 261
Preußische Jahrbücher, 100
Prince of Wales (Albert Edward), 111
prisoners of war, 92
Progressive Party, 55
proletariat, 190, 193
protest, political protest, 5, 28
Protestantism, Protestants, 17, 26, 27, 50, 117, 146. See also religion
Protestant Workers' Associations, 222
Prussia, 16, 20–2, 46, 47, 49, 51–2, 55, 56, 58, 60, 63, 64, 65, 68, 107–28, 146–7, 154, 192, 196, 203–4, 207, 215–16, 222, 237, 245, 252, 262, 294, 296, 312, 314–15; army, 23, 111, 112–16, 119, 124–5, 195, 299, 304, 307–8; Association Law, 305–6, 307; civil service, 27; diplomacy, diplomats, 60, 66, 67, 69, 70–1, 118, 188, 192, 210; East Prussia, 26, 216; Greater Prussia, 262; officer corps, 24. See also Landtag (Prussian)
Public Record Office, Kew. See under Britain, National Archives
public sphere, 265, 296
Putbus, 117
Puttkamer, Robert von, 70, 71

race, racism, *Volkstum*, 49, 145, 225
Radbruch, Gustav, 261
Ramm, Agatha, 48
Raphael, 155; *Madonna and Child*, 155
Raumer, Friedrich von, 293

Realpolitik, 22, 23, 189
reform, 5, 21, 50, 58, 63, 108, 192, 252, 266, 288, 314. *See also under* conservatism
regionalism, regional diversity, 5, 10, 14, 27, 44, 51, 60, 94, 107, 238, 243, 249, 250, 312
Reichstag, 20, 26, 56, 58, 65, 66, 68, 69, 70, 125, 126, 190, 193, 195, 196–7, 203, 210–12, 215, 222, 227, 239, 242, 243, 244, 250, 251, 266, 267, 268, 269, 272, 286, 288, 294–6, 298, 303, 304, 305–6, 309, 311, 313–14, 318; election of 1893, 244–5, 247, 249, 314
religion, 17–19, 68, 269, 293. *See also* Catholicism, Catholics; Jews; *Kulturkampf*; Protestantism, Protestants
Renoir, Jean, 71
Repp, Kevin, 266
Rétablissement (Saxon), 108
revolution, 5, 56, 58, 60, 71, 188, 193, 197, 252, 288, 293, 298, 300
Rhine-Ruhr district, 296
Rhineland, 26, 123, 124
Richler, Mordecai, 140, 145, 170
Riehl, Wilhelm Heinrich, 141
Riezler, Kurt, 209
Ritter, Gerhard A., 288
Robbins, Keith, 148
Rohe, Karl, 240–1, 286
Röhl, John C.G., 293, 306, 310
Rokkan, Stein, 240, 286
Roman Catholicism. *See* Catholicism, Catholics
Rose, George H., 57
Rosenberg, Hans, 8, 241, 266, 270–1, 280
Rosenhaft, Eve, 272

Rosenzweig, Roy, 87
Ross, Ronald J., 259
Rüger, Jan, 48
rule of law, 239, 261, 273
rural communities, rural life, 7, 10, 11, 15, 94, 125, 141, 195, 245. *See also* agriculture; localism; regionalism, regional diversity
Russell, John, 58
Russell, Odo, 48, 53–4, 55, 58, 61
Russia, 22, 45, 46, 49, 51, 57, 61, 108, 149, 213, 216, 307

Saarbrücken, 99
Saarland, 296
Sächsische Arbeiter-Zeitung, 315
Salisbury, Lord (Robert Gascoyne-Cecil), 47
Sand, Karl, 57
Sanford, H.S., 65
Savigny, Karl von, 117–18
Saxe-Weimar-Eisenach, Grand Duke of, 117
Saxon Central State Archive, 65–6, 313
Saxony, Kingdom of, xii, 18, 46, 50, 51, 53, 57, 61–2, 63, 65–6, 68–70, 107–28, 138–70, 191, 196, 245, 247, 249, 262, 266, 267, 294, 298–300, 302–5, 306–7, 310–16, 317–18; army, 113, 115, 120, 123, 124, 151, 216; Association Law, 299, 305, 312; civil service, 62, 121, 122, 299; court, 109; diplomacy, diplomats, 46, 51, 68, 71, 108, 110, 120, 316; Progressives in, 313, 315. *See also* Landtag (Saxon)
Saxony and the North German Confederation, anon. [Cäsar Dietrich von Witzleben], 121
Scandinavia, 55

Schack, Hans von, 121
Scharnhorst, Gary, 159
Schattschneider, Elmer Eric, 251–2
Schelling, Hermann von, 194
Schiffer, Eugen, 208–9
Schiller, Friedrich, 47, 151
Schönberger, Christoph, 262, 288
Schöneberg, 203
Schorske, Carl, 270, 280
Schultz, Andreas, 302
Second World War, 88, 94, 147, 281
Sedan Day, 5, 24, 55, 62, 144, 312
Seven Years' War, 108, 111
Seward, William, 65
Sheehan, James J., 50
Sidgwick, Cicely, 64, 164; *Home Life in Germany*, 164
Silesia, 203, 208, 213, 216
Simplicissimus, 59, 67, 285
Six Articles (1832), 54
Smith, Helmut Walser, 271, 281, 282
Social Democratic Party of Germany (SPD), Social Democrats, 12, 14, 19, 25, 26, 28, 55, 62, 63, 65, 68–71, 186–8, 190, 192, 193, 195, 196, 197, 210, 212, 213, 222, 225, 239, 241, 243, 244, 246, 267, 268, 269, 271, 272, 295–7, 298, 299, 300, 302, 304, 305, 306–9, 311, 312, 313–16, 317–18. *See also* Anti-Socialist Law; socialism, socialists
social insurance, 19–20, 145, 192
"social question," 19–20
socialism, socialists, 21, 69, 70–1, 186, 188, 223, 239, 240, 243, 261, 268, 272, 295, 296, 304, 307, 314; opponents of, 272, 281, 299, 302, 313. *See also* Anti-Socialist Law; Social Democratic Party of Germany (SPD), Social Democrats

Sonderweg, xiv, 50, 72, 139, 239, 258, 262, 264, 280–1, 283, 288, 299
Sontag, Franz, 207, 225–6
South-West Africa, 24
Soviet Union, 47. *See also* Russia
Sozialdemokrat, Der, 70
Spain, 51, 149
Spenkuch, Hartwin, 261–2
Sperber, Jonathan, 94–5; *The Kaiser's Voters*, 241
Spitzemberg, Hildegard von, 211
Sportpalast, 100–1
Stände. *See* estates, social
Steinbach, Peter, 238, 286
Steiner, Zara, 45
Steiniger, Karl, 225–6
Stirk, Peter, 264
Stöcker, Adolf, 222
Stoppard, Tom, 242
Strachey, George, 51, 53, 62–3, 69, 70, 127–8, 302–3, 311–12
Stübel, Paul, 191
student fraternities (*Burschenschaften*), 57, 60
Stumm-Halberg, Carl Ferdinand von, 11, 296
Stuttgart, 56, 58, 61
suffrage (universal manhood), xiv, 28, 29, 49, 58, 60, 63, 65, 116, 164, 193, 196, 197, 213, 237, 238–52, 258, 264, 266, 270, 286, 286, 294, 296, 299, 304, 306, 313–15; Prussian Suffrage Reform (1910), 206. *See also* democracy, democratization; parliament, parliamentarism
Suval, Stanley, 258, 266, 267
Sweden, 51
Swiss Confederation, 60
Sydow, Reinhold von, 209

Taylor, Bayard, 65
Tell, William (national figure), 148
Teplitz, 120, 124
Third Reich. *See* Nazi Germany
Thöny, Eduard, 59
Thompson, Alastair, 271
Times, The, 54, 125
Togo, 25
Tönnies, Ferdinand, 284
travel writing, 45, 146–7. *See also* Hawthorne, Julian
Treitschke, Heinrich von, 72, 100, 122–3, 163–4, 247
Turkey, 51
Twain, Mark, 45, 64, 139, 140, 150, 155, 168; *Innocents Abroad*, 45, 139, 140, 145, 154

Uhde, Fritz von, 16
Ulk, 287
Uncle Sam (national figure), 148
unification. *See under* Germany
United States, Americans, 64, 108, 109, 146, 153, 154, 165, 216, 242, 245, 298; Civil War, 65, 146; diplomats, 64, 65, 116, 124, 146; Jews of, 247; views of Germany, 56, 139, 145–6, 170
universities, 57, 146, 187
Urbach, Karina, 48, 53–4, 56
urbanization, 7, 10, 61. *See also* municipalities

Valentini, Rudolf von, 211
Vaterland, Das, 315
Versailles, 53–4. *See also* Hall of Mirrors
veterans' associations, 269
Victoria (Queen of Great Britain), 48, 55

Vienna, 47, 58, 120, 121, 123, 124, 310
völkisch movements, 224, 266
Volksfreund, Der, 268
Volksgemeinschaft, 250, 284
voluntary associations, 272, 286
Vorwärts, 69, 187, 312

Wagener, Hermann, 249
Wagner, Richard, 16, 144; *Parsifal*, 16
Waldersee, Alfred von, 306, 307, 308, 309, 310
Ward, John, 48, 52
Wars of Unification, German, 20, 22, 24
Watch on the Rhine, The (Max Schneckenburger), 16
Weber, Carl von, 114
Weber, Max, 4, 261
Wehler, Hans-Ulrich, 264, 271, 280
Weimar Republic, xiii, 92, 93, 202, 222, 241, 259, 288, 295
Weitz, Eric, 92, 93; *Weimar Germany: Promise and Tragedy*, 93
Welsh, Helga, 91, 92, 95, 97, 99
Werner, Anton von, 21, 263; *Kronprinz Friedrich Wilhelm auf dem Hofball 1878*, 263
West Germany. *See* Federal Republic of Germany
Westarp, Kuno von, 202–27; *Konservative Politik im letzten Jahrzehnt des Kaiserreichs*, 204; *Konservative Politik im Übergang*, 215, 216–17, 223
Wettin dynasty, 107–8, 121, 159. *See also* Johann (King of Saxony)
Whitman, Sidney, 64
Whitman, Walt, 146–7; *Song of Myself*, 169
Wilhelm I (King of Prussia, Kaiser of Germany), 19, 20, 21, 24, 29, 55,

62–3, 68, 117, 118, 120, 122, 123, 127, 159, 248; as Prince Regent, 58
Wilhelm II (King of Prussia, Kaiser of Germany), xi, xii, 19, 22, 23, 24, 28, 30, 62, 63, 109, 191, 193, 195, 196, 206, 211, 239, 243, 252, 288, 293, 294, 295, 296, 298, 299, 304, 305, 306–7, 308, 309, 310, 312, 314, 316, 317
Winzen, Peter, 306
Wolff, Theodor, 208
women, 14, 94, 100, 115, 151, 160, 188, 222, 268, 300, 302; educational opportunities for, 14, 18; movements for emancipation of, 4, 12, 160, 272. *See also* families; education

workers, 12, 19, 28, 62, 212–13, 225
Wright, Joseph A., 64
Wurmb, Lothar von, 114–15, 116, 120–2, 127
Württemberg, 21, 51, 56, 58, 63, 211, 216, 262, 294, 303, 307

Yeats, William Butler, 249

Zehmen, Ludwig von, 120
Zetkin, Clara, 14
Ziblatt, Daniel, 241
Zollverein (Customs Union), 48, 57
Zuckerberg, Mark, 87

German and European Studies

General Editor: Rebecca Wittmann

1. Emanuel Adler, Beverly Crawford, Federica Bicchi, and Rafaella Del Sarto, *The Convergence of Civilizations: Constructing a Mediterranean Region*
2. James Retallack, *The German Right, 1860–1920: Political Limits of the Authoritarian Imagination*
3. Silvija Jestrovic, *Theatre of Estrangement: Theory, Practice, Ideology*
4. Susan Gross Solomon, ed., *Doing Medicine Together: Germany and Russia between the Wars*
5. Laurence McFalls, ed., *Max Weber's "Objectivity" Revisited*
6. Robin Ostow, ed., *(Re)Visualizing National History: Museums and National Identities in Europe in the New Millennium*
7. David Blackbourn and James Retallack, eds., *Localism, Landscape, and the Ambiguities of Place: German-Speaking Central Europe, 1860–1930*
8. John Zilcosky, ed., *Writing Travel: The Poetics and Politics of the Modern Journey*
9. Angelica Fenner, *Race under Reconstruction in German Cinema: Robert Stemmle's Toxi*
10. Martina Kessel and Patrick Merziger, eds., *The Politics of Humour in the Twentieth Century: Inclusion, Exclusion, and Communities of Laughter*
11. Jeffrey K. Wilson, *The German Forest: Nature, Identity, and the Contestation of a National Symbol, 1871–1914*
12. David G. John, *Bennewitz, Goethe, Faust: German and Intercultural Stagings*
13. Jennifer Ruth Hosek, *Sun, Sex, and Socialism: Cuba in the German Imaginary*
14. Steven M. Schroeder, *To Forget It All and Begin Anew: Reconciliation in Occupied Germany, 1944–1954*
15. Kenneth S. Calhoon, *Affecting Grace: Theatre, Subject, and the Shakespearean Paradox in German Literature from Lessing to Kleist*

16. Martina Kolb, *Nietzsche, Freud, Benn, and the Azure Spell of Liguria*
17. Hoi-eun Kim, *Doctors of Empire: Medical and Cultural Encounters between Imperial Germany and Meiji Japan*
18. J. Laurence Hare, *Excavating Nations: Archaeology, Museums, and the German-Danish Borderlands*
19. Jacques Kornberg, *Pope Pius XII's Dilemma: Facing Atrocities and Genocide in World War II*
20. Patrick O'Neill, *Transforming Kafka: Translation Effects*
21. John K. Noyes, *Herder: Aesthetics against Imperialism*
22. James Retallack, *Germany's Second Reich: Portraits and Pathways*
23. Laurie Marhoefer, *Sex and the Weimar Republic: German Homosexual Emancipation and the Rise of the Nazis*